MW01136961

Funny Because It's True

Funny Because It's True

How
THE ONION
Created Modern
American News Satire

CHRISTINE WENC

RUNNING PRESS
PHILADELPHIA

Running Press
Hachette Book Group
1290 Avenue of the Americas, New York, NY 10104
www.runningpress.com
@Running_Press

First Edition: March 2025

Published by Running Press, an imprint of Hachette Book Group, Inc. The Running Press name and logo are trademarks of Hachette Book Group, Inc.

The Hachette Speakers Bureau provides a wide range of authors for speaking events. To find out more, go to www.hachettespeakersbureau.com or email HachetteSpeakers@hbgusa.com.

Running Press books may be purchased in bulk for business, educational, or promotional use. For more information, please contact your local bookseller or the Hachette Book Group Special Markets Department at Special.Markets@hbgusa.com.

The publisher is not responsible for websites (or their content) that are not owned by the publisher.

Photo credits
cover © Associated Press
featuring left to right: (background) Chris Karwowski, John Krewson, Mike Loew, Chad Nackers, Carol Kolb, and Todd Hanson; (foreground) Robert Siegel and Tim Harrod

This is a work of deeply researched nonfiction and based on interviews with many of the key figures. The author has sought to recount relevant events as faithfully as possible, while recognizing that others who were present might recall things differently.

Print book cover design by Amanda Richmond
Print book interior design by Sara Puppala

Library of Congress Control Number: 2024949312

ISBNs: 978-0-7624-8443-0 (hardcover), 978-0-7624-8445-4 (ebook)

Printed in the United States of America

LSC-C

Printing 1, 2025

For all
Onion staffers
and Onion readers—
past, present,
and future

CONTENTS

PROLOGUE

The Onion's story begins in the 1970s with a real newspaper: the *Hammond Times* of Hammond, Indiana. Hammond borders the southern end of Lake Michigan and is part of the larger Chicago metropolitan area. The story also starts with a real newspaper editor named Edward Keck and a real reporter, Janet Keck (née Janet von Hoff).

Most American newspapers were, and still are, a business—sometimes a highly profitable one, sometimes one that sends owners into bankruptcy. Whether a newspaper is successful, whether it can *stay* in business, depends on much more than the quality of its content—though that can matter quite a lot. Newspapers have always been more than sources of information. Since the creation of mass-production (and its required corollary, mass-consumption) culture in the nineteenth century, when the beautiful flora and fauna of planet Earth started to be mutilated at enormous scale into products to be packaged, purchased, used, and thrown away, all powered by the burning of coal and oil, newspapers were there to tell us both how to live in this new world and what it all meant. Separation from nature—from our own experiences and observations unmediated by sensory-overloading news, entertainment, and information technology—meant not understanding how things worked anymore. We were now in a world where media told us what was real, what was important, and what was *not* real or important. Which was anything that did not appear in the media. If you have the power to tell people what reality is, you can do all kinds of things.

Wealthy investors bought local papers, became newspaper publishers, and thereby gained even more influence and power. Even if they didn't own the newspapers in a legal sense, big business and political operatives and public relations firms skilled in applying economic pressure and manipulating public opinion could affect what newspapers printed in all kinds of ways. The idea of "objectivity" has always been complicated. But the press has always fought back against external forces trying to shape its messages. Some versions of reality are better than others.

In the 1970s, newspapers were not the sad, thin remnants of themselves supported by half-page ads for hearing aids and erectile-dysfunction products you see today. They were big and fat, read by everyone, and packed with stories and advertising. You could say newspapers existed *because* of advertising, in fact. Selling display ads and classifieds could actually be thought of as every newspaper's real business. No ads, no newspaper. Newspapers might have reported on the catastrophes wrought by mass consumption, but, in many ways, they also depended on them. On the other hand, no newspapers meant no ads. The content did matter—in ways that often had nothing to do with making money.

In the 1970s, Janet Keck—a native of Oshkosh, Wisconsin, and a University of Wisconsin–Madison journalism and political science graduate—was a star environmental reporter at the *Hammond Times*, where she had started working after getting her degree. She had met her husband there, news editor and columnist Edward Keck. They had three children: Michelle, Kathleen, and Tim.

Janet was an ambitious, energetic reporter. Soon she was publishing multiple times a week on environmental and labor issues large and small, and developing a network of local contacts. Environmental journalism was a new field in the 1970s, and Janet Keck was in the vanguard of this new reporting beat. There was a lot to write about. Rachel Carson's best-selling book *Silent Spring* had been published in 1962, and in its wake the modern environmental movement took shape, alongside the civil rights, feminist, gay rights, antipoverty, antinuclear weapons, and antiwar movements, all of which pointed out the incompatibility of corporate capitalism with freedom and justice—and health and well-being—for all. One of the goals of this reporting was to influence public policy, and federal clean-air, clean-water, and endangered-species legislation was passed in the 1970s by Republican president Richard Nixon. *Silent Spring*, about the persistent organochlorine pesticide DDT and the way such chemicals moved through the food chain, decimating species far removed from the ones that had been the original target of the poison and staying in the environment for generations, had taught other writers how to research and report on environmental issues. (DDT was finally banned in 1972 after a lawsuit led by Wisconsin bird-watchers and University of Wisconsin scientists.)

Janet's husband, Edward Keck, had come to the United States in the 1940s as a small child in extraordinary circumstances: He and his family were Volga Germans, ethnic Germans who lived in Ukraine and environs in the Soviet Union. In World War II, however, Stalin decided to purge this population, and more than a million people were killed, deported, or sent to internment camps. Edward's extended family were all murdered. Relief organizations resettled many of those who were able to escape, and a lot of them went to the midwestern farm states—Indiana, Iowa, Illinois, and Wisconsin. As a kid, Tim's dad worked in the onion fields of southern Illinois with his family as a migrant laborer. Eventually, he dropped out of college and became a journalist and newspaper editor with much influence in the region, rising to become the president of the Chicago-area newspaper association and the city editor at the *Hammond Times*, where he published Janet's award-winning environmental and labor reporting. Before Tim was born, Edward also narrowly won a single term as a Republican state representative.

Edward also had a serious heart condition. In fact, he had been sick for Tim's entire childhood. At one point, he had an artificial valve implanted—but it was poorly made, and little bits of it would break off and go into Tim's dad's bloodstream. The bits caused his dad to have small strokes. Tim's dad was not only a newspaperman but also a pianist, and the strokes slowly eroded his abilities. "And his heart had gotten so scarred over they couldn't take the valve out, or it would kill him," Tim said. "So he kept having strokes. From when I was in kindergarten through sixth grade, he had like 100 strokes." All of a sudden, Tim said, "he'd wake up and couldn't play the piano anymore. Then he couldn't drive. Then he couldn't write."

In 1978, when Tim was in sixth grade, his dad died. "Every single one of his pallbearers were reporters," he said. "Everybody who spoke at the funeral, except for my drunk uncle, was a newspaper person."

Growing up in a newspaper-saturated environment was thrilling for Tim. "Newspapers were my life," he said. "Newspapers were just every part of our life, all my parents' friends' social life." Mike Royko, the famous *Chicago Tribune* columnist, was a family friend; he wrote Tim's sister's birth announcement. The scope of influence was the entire Chicago metro area. And Tim was surrounded by it all. "In Chicago, newspapers, especially in the '70s, were amazing," he said. "There's a huge amount of newspapers. There was the *Chicago Tribune*, the *Sun-Times*, there was the *Chicago Reader*, which is the classic alt weekly there, and a zillion ethnic and religious and labor and millions of different newspapers. It was a really rich newspaper environment. I was just swimming in it. Even after my dad got sick, newspapers were just what my family lived and breathed."

With Inland Steel, one of the biggest steel mills in the country, in her back-yard dumping toxic waste into Lake Michigan and poisonous black smoke into the sky, Janet Keck had plenty to report on. It seems she was absolutely driven. Tim said she even got her pilot's license and would fly small planes over the enormous Inland Steel plant, looking for destructive environmental activities. She also befriended a group of steelworker union members, including Mike Olszanski, who had started an environmental advocacy wing at the plant and became one of Janet's key informants.

Olszanski was an electrical technician at Inland who organized the first United Steelworkers of America Environmental Committee. He was also the environmental chair from 1977 to 1981, when he focused on building a coalition of union members, environmentalists, and people in the community. Unions and environmentalism were not natural allies at first. As the saying went, skies full of black smoke meant a plant full of jobs. However, when Olszanski helped people see that the black smoke affected their own personal health as well as the health of their families, not just an abstract thing called the "environment," he had better luck.

Olszanski recalled that one of the first big stories Janet worked on with them was about air pollution. The plant would be in its usual state of blowing tons of carcinogenic greenhouse gases into the air until the Environmental Protection Agency (EPA) announced an inspection, whereupon Inland would shut every-thing down in time to make the pollution level appear lower. So the steelworkers started taking photos of the smoke and sending them to the EPA directly.

This behavior was risky. But such things were possible, Olszanski said, because the union would protect their jobs. Being public would keep their jobs safe too. "Our thinking was," he said, "the more public we are, if they tried to fire anybody, they're not going to be able to just sneak it by, you know what I mean? They're going to have to face the public." Olszanski told me that indeed there were no repercussions. "If anything, they were scared of us for that. For those reasons. The union plus the public exposure." They were going after it from inside the plant, from the viewpoint of steelworkers, he said, and Janet was "shining a spotlight" from the outside.

No repercussions for union members, that is. Janet Keck was not in the union. A few months after Edward Keck died—leaving Janet without her husband and *Hammond Times* ally—Inland Steel executives pressured the *Times* first to move Janet off the labor beat and then off the environmental beat. The now spineless *Hammond Times* transferred her to the local government beat twenty-three miles away, in the town of Crown Point, the county seat. For a widowed single mom with three kids at home, the daily commute and erratic legislative scheduling made this new beat impossible, and Janet resigned.

Writing for the local steelworkers' union newsletter, Olszanski described her departure with bitter words in a 1979 article, "*Times'* Keck Forced Out by Inland. Area Reporter Too Honest":

The region has lost a truly great investigative reporter with the resignation of Janet Keck from the *Hammond Times* in January. Janet not only accurately reported the stalling tactics and intransigence of corporate polluters such as Inland, but dug out and exposed their hushed-up dealings with State Air Pollution authorities.

Janet was never afraid to "tell the truth on 'em." She was removed from the Labor beat several years ago, subsequent to her candid and accurate reporting on area union politics. After a confrontation with five Inland execs in mid 1978, Keck was transferred to Crown Point.

... We've all heard the cry of "freedom of the press" by the newspaper giants, including the *Times*. Yet for telling the truth, they have forced out a top rate reporter. Her crime, really, was being too good at her job.

Janet worked for the Chicago branch of the EPA for a couple of years, then moved the family up to Omro, Wisconsin, to care for her aging father and take a job at UW–Oshkosh, editing the annual college magazine. Her award-winning environmental journalism career was over, though she later used her piloting skills to help scientists observe melting ice in Greenland and traveled the world doing "grunt work," as Tim put it, for other environmental research, like bird banding in South America.

Now living in the woods of rural Wisconsin, where the nearest neighbor was five miles away and the city of Oshkosh was twenty miles away, Tim said, "I went from having a life filled with newspapers and a social life to no newspapers and no social life." Only one newspaper was available in Omro: the *Oshkosh Northwestern*. Tim said:

My mom and I used to call it the "Oshkosh Nowhere." But I didn't realize how incredibly influential the *Northwestern* would be to me. First of all, I had nothing to do, so I would read the *Northwestern* from cover to cover. And I just adored it, because it was horrible. Every newspaper had its good days and bad days, and in Oshkosh in the mid-'80s, the *Northwestern* was having its bad days. The headlines were hilarious, unintentionally hilarious. Anybody could have a column. Crazy insane Christians, weird bar owners. They had a social column where if you went out to dinner at somebody else's house it was written up. And they'd talk about little things and make them big, and it was awesome.

I had two older sisters, but they had already moved out, so it was just my mom and myself. And she just does not like sound at all. All she does is write, so the only sound you'd hear in my house would be a manual typewriter that she would just hit so aggressively and hard. There's no way we could have a TV or music on, and the only time she would stop writing would be to talk about headlines. And we would joke about the headlines in the *Northwestern*. To this day, that's how my mom and I bond. We talk about news and stuff.

During Tim's sophomore year in high school, a second newspaper came to rural Omro. "It was incredibly exciting," he said.

USA Today had already started working its way across the country, but this was the first time that I could get it in Omro. It was delivered a mile and a half away from my house, and I'd ride my bike to go pick it up.

Cassette player stolen

Truck strikes car

GREEN LAKE — A semi-trailer truck struck a car at

Jeweler attends conclave

Herbert Reimer of Reimer Jewelers Inc., 11 Waugoo Ave., Oshkosh, attended the recent 1980 American Gem So ciety Conclave in Dallas Texas

Balloon crosses America

MATANE, Quebec (AP) — Maxie their return Anderson and four 18th sons 82th today i— Trying to get into the clearing was

Area man named vice president

Jeffrey L. Werch, 27, a 1971 graduate of Berlin High

Right - turn law is clarified

The state Department of the nearest highway to turn — a comparatively rare situ- Transportation's office for right into the second highway. tion highway safety said today that. The department said driv-
The department empha-

Shoe store in expanded facilities

RIPON — A short move has Merchandising space for semi-self service section of former location for nine moved a major expansion for the shoe business has been men's work shoes, boots and years. It will be remodeled sparts tripled from 800 square large selection of shoes will be and occupied by Goodrich

Two attend workshop

'Tightening up' asked

kosh housing inspector family dwellings would still in the state which doesn't

Fire damages Hardee's

Fashion show
set for Tuesday

Masons to celebrate

Grain prices plunge

Doctorate received

Corner congestion looked at AIDS victim blood used

ST. PAUL, Minn. (AP) — American Red Cross he

Tugboat all set to 'chug' up Fox River

Wittman Field budget
includes new hangers

Zoo to salute
senior adults

Jobless
rate holds
at 9.5%

Omro High School alumni look through scrapbook

Outrage mounts around the world

Headlines from the Oshkosh Northwestern, *circa 1983.*

And *USA Today* was the opposite of the *Northwestern*. It was slick, professional, color, you know? It was like the *Falcon Crest* version of a newspaper. Everything was upbeat; it glossed over everything. It was just soulless and horrible. And the combination of the *USA Today* and the *Northwestern* was really a great thing.

After graduating from Omro High School in 1985, Tim went to college at his mom's alma mater, UW–Madison. He didn't know it yet, but a newspaper was about to become a big part of his life again. Just not in the same way it had been for his parents.

Chapter 1

Before we get any further into this story, I'd like to invoke an important figure: the trickster.

The trickster is a powerful archetype that goes way back and seems to be something inherent to the human species. Almost every tradition and culture includes it in one form or another. The trickster is a mediator between the visible and the invisible, a force of anarchy amid rules and tradition, throwing in a wrench just when you thought everything was perfectly calibrated. The trickster also tends to appear at points of change or origination. By destroying what exists, new things can arise. By going on a wild goose chase, you discover something you might never have otherwise considered. Are these things good or bad? Does the trickster help us or hurt us? Yes.

Jim Leary, professor emeritus of folklore at UW–Madison, described the trickster as "a manifestation of natural forces and cultural forces. Of forces going on within individuals. There's the capacity and possibility to do great things— and terrible things. The yin and the yang. Your strengths or your weaknesses. The solar power of the sun can give us light and then growth, but also scorch."

Martha Crawford is a psychotherapist who studies depth psychology, dreams, and death, and how they make life more meaningful. She told me the trickster archetype is not just one but many things:

In the West, we generally draw on archetypal images that lead back to Greece, and that is the hermetic, quicksilver archetype. Hermes is the god of thievery, of lying, of deceit, but he also has very important functions. He's a psycho-pomp who guides people from this life into the next. . . . You pray to Hermes at the crossroads, and acknowledge him. Because if you step into the crossroads, you could end up going into a very, very different direction than the one you anticipate. And if Hermes is annoyed with you or not on your side, he will absolutely send you in a direction you don't expect to go.

In the Indigenous American communities, there's the raven and the coyote. Both of those have very sacred and important trickster functions. They're tricksters that are often in service of people. They go and grab the light of consciousness to shine on the darkness. The raven goes in, like a Prometheus-like character, to capture the first light and bring it to the earth. Some of this is about shining the light of consciousness and awareness into places that are obscured and perhaps not revealed or not easily seen.

The other interesting or important aspect around that is its relationship to clowning and buffoonery. The kinds of archetypes you see around this are dell'arte-like constructs. We think of Pucks very often as trickster archetypes. They're mischief-makers, right? They will steal the grain if you leave it out at night; they will sleep with your daughter if she's not where she's supposed to be. They're mischievous, and they turn rules upside down. They're slippery and tricky. They upset your expectations. That's the function of the trickster archetype.

Lewis Hyde, author of *Trickster Makes This World*, wrote that most "liars, thieves, and shameless personalities of the twentieth century" are not actually tricksters. "Their disruptions are not subtle enough, or pitched at a high enough level." The trickster's aim is to "disturb the established categories of truth and property and, by so doing, open the road to possible new worlds. When Pablo Picasso says 'art is a lie that tells the truth,' we are closer to the old Trickster spirit."

The trickster spirit had been a well-known and much-loved component of Madison, Wisconsin, since at least the 1960s, and it was still alive and well in the 1980s and 1990s. Madison was a great place for young people then—especially creative young people. A beautiful small city between two lakes, Mendota and Monona, Madison offered a low cost of living and a vibrant economy filled with prosperous small businesses that helped maintain an exciting and innovative local arts and journalism scene. Madison had two things that helped guarantee that local economy: the state government and a huge public university. Future *Onion* editor Ben Karlin, a student then, said, "So Madison never really dips. Not to say there aren't problems with it. But it just feels like it's a city that's constantly doing okay."

Madison, however, was also in something of a cultural crossroads. It wasn't the 1970s anymore. The city's Vietnam-era protests were now in the past. "People were really proud of Madison's history of protest and dissent, born out of the '60s and the antiwar movement," Karlin said. Madison's nickname was "the Berkeley of the Midwest." That was very appealing to him. "The tradition of student protest and activism seemed very intriguing. It seemed like an engaged thing that, frankly, growing up in the '80s in the suburbs of Boston, there was nothing. There was nothing like that. There was no stimulation like that there at all." Wisconsin, though historically a progressive state, is also a purple state, and many of us attending college in Madison grew up elsewhere in Wisconsin amid political complexity. There are a lot of contradictions. Frank Lloyd Wright and Jeffrey Dahmer. "Fighting Bob" La Follette and Joseph McCarthy.

At the time, UW–Madison had a much more relaxed admissions policy than it does today. As long as you were in the top half of your high school graduating class, you were in. Madison was also cheap. A land-grant university, it was still being generously funded by government then—and in the late '80s tuition was only about $800 a semester. (No, I did not leave off a zero.) Tim Keck worked at a gas station in high school and saved enough money to cover his costs for two years. Another friend waitressed her way through Madison— and not at a fancy restaurant. At a diner. Like Karlin, there was also a smattering of out-of-state students, mostly from the East Coast. Otherwise, the student body was almost entirely Wisconsinites.

It was also huge: forty thousand students in a city of around two hundred thousand. And just about anything you'd ever want to study was available: humanities, science, art, medicine, music, and more. For Keck, arriving in Madison was like discovering a secret little door in your bedroom. "You open it up, and you go into another dimension. Madison was amazing." They had these things called "burritos," he said. "Fucking amazing. And bars, cafés, and kids. Rich kids, farm kids, foreign kids. Drugs. My first two weeks in Madison, I lived twenty lives. It was fantastic. And I dove right into school. I took the hardest courses I possibly could. I took a Japanese class, I took some high-level math classes—why, I don't know—but I just wanted it all, and I just loved it."

I knew exactly what he meant. Though I had grown up only about forty miles away, in the country outside the rural town of Spring Green (population twelve hundred), for most of the people in that area Madison was another planet. For me, it *was* my planet. As soon as I moved into my freshman dorm— the same one Tim Keck was in—I was like a kid in a candy store. I took a lot of classes in this fantastic core-curriculum, cross-disciplinary program called Integrated Liberal Studies. Every single one was absolutely brilliant. Plants and Man. Science, Technology, and Philosophy. A semester-long seminar on the history and social context of AIDS. I ate it up with a spoon. The very first class I took, ILS 101: Critical Thinking and Expression, remains with me to this day. (If you've never read Darrell Huff's *How to Lie with Statistics*, I recommend it.)

Many of the people who worked for *The Onion* in the early years identified as outcasts and misfits and weirdos or were treated that way by others, and that includes me. In high school I was one of only a handful of kids who were into punk, new wave, and postpunk music; I got good grades, which in rural Wisconsin back then automatically made you suspect; and I wanted to do something different with my life. And I knew that was possible in Madison—a place some of my friends' parents were so unfamiliar with they wouldn't let their kids go there and see movies with me. They were afraid of downtown Madison, Wisconsin. My dad, on the other hand, had an office near campus when he worked for the state as a social worker for a while, and sometimes he'd let me hang out with him. My absolute most favorite place in the world was Library Mall, this big pedestrian area with grass and trees by the huge central campus library a block from Lake Mendota. It was always filled with students and food vendors and people playing guitar and Frisbee. All kinds of stuff happened there: fire-and-brimstone religious speeches, political rallies, hippies juggling bowling pins in crazy outfits. I'd climb in the big circular marble fountain in my bare feet. Play with the giant chess set. Buy "Question Authority" buttons and feminist T-shirts. Learn how to tell the Moonies and evangelicals to fuck off when they tried to recruit me. I was around twelve years old.

Not far from State Street—downtown's main drag and my other favorite place in the world, a mile-long stretch of car-free street lined with shops, cafés, and bars always filled with people walking, talking, and hanging out—and the UW campus were the legendary rock clubs O'Cayz Corral (the CBGB of Madison) and Club de Wash, where you could see every great touring indie and underground band as well as great local ones for five bucks a pop. Bigger acts came through too, at bigger venues.

The Cardinal Bar was a tiny nightclub near the capitol where you could go on New Music Night and dance to New Order, the Cure, Shriekback, and all those guys and check out (or show off) Madison's supply of new-wave haircuts and gender-bending fashion. The Plaza was a classic dive bar and bar-food joint off State Street where all the punk rockers hung out mixed with whoever else happened to be passing by. Madison was big enough to have a bunch of different scenes but also small enough that you'd routinely see skinny hippies in long hair and tie-dye next to people with mohawks next to preppy frat boy–looking jocks next to sweet-faced chubby farm girls in red Wisconsin sweatshirts next to sexy, artsy earth-goddess bohemian freaks. (Important to note that despite this idealized picture, liberal, artsy, intellectual Madison in the '80s was also extraordinarily white. It still is today, but in the '80s it was even more so. There were a lot of different kinds of white people for sure—Madison was the New York of Wisconsin, a place where you could finally be yourself without being called "weird" or "different" [the worst things you could be in the Midwest]—but that's mostly where the diversity stopped. Parts of Madison had been redlined in the not-so-old days, and even an Italian neighborhood had been bulldozed at one point. Though there is ongoing effort to change this picture on multiple levels, Wisconsin continues to have some of the worst levels of racial disparities and inequality in the United States.)

State Street and the nearby blocks were also packed with inexpensive bars and cafés. Tons of reasonably priced rental housing were just a few blocks from the lake and downtown in big old multifamily houses with hardwood floors, fireplaces, and huge porches. If you were really watching your pennies—or if you just wanted to be in a hippie environment where you were guaranteed an active social life—you could join one of the many housing co-ops on campus, some of them in converted mansions, smack in the middle of everything. (Wisconsin has a long-established co-op tradition not just in housing but in other areas like agriculture.) A minimum-wage job at a local independently owned retail store, restaurant, bar, or business was usually enough to get by.

5

Madison also had many local publications. Dan Kaufman, Madisonian and author of *The Fall of Wisconsin: The Conservative Conquest of a Progressive Bastion and the Future of American Politics*, told me, "The Midwest has an amazing press history." This included *Appeal to Reason*, the socialist newspaper published in Girard, Kansas. Victor Berger, who founded the Sewer Socialists in Milwaukee in the 1920s, also published a couple of newspapers. Going back a bit further was Sherman Booth's Milwaukee abolitionist newspaper. "Wisconsin became this bastion of this sort of enlightened citizenry. And the press was hugely important to that," Kaufman said.

Madison's local media scene was anchored in part by the *Progressive* magazine, which was founded by Senator "Fighting Bob" La Follette in 1909. He dedicated the magazine to "winning back for the people the complete power over government—national, state, and municipal—which has been lost to them." Norman Stockwell, the current publisher of the *Progressive*, told me about Madison's strong alternative-media history. *Radical America*, the Students for a Democratic Society publication, he reminded me, started in Madison in 1967. *Isthmus* was the mainstream alternative weekly in the 1980s; it is still around today. The 1980s also had an alternative alternative weekly, the *Madison Insurgent*, and an alternative alternative alternative weekly, the *Madison Edge*. Annie Laurie Gaylor, the daughter of Anne Gaylor, who started the Freedom from Religion Foundation, ran *Feminist Connection*. Freedom from Religion in turn had their own newspaper, *Free Thought Today*. A paper devoted solely to comics was called the *Comic Times*.

Madison also had an interesting zine culture oriented around an East Side couple named Liz Was and mIEKAL aND, who ran a press called Xexoxial Editions from a home called the "Church of Anarchy," where they put together "zines and books and all kinds of really avant-garde art stuff," Stockwell said. In the '80s and '90s, as an article in *Isthmus* put it, they also "produced art events the way others take daily showers." The article quotes aND, who now lives in rural Wisconsin: "There's a concept in permaculture called edges. Like where a hillside meets a pond. Those edges are the highest percentage of diversity and potential."

Broadcast journalism in Madison was also excellent, especially at Wisconsin Public Radio (founded in 1917, WPR is one of the oldest public radio stations in the country), Wisconsin Public Television, and the Madison community radio station WORT. WORT took the "community" part very seriously and is still a constant and reliable source of local news, information, and music. (I hosted a late-night music show there in the early '90s.)

Along with all the free niche papers, there were also two big local daily mainstream newspapers that (unless you found one lying around in a café) you had to pay to read: the *Capital Times*, which was the more liberal one that came out in the afternoon, and the *Wisconsin State Journal*, which was the status quo, conservative morning paper. The *Journal* had the big fat Sunday paper with the color comics, *Parade* magazine, and a stack of loose glossy coupons in the middle. Both newspapers were high quality and professional, with competent, experienced reporters. And both were filled with ads.

Growing up in Spring Green, you could buy the *Wisconsin State Journal* and the *Capital Times* at the grocery store or the truck stop. There was also the local paper, the *Home News*, which was mainly made up of stories about the school board, pictures of the high school sports teams and band concerts, and this actually really good nature column by Helen Taggart Birkemeier. Nothing resembling investigative reporting at all. But as far as I remember, the *New York Times* and *Wall Street Journal* were not sold anywhere in town. I'm not even sure they had the *Chicago Tribune* or the *Milwaukee Journal*. You could, however, buy the *National Enquirer*. I'm guessing that was pretty much the only nonlocal newspaper a lot of people there ever saw. That's what passed for "alternative journalism" in rural Wisconsin in the 1970s and 1980s. They sold it in the grocery checkout line. I remember people talking like they really believed it. "Giant Ant Terrorizes the Topeka County Fair" or whatever. Because it was in print, right?

In 1988, however—the same year *The Onion* would begin—a new alternative source of information appeared on the radio that would reach a substantial rural audience, *The Rush Limbaugh Show*. After President Ronald Reagan suspended the Fairness Doctrine in 1987 alongside other forms of media deregulation, right-wing media programming quickly expanded. The Fairness Doctrine had been in place since 1949 and mandated balanced and fair news reporting by TV and radio broadcasters, who were required to present controversial issues of public interest from different points of view and give opposing political candidates airtime. Its demise is often marked as the beginning of today's deep political polarization, as well as the highly strategic use of media by conservative Republicans and political operatives. It also, however, opened the door to new kinds of media. In her introduction to a special issue of *Cinema Journal* on the right-wing media,

media historian Heather Hendershot wrote: "In the regulated pre-Reagan environment, news coverage did indeed attempt to be 'balanced,' but regulation often seemed to promote not so much political parity as utter blandness. . . . It was most often not left- or right-wing speech that thrived but centrist, moderate speech." The days of moderation, however, were now on their way out.

There were two primary UW–Madison campus newspapers: the *Daily Cardinal*, which, as Stockwell put it, "was antiwar and anti-intervention in Central America, and exposed the university's complicity with the military industrial complex, and so on;" and the *Badger Herald* "was like, Rah Rah Republican, Go Reagan." As a student, Tim Keck did a little writing for the *Cardinal*. "Aside from the comics pages, everything else in the *Cardinal* was painfully serious, you know?" Keck said. "The *Cardinal* was filled with good kids, but they were just discovering racism and sexism and that there was disparity, and people were starving, and they just really were feeling the weight of the world, and they were very serious about their writing." Karlin also worked there for a time. "The *Daily Cardinal* pretty proudly identified itself as advocacy journalism," he said. "'We have a political bias; it's baked into the way we cover things. We're saying that up front.'" Though his inclinations aligned with the *Cardinal*, Karlin wasn't comfortable with the overt politics, so he wrote about sports. Carlos Yu, a student who also spent time at the *Daily Cardinal* (and who was later friends with a number of *Onion* writers), remembered, "In 1975 when Saigon fell, they ran the headline 'VICTORY,' and people would look it up in the archives and go 'Oh my God.'"

The *Badger Herald*, on the other hand, as Keck put it, "was funded by the John Birch Society." (It was actually the Collegiate Network—an organization that provided financial support for college Republican and libertarian newspapers—as well as a campus fundraising event hosted by William F. Buckley.) These Young Republican journalists "thought it was really cool to go to Madison, which was this big liberal hippie fest, and put why apartheid was actually a good thing in their paper. They're kind of like right-wing trolls. So everybody kind of hated both newspapers." Matt Cook, a student who would later write for *The Onion*'s first year, said, "About the only reason you picked up the *Cardinal* was for the comics. The *Badger Herald* was, of course, the knee-jerk, right-wing, reactionary paper. Which nobody picked up for any reason, other than the crossword puzzle. Because they had a decent crossword puzzle."

Madison may have been amazing, but something was changing. You could feel it in the air. Among people my age, it was becoming evident that the world we'd grown up in was not going to be the world we would be adults in. Neoconservatism and the associated government-program budget slashing, industry deregulation, union busting, and social safety–net shredding of the Reagan years—all the stuff he and his cronies did to undo what had been accomplished in the '60s and '70s, which were regularly celebrated on the *Badger Herald* editorial page—were just starting to have real everyday effects.

A new preoccupation with money and status was also trickling down. "Conspicuous consumption" was now a thing. Labels were starting to appear on the *outside* of clothes. An ordinary, middle-class, three-bedroom-one-bathroom style of living that had seemed perfectly fine before was being replaced by far more resource-sucking "luxury" aspirations. It was even happening in Madison. "There was this competing kind of dynamic in the city," Karlin said. The hippie-bohemian vibe was still very strong, but "there was also this prosperous midwestern city that was attracting industry, and *Outside Magazine* is saying it's one of the best cities in America and all that. That yuppie force and that hippie force were coming to a head a little bit." Meanwhile, in a world totally outside the yuppie perspective, the AIDS epidemic was in full swing. Legions of young gay men were dying, abandoned by families and treated like lepers by health-care providers, and nobody seemed to be doing anything about it. Sex could kill you now.

Reflecting this new reality, protest styles were evolving in Madison. Dan Savage, who would later become a famous advice columnist, lived in Madison at this time and worked as a clerk at a local independent bookstore and video rental place, Four Star Fiction and Video. Everybody knew him as the wise-cracking guy in the ACT UP T-shirt at the checkout counter when you were renting your VHS copy of *Battleship Potemkin* or the complete works of Robert Altman. (Though Savage was never employed by *The Onion*, Four Star later became an advertiser.)

Savage was a member of a Milwaukee-Madison branch of ACT UP and a part of Madison's out gay and lesbian scene. One of their most famous demonstrations in Wisconsin took place after a prisoner died of AIDS behind bars. "People with HIV were being dumped into Wisconsin prisons, mostly people of color," he said. And there was no real treatment for people with HIV in prisons.

Savage said the nutritional supplement for prisoners with AIDS was a peanut butter and jelly sandwich. "It was not actually going to help anybody," he said.

"The genius of ACT UP was that there was this core in every city, in New York, in Chicago, this core of people who made it like what they did twenty-four hours a day," he said. Other people could then show up at a demo, equipped with signs and shirts that ACT UP gave them, and leave. "There was no 'Well, you weren't at the meeting. Fuck you.'" When lives are at stake, getting stuff done matters more than "lefty bullshit."

The AIDS-in-prison demonstration took place at Governor Tommy Thompson's office in the capitol. "We showed up with about thirty people, crowded into the little receptionist area, and threw peanut butter sandwiches everywhere," Savage said. "Dumped them on his desk, a couple hundred of them. And then we would deliver one every day to his office." Eventually, the Thompson administration agreed to work with the Milwaukee AIDS Project and altered some of their policies.

"For us, it was a really effective demo because we didn't guilt-trip anybody for not being one of the six of us weirdo crazy people who were at every meeting, and we made it look to the Thompson administration like there were hundreds of us," Savage said. They didn't get everything they wanted, "but it was effective. ACT UP was really good at effective activism because it was a party and because we didn't guilt-trip people."

This was the world in which my generation was coming of age. And it kind of felt like we had been left to sink or swim on our own. People joke about how Generation X is the overlooked middle child, but it's sort of true. A lot of the stuff millennials talked about later was first experienced by us. It *is* the case that we were still able to take advantage of the last bits of societal things like affordable public university tuition and interesting cities where you could live on minimum wage and still have time for projects and a social life. That world is mostly gone now. But at the time, one media thing after another described Generation X's miserable life prospects, on the one hand, and how we were all cynical slackers with bad attitudes, on the other. We were graduating into a major recession. Unemployment was very high. Full-time jobs with pensions were rapidly being replaced by temp jobs with no benefits. The jobs that did exist seemed pointless. Nobody I knew had health insurance. We were called "the first generation expected to do worse than their parents." So, the bad-attitude thing was actually kind of true. I used to think millennials got angry because they grew up feeling like they were promised something and then that promise turned out to be trash. But this wasn't a shock for us. We understood the game as having been rigged from the start.

Johanna (Jonnie) Wilder, a Purdue dropout who had recently moved to Madison and would soon play a key role in *The Onion*, said that in 1988, "Madison was an island. It was a very political town, and everyone seemed to have a high level of local, national, and world political knowledge." Ronald Reagan was going "obviously senile" and had "just gotten away with the Iran-Contra thing." Jesse Jackson's Rainbow Coalition had lost the Wisconsin primary to Michael Dukakis "and the boring Democratic Party who didn't connect with young people." The Berlin Wall would fall in November 1989, "but the cracks had been spreading for years before." The Tiananmen Square massacre took place that same year.

The world was in a bad way, Jonnie said, "run by crooks and spies. Big media that we'd grown up with as this completely trustworthy source was starting to show wear at the seams. McPapers like *USA Today* were starting up that printed news as entertainment. The free spirits of peace and love of the '70s were giving way to the 'greed is good' capitalists of the '80s. George Bush Sr. was the new president. It was horrific to watch." Jonnie added, "Maybe it's just how it looks from the perspective of now, but it sure feels like we were watching the initial stirrings of the monstrous horrors that roam the earth today."

Todd Hanson, future *Onion* head writer, was a UW–Madison student from "1986 to 1986," as he puts it. He said, "What was Madison like then? I mean, it was Generation X." After his first year—he did register for classes for the spring 1987 term but apparently never attended them—Hanson dropped out, got a minimum-wage job, and wasn't in school anymore. "A lot of people I knew were still students," he said. "And eventually the people that were in school graduated. And then we were *all* working minimum-wage jobs, you know?"

The creeping pointlessness and anxiety we were feeling, however, could also be seen as allowing an opening. It was actually freeing in a way, because you didn't have anything to lose. You could take chances. You could take risks. Since your future was screwed anyway, you might as well do something interesting.

Chapter 2

Madison, famous for its weirdos—one of its nicknames was "Mad City"—had something of a prankster history. The most locally famous was the Pail and Shovel Party in the 1970s. As the Wisconsin Historical Society describes them, the group was "an absurdist contingent of UW–Madison students who won control of student government in the spring of 1978 with the campaign slogan, 'Are you nuts enough?' and conducted a series of classic pranks." Led by Leon Varjian and James Mallon, the Pail and Shovel Party was responsible for the often-photographed "submerged" Statue of Liberty replica constructed on the winter Lake Mendota ice. In another famous prank, on the first day of classes, September 4, 1979, Madison students awoke to find more than a thousand pink lawn flamingos covering the university's Bascom Hill. Kentucky Fried Theater was another comedy institution that came out of Madison, created in 1971 by David Zucker, Jim Abrahams, and Jerry Zucker. The trio would go on to write and direct the films *Kentucky Fried Movie*, *The Naked Gun*, and *Airplane!*

Tim Keck carried on that prankster tradition in his normal, everyday life. Something was always happening in his mind, and it came out constantly in ways that were very silly, witty, and sometimes intense. He cracked jokes continually, including about himself. Andy Dhuey, a mutual friend since our freshman year in the UW–Madison dorms, described him as very personable and "really wickedly funny." They were hanging out and smoking dope together almost right away. Keck was also "scatterbrained. I don't know if it's attention deficit disorder—he probably has a diagnosis for it—but it's pretty hard for him to stay in a straight line on any topic for very long." But, Dhuey said, he also "has a way of seeing patterns in the world and then imagining something that can work in a way that nobody's really thought of yet."

Keck and I also became friends that year. It was weird and fascinating for me that someone who didn't appear to be bohemian at all could be such an anarchist. We appeared to have little in common at first. I was into new wave and postpunk, but he was preppy. He didn't seem to be interested in art or writing or music, while to me this was the only thing that mattered. He was also interested in business, which by definition made you uncool. At that age, I was one of those people who judged you on how obscure your record collection was. Yet somehow he still had a completely unique outlook on the world. I was very tired of predictable, conformist people, and with him you never knew what was coming. Keck was also very good at getting in trouble, but in ridiculous, silly ways that made you like him instead of wanting to kill him—most of the time. If you had a box of cookies in your room, the kind that slide out in a little plastic drawer, Keck would grab them, open the drawer, and lick every cookie while you watched so that you had to give him the whole box. If he was hungry and you were eating something, he would come up to you, chirp like a baby bird, and point to his open mouth until you put some of your food in it.

He was also impulsive, and would sometimes go over the edge. Once when I was biking to class down State Street, Keck suddenly came up behind me on his bike, started pretending we were race cars, and clipped me. I wiped out in the middle of the street. Another time, our friend Rachel was walking home alone as night was falling, and he sneaked up behind her and grabbed her as a joke. She freaked out, as well she should have. (He did apologize for that one.) Still, whenever Keck stepped over the line, he'd always get out of it because he was funny and cute. He was like a brother. A cute little brother that you loved but also wanted to strangle.

After our freshman year, Keck moved out of the dorms and into an apartment on Mifflin Street with Dhuey and some other friends. He continued to love Madison, he said, "but my grades were horrible. My education at Omro High School wasn't fantastic, and, also, at that time, dyslexia wasn't really a known thing. But I'm a bit dyslexic." Keck said he "started to feel like my friends were doing well in school, but I was doing horribly. I felt like I was smart, but I demonstrably wasn't. I could never really focus on what the professor thought was important."

Then things got worse. The money he'd made working at the gas station in high school was running out. He needed to do something. Keck had been involved in AIESEC, an international youth business internship and leadership organization, in our freshman year. And he seemed to have learned something there. "I had a business idea," Keck said. He had been writing for the *Daily Cardinal*. "And there was a comic artist named James Sturm in there. He was good. The comic was called *Down and Out Dawg*, and it was your classic underground cartoon. It was really funny."

James Sturm was from New York and found inspiration for *Down and Out Dawg* from 1960s underground comics, which he'd discovered in Madison. They blew his mind. *Dawg* was a huge hit on campus. "It seemed like everybody read *Down and Out Dawg*," he said. "I've probably never done anything that popular since. I mean, there were *Down and Out Dawg* T-shirts. There was a *Down and Out Dawg* book." (Sturm would later become an accomplished comics artist and cofound the Center for Cartoon Studies in Vermont.)

Keck and Sturm made a deal. They would produce a monthly calendar together that would be distributed to students. Sturm would do illustrations for every month based on the *Down and Out Dawg* character, and Keck would sell ads to display around them. "We shook hands and smoked a bowl, and that was that," Sturm said. Keck said the project did "spectacularly well" because he was able to advertise right into people's dorm rooms. "That's how I made a living," he said, along with selling some pot to fraternities. Keck said they made around $1,000 for each calendar—a new one-pager for each month—which he and Sturm split fifty-fifty. "I thought of it as my rent," Keck said. "I remember saying, 'James, you're making 500 bucks doing this! Dude, I'm talking to Jimmy Dimitri for ten minutes and making $500!'" (Jimmy owned Zorba's, one of two dueling gyro restaurants on State Street, funded entirely by a steady stream of drunk, stoned college students getting takeout. It was probably like printing money.)

Sturm, Keck said, "did all the artwork in like four hours or less. And two days late. I'd be like, 'James, it's November third. We're selling a *calendar* here, man. I gotta take 'em to Kinko's.'" Once things got rolling, Keck said, "James and I just would do that calendar and smoke pot and eat and live like kings. It was kind of a brilliant marketing thing, and it totally worked. And it also flicked a little something in my head, a thing that was like, 'You're not a complete loser.' And if you feel that and that thing clicks, you just want more."

Keck and Sturm's calendar for April 1988 (they forgot to add the year). *Down and Out Dawg* is in the center with a headache. Keck's business entity was called Keko's Evil Clown Enterprises.

Keck decided to start his own newspaper. "I didn't really have a good idea of what that was; I just knew I wanted to start a newspaper. I was going to quit school and do this newspaper. And then I met this guy in a history of science class, part of the Integrated Liberal Studies program at Madison. His name was Chris Johnson."

Keck said they were reading Lewis Mumford, who wrote about how society influences technology as much as technology influences society, and Thomas Kuhn, the man responsible for the term "paradigm shift," which for Kuhn took place in science when anomalous ideas and details around a research topic or scientific field accumulated to such an extent that the original paradigm that everyone had believed was adequate to that point could no longer apply. "You know how you go into the big lecture hall and you always sit in the same place?" Keck said. "[Chris] sat behind me.

"He's one of those people that just has a weird light and energy around them. Completely fearless," Keck said. "Can make a trip to the grocery store weird and uncomfortable and electric. He had this crazy childhood in Brazil and Poland and Sweden, and then he went to high school in Lodi, Wisconsin." (Lodi is a town of three thousand on the Wisconsin River, about thirty miles from Madison.) He had also started college early after leaving high school and taking the GED instead; though a sophomore, Johnson was only eighteen years old. The rest of us were about twenty. "When I met Chris," Tim said, "I was like, 'That's the guy. I can't do this on my own. I need somebody like Chris to do it with me.' I talked to him about the idea, and he immediately jumped in." Amy Reyer (Amy Bowles at the time, who would sell ads and write for *The Onion* in its first year) said, "Tim has a healthy dark streak that draws him to the most complicated, brilliant people. He's genuinely curious about what makes someone tick. The weirder, the better."

But then, out of the blue, not long after they'd started brainstorming, Johnson said he was going to drop out of school and move back to Brazil with his dad to work on a business venture. Tomorrow. He packed up his stuff and vanished.

Keck was shocked and bereft at the abrupt loss of his friend and purported business partner. At the same time, he was impressed by the boldness of it all. The disregard for convention. The hugeness of the move. He kept on working on the newspaper idea, but found he didn't have the confidence to do it by himself. So he decided to go to Brazil on a cheap courier flight and convince Johnson to come back. He returned victorious and very hungover ten days later. Johnson had said he would return in six months.

Keck had taken a room in my apartment around this time, and I remember him telling me about the newspaper idea when he got back from Brazil. He said they wanted me to be the art director, whatever that was. (Though I did do some drawings now and then, I actually became the copy editor.) I hadn't met Johnson yet, but I was excited enough that I wrote about it in my diary: March 3, 1988.

Johnson finally got back to town, and then it was time to rock. "We didn't have editorial ideas or anything complicated like that," Keck said. "We just wanted to start a newspaper." Keck's mom loaned them $3,000, and they rented a shitty three-bedroom apartment on East Johnson Street, a few blocks from both State Street and the capitol, to be the office—and their home. The living room was the production and editorial area, and Andy Dhuey was brought in to live in the third bedroom and help pay the rent. Keck's mom would also be their advisor.

The first problem was what to call it. The only requirement was that it couldn't be serious. Maybe *The Rag*? How about *The Paper*? Then one day they were visiting Johnson's uncle Nels, who lived in Madison. "We ate onion sandwiches a lot," Keck said. "Why, I don't know, but we did, and Johnson's uncle said, 'Why don't you call it *The Onion*?'" Keck added, "I'm sorry I don't have an interesting story about why we called it *The Onion*; that's it. We made a lot of snap decisions in those days." Reyer's roommate, Pete Haise (pronounced "hi-zee"), told me, "And then I think somebody drew a pretty good onion, and that was the clincher."

Keck wasn't sure how you charged for advertising in a newspaper, so he called "every publication in New York" to get their media kits. "A media kit is a thing that says how big ads are, how much the ads are, all that kind of crap. But I didn't know any of that stuff. So I called *New York Magazine*, I called the *New Yorker*, I called the *Atlantic*, I called everybody. Nobody sent me anything except for the *New Yorker*." Keck took the rate card, whited out the *New Yorker*, and put *The Onion* on it instead. (He left the rest the way it was.) Keck then called up his *Dawg* calendar advertisers, told them about his new project, and gave them the rate card. There would also be coupons on the bottom of the front page, he said. "They were all thrilled with me because of the coupon concept. Everybody loves coupons."

Sturm agreed to let the new paper publish reruns of *Down and Out Dawg*. Keck also found another cartoonist he wanted to publish: Scott Dikkers, the creator of *Jim's Journal*. As Keck put it, "The *Daily Cardinal* paid them five dollars a comic strip. I paid them ten."

Jim's Journal was just as popular on campus as *Down and Out Dawg*. The polar opposite of Sturm's crazy psychedelic style that literally went outside the lines on a regular basis to express Dawg's insane adventures, *Jim's Journal* was the epitome of minimalism in both style and content. "Jim" was basically a stick figure, as were the other characters in the strip, and his "adventures" consisted of, say, waking up in the morning, going to class, playing with his cat, and starting his work shift at McDonald's. These would be the topic of four different strips, by the way—not one. Though he stayed inside the lines on the page, Dikkers liked to work outside the system and self-published a collection of Jim cartoons called *I Went to College and It Was Okay*, which pretty much summed up the level of invigoration expressed by Jim in any situation. Dikkers, a college dropout himself, had also syndicated the strip in college newspapers across the country and was making a living selling *Jim* books, T-shirts, and merchandise. The book did so well that it ended up on a college best-seller list.

People thought *Jim* was brilliant. Where *Dawg* was explosive, *Jim* was Zen. It was so minimal, it seemed deep. You could project all kinds of things onto it. The deadpan style also made the smallest joke very funny. Dikkers agreed to draw a bunch of other cartoons for *The Onion* too, all in different styles, so that it would seem like several different people were contributing. These included his comic *Plebes*, which made fun of ordinary people's stupidity, as well as a *Ripley's Believe It or Not!*-style one-panel cartoon about nonexistent historical events. Keck also asked me if I wanted to collaborate on a comic strip with him. Keck would write the story, and I'd draw the pictures. The cartoon was called *Jake the Weasel*, about a young man who seemed wholesome and nice but was actually horrible.

"So now we had some advertisers," Keck said. "We had a name. We rented a Mac. This is in 1988, so it was a shitty little Mac, the ones where you had to put the floppy disk in and out and change it eighty times just to run a program. But we didn't have any idea about the content in the publication." They had no editorial mission. No cause they wanted to promote. No message they wanted to send. They did love *Spy* magazine. Doing something in that spirit would be cool. But, otherwise, no topic fascinated them enough to make an entire newspaper about it.

As far as I know, only one other person from my high school class besides me graduated from UW–Madison, a guy named Todd Brown. He was good looking, funny, and charismatic, with parents from the Twin Cities. One day I went to visit him in his dorm during our freshman year, and he had a new friend there, a guy he'd met at the Ark Improv, a little independent theater a few blocks from State Street where he'd been taking classes and performing: Matt Cook. (Improv was invented in the Midwest, at the Brave New Workshop in Minneapolis and Second City in Chicago and ComedySportz in Milwaukee. Maybe that's why improv is more about the collective performance than any one individual star.)

Matt and I hit it off right away. He was from Chicago, he was really funny, and he was wearing a Joy Division T-shirt. We started hanging out all the time. That summer at a party at my first apartment, a tiny, sweltering attic two-bedroom on Conklin Place I shared with our friend Rachel, I introduced Keck to Matt Cook. Several of us were hanging out on the street—really an alleyway—waiting for Matt to show up. "The first time I saw Matt Cook," Keck said, "he was roller-skating with a refrigerator box on top of him down the street and then intentionally running into shit. Like 'Oh no! Oh no!' and then 'It's okay, I'm okay!' Like doing tons of pratfalls." The box was so big it covered Matt completely, making it look like it was zooming around all by itself. He careened around bashing into things, and we all just about died laughing. Keck said, "Matt is really funny, and he's self-hating, and creative, and not afraid to make a fool of himself. He kind of likes it. And that's the ingredients of a great comedian."

Keck said, "If there was a person who created *The Onion*'s voice, it would be Matt Cook."

Cook was born in South Bend, Indiana. His dad was a physicist, teaching or maybe doing postgraduate work at Notre Dame at the time. "Particle, high-energy, nuclear?" he said. "I don't actually know." Cook's parents were "your typical midwestern white Catholic parents. As they say, the Jews invented guilt, and the Catholics perfected it."

His dad unfortunately did not get tenure and started teaching himself computers instead, eventually landing a job in the University of Chicago Computer Science Department around 1974. First, they lived in Homewood, in the south suburbs of Chicago. "And that was a relatively integrated place," Cook said. But then they moved to the northwest suburbs of Chicago, where he went to high school. "And it was the whitest place in the universe." He added, "You probably won't be surprised to hear I was a bit of a weirdo in high school. You know. Into whatever was the cool music of the time. Punk, postpunk, new wave."

Brian Stack, who later became a writer and performer with Second City, Conan O'Brien, and Stephen Colbert, started his performance career at the Ark Improv in Madison. He told me that Matt Cook was in the first show he ever saw there. Cook joined other interesting performers from that era, like Joan and Bill Cusack. And also, "Chris Farley, the late great Chris Farley," was there too, "with his bandana and his Marquette rugby jacket." Cook said, "I was Chris Farley's first director. I taught him everything he knew about comedy except for cocaine and hookers and booze, because he learned that stuff by himself." Stack praised Cook and his creative style:

Matt was one of the most original thinkers I've ever met. He would do very, very fun experimental things with the Ark that were very conceptual and weird in wonderful ways. He would also do really fun video projects. I remember him doing a short film where the visuals were just him going through his normal day, like getting up and brushing his teeth, putting his backpack on, walking to class, sitting in class, eating lunch—but the only soundtrack was him crying.

It was so simple, and funny, and also kind of heartbreaking, because I'm sure some of it was rooted in his daily sadness that we all go through. But it was also very, very funny. The juxtaposition of this mundane guy who's not crying is going through his day with this sadness underneath it all.

One day, Keck and Johnson asked Cook to meet with them. "It was this baby-businessman thing," Cook said. The calendar had been pretty successful, Keck and Johnson said. Now they wanted to do a newspaper. Cook asked them what kind of newspaper, and they said that's why they'd invited him to the meeting. "So sitting there at that time, at that very meeting, I said, 'How about we just make it all up? Have all made-up stories, but play it like it's a real newspaper?'"

Keck remembered that the *Cardinal* did an April Fools' Day parody every year that was always really popular. "Well, I'm just gonna fucking do that," he thought. *The Onion* would not be a real newspaper. It would be a comedic parody of one.

Keck and Johnson finally had their concept. They went to Reyer and Haise's place and said, "Okay, we're gonna unveil this thing. You're sworn to secrecy." (Their other roommate was Deidre Buckingham, who became the photographer for *The Onion* in the first year. Buckingham, a skilled photographer and darkroom developer, told me that she had always wanted to be a photojournalist, but had flunked the skills test to get into UW's journalism school because she couldn't spell. *The Onion* became her outlet instead.) Reyer said, "I didn't even know them well enough to guess what it was. I was so sure it was gonna be lame." They unveiled the concept and explained: "We're gonna make up fake news. And people are going to believe it."

They said it was going to be called *The Onion*, and Reyer said, "Please tell me that it isn't like the onion has these deep layers of meaning. Is it just random?" Johnson and Keck said, "It's totally random. People will think it means something, but it doesn't."

"That was the beginning of it," Reyer said. "And it actually was a big deal. It never felt like that at the time, though." They asked Reyer if she wanted to help out, and she immediately said yes; she had a huge crush on Keck. She began selling ads, brainstorming, and eventually doing a little writing. Buckingham signed on too.

Amy Reyer was born in New York City. Her dad's work on a traveling medical ship called *Project Hope* had taken them all around the world when she was little. They eventually landed in Washington, DC, where she attended the school Sidwell Friends. "It was a private school with some really smart fucking kids," she said. "And I did not feel like one of them." For college, she wanted something completely different. "I thought, 'I want to go to a Big Ten school. And I want to be anonymous.'"

Anonymity was important. Amy has a very famous older sister, Julia Louis-Dreyfus, a Second City and *Saturday Night Live* alum who had been working in film and would soon be cast in a lead role on *Seinfeld*. Amy's younger sister is actress Lauren Bowles. Amy, the middle child, said she was a theater kid too. "But it's not what I wanted to do. I was good at it, but it's not what I wanted to do." She was also tired of being in a small place—her Sidwell class was only about a hundred people—as well as "sort of being labeled as a dumb blonde" there. "That sucked," she said. "It really sucked. And UW–Madison, when I visited, I thought, 'Oh my God, this is so great. It's, like, 85 percent blonde. Nobody will notice me. I'm just gonna be a regular person here.'" She had also visited the University of Michigan at Ann Arbor, another popular destination for East Coast kids, but thought people were too serious about school there. "And I was looking for a vibe where people didn't take themselves too seriously. That was important to me, to go to a school where everyone wasn't going to go on to do amazing things."

Keck and Johnson asked Haise if he would sell ads. He said no. Though he used to do ad sales for the *Cardinal*, he was done with that. He had gotten fired from the *Cardinal* for skipping too many meetings. And he had other jobs now: he rented apartments and he bartended. Whatever worked to keep him cruising. But after being asked "five times," he finally caved, and within a few weeks he was the advertising manager.

Haise saw it as "rallying around a cause," saying, "I never thought there could have been a better job." Haise was from Wauwatosa, a suburb of Milwaukee, a place for which he had great affection. His parents had divorced when he was young, and it may not have been a great time for him. Luckily, Haise was a very outgoing and social guy, and he had his hometown to give him a foundation even if his parents were not together. At the time, I saw him as this sort of surfer-dude Deadhead. According to Reyer, he was "baked all the time." (He had also been in AIESEC.)

The first issue of *The Onion* came out in the fall of 1988, with the front-page story "Mendota Monster Mauls Madison," written by Matt Cook under the pseudonym Gunnar Downes (they wanted the most macho-sounding name possible), about a mythical lake monster named Bozho. The purposely blurry photo by Deidre Buckingham showed the head of the "monster" breaching the water. It was actually Tim Keck's arm with a stocking over it; Photoshop had not been invented yet. (I remember seeing him at the office afterward and asking why he was all wet.) The rest of the issue was a pretty anarchic mix of stuff. Most of it was written in the week or two before the first issue came out. In addition to copy editing, I wrote occasionally that year too; in the first issue I have a little story of the sort that would later be called "flash fiction." We also published a story by a creative writing friend of mine. The issue also ran excerpts from the campus police blotter—gossipy content that people would want to read, but that you didn't have to pay for. Lorin Miller and Sandra Schlies wrote soap-opera summaries, which turned out to be one of the main reasons people picked up the paper. To create some buzz before the first issue hit the streets, Keck and Johnson printed out stickers with *The Onion*'s name and the motto they'd invented, "Witty, Irreverent, and a Little Nasty," and stuck them up around town.

Keck said, "And it was just a pile of crap. When I saw it, I was like, 'This is really, really bad.' But strangely, it was successful. Like, right off the bat."

A student at Madison at the time, future *Onion* writer Joe Garden said, "I remember being kind of impressed by it because back in those days, you had the regular alternative weekly, you had the socialist weekly, you had the feminist weekly. You had a second socialist weekly. The music weekly. You had all these free papers, all these free papers everywhere. And *The Onion*, even as raw and primitive as it was with the 'Mendota Monster' issue, it stood out from the rest of them."

I reread the "Mendota Monster" story in 2018, when I started researching this book during the Trump administration. Until I accidentally saw a reference to Bozho in a public library book about Wisconsin folklore one day—which I picked up while waiting for a study room to open—I thought that Matt had invented the name. However, the name, short for "Winnebozho," was derived from an Algonquin trickster of the same name—and borrowed by white settlers in the Madison area.

Lake Mendota is one of four lakes around Madison. The area is called "Dejope," the Ho-Chunk word for "four lakes." The Ho-Chunk are the Indigenous nation that lived in the Madison area for thousands of years before European settlement and still do today. In 1942, Charles Brown, an archaeologist at the Wisconsin Historical Society, published a pamphlet called *Sea Serpents in Wisconsin Lakes*, which mentioned a friendly Lake Mendota serpent. In the early 1960s, playwright Robert Gard reprinted Brown's stories about this serpent. "And in these sources," Professor Jim Leary said, "this figure was referred to as a lake monster named Bozho."

THE ONION

free campus weekly   monday august 29, 1988   volume 14 number 1

august

S	M	T	W	T	F	S
28	29	30	31			

septemeber

S	M	T	W	T	F	S
				1	2	3

under the skin...

UW SNAPSHOTS

Superfluous statistics that really don't shape much of anything

Unhappy Bike Owners

Every year many bicycles are stolen because people are careless, or worse yet trustworhty of their species. The simplest way to avoid such an unpleasant situation is to lock your bike. Remember lock it or lose it!

Number Of Stolen Bicycles Per Year

1987	154
1986	125
1985	148
1984	164
1983	188

Source: UW-Madison Police and Security Report

Mendota Monster Mauls Madison

What exactly is happening in the once peaceful town of Madison, Wisconsin? See page 4 for the scoop by Gunnar Downes, two-time winner of the Provo, Utah -- Reporter of The Year Award. Gunnar exposes the dirty truth.

The first issue of The Onion: *August 29, 1988. The blurry-on-purpose photo of Tim Keck's arm sticking out of Lake Mendota was taken by Deidre Buckingham. The issue created a pain in the neck for all future* Onion *archivists by beginning with "Volume 14."*

The real Indigenous trickster named Winnebozho was "a kind of cultural hero of the Algonquian people," Leary said. However, "In Wisconsin, the Algonquian people are Potawatomi Menominee, and the Ho-Chunk linguistically are Siouxan people." The two groups live in different areas of the state as well. In other words, "Winnebozho [the real one] is associated with people who did not live in the Dejope area at all." Yet somehow Lake Mendota, in Ho-Chunk land, now had a sea serpent that settlers had given the same name.

Why settlers had wanted there to be a mysterious serpent in the lake in the first place is another subject. I asked Colin Dickey, author of *The Unidentified: Mythical Monsters, Alien Encounters, and Our Obsession with the Unexplained*, about settlers of European ancestry borrowing Indigenous stories and moving them into different places. His book discusses a period in the nineteenth century "when the way we understand the world is divided into two spheres—religion and theology on the one hand, and science on the other," creating a desire for things that didn't fit into either sphere. He thought the "borrowing of Native American tropes and mythologies and cultures has a lot to do with a longer-running kind of fetishization of these cultures that white people sort of simultaneously oppressed and murdered, but still sort of romanticize because they represent a kind of 'uncivilized' freedom. Which is bullshit, but."

I sent Matt a copy of his "Mendota Monster" story to see what he thought after thirty-five years. He said, "I was clearly twenty. It is not the writing of anyone who has put in many hours on the planet." In his story, Bozho is a long-dormant monster submerged in the lake. Then, in 1988, he comes out from the depths and starts terrorizing everyone. Experts and officials dismiss the evidence and say the people who saw it must have been deluded. The state Republican administration, led by Governor Tommy Thompson, denies what's happening while secretly helping the monster in its path of destruction.

I used to be so sick of Tommy Thompson. These days I'd love to fill the GOP with clones of him. He listened to ACT UP, you know? Rereading the story in 2018, during the Trump administration, I didn't see it as having much to do with Thompson anymore, but instead found it creepily prescient. Yes, the story was written by a twenty-year-old improv comedian, but now it felt like Bozho could be read as an allegory of what neoliberalism and the GOP and inequality and the concentration of power into ever-fewer hands had done since the 1980s to institutions like the media and our sense of safety in everyday life.

In the first issue of *The Onion*, intrepid reporter Gunnar Downes has noticed something, and he is warning us. The monster might only be killing swimmers in the lake right now, but soon it will be much worse. In fact, the monster's appearance is the beginning of the end of the world.

The Onion
MONDAY, AUGUST 29, 1988
Mendota Monster Mauls Madison (excerpt)

GET YOUR HEAD OUT OF THE SAND
AND STICK IT IN THE WATER
by Gunnar Downes

Listen up, it's time for all you idealistic, college time-wasters to get your head out of the clouds and start paying attention to scandals right in your own back yard. While the population of this sissy, pseudo-liberal town has been running around like chickens with their heads cut off over some foreigners in Central America, our friendly Gov. "Tiny" Tommy Thompson has been tiptoeing through the taxpayers. He and his Republican cronies have been perpetuating the biggest cover-up in Wisconsin history. Don't pretend you haven't heard the rumors. You know exactly what I mean. I'm talking about the fearsome beastie known as Bozho, the Lake Mendota monster.... Oh, it's not really going to happen if we get off our collective asses and stop it. Inside the pea brains of state officials however, Armageddon is a distinct reality.

... The plan remains simple for the time being. Bozho surreptitiously kills swimmers by holding them under long enough to drown, without marking them in any way. And who are these swimmers? Why they're the nature-loving, liberal types who are most likely to vote against Thompson. With only Republicans left alive in this state, "Sachead" Thompson will easily win the next few elections and thereby build enough credibility to become president.... Who controls the red button then?

Chapter 3

Wednesdays and Thursdays, Chris and I would go around selling ads; that's when our week would start," Tim Keck said. "Friday was when we'd start writing and laying out the newspaper," a "painful" process. Then they would "put it on three hundred floppy disks, ride our bikes to the computer lab, print it out." And never, for a year, "never ever, there was *never* a time we slept on a Sunday night, because the paper had to be at the printer early Monday morning."

The printer (the first of several *The Onion* went through in its time) was a half-hour drive outside of Madison. They'd drive the pasted-up boards there, come home, and crash for a couple hours, Keck said. "Then a truck with all the *Onions* would arrive. We'd take them out of the truck, put them in my Jeep, and then go out drinking or whatever. And then next morning, five o'clock in the morning, we'd deliver the papers all over Madison." Circulation was 12,500. Repeat every week for an entire school year. Keck used the huge old decrepit Jeep Cherokee his mom had given him for distribution. Once, the engine caught on fire while parked in the office driveway packed with *Onions*. Keck frantically put it out before the entire week's work went up in flames.

To fill space, they often used deadheads—little boxes with words and a picture in them that helped to fill up any openings left over after the ads and written content went in. Some were ads for *The Onion* itself. Others were basically absurdist Zen that came off the top of someone's head at the last minute, like "Toast is life." Pete Haise said they ran that deadhead all the time because toast was a big meal.

The computer sat in Chris Johnson's bedroom. Photographer Deidre Buckingham told me it was the first computer she had ever seen. "This is of course Year Zero for desktop publishing," Matt Cook said. "Everything I wrote for that paper I wrote on that Mac Classic, in that room, because I didn't have a computer. Nobody did." You had to physically come to the office and type your article into it. Everybody took turns. There was no printer—hence the bike rides to the campus computer lab.

The second issue was rather less portentous than "Mendota Monster." The front-page headline was "Crazed, Drunken, Back-Stabbing Sorority Girls." There was no story, just a jump to a rather tasteless (but funny) drinking board game that ridiculed Greek life. Keck had me draw the pictures for the game, which featured much fluffy 1980s hair. The rest of that issue's content was similar to the first. Issue 3, with "Wild Boy of Picnic Point," also by Gunnar Downes, featured a blurry rear view photo of a naked, mud-covered Tim Keck running through a dark forest on the shores of Lake Mendota. Deidre Buckingham took that one too.

Other front pages that year include "World to End Thursday," an article by staff psychic Elisha Caldor (the photo was Matt Cook in drag), and "Six Youths Roto-Tilled to Death in Gang War," a collaboration between Keck and myself about the rural Wisconsin turf battle between the Fleet Farm Knights and the Lords of Farm and Fleet.

Despite their early success, the staff's lack of computer skills was becoming a problem. The universe, however, was about to send *The Onion* the first of many timely gifts. Jonnie Wilder was recruited to the paper "on a chilly September evening in 1988." Jonnie had just finished up a Narcotics Anonymous meeting and was walking up State Street with some friends toward the capitol. "I heard music, some sort of jazz torch song, floating out into the street," Jonnie said. "I felt a strong pull to go inside. My friends said it was a bad idea to go into a bar, that I would end up drinking. But I felt the pull so strongly."

(Jonnie came out as transgender several years later. "I won't say that I had a fixed idea of what sex and/or gender I was back then," Jonnie wrote me. "I don't want to make up memories with my imagination." Jonnie told me it was okay to refer to her as "he" in this book, since that's how she identified in those days. I've done that in places when events are narrated in the past tense. Jonnie said, "I'm not going to try to claim that I had a female-identity or woman-identity back then. And as everyone knows, we don't actually realize we're trans until we get access to the internet and that wouldn't be for a few more years for me." She was credited as Jonathan Hart Eddy in the *Onion* masthead.)

A sign on the door said "Onion Night." Johnson's sister Elizabeth, who had been helping with ad sales and many other things—including regularly feeding Keck and Johnson at the nearby hotel buffet where she worked—greeted Jonnie at the door. "This is *The Onion*," Elizabeth said, and asked if he read it. Jonnie said no. "She said they were looking for volunteers, and would I be interested? They were always looking for writers and artists. And advertising salespeople, of course. Oh, and if I knew anything about desktop publishing, that would be helpful."

Jonnie immediately paid closer attention. Because "that was my thing; that's what I did. I was one of the few kids on my block who had their own personal computer, a Macintosh Plus, with a 20-megabyte external hard drive. I had made zines and was into self-publishing. My job at the time was working for a place called CompUType. The guy who owned it was a journalism professor, Roy Caldwell, and this was his side gig." The business was mostly printing out résumés on a laser printer and renting computers by the hour.

Inside, Jonnie met Johnson, Keck, and Amy Reyer. "Everyone was super drunk," Jonnie said. "It was pitched to me as a parody of the *Weekly World News* and *National Enquirer*, but with a focus on life at the UW. So, like, *Weekly World News* meets *National Lampoon*. I liked the idea, and looking through the current issue, I thought I could make it look nicer. Because it looked terrible." Jonnie told them about CompUType and having access to multiple Macintoshes and a laser printer, which was closer to the office than the computer lab and could make their production process much easier. "I was really excited by it," Jonnie said. "I could really help here."

Jonnie stated the plain facts in the situation. "I am a slightly above-average smart person," she said. "But I had a skill that very few people had back then. I knew how to use a Mac, and I knew about desktop publishing. In Madison in 1988, there couldn't have been more than five to fifteen people who had that skill set in the entire city. I was in the right place at the right time."

Johnson was so excited, Jonnie said, that "he offered me Amy." They told Jonnie to come in to work the next week, which Jonnie did. It may have been something of a surprise. Reyer told me that Keck and Johnson had been in the habit of drunkenly telling people to come to work, forgetting about it, and then having no idea who they were when they actually showed up. Jonnie, though, was different. "I started upgrading right away," she said. "The first thing I did was start laying out as much of the paper as possible in Aldus PageMaker. This gave us a cleaner look and saved more time doing layout since we didn't have to cut so much stuff out. But it basically required using my Macintosh with the external hard disk. Which started to become a problem when the external hard disk started failing and needed to be sent away to be repaired. For a while, I could get it to start again by kicking it, like the Millennium Falcon." Jonnie was soon an essential (and unpaid) part of *The Onion*'s operation.

Jonnie was raised in Rockford, Illinois, by a single mother who worked full-time as a bookkeeper and occasionally as a substitute teacher, "and mostly abandoned by an alcoholic father." Jonnie's mother remarried "a decent and gentle man who managed several Sears department stores across the central Indiana sales district." Unfortunately, Jonnie said, "I was bullied relentlessly by students who carried knives on their belts and rifles in gun racks displayed in their pickup trucks parked in the school parking lot." Ultimately, it worked out, however. In order to get promotions, Jonnie's stepdad had to keep changing Sears stores and moving the family. "By the time I would get a good group of bullies that really wanted to kick my ass, I was out of there . . . I survived. A lot of kids don't."

Jonnie redid the masthead "so it could be reprinted each week with different dates and a different wacky banner. We moved a lot of our production to the offices of CompUType on evenings and weekends." They bartered an ad each week to use the equipment. Layout Hell weekend was "the highlight of my life," Jonnie said. "We'd produce most of the newspaper over the forty-eight-hour period from Friday evening to Sunday evening." By the end of the first year, "we had a pretty sweet little system and were producing a high-quality product . . . We'd listen to the community radio station, or I'd bring cassette tapes from home to play," Jonnie said. "I don't think I was allowed to play Grateful Dead or anything prog rock, so I'd bring Steely Dan tapes instead." Johnson loved Brazilian samba and bossa nova, bootleg cassettes he'd brought back from Rio. The vibes in that room, Jonnie said, were incredible.

In Johnson, Keck had chosen a bold, funny, rule-breaking business partner who seemed to have little fear of anything, and they became good friends. He had also unfortunately chosen someone who was often difficult to be around. Johnson's schtick was to be just absurdly, over-the-top rude to everybody, insult-comic style. Sometimes it was indeed funny. But, most of the time, it was too much. Looking back, there was probably some self-protection happening. Growing up, his family had not always been the most nurturing. He and his sister, Elizabeth, were very close and had supported each other through some difficult times.

"Chris and Tim were very different kinds of businesspeople," said Peri Pakroo, a Madison student then who later worked with both Keck and Johnson on subsequent newspapers. "Chris was more of a micromanager, which is kind of interesting and weird. It seems like he would be the type of person who wouldn't want to do that. Tim was more hands-off and allowed people to do their own thing. But Chris just has a mean streak. I mean, everybody will say the same thing." He would get "borderline abusive to people, for no reason. And that was a bummer, and we fell out," Peri said. "It's sad that Chris has to be so mean, because everybody who's ever been friends with him, he's the most fun. The most interesting, hilarious person." Some staffers avoided coming to the office because of Johnson's behavior.

Jonnie said Johnson was "insanely abusive, which, oddly enough, just made him more appealing. People do it a lot. You're abusive to somebody, and it just makes them want to try harder to make you like them." Haise, however, wasn't impressed. "Johnson was just a punk," he said. "Definitely the self-proclaimed smartest guy in the room. And a total asshole." Haise told me that Johnson used to actually wrestle him in the office. "Johnson has an incredible ability to make you feel bad," Haise said. "And he would just pin me and push my face into the carpet. I'd be like, 'Dude, come on, look at me. I'm five-seven, 150 pounds.'" Haise said, "They managed by insult and apology. I think Chris and Tim actually did that very well in the year they ran the paper. Chris was a fantastic bad cop, and Tim was a fantastic good cop." Buckingham, who has known Johnson for decades now, said he was a "brilliant, brilliant guy" who was also "complicated." "There's definitely an edge to him. There always has been."

Jonnie said Johnson "had an energy inside of him that was, 'Okay, we're doing this, now!' He was funny; he was exciting. You never knew what was going to happen next." Jonnie remembered Johnson and Keck pinching the backs of her arms at the computer to prompt faster work. Keck said, "Jonnie and Matt were under Chris's spell. Chris would just ask them to do shit, and they would do it." Matt Cook remembered, "I think it was the cheese-plate piece. Chris locked me in the office and wouldn't let me out until I gave him six column inches. It was a fake home-and-gardeny sort of dining recipe piece. Fluff piece. How to make an elegant cheese plate. Which I'm sure isn't very funny, given the conditions it was written under."

Peri Pakroo said, "The thing about Chris is that he has a lot of anger and hurt. You know that tension that every businessperson has between wanting your product to be really quality, you want your creative passion to be shown in it, versus you want to make money doing it? There's something about that tension that just brought out the worst in him. It's almost like, the more you cared about what you were doing—and these are young writer people who care, you know?—the more Chris would want to squish you down."

Keck said Johnson had good relationships with several advertising clients, including the owner of the Cardinal Bar, a guy who booked entertainment at the Memorial Union, and the owner of a Chinese restaurant, all of whom he began hanging out with socially. All three were immigrants, which may have reflected Johnson's own experience of living in multiple countries growing up. Johnson was also bilingual—he was fluent in Portuguese from his years in Brazil—so he had that in common with them as well. His frame of reference at his small rural Wisconsin high school must have been on a different planet from many of his classmates.

I asked Keck what Johnson brought to *The Onion*—what work he did, as well as how his approach to life affected that first year—and he wrote: "I've always considered Chris' effort to be equal to my own (or more). He wrote, edited, sold ads, worked on layout, collections, distribution, accounting, etc. We never took a day off except during school holidays. Rarely there was a workday that wasn't over 14 hours." Keck said he couldn't have worked like such a maniac if Johnson wasn't doing the same. "Chris' super-dark humor and intense worldview completely matched the vibe of the endeavor. I know it wasn't war or famine or anything and this was something we chose—we were college kids. But *The Onion* had that kind of sustained intensity that scratches an itch that's hard for me to explain or understand."

This first year, *The Onion* also featured Mark Pitsch, a writer at the *Daily Cardinal*, who wrote an oddball little stream-of-consciousness column called "Catch the Pig." Readers loved it. Pitsch later became the assistant city editor of the *Wisconsin State Journal* and president of the Madison chapter of the Society of Professional Journalists. Today, he is the director of media relations for the University of Wisconsin System. He told me, "When I was in college, I was pretty straight. And I liked hanging out with guys who maybe had a little more edge than I did and were willing to take more risks. Tim and Chris were definitely in that camp." Keck told me that Mark's good friend, the future Pulitzer Prize–winning international reporter Anthony Shadid and a fellow *Cardinal* writer, also wrote "little jokey pieces" that year. Keck said he remembered Shadid saying, "Please don't let anybody know. My job at the *Cardinal* is important to me." (Shadid unfortunately died in Syria in 2012 of an asthma attack while reporting for the *New York Times*.)

Along with his cartoons, Scott Dikkers occasionally helped with layout that fall, and he and Keck brainstormed sometimes as well—the same kind of thing all of us did that year. Keck said, "Scott was disciplined; he was funny and disciplined. But he had a big turmoil in his heart because he really wanted to do *Jim's Journal* and he felt like *The Onion* was sapping his creative juices. And every time he was working at *The Onion* it was hurting *Jim's Journal* somehow, which was going to be his future. Scott quit fourteen times in the first year."

Keck said Dikkers believed you had a limited amount of creativity, so you had to spend it incredibly wisely. "He thought that the more you used it, the less you had. It was a zero-sum game. So we would always joke about it." They had to be cautious about how much Scott they got "because he had this real genuine belief that once it was used, it was gone." Still, "I have to say, some of the most fun work I've ever had in my life was brainstorming with Scott" about *Onion* articles, Keck said. They would meet at Wisconsin Public Radio sometimes when Dikkers was doing a board-op shift. "There was a lot of Dionysian shit in the early *Onion*, but there wasn't a lot of Apollonian, and he was very mathematical and an excellent editor."

Through all of this, Andy Dhuey was a fixture in the office. After all, he *lived* there. And Dhuey almost never went to class. So whenever anyone was waiting to use *The Onion*'s computer, Dhuey was always there to hang out. He was a relaxed, amiable companion, interested in pretty much everything and

THE ONION

Free Campus Weekly   Tuesday, September 20, 1988   Volume 14   Number 4

The Onion's Early Years

by Sylvia Hein

Remember "Rap" music, or "Heavy Metal?" How about lycra bike-racing shorts? Perhaps you remember going to the local movie house to see silver-screen idol Tom Hanks wooing captivated teens in his latest picture, *Big*.

It was a quaint and almost mythical time, back when the voices of George Michael, Robert Palmer and Tracy Chapman were emanating from radios all across the land. Such minstrels crooned truisms of a simpler era, an era of President Ronald Wilson Reagan, *Who Framed Roger Rabbit*, and Orville Redenbacher's Microwave Popping Corn.

The Midwest was stepping out of its hottest, drought-stricken summer in over half a century. And the nation mourned over still another delayed launch of the space shuttle Discovery— this time a loose coping capnut in the emission cooling system. But President Reagan's soothing, patriotic radio addresses reassured a country at peace.

With wildfires raging in the Western United States, regional unrest in the Soviet Union, and student demonstrators in Seoul, South Korea shedding a foreboding shadow over the pageantry of the Olympic games, Americans turned

See **Look Back, page 5**

UW Snapshots

superfluous statistics that really do not shape much of anything

Hurricane Gilbert

Amount spent on local media coverage of Hurricane Gilbert:

$7,322

Amount of local property damage caused by Hurricane Gilbert:

$0

A rare photograph of T. Hermann Zwiebel, the famed newspaper mogul, who fashioned the world of print media to conform to his expectations. He is shown here reading the first issue of *The Onion*.

photograph courtesy of State Historical Society

Scott Dikkers (left) as The Onion's *fictional founder, T. Hermann Zwiebel. (Later, the spelling of the name would change to "T. Herman Zweibel.") Unidentified companion on the right. The State Historical Society photo credit is also fictional. Photo by Deidre Buckingham.*

always ready to chat. Keck said Dhuey would lounge in his brown velour bathrobe listening to Steely Dan and watching *Raging Bull* "for the five thousandth time" with whoever was around that day.

Dhuey grew up in suburban Milwaukee and had twelve years of Catholic education all the way through Jesuit high school. He said he actually felt different our first year in the dorms. "Most people were from public high schools throughout the state and didn't have my kind of slightly snotty college-prep background." Though socially liberal, back then he also usually voted Republican. Dhuey is now an intellectual property lawyer with an independent practice. And that year he got a little experience by serving as *The Onion*'s source of legal knowledge. Yes, Dhuey's IP law career began as a pretend lawyer for a fake newspaper. Today he is probably best known for being the attorney representing the human photographer in the "Monkey Selfie" case brought by PETA. (I encourage you to look up his brief. I will, though, say that giving legal personhood to animals, rivers, and land is a compelling idea. I mean, if a corporation can be a person now, why can't Lake Superior?)

Dhuey also happened to be the business manager of the *Daily Cardinal*. In other words, they had an informant from their biggest competitor living in their office. Keck said, "I would just say, 'Dhurod [Andy's nickname], if I want to sell an ad, who do I want to talk to at the Orpheum?' Or, 'Hey, Dhurod, what the fuck do you think of this?' for some legal thing." Still, Keck said, "I don't know why Dhurod lived with us. I mean, it was a fucking hellhole. It was just disgusting. We all smoked. There's beer cans and disgusting old coffee and piles of cigarettes and bongs—and Dhurod."

Issue 4 saw the first appearance of T. Hermann Zwiebel, *The Onion*'s illustrious fictitious founder. Played by Dikkers with a big grin in the front-page photo—he seemed to enjoy pretending to be *The Onion*'s eccentric originator—Zwiebel (German for "onion") would become a running character in the publication for decades. (The spelling of the name would change, however.)

Keck also loved contests and gimmicks and events that got people interacting with the newspaper. One was the "Win a Cheese Sandwich" contest. In issue 6, entrants were asked to write essays called "Why I Think America Is Neat" and submit them. The next week, the cover featured Keck and Johnson awarding the sandwich to twenty-three-year-old first-year law student Ralph Sczygelski from Merrill, Wisconsin. His winning essay was written in poetic stanzas:

THE ONION

| Free Campus Weekly | Tuesday, October 11, 1988 | Volume 14 Number 7 |

Cheese-Sandwich Winner

by Sylvia Hein

One week ago, when The Onion announced that a cheese sandwich would be awarded to the author of the best "Why I Think America Is Neat" essay, euphoria struck the literary community. Everyone with a knack for words was starry-eyed—everyone from renowned essayists, poet laureates, and best-selling authors, to the goofy-looking kid with the chewed-up pencil who sits behind you in writing class and sniffs like he has a cold even though he doesn't. Patriots of every stripe mused over blank sheets of paper with the proverbial fountain pen in hand, yearning for the inspiration to transfer that lyrical stream of heart-stopping prose vacillating in their thoughts onto the page with lucidity and eloquence.

Judging the entries was not an easy job. When all the essays were in, The Onion's panel of judges agreed that all the essays were excellent and each deserved to win. After hours of heated deliberations, the winner was chosen: Ralph Sczygelski, a 23-year-old first-year law student from Merrill, Wisconsin.

See Cheese on Page 5

PHOTO BY FRANK MILLER

Co-chairpersons of *The Onion's* Committee for Civic Awareness, Albert von Hoff (left) and Billit Shervick (right), award Ralph Sczygelski a cheese sandwich for his essay, "Why I Think America Is Neat."

UW Snapshots

Pointless drivel that you heard here first.

Tripping in Madison...

Onion operatives staking out the Library Mall watched people tripping and observed the following behavior.

46%

Looked back at whatever it was they tripped over.

32%

Broke into a brief sprint..

18%

Fell to the ground and feigned death.

The cheese sandwich winner receives his prize. Tim Keck is on the left and Chris Johnson is on the right.

America is really neat.

We have a solid naval fleet.

The food is good. The sky is blue.

The water's wet. The beer is too.

Our constitution sets it straight.

I'm free to speak. I'm free to date.

I like it here and so should you.

Shoobydoobydoobydoo.

The Onion also got a little taste of the power of the press to influence politics. In the second semester of that year, they came up with two write-in cocandidates for student council president and promoted them, as a joke, over two issues: "WSA Conspiracy Keeps Crusaders Off Ballot" and "Alien Invaders Campaign for Student Print Notes with Help of Local Meteorologist." Shockingly, the endorsement almost worked. Amy Reyer remembered the staff freaking out a little. Their joke candidates were getting a lot of momentum, "like for real, and he's gonna *win*," she said. "Which was never part of the range of possibilities, I don't think, in anybody's mind." They were just hoping to sell more ad space, and now somehow they were picking who was going to become the next president of the UW student body. Then they found out that one of the candidates—nobody had vetted them, since it was a joke—apparently had political opinions they abhorred. Reyer said, "That was one of those early moments or red flags where I thought, 'This is not cool. We're colliding with the real world here.'"

Looking back, Keck believes that "Dead Guy Found," from February 1989, written by Matt Cook, was the "first real *Onion* article." He said, "It has all of the rules. You put it in the structure of a newspaper article, make little things big, big things little. You're really in a genuinely interesting way messing with the form. It's not an obvious satire about anything. It's an environmental satire, you know? It's a satire of a feeling of what newspapers are, rather than a specific political thing."

Matt Cook agreed. "I think maybe that 'Dead Guy' article was the first hint of what *The Onion* would become," he said. And yes, "that's me in the photo buried head down in the snowbank." He added that the story was written in "faceless, AP reporter-type style, with quotes from the sheriff and the chief of police."

Haise worked with Keck and Johnson to sell the ads that kept *The Onion* alive. I would run into him occasionally at the office when I came in to copy

St. Patrick's Day Shopper

THE ONION

Free Campus Weekly | Tuesday, February 21, 1989 | Volume 15 • Number 6

DEAD GUY FOUND

BY LISA COOPER

Madison, Wisconsin—A dead guy was found buried head first up to his waist in a snowbank this Monday morning, apparently the result of an accident with a snowplow.

"I was just out shoveling my walk when I noticed this pile of clothes and stuff," said 28-year-old insurance agent, Timothy Specht. Specht said that he and a neighbor's further investigation lead to the discovery of the dead guy.

Kairen Juniper, 19, an exotic dancer, also saw the dead guy. "One minute I'm walking down to pick up my daily paper, and the next minute there's this dead guy," she said.

Speculation by the Police Department as to the dead guy's situation immediately before his immersion in the snowbank has lead to almost nothing. "About the only thing we have gleaned at this point is that the dead

guy was probably unaware of the alternate sides parking law enforced in conjunction with heavy snows and that he was walking on the wrong side on that morning," said Madison Police Liaison Mary Ann Thurber.

The Dane county coroner's office has been working since Monday to determine the cause of death. A Coroner's office employee said work had slowed to a

See Dead Guy on page 7

UW Snapshots

A brief glimpse of the reality you participate in every day

Donna Does Emerald City

Onion Operatives polled 100 students to see which character in *The Wizard of Oz* Donna Shalala resembles most.

86% King of the Flying Monkeys

13% Mayor of Munchkinland

1% Glinda, the Good Witch of the North

*Onion Operatives were happy that no one mentioned either Wicked Witch because of their profound respect for Donna Shalala.

Matt Cook as the Dead Guy on a typical Madison winter day in February 1989. Today temperatures occasionally reach 70 degrees in February and snowfall is a fraction of what it once was. Photo by Deidre Buckingham.

edit the paper every week. I didn't talk to him much, though. I was a total snob about the business side, especially around advertising, and I did not appreciate what Haise did. Just the word "salesman" made me dismiss anything that person might otherwise have had to offer. So I looked down my nose at Haise, who wore Grateful Dead T-shirts, talked in stoner business jargon, and appeared to have no interest in literature, philosophy, art, or anything I thought made a person worth socializing with. He was a *salesman*.

Like so many other things I wouldn't understand until many years down the road, I was completely wrong. Haise was probably the most consequential person on *The Onion*'s staff.

In only ten months, Keck and Johnson had made *The Onion* out of nothing into a highly popular campus presence. They had also earned enough money to keep the lights on, pay the printer, and—most important—pay Keck's mom, Janet, back.

They were also exhausted. Haise recalled, "One time I was sitting next to Tim on the couch, and I just said, 'Do you ever just kick back and say, "I own a newspaper!"?'" And Keck told him, "Look at me. I'm out of school. I have no money. I have no clothes. I can't sleep. Are you fucking kidding me? Like I have time to look back and enjoy any success? This is a huge disaster. No. Never."

Keck said, "It was a grueling schedule, and it had started to become kind of unfun. Though the paper was just getting more and more popular. We went out to a bar, and we just decided, 'Let's stop this. Let's just move on. I want to get out. I hate Madison. Don't you hate Madison? Let's get out of here.'"

So Keck and Johnson decided to sell *The Onion*, and they knew who they wanted to sell it to: Haise, Dikkers, and Jonnie. Haise would be the business guy, Dikkers would be the editorial guy, and Jonnie would be the computer guy. The cost was (as people recall it) $16,000. According to Haise, they were "bullied" into buying it. If they didn't, Keck and Johnson told them, *The Onion* would die. Jonnie told me that Haise didn't want to do it. Why don't we just make our own newspaper? Haise asked. With a new name? We can keep all the advertisers. Jonnie said Dikkers felt that *The Onion* name and reputation were worth it.

Keck and Johnson won. The deal (as much as people could remember) was that each of the three had to come up with $3,000 for a $9,000 down payment— which for Dikkers, at least, was "all the money [he] had in the world"—and then had one year to pay down the balance. If they didn't pay it off in a year, the business went back to Johnson and Keck.

The deal was inked, Keck and Johnson were free, and Haise, Dikkers, and Jonnie . . . were not. Reyer remembered being aghast when she heard the price: "That's madness," she told Keck. It was completely ridiculous, absurd. "I thought it was insane that somebody could possibly spend that much money on *The Onion.*" She said Keck was like, "I can retire now!"

Jonnie also had a change of heart about Haise with the passage of time. Back then, she said:

I hated Pete. But as I've grown older, I realized what an asshole I was to him. Because I'm a hippie, right? I have always thought capitalism was evil. And Pete was a capitalist because Tim was a capitalist. Chris and Tim were both capitalists. Pete was about sales, which is the army of capitalism. And Pete was the guy who had to take a lot of shit for making capitalism actually work, right?

Pete is a guy who wants to be liked, and who has very high emotional intelligence. To be a good salesperson, you have to be. I always used to be like, "I'm so much smarter than Pete." I'm making myself sound like an asshole. But you know, I realized that being clever is not the most important thing in the world. Because I knew at a very early age I was clever. But I was failing at life. And people who were way less smart than me in that sense were doing great. So I have a lot of respect for Pete now, because he sold ads. He fed the monster.

Keck and Johnson decided to see just how far they could stretch their *Onion* money. Johnson took up residence in a cabin on the Mississippi River. Keck joined him for a while, and they lived off homegrown veggies and fishing. Then they hitchhiked to Brazil, stopping along the way to take a job loading fruit trucks until they had enough money for plane tickets for the final hop. Finally, they made their way to Rio. Not long after, Johnson moved to Albuquerque to start a real alt weekly, *NuCity.* Keck went to Seattle to start an alt weekly as well: the *Stranger.* He would bring along Peri Pakroo (editor) and most of the first-year *Onion* staff, including Sturm (art direction), Cook (editor/

writer), Jonnie (computers), and a few months later me, as the full-time editor-in-chief, to get it going in a way very similar to *The Onion*'s start-up. He also brought Dan Savage, the hilarious clerk from Four Star Fiction and Video in the ACT UP T-shirt, to be the *Stranger*'s advice columnist. Keck would go on to become one of the most respected alt-weekly publishers in the country.

Keck and Johnson's final signoff in *The Onion*'s last issue that year was something longtime readers will recognize. There is a placeholder dummy text used in typesetting and publishing known as "lorem ipsum," a long text in Latin that is inserted into pages and columns while waiting for the real text to be completed. PageMaker included it in the version the team was using then. The text, www.lipsum.com tells me, comes from a popular Renaissance treatise on ethics, *De finibus bonorum et malorum* (The Extremes of Good and Evil), by Cicero. Keck and Johnson, however, made up their own text: "Passersby were amazed by the unusually large amount of blood," repeated again and again until the empty space was full. It would be used as a recurring *Onion* joke for the next twenty-four years.

THANX

to our readers

BY CHRISTOPHER JOHNSON AND TIMOTHY KECK

PASSERSBY WERE AMAZED BY THE UNusually large amount of blood. Passersby were amazed by the unusually large amount of blood. Passersby were amazed by the unusually large amount of blood. Passersby were amazed by the unusually large amount of blood. Passersby were amazed by the unusually large amount of blood. Passersby were amazed by the unusually large amount of blood. Passersby were amazed by the unusually large amount of blood. Pas-

sersby were amazed by the unusually large amount of blood. Passersby were amazed by the unusually large amount of blood. Passersby were amazed by the unusually large amount of blood. Passersby were amazed by the unusually large amount of blood. Passersby were amazed by the unusually large amount of blood. Passersby were amazed by the unusually large amount of blood. Passersby were amazed by the unusually large amount of blood. Passersby were amazed by the unusually large amount of blood. Passersby were amazed by the unusually large amount of blood. ∅

KIDS
from page 11

a five-month second honeymoon with Brooke. She also finds out that Brooke knows the truth. She forces Adam to choose. He chooses...Dixie! They kiss and hug and, of course, Brooke walks in. Dixie's totally freaked. "Abject fear" best describes the look on her face. How will Adam talk his way out of this one?∅

Tim Keck and Chris Johnson's signoff in May 1989. With a lot of hard work and the help of their friends, they had created a successful and popular local weekly publication in only 10 months. (The other part of this image is a jump from the soap opera summaries—dramatic ongoing stories told in installments that were a big reason people picked up the paper.)

James Danky, the retired alternative-publications curator at the Wisconsin Historical Society in Madison, cofounder of the Center for Print Culture, coeditor of the book *Protest on the Page: Essays on Print and the Culture of Dissent Since 1865*, and one of *The Onion*'s first subscribers, told me:

> Tim and Chris's genius was to have the ability to figure out how to make *The Onion* into something that could be printed and continued. And that's too easily discounted. Underground papers in the '60s were sold. They weren't free distribution. They were co-ops or not-for-profits that were never going to make any money anyway.

> It's not unique to *The Onion*, but *The Onion* certainly was an enthusiastic participant in free distribution. You make your money on ads. And that's the dominant model that kills off purchased publications, because you're not gonna pay fifty cents for something when you could have it for free.

Almost everyone on the original staff eventually went on to start their own businesses or be self-employed. When you get to have total creative control over a popular publication, make your own schedule, and basically do whatever you want at a job in your early twenties, even if the pay is terrible, it is really hard to go back to being a plebe. That's something Keck and Johnson taught us: going your own way was an option. You didn't have to do what the so-called people in charge said.

Keck and Johnson were profiled in an April 1989 article in Madison's afternoon newspaper, the *Capital Times*, by media critic Patrice Wendling about seven months after the first issue. The profile begins: "Predictability. You find it in Madison's dailies, the two establishment campus clones and even our city's 'alternative' weekly. . . . Delightfully, and often devilishly, ignoring the expected is *The Onion*. The irreverent campus weekly has made its mark this academic year with a successful business strategy and outrageous editorial content."

The article includes quotes by both Keck (who "sports a shock of dark, wild hair that towers over his slight frame and draws attention to his brown eyes and wide-mouthed grin, which is offered up frequently in conversation") and Johnson (who "appears more conservative with a short cropped coiffure topping his 6-foot frame and a pair of tortoise shell and gold glasses that shield a pair of steely blue eyes").

"We do spoofs or real stretches of the truth," says Keck. "I'd rather people believe some of the stories are true. It keeps them guessing."

"There's always people out there who'll say, 'Is this real?'" laughs Johnson. "Even people that know us ask if certain stories are true. There's always that question—what is this thing?"

Toward the end of the piece, Keck says, "Everything is becoming boring."

"The thing with journalism is that the people who run the news have changed. They're real slick now. The newspapers were in there digging before," he says. "Look at how the press went after Nixon but didn't touch Bush or Reagan. The press represents what the people want."

"It gives them the USA Today type news—how many people eat hot dogs and own a microwave," says Johnson. "We're not claiming to be news."

The very first time someone thought an Onion article was real in my presence was after the publication of the ninth issue on Tuesday, October 25, 1988. This took place—not kidding—in a big UW–Madison lecture course I was taking called "The Effects of Mass Communication."

I wasn't a big fan of the class. The arguments the professor made seemed very simplistic. (Scholar James Carey's famous book Communication as Culture, which would transform the field after publication in 1989, hadn't come out yet.) I remember a big, basic graphic the professor put up, with arrows indicating the flow from media to society, and thinking it was really lame. I also found the idea of mass-media "choice" absurd. It seemed blindingly obvious that most people just passively consumed whatever was placed in front of them. The sort of cultural analysis I was interested in came more from people like musician Laurie Anderson, spoken in her song "From the Air," from her 1982 debut album, Big Science:

This is your captain.

We are going down. We are all going down, together.

And I said, Uh-oh. This is going to be some day.

Stand by.

This is the time. And this is the record of the time.

This is the time. And this is the record of the time.

One day I got to "The Effects of Mass Communication" a little early. That past week we'd finished up the ninth issue, with the front-page headline and story "Portrait Cries Real Tears," and it had just hit the streets.

The story was about "real tears" flowing from the framed photograph of Helen C. White on the first floor of the English Department building named for her, which stood tall over near the lake next to the Memorial Union, a large, beautiful 1928 building with a cavernous rathskeller, a cafeteria, study rooms, a theater, and a big outdoor terrace on the lake that was one of the most beloved public hangout spots in Madison. Helen C. White had been a legendary UW English professor, in 1936 the first woman to become a full professor in the College of Arts and Sciences. Miss White, as everyone called her, always wore purple and, in the nomenclature of the time, "never married."

I came into the big lecture hall and sat down in a middle row. A group of three—two girls and a guy—sat down behind me with a copy of the new issue of *The Onion*. I listened to them talk about it. It was still interesting and weird to overhear total strangers discuss something I'd helped to create.

"Oh my God," one girl said. "Did you see this? Portrait of Helen C. White cries real tears."

"No way," said the other girl. "Really?"

"Whoa," said the dude.

They talked for a minute about the article, and I realized, to my astonishment, that they thought the story was real. They didn't know they were reading a joke. Their conversation wasn't ironic. It was completely sincere. I could not believe it.

"You guys," the first girl said, "we have to go over there and check it out." They then made plans to walk over to the building after class. I wish I had followed them.

Chapter 4

The Madison economy back then was like a native midwestern prairie ecosystem. The diversity, creativity, local focus, and interconnectedness made it healthy and resilient. Pete Haise said, "Madison was just an incredibly viable economy. A very open media market. And the only place and time that I would say that *The Onion* could have ever come from and existed."

That summer, Haise, Scott Dikkers, and Jonnie created their business entity, which was called the Welles Group, after filmmaker Orson Welles. I can still hear Dikkers quoting the famous line from *Citizen Kane*, "I think it would be fun to run a newspaper!" Kane, of course, was modeled on William Randolph Hearst, the Gilded Age newspaper tycoon who monopolized ownership of many of the nation's newspapers and carried on a long battle with his rival, Joseph Pulitzer. In the film, after a long career, Kane ends up eccentric and alone in his huge mansion after alienating everyone he was once close to.

None of them knew what they were doing. Haise, who was about twenty-two at the time, was "owner, ad manager, business manager, president, publisher, CEO, distribution manager. I did absolutely everything." (At one point, Haise was even driving the completed boards all the way to a printer in Platteville by himself, ninety minutes away, every single week at four in the morning, for a year and a half.) He patched together their incorporation documents and found advertising reps in spare moments during a summer real-estate internship he was doing in Chicago. And at that internship, "I got ahold of their articles of incorporation and bylaws, you would call them, of a real-estate partnership," he said. "And I took those bylaws and just rewrote them all in the form of a newspaper and a publishing entity. I just transposed the words, like 'condominium complex' with 'newspaper.' Scott and I turned them in to an attorney, who we paid a hundred bucks or whatever, and we signed off on them and formed a legal entity.

"We just made it up. Just made it all up. There wasn't a journalism major or a business major in the crew." (Haise said he did technically graduate from the business school, actually, but his degree was in real estate and risk management. Apparently, in their first year, Haise was paid in part via Chris Johnson typing his class papers for him.)

The office had moved from the dumpy student apartment on East Johnson and was now in a real office in a small, nondescript pale-brick 1960s-era building on Gilman Street—just off State Street—where they worked in a cheap two-room suite in the basement. Madison in 1989 was the kind of place where a small business run by three people in their twenties could afford an office one block from the city's most central hub. The front room was the business office, and the back room was the production office. The Coke-machine room had a little table for meetings too. Jonnie said, "It was fantastic." Jonnie's father had been asked for a loan so they could buy a Macintosh IIcx as their production computer, "which would have been like going from a sedan to a sports car." He turned them down. The computer cost about $5,000—about $13,000 today. "Pete worked some magic, and we were able to buy one. It was a big deal."

Dikkers faced some challenges as the 1989 school year started. Unlike Haise, who had spent much of the past year selling *Onion* advertising and, before that, had sold ads for the *Cardinal*, Dikkers's previous newspaper production involvement—aside from his *Jim's Journal* publication success—seems to have been mostly limited to some brainstorming sessions with Tim Keck, line editing a few stories, and helping with pasteup for a couple of months in the fall of 1988. Now, Dikkers was the editor-in-chief. Dikkers also had to contend with the loss of the central writing staff. Pretty much the only first-year staff members to continue into the second year were the soap-opera summary writers, an occasional story by Keck writing under the pseudonym Ike Alberts, and me. Despite these challenges, Dikkers told me that he did nothing to prepare for the fall opening of *The Onion*'s second year in business. In his memory, the sale happened in August right before the fall semester began. "And then all of a sudden I'm like, 'Holy shit, I have to do all this,'" he said. "It's a lot of work."

They all got a salary, but it wasn't much. Jonnie recalled it being around $600 a month, "which was a shit-ton of money back then, at least for me, who was more used to living on $450 or $500 a month." Haise said they also split profits, and when they got paid in cash for ads, such as by the bar Jocko's Rocket Ship—later busted for being a center of Madison's cocaine trade—they would divvy it up.

Haise and Dikkers also made a very important agreement at this time: a firewall would be erected between editorial and business. They might discuss things together as needed occasionally—or complain about each other, editorial about business especially—but otherwise business had no right to tell editorial what to do and vice versa. This deal would become the backbone behind *The Onion*'s coming years of experimentation and growth. Haise would keep the lights on and the bills paid, and the writing staff would be left to do whatever they wanted.

At this early stage, however, Haise said neither he nor Dikkers took *The Onion* very seriously. If the oft-repeated dismissal that the early issues were just a few paragraphs of thrown-together content wrapped around a bunch of pizza coupons ever actually applied, it seems to have been in the fall of 1989. From a personality perspective, Dikkers, Haise, and Jonnie were also about as different from each other as three people could possibly be. It was almost as if Johnson and Keck had deliberately orchestrated a messed-up psychology experiment. As Haise put it, "If it weren't for *The Onion*, and [Dikkers and I] weren't forced into working together, basically, there's not a chance we meet, ever in the world." Haise was extroverted and social; he was pretty much "required" to have a cocktail with the owners when he went to sell ads to bars and restaurants. Dikkers, on the other hand, actively avoided other people. And Jonnie was a first-generation digital native working with two guys who knew next to nothing about computers.

Scott Dikkers grew up in Minneapolis with two brothers and his mom (his parents divorced) and says they were very poor. His mother remarried, and they moved to Ellsworth, Wisconsin. Unfortunately, his stepdad was abusive. "Life in general was a pretty humorless affair for me," he said in a 2021 speech. He cheered himself up, however, by discovering *MAD* magazine and other comedy and humor. That sent him down a path of working on his own comedy projects as often as he could—radio skits, stories, cartoons, and films—by himself and with friends. Still, as Amy Reyer recalled, "Scott was really dark. And really pessimistic." Jonnie said Dikkers "seemed to have at a very young age an intense dislike for common people."

Dikkers told me he would analyze episodes of *Monty Python*, TV comedian appearances, and sitcoms by recording them on cassette, transcribing every word, and studying the structure of each joke to figure out the formula for what made them funny or not. In other words, by the time *The Onion* came along, "I had been doing comedy almost like it was a job since junior high school."

His original goal was to become a movie director; his idol was Steven Spielberg. "I was shooting for the top," he said. He had started at two different colleges with strong filmmaking programs—including the University of Southern California in Los Angeles—but dropped out of both soon after starting. In his USC freshman year, Dikkers had attended a student film screening. It was a big disappointment. Though there was a high level of technical skill, "the kids who produced films seemed like all they had ever done was study film, and they hadn't actually lived," he said. "Their stories were just so derivative and shallow." They looked amazing and sounded amazing, but they had "terrible, terrible stories. Like no stories, really, just good-looking pabulum. And I was like, 'Am I gonna spend all this time and money pursuing this to end up like that?' What's the point? I want to do something real."

He dropped out and decided to concentrate on cartooning instead, which had a pretty straightforward profit model. To figure out where to send his cartoons, Dikkers stole a book from the USC library—a reference book listing the address and phone numbers of all the newspapers in America. Just before he moved to Madison from California, the *LA Downtown News* wanted to run his cartoon. They paid him forty dollars. His professional cartooning career had begun. But his filmmaking dreams did not go away.

In the second year of *The Onion*, Dikkers and I hung out a few times, getting lunch or just sitting and talking. Or, rather, Dikkers talked and I listened. He opened up a bit about his life philosophy and other things. It's been more than thirty-five years, but this is what I remember: He was an ethical vegetarian who felt very strongly about animal rights. He had a couple of cats whom he loved in a charming way. He did indeed think most people were very stupid and could be counted on to make bad choices. I recall him going into an especially intense level of detail about his life philosophy one time and being shocked by not only how bleak but also how specific it was. And I argued with him a bit because I was offended by it. Dikkers's view of the world wasn't a mood or an aesthetic; it was a detailed, ironclad conclusion supported by a well-articulated list of premises, and it seemed to have been reached without input from anyone or anything else.

Almost anyone else, that is. Weirdly, Dikkers was a big Tony Robbins fan—the self-help guru who tells people to "unleash the power within." I barely knew who Robbins was other than that he was a popular motivational speaker who drew in giant crowds—and I was always suspicious of that kind of thing. As a multipart 2019 BuzzFeed News Investigation put it, "Victims of sexual and physical abuse, along with people who struggle with addiction and have mental illnesses, pay thousands of dollars to see him on the promise he has the power to 'transform your life' and 'rewire your brain.'" But anything that had mobs of people yelling in unison gave me the creeps, and Robbins has been (as I'm sure you'll be shocked to hear) accused of abuse and misconduct, including sexual assault.

So on the one hand, Dikkers was incredibly dark and singular in that darkness. On the other, he was into cheesy-ass and possibly malevolent motivational speakers. (And still is: as recently as December 2023 in his Substack, Dikkers described Robbins as the man who "sold his programs and built his platform and ignored the overwhelming, decades-long flood of haters. And look at him today. He's a beloved figure. He's the undisputed Jedi master of self-improvement who's helped millions of people achieve their dreams.")

That wasn't the only surprising thing I would learn about Dikkers. One day, he told me he was married. He asked me not to tell anybody. What? He was *married*? I had known him for a couple of *years* at that point, and he had never mentioned it. Nobody else had ever mentioned it, either. And who was his wife? Why had nobody ever met her? Was she a madwoman in the attic or something? It was completely bizarre—not so much that he was the only person I knew in Madison who was married, but that he'd kept it a secret from everyone. (I later met and worked with Dikkers's wife in a State Street bookstore called Pic-A-Book, and she was a totally normal person.) Haise had a story of his own about this. He told me Dikkers used to talk all the time about how marriage was a scam and a joke, a terrible idea, nobody should ever get married, and so on. And then one day Haise learned that Dikkers was married himself. When I asked Dikkers why he didn't tell anybody, he said it wasn't anybody's business.

Overwhelmed by the huge amount of work involved in putting out a weekly paper, Dikkers asked his friend Jay Rath—a local cartoonist, entertainment writer, and theater creator a few years older than Dikkers—to help. It was the start of what became a mostly uncredited arrangement that went on for more than twenty years for both *The Onion* and Dikkers's personal projects. Rath *did* have newspaper experience—a lot of it. Rath said, "Scott and I were frequent collaborators on a variety of projects over a period of decades. At times we had formal meetings twice a week. We were very close, professionally and socially."

Jay Rath was from the Madison area and had graduated from UW–Madison in 1985. He had aspired to be a humor writer in the Thurber/Benchley vein. When he was a freshman, he learned that there had once been a humor magazine on campus called the *Octopus* in the 1930s and 1940s. He got some UW funding to get it going again, but it ended up being much too large a project for a single eighteen-year-old. Rath then started doing entertainment writing and cartooning for Madison newspapers and thereby met and befriended both James Sturm and Dikkers. He and Dikkers especially seemed to have many tastes in common.

Dikkers also enlisted a couple of other friends to provide content and renamed the arts and music-review section the Audio Visual Club, replacing Matt Cook's first-year review section, the all-lowercase "some reviews." (These sections were the precursors to the "Entertainment" section created by Stephen Thompson in 1993—renamed "The A.V. Club" in 1995—and consisted mainly of whatever staffers felt like covering. It wasn't until Thompson that the arts-reviews section gained identity and focus.)

During the second year, the paper looked pretty much identical to what it had been before, except for being noticeably thinner on the editorial side. Dikkers, Haise said, was "not putting in any effort at all." The paper had very few actual stories and consisted only of the soap summaries, "Who's Busted" (the campus police blotter), and cartoons. Haise said they actually started buying content—mainly cartoons—to fill each issue. "Scott's doing everything he can to do nothing" at that point, Haise told me. Dikkers did enlist Rath to set up a side project called Onion Features Syndicate, which focused on syndicating *Jim's Journal* and a few other cartoons to college and alternative newspapers around the country.

Though the editorial content was slim, *The Onion* was otherwise, as Haise put it, "loaded with fucking ads." If they did not make their payments on time, Keck and Johnson would get the paper back. "And that was something I wasn't gonna let happen," Haise said. He estimated the pages were 70–75 percent advertisements. Each one got them a little closer to paying their debt. "I went from morning till night," he said. "Nonstop. Everyone has their 'how I supplemented my *Onion* habit' story. There was a time where I was bartending, renting apartments, going to school, running *The Onion*, taking bets, making book, and selling weed, all at the same time."

Haise said at the time, he loved Dikkers's "natural gift for content design and the future of *The Onion*. He just kind of saw it better." Haise, however, was always engulfed in "the daily grind for survival," while Dikkers came in "a couple of times a month." Jonnie did the graphics and layout for each issue and was around much more regularly. Still, for Haise, "it didn't take me long to realize that I had ten jobs, and they each had one. And how the equal split of that in any way, shape, or form was just stupid on my part.... Probably the worst business deal I've ever made in my life was the way I allowed things to get chopped up in terms of ownership when we all took over *The Onion*."

There were so many things with which they had no experience. Improvisation was often required. One day, early on, the phone rang. It was a caller asking to speak with the publisher. Haise told me that nobody knew what a "publisher" was. So they made up a name, took a message, and, once they'd had a chance to get out a dictionary, had someone posing as the publisher return the call. It was a trick they had used before. Haise said in their first year, Johnson told him he would never get anyone to pay overdue accounts because he looked so young. Haise "took that to heart right away"; he and Dikkers made up someone called Robert Taylor to be their accountant, complete with letterhead. People would call the office and ask "Can I talk to Robert Taylor?" to which they would answer, "Sorry, he's not in."

Not long into the fall semester, a new contributor joined the staff: Rich Dahm. Dahm was from Waukesha, a suburb of Milwaukee, and was the son of a plumber and a housewife. Like Tim Keck's father, Dahm's dad had also been an ethnic German living in Soviet territory and had also fled as a child from Stalin's marauders to the United States with his family after World War II. Dahm had just graduated the prior spring from the UW with a degree in communication arts, where he had been in video production classes with first-year writer Matt Cook. They had collaborated on several class projects, including a parody of the old commercials for pop-song compilation albums sold on TV. They used punk songs for their parody and, instead of pop stars, had a priest lip-syncing the 1980 Subhumans song "Slave to My Dick."

Dahm had admired *The Onion* since it began. "I loved it," he said. "I would pick it up every week, and it was always hilarious and unpredictable. It had this great 'we hate our readers' attitude that I quite enjoyed." Then he graduated, "and I was like, 'I don't know what the hell I'm going to do.'" He was dating someone at the time who had another year of school, so he thought, "Maybe I'll just stay in Madison and find something to do. Maybe I could work at *The Onion*." Dahm had spent the prior three summers working at a water park in Wisconsin Dells, one of Wisconsin's biggest tourist spots, so he submitted a funny travelogue about it. Dikkers liked the piece but wanted to make some changes. "It was eye-opening, let's just say," Dahm said. They rewrote it together, "and we kind of hit it off."

Dahm waited and waited for the article to be published, but nothing happened for a couple of weeks. "I was like, 'What? Why would you print an ad and not my article?' . . . That was my naïveté. Eventually, it did get published, and I was really excited about when it was coming out, and . . . it was in the 'Penis Fear' issue."

The only front-page article I ever wrote solo for *The Onion* was "Penis Fear," published on September 19, 1989. I recall that I was interested in what it would be like if the whole phallic-symbol thing was reversed. I thought, "What if we lived in a world where everybody was scared of and weirded out by penises instead of vaginas?" Or something like that. The article didn't exactly express all of this, but I was still happy with how it turned out, even though Dikkers punched it up a little without my knowledge in ways I didn't like, including adding a stupid joke about Snuggles, the fabric-softener bear, "sporting a lifelike phallus." (Okay, it is a little funny.)

The story, which had a big drawing of a penis on the front page, created a bit of a stir. Two different friends told me their professors had used it for class discussion. Randy Jones, who was helping with graphic design work around that time, said, "I remember the cover well. It was the most requested back issue. We ran out of it right away." Jonnie felt the issue was the one that put the publication on the map, adding, "It was early in the second year. 'We're gonna do this right. We're gonna make it professional.' . . . 'Penis Fear' was when we became smart comedy."

Dahm, anxious for his first *Onion* article to appear so he could show his family, excitedly went to get copies—only to discover there was a big penis on the cover. "I thought, 'Oh, great.' My parents were already getting a little worried about me. I was done with school, but I'm still working low-paying jobs in Madison. But I'm reassuring them, 'It's okay! I'm writing for this newspaper called *The Onion*! I'll send you a copy when it comes out!' And then it comes out and I'm like, 'Shit.'"

Everybody liked Dahm a lot. He was very funny and very modest, with a goofball, absurdist sense of humor paired with the ability to make you feel warmly welcomed all the time. People felt safe around Dahm, and that let them open up and stretch. He would often crack you up by making observations or commentary in various silly voices, like a faux dumb guy or an overexcited nine-year-old. (When interviewing people for this book, I heard pretty much everyone who worked with Dahm do an impression of his silly voices.) As writer John Krewson put it, Dahm was "fucking Dick Van Dyke in real life." Dikkers said Rich was "a delight." Dahm also had an encyclopedic knowledge of popular culture and an almost photographic memory. On top of this, he was a smart, conscientious, and competent person who could get the job done. This impressed Dikkers—and also perhaps showed him how he could escape *The Onion's* weekly grind and get back to his real projects. Dikkers, who had a penchant for 1950s black-and-white TV *Leave It to Beaver*–style aesthetics, nicknamed Dahm "Chip."

Dahm brought other silly ideas. "I did this VapoRub story about how VapoRub is a drug. VapoRub, the silent killer," he said. That was just the beginning. Dikkers paid him "some pittance, twenty-five bucks a week or something, to come in and hang out and work." Dahm said he was excited that people were going to read what he wrote and laugh. "The fact that there wasn't a financial reward at that point didn't matter that much, even though I desperately needed money to pay rent. I was working other jobs to supplement it. I was driving a school bus, cleaning apartments." Dikkers took him under his wing in those early days, he said, which was good because the girlfriend he'd stuck around for dumped him. Now, though, "here was an opportunity to write whatever I wanted and put it in twenty-five thousand newspapers."

the ONION

Free Campus Weekly | 19–25 September 1989 | Volume 16 • Number 4

OUR SOCIETY IS IN THE GRIP OF
PENIS FEAR

by Kate Wendimeir,
Onion **Genitalia Reporter**

Penis Fear—What is It? Ever since Freud's theory of Penis Envy was debunked, experts have disagreed over what role the penis plays in society. Feminists have promoted the idea of Penis Indifference, which states that, contrary to Freud's notion that all women feel incomplete because they lack a
See Penis on page 5

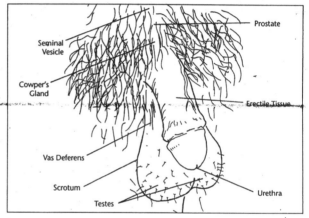

Labels: Prostate, Seminal Vesicle, Cowper's Gland, Erectile Tissue, Vas Deferens, Scrotum, Testes, Urethra

Does this image make you uncomfortable? Of course it does. Like most people, you have *PENIS FEAR*. A prominent UW psychologist has coined this catch-phrase to get more media attention than any other psychologist ever. *MORE SHOCKING SCIENTIFIC LINE DRAWINGS INSIDE!*

UW Snapshots
Numbers that add up to lifelong learning.

Cryme is Money
Onion Operatives "monkey wrenched" automatic teller machines around town to make them suck up Tyme cards. Here's how patrons reacted:

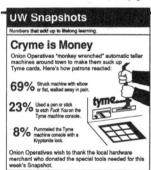

69% Struck machine with elbow or fist, walked away in pain.

23% Used a pen or stick to etch *Fuck You* on the Tyme machine console.

8% Pummeled the Tyme machine console with a Kryptonite lock.

Onion Operatives wish to thank the local hardware merchant who donated the special tools needed for this week's Snapshot.

The infamous "Penis Fear" cover. September 19–25, 1989.

Soon Dahm and Dikkers were staying up late talking and joking, drinking Coke and eating pizza, and writing silly front-page stories together. Dahm also began writing a column called "Rich's Kids" about his adventures as a school bus driver. One night, Dahm said, he and Dikkers stayed up until four planning the front page for every issue until the end of the school year "and just riffing on funny ideas all night." Rich remembers this as one of the best times he's ever had hanging out with anybody.

From their late-night brainstorms came the Belt-sanding Hoodlum. "This was a newspaper," Dahm said, "so we should have a character who's like Superman. And we came up with this dumb idea of a guy who murdered people with a belt sander, but had turned good." The first story was "Belt-sanding Hoodlum Rescues Drowning Child" (February 27–March 5, 1990). The Belt-sanding Hoodlum saves the child but is also constantly possessed by his desire to belt-sand people. "It's the demon within. A constant battle between the good and the abrasing-people-to-death thing," Dahm said. Later, the Belt-sanding Hoodlum wins a citizenship award. For the photos, the Belt-sanding Hoodlum was played by a friend of Dahm's, who was also Matt Cook's roommate on Jenifer Street in Madison's bohemian near east side for a while: Todd Hanson, in his first appearance in the paper.

Sometime that year, Jonnie decided that co-owning a newspaper was not what he wanted to do after all. A fan of role-playing games, Jonnie had taken a trip to GenCon, the largest gaming convention in North America, where he handed out issues of *The Onion* to show his design work, and was offered a job at Iron Crown, the "Apple" of game-creation companies, based in Charlottesville, Virginia. (TSR, the company in Lake Geneva, Wisconsin, that created *Dungeons and Dragons*, was the "Microsoft," according to Jonnie. Jonnie wanted to work for the cooler one.) Jonnie said of *The Onion*, "We did good work, but I thought it was just shenanigans . . . just stupid bullshit, and I wanted to do the real work." Jonnie told Dikkers and Haise that he wanted to sell his portion and leave.

Though everyone admits their memories are vague at this point, Jonnie described her exit by saying, "Negotiations weren't going well, and I was young and reckless and very, very stupid." Dikkers believes the trigger was when he said Jonnie was on the wrong side of a power imbalance—he and Haise were on one side, and Jonnie was alone on the other. Perhaps to show he did indeed have power in the situation, Jonnie then locked their single computer with a password and left, knowing nobody else in the office would be able to unlock it. Haise said, "He held all the files, disks, and all *The Onion* stuff hostage." Jonnie did finally unlock the Mac, sold his shares for $15,000, and left the Welles Group—though only ever received the first two $5,000 installments of the $15,000 payment. Dahm said, "I want to say nice things about people. It was a tense situation. It was a contentious situation, and then it ended." Haise and Dikkers reincorporated the Welles Group under a new name: Onion, Inc.

While they searched for a replacement, Randy Jones helped to fill the gap Jonnie had left behind. Jones had been working for Madison Newspapers, the group that published both of Madison's daily papers, where he learned layout and how to "crunch out ads." Jones was also into fonts, an interest that had started years before, "to the point where I had some talent and some practice in it and was able to do professional work when I was nineteen or twenty." Jones, whose dad was one of the first computer programmers in Madison—he worked in astronomy—was also a musician and digital artist. (Jones wrote his first computer program on punch cards when he was a kid.)

Jones inherited the long hours and late nights of his predecessors. "I remember a lot of times rolling out of there at 2:00 a.m.," he said. But the fun part of his job was Photoshop, which had just been released. "Scott would come in and say, 'We need a big pickle' or something. And I'd have to find some photos to scan and put them together in Photoshop and do a halfway decent photo collage to illustrate some funny idea." They looked at *USA Today* charts a lot, "like, '47 percent of Americans don't know what country the Eiffel Tower is in,' or something like that. And, so, we'd illustrate that and bring out whatever made that even dumber than it actually was. Kind of accentuate the dumb, I guess."

Jun Ueno was another early designer who would join the staff the following year in 1991. But he was already reading *The Onion*. Even at this early stage, he said, "*The Onion* was a totally different thing." It was subversive and hilarious. "For those of us who didn't like watching MTV, or weren't into novels or comic books, it was easy to find and really spoke to us," he said. It was also free. College kids sometimes couldn't afford to even rent movies. (Ueno grew up in Evanston, Illinois, and went to UW–Madison to gain a horticulture

the ONION

| Propaganda Instrument of the UW | 24–30 April 1990 | Volume 17 • Number 15 |

Belt-Sanding Hoodlum Receives 'Outstanding Citizen' Award

IN A GRANDIOSE GESTURE OF CIVILITY, THE MADISON COMMU-
nity Improvement Network presented its annual 'Outstanding
Citizen' Award to the Belt-sanding Hoodlum Monday afternoon.
The Belt-sanding Hoodlum, a former criminal notorious for belt-
sanding his victims beyond recognition, was rewarded for uncom-
promising service to the betterment of the community. Madison
Community Improvement Network President Dick Abercrombie
cited the Belt-sanding Hoodlum's "heroic deeds" that began this
winter, when he plucked a drowning child from Lake Mendota.

"The Belt-sanding Hoodlum is the kind of citizen Madison
needs as we enter the nineties," Abercrombie read in a prepared introduction. "He's a kind soul, and deserves our respect and grati-
tude," he said.

As the Belt-sanding Hoodlum approached the podium to accept

see Belt-sanding Hoodlum on page 7

**Madison Community Improvement Network President Dick
Abercrombie presented the 'Outstanding Citizen' Award to the
Belt-sanding Hoodlum moments before staving off his attack.**

UW Snapshots

Statistics for people whose elevator doesn't go all the way to the top floor.

Gimme a Lift

ONION Operatives caused various campus elevators to get stuck between floors. Here's how the inconvenienced elevator users reacted:

58% Killed and ate the
weakest member of
the group to survive.

26% Stood in the
elevator politely and
didn't look anyone
else in the eye.

8% Became
nihilists and
refused to
believe the
outside world
existed.

ONION Operatives offer this advice to those who find themselves
stuck in elevators: Use the stairs next time, you lazy asses.

Todd Hanson (right) as the Belt-sanding Hoodlum with Jay Rath bestowing the Outstanding Citizen Award.

degree, but ended up in the campus computer lab learning Photoshop. Then he saw an ad for a graphic designer at *The Onion*. Ueno thus began a twenty-year *Onion* career.)

In those early days, Ueno told me, *The Onion* had a real mystique. There were no bylines. Were Pete Haise and Scott Dikkers even real? Were the names in the masthead fake? Nobody knew. It was a "black box" that allowed readers to imagine all kinds of things.

Chapter 5

By the fall of 1990, day-to-day editorial production had been left entirely in Rich Dahm's hands. Dikkers had given him a crash course on everything that needed to be done to get the paper out each week and officially hired him to be *The Onion*'s editor. And then Dikkers went back to his old life. It was a nice deal for him. As he told me, "Boy, there was probably a good year in there where I just played a lot of pool. Enjoyed my life as a business owner who had a lieutenant who was, you know, minding the store. So that was pretty sweet."

Dikkers had offered Dahm a base salary, "plus he would kick in a portion of the profits that he would get from the paper and give me that as sort of a bonus," Dahm said. "I mean, it was still very much a barely subsistence level of income. But it was Madison, so you could live pretty cheaply." And Dikkers was letting him do everything for the paper—making decisions on stories and doing all the editing and the layout. "Which was fun, though it was a little lonely." He was also designing something like half the ads at one point. As a reward, Dikkers and Haise offered Dahm a chance to buy into *The Onion*. "Which I foolishly did not do," he said, "because I was broke. I mean, where would I even get the money, you know?"

The relentless weekly deadline was brutal, and Dahm was doing it all almost entirely alone. Meanwhile, Haise and his crew were out selling zillions of ads. Which, if you didn't want the pages to be a solid wall of advertisements, made the paper bigger. Which meant more open space to fill with content, sometimes at the last minute. "I used to work really terrible hours," Dahm said. "I was a night owl then, so I'd come into work at ten and work until six in the morning. It was insane. How the hell did I do that? How did I stay alive?" For a while he was putting in fifteen-hour days.

Now With More Real Fruit!

the ONION

Free Campus Weekly   19 June–16 July 1990   Volume 17 • Number 18

THE ONION Acquires a New Envelope Moistener

by Yule "Orange" Schweppe
ONION Sculling Corespondent

The newest member of THE ONION's office-supply family is a Sterling "Master" sponge-top envelope moistener. Purchased by copy boy Miron Semms from a respected local retail establishment that advertises in THE ONION, the utensil came aboard just a

see Moistener on page 9

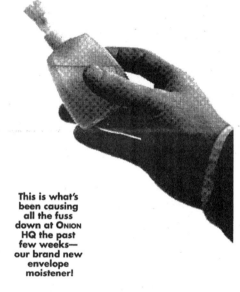

This is what's been causing all the fuss down at ONION HQ the past few weeks— our brand new envelope moistener!

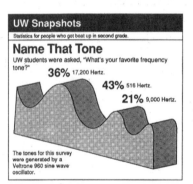

UW Snapshots

Statistics for people who got beat up in second grade.

Name That Tone

UW students were asked, "What's your favorite frequency tone?"

36% 17,200 Hertz.

43% 516 Hertz.

21% 9,000 Hertz.

The tones for this survey were generated by a Veltrone 960 sine wave oscillator.

A front page most likely created a few hours before the printer deadline. (The Onion started publishing summer issues to generate more ad revenue.)

He was also writing, "like, *all* the stories," he said. "Scott would come in and write with me sometimes, but it was primarily me for about a six-month stretch." Dahm also loved movies, so he was reviewing them for *The Onion* every week too. "As if I didn't have enough on my plate." It was okay, Dahm said, because he loved being there, "but you know, I had a new girlfriend I wanted to hang out with, and I started to lose it a little bit."

Haise was also now left without his business partner and co-owner much of the time. A hardworking, boots-on-the-ground scrapper who did whatever it took to get deals done, Haise came to be very disillusioned with Dikkers, whose goal seemed to be to do as little work as possible and call it a day, even if he left a mess behind for someone else to clean up. "I'd be like, does anyone know where Scott went?" he said. The office was only two rooms, so he would check the hallways and walk around trying to find him. Nothing. "I'd be like, 'Guess he's gone.'" Dikkers, Haise said, wasn't aware of "half the stuff that went on" there. His absences caused resentment and inconvenience not just for Haise, but also for many others down the road: "He would come to meetings every now and then; he would come in and steer the ship, and again, it's so genius, and such a beautiful vision for what *The Onion* is and became and should be," but, as Haise said, "he did not fight through the hard times. I guarantee you Scott Dikkers didn't experience one hive from the fear that *The Onion* would collapse one day. I assure you. I assure you that. He was never in the trenches. He was always very, very white collar."

One night, staring down a blank empty space a few hours before the printer deadline, and thinking in his goofball fifth-grader voice, Dahm did something that at the time was more or less tossed off but was actually momentous. He wrote "You Are Dumb" in a box and pasted it in. Rich Dahm had just invented *The Onion*'s motto. As Todd Hanson would point out later, Dahm had also inadvertently reproduced the famous line spoken by Puck, the trickster in *A Midsummer Night's Dream*: "What fools these mortals be!"

The innate foolishness of human beings has been the basis of satire for thousands of years. Other elements can be laid on top of that—politics, social conventions, and so on—but at its heart satire is about how dumb people can be and all the ways they either don't notice or try to justify it. *The Onion* would go on to take ridiculing humanity—especially American humanity and how it uses the media to both enact and enforce its stupidity—to amazing heights and depths. As Hanson said, "I thought that even though it is something a six-year-old would say, it really captures the whole point of satire, which is to criticize the stupidity of the human race." Politics, culture, fashion, ideology, technology—all of that changes over time. But the one thing you can count on, no matter how "advanced" we are, is people being dumb.

Dahm soon became overwhelmed trying to do everything almost entirely alone. Dikkers's passive approach to bringing in talent wasn't yielding much. Dahm said they were getting submissions through *Writers Market* "from retirees in Florida writing hilarious columns about how funny the dentist is, or how bad their wife's cooking is. 'My Wife the Cook.' It was hard to find new people." So Dahm decided to start asking friends to help. The first two people he brought on board as writers were Todd Hanson (no longer just a photo model) and John Krewson. Both would become *Onion* legends.

Hanson was born in Chicago, but went to high school in Wisconsin Rapids, Wisconsin. His dad was a Lutheran minister "who entered the seminary in the mid-'60s because of his convictions about the civil rights movement. His heroes are Gandhi and Martin Luther King. He's the kind of pastor who makes his congregation listen to him sing antiwar Dylan songs on the acoustic guitar in church," as he shared in a *Moth* performance. Hanson's mom . . . seems to have had some issues. In the same performance, he said she was a "psycho neurotic batshit insane loony freak-ass mother." After his parents divorced, he moved all around the Midwest before going to UW–Madison for college.

Dahm and Hanson had a serendipitous first meeting during their freshman orientation, where an ice-breaking activity had everyone going around in a circle, introducing themselves, and saying, if they were a car, what kind of car they'd be, which they both thought was dumb. Dahm said:

> I don't give a shit about cars. And all the guys were like "I'm a Camaro" or some sort of muscle car, [and] the women would be like "I'm a little red Corvette," you know? . . . And then they got to Todd, and his answer was something like, "I would be, I was going to say hearse," and that got a laugh, "but I guess I'll say Magic Bus."

And then they got to me, and I said, "I would be a Metallic P-Wagon Family Truckster," which is the car from *[National Lampoon's] Vacation*. Which got a big laugh, because it was the uncoolest thing you could possibly come up with.

Hanson said, "He laughed when I said my answer, and I laughed when he said his answer. So we literally bonded at the special bonding meeting with the bonding exercise. Like, it actually worked. But it only worked because we were making fun of it. So our very first bonding moment was one of mockery."

Unfortunately, Hanson said in another *Moth* performance, he "basically started bombing out right away" at the university. "I was just so much more interested in being part of the counterculture at Madison than I was interested in actually doing homework. Smoking pot with your friends and listening to music and talking about shit seemed just as important as going to class." He dropped out of school and then "lived for years and years and years just bumming around Madison." He worked for a medical answering service, as a retail clerk, and as a dishwasher. And "every second that you weren't slaving away at your shitty minimum-wage job, you were sitting in your living room, sitting with your friends . . . trying to wring every last ounce of leisure out of the remaining hours before your shift at the job you hate starts again."

Despite his dropout status, Hanson was an intense autodidact and given the briefest prompt could spontaneously spin PhD-level analyses of anything and everything—music, films, TV, anything cultural or political—while also emitting a steady flow of extremely dark and extremely funny jokes. I think he warded off despair by talking. Hanson also kept drawing a cartoon for the *Daily Cardinal* over the next several years called *Badgers and Other Animals*. His first *Onion* story was "Canada Signs Nonaggression Pact with United States" (November 27–December 3, 1990).

Hanson said he had a "very distinct memory" of Dikkers, whom he knew as a fellow *Cardinal* cartoonist, also approaching him at some point and saying that Hanson was one of the most creative minds he knew and that he should write for *The Onion*. "So, he approached me with like flattery or whatever, and it worked. But I'm pretty sure it was Rich who hired me and not Scott." As Dahm said, Hanson "was a genius and a natural comedian—perfect for *The Onion*. He's someone who made me laugh so hard, I knew I had to bring him in."

John Krewson grew up in Verona, a town outside Madison that is now a rapidly expanding boomtown due to its being the headquarters of Epic Systems, the electronic medical-record software hated by health-care workers around the world. He told me some stories about his family. His dad was a banker who worked on the Capitol Square. "He didn't like being a banker," Krewson said, "but he's part of that weird generation that's a lot like Generation X and is the parents of Generation X" called the Silent Generation. "I would like to say that we had happiness because we had each other, but my family was troubled. My little brother is developmentally disabled. That's hard on families to have that." Krewson said his little brother was one of the reasons he developed his sense of humor. "There's no better example to you that the world is a cold, uncaring place full of cruelty and utter indifference than to grow up with a special-ed brother or sister."

When Krewson was in middle school, his mom went back to work as a secretary at UW–Madison for the Botany and Zoology Departments, which was "pretty magical." Krewson spent summers hanging out on campus with his mom, wandering around "terrorizing the university," exploring old elevators with doors that "scissored closed" and the steam tunnels underground. As a UW–Madison creative writing student, Krewson supported himself by working as a bartender at Club de Wash. "I always thought you had to be twenty-one to work in a bar. Turns out you don't." Krewson said his mom had also been a secretary for the Physics Department in Sterling Hall, where she worked on a fancy mathematical typewriter that had keys "for, like, conic sections." She always knew when the space capsule would be coming in because NASA used Sterling Hall for calculations. "The people doing the actual work were highly to moderately classified government employees, but they would just hand off the documents to my mom to type them up, and she'd come home and talk about them at the dinner table."

His mom was working in Sterling Hall when it was bombed by antiwar activists in 1970. Even though he was "tiny small" at the time, as a result, "I grew up with a very negative view of extreme activism, which I hold to this day." His mom didn't like talking about it. "But yeah, there was a big smoking hole where her desk was." It was blown up just "because it was called the Army Math Research Building. They did ballistics work in there, but they didn't do actual, as far as I know, military ballistics in the building. It's just a sloppy piece of activism all around. The IRA had better fucking planning. And the IRA is a bunch of dipshits."

Krewson said his mom also became the undergraduate advisor for the English Department, where he was taking creative writing classes. "She's a capital-M mom, and for her to be mom to like ten thousand kids was a dream job. My mom still gets cards in the mail, like, "You were the best advisor. I just had a child; here's a picture," or "I'm on the board of such-and-such publication. It's all because of you helping me through."

I mentioned to Krewson that I had actually been an English major at the time myself, also taking creative writing classes, and his description of the department's advising was nothing like what I remembered. He said that, actually, his mom "was a utility infielder of the advisory department. If you didn't have a major problem and didn't need to actually talk to any professors, you would have gotten Carol," a different person, "because she was contractually obligated to be there. She's playing out the string. She had six years to go to retirement; she'd been shuffled around every department. She knew the bureaucracy of the university, but she was basically a creature of that bureaucracy. Not a lot of help. Knew what boxes to tick, but she wouldn't lift the phone."

Here is where I should mention that during the course of my research for this book, many people warned me that Krewson was, shall we say, a habitual confabulator. Symptoms include telling long, overly detailed stories salted with clever turns of phrase that don't actually make sense when you go back and examine your interview transcripts. Krewson's rather astonishing spontaneous storytelling abilities were helpful for some things. Dahm said one of Krewson's best attributes was that he was good at writing fast. "Procrastination was in the lifeblood of *The Onion*, when we'd all give ourselves a lot of stuff to do at the last minute," Dahm said. Indeed, several people told me that Krewson was the best writer of the entire Gen X staff, amazingly gifted with wordplay and generating perfectly formed prose on the spot that would all just spill forth effortlessly.

Dahm said the first time he, Hanson, and Krewson ever hung out together was one night at Krewson's house to watch the acclaimed 1988 Japanese animated cyberpunk film *Akira*. Since the film was so new, the only version they could get was in Japanese, without subtitles. They had to figure out what the story was based on the visuals alone.

Krewson told me that on the *Akira* night, he "met the yin and yang of *The Onion* at the same time." He said, telling the truth, I think, this time:

I have very strong memories of that as one of the formative moments of my entire life. And it's weird because, you know, life doesn't work that way. It's very rare that there's one event in your life that you can say, "Wow, this really shaped a lot of things that happened for years afterward," but hanging out with Todd and Rich watching *Akira* together was one of them. It really was.

Because nothing actually happened then. We didn't all go into a room during intermission and say, "Oh, by the way, let's forge a satire empire that will influence things for decades to come." We were just like, "We have to go to each other's parties!" But that was enough, you know? That was enough.

Dahm continued to build out the writing staff with *Daily Cardinal* cartoonist Dan Vebber. "We had a lot in common because he was into Devo in high school, and he's from the Milwaukee area, and we were into all the same damn things," Dahm said. Vebber grew up in Whitefish Bay and said, "I can't remember a time when I didn't want to be a cartoonist." His *Daily Cardinal* cartoon was called *Adventure!* and ran alongside Hanson's. After Dahm asked him to join an *Onion* writers meeting, "it very quickly became a very big part of my life." As with Hanson, Vebber's style was darker than Dahm's. Like Dahm, however, Vebber had a taste for extreme silliness. Dahm put Vebber's very first story on the front page: "RUN FOR YOUR LIVES!" Placed beside a photo from *Invasion of the Body Snatchers* featuring a crowd running in panic was a huge paragraph composed entirely of variations on "Run for your lives! The hour is at hand! The hound of ill omen has bayed for you!" and so on—the only text in the story.

Cartoonist Maria Schneider also joined from the *Daily Cardinal*. "Maria was really funny and had a great ability to write in other voices, in archaic voice," Dahm said. "When we did the T. Herman Zweibel columns, she was great for those." Schneider grew up in Madison and graduated from UW–Madison with a BA in history. "So I'm a townie," she told me (a townie who got her BA from one of the most highly regarded history departments in the United States). She said, "I just thought I'd go to the nice big university in my hometown. It seemed pretty good." When she started writing for *The Onion*, she also remembered thinking, "I should keep up with this. I think I might have some talent in this. And I think it's going to go somewhere."

Graeme Zielinski joined the staff in 1992. Zielinski grew up mostly on the south side of Milwaukee in a working-class family with a Mexican immigrant mom; he said maybe one or two people from his class went to college. Zielinski is probably the only writer in *The Onion*'s entire history who specialized in nonfiction "real" stories. (*The Onion* was still experimenting at this time, and Zielinski wanted to be a reporter.) He used his nonfiction reporting for comedic effect, however. "I was and am super-Catholic," he said, but it was "a left-wing socialist Labor Catholic family." And at *The Onion* he had a column called "Graeme Zielinski's Pope Watch," where he would write that last week the bishop of Rome visited the shrine of the blood of the martyrs or whatever it was. Zielinski also tried to buy a nuclear bomb, interviewed Governor Tommy Thompson, and did a profile of a pro wrestler and other goofy "real" comedy reporting. He left in 1994 to do noncomedy journalism.

Another Milwaukee native, Kelly Ambrose wrote for *The Onion* during this time as well. He was hired after sending in his *Family Carcass* cartoons, repurposed *Family Circus* cartoons with deranged captions like "Mommy, what's a juhbortion?" or "Hide-and-seek is fun. Billy found a hiding spot in the fridge and he's been there all day." Ambrose believed he brought a different point of view to *The Onion*. Since the staff was from the *Daily Cardinal*, Ambrose said, "they were all pinkos. It's not funny to be left-wing where everyone is that, so I had to disrupt their reflexive attempts to politicize, and we ended up having a more balanced comedy." Ambrose's humor seems to have been in the shock-comic vein, with a surreal spin. His first published headline was "New Railway Line to Be Built Straight Up Your Ass."

Ambrose, as Hanson put it, was "a really major creative force at *The Onion* for many years." Zielinski said Ambrose was the one who came up with the "News in Brief" feature and "took the horoscopes to the next level." He was "absolutely indispensable to the story of *The Onion*." Unfortunately, Ambrose also seems to have had some pretty serious demons. Vebber compared him to Andy Kaufman, saying that the line between his real life and his comedy life was blurry. Other staffers agreed that it was often hard to tell if he was joking. One writer said he was a "pure misanthropist." His alcohol and drug use was described as completely off the rails.

The staff also recruited a friendly goofball guy with a healthy streak of weird, yet amiable, performance art named Joe Garden from his job at Badger Liquor, a store on State Street. Garden was kind and generous, the opposite of a misanthropist. He came to *The Onion* because the staff, like everyone else in Madison, would walk past Badger Liquor and laugh at the witty, silly, booze-related handmade signs that Garden and the other store clerks would write with markers on big sheets of paper they'd put up in the windows, some of which were basically short stories—so one day Vebber went in and invited Garden to a writers meeting.

Garden was from Richland Center, a town about twenty-three miles down Highway 14 past my hometown of Spring Green and about an hour and a half from Madison. Like me, he also grew up loving Madison's vibe. He was also one of the few people in his rural town who was into punk and new wave music. He said, "Now every time I go back home to Richland Center, I say, 'It's beautiful. I wish it was economically viable to have a place here.' But it's not, because there's no business. There's not even a grocery store if it's not a Walmart. . . . It's depressing."

Vebber was now spending countless hours alongside Dahm as his assistant editor. "I've never worked as hard in my life," he said. They would be on duty together from "Friday evening until, like, 5:00 a.m. Monday morning. We just did not sleep," getting everything ready for the printer. Along with Garden, other new members of the writing team included Heather Donohue (née Heather Ekey), Shaun Mulheron, and Ben Wagner. Susan Rathke became the new soap-summaries writer. Garden's Badger Liquor colleague Rick Streed also contributed material.

Now that he had a full staff of writers, Dahm began the famous *Onion* brainstorming meetings, where people would pitch headlines. "Everyone would bring a bunch of ideas, ten ideas or twenty ideas, and they'd pitch 'em around," he said. "We paid like ten bucks a story or something and five or ten dollars a week for your ideas." Designer Randy Jones had high praise for Dahm's management abilities. Dahm recognized that the people over in the corner "busting out ads" were working hard at their screens while people on the other side of the room were having fun pitching stories. In that case, "It's hard to resist putting your oar in sometimes," Jones said. So Dahm found opportunities for the people who were creative but not so great at the craft of comedy to put some funny stuff into a coupon or a deadhead. "You know, 'Can you write "You Are Dumb" in this size box?'" Jones said. In this way, Dahm helped people feel included and engaged, which was "a really nice thing," a "managerial move that you had to have a certain amount of maturity to pull off."

The Onion, though still a news parody, was almost totally free-form at this time. One week, the crew could not think of anything for a front-page story. "I remember we were at my apartment, and we were just throwing ideas out," Dahm said. "Nothing was sticking. And I think it was Krewson who suggested 'Guilty Trout to Fry in Pan.' For whatever reason, 'Guilty Trout to Fry in Pan' made us all laugh, so it was like, that's it! That's the winner!

"I remember Dikkers didn't particularly love that one," Dahm said. "He was like, 'Well, if that's what you're doing.' Because it seemed sweaty and out of desperation. Someone told me they read it not that long ago, and it's actually a pretty funny story." Dikkers said, "I thought, 'Oh, boy, *The Onion* has lost its way.' . . . The graphic was awful, and it was just so silly, and it didn't have any intelligent subtext at all. And I was like, 'Okay, I'm taking over.'" Dikkers came in, "steered the ship" for a little while, and then left again.

Dikkers was not only developing his own very particular ideas about *The Onion*'s voice, but in his typically idiosyncratic way also developing a management philosophy—one that was pretty different from Dahm's. Dikkers had a side job at Wisconsin Public Radio, where one day he was given the project to edit a series of audiotapes on a famous workplace-management consulting guru named W. Edwards Deming and his "Total Quality Management" system. (Dikkers helped both Dahm and me get jobs as news announcers and production assistants at WPR as well.) Deming taught his system to the Japanese after World War II to help them rebuild their economy after it had been "bombed to smithereens," Dikkers said. And "within forty years Japan was one of the world's leading economies. Total Quality Management was all about the concept of putting the customer first and continual improvement. And by editing these tapes, I was unwittingly getting this lesson in how to build a great company. And how to create a great team. And how to really satisfy customers."

Other twentysomethings were interested in existentialism or electronic music. Dikkers was fascinated by a post–World War II manufacturing-industry management philosophy created by a guy who was born in 1900. "I learned so many tips and tricks and tactics about how to do things that were super-high-level," he told me. "Like always being open to new ideas. And not letting my ego get in the way." And when the inevitable strife occurred—"It's a bunch of twenty-year-olds, a bunch of hotheads who think they're funny. It's so easy for that to deteriorate into a bad rock band just breaking up all the time," as Dikkers put it—"I knew how important it was to remain this sort of egoless head of it to defuse anything like that and to encourage people and compliment people on their great work and make them feel good about what they were doing."

Jones said, "It was a real positive experience overall working with Scott. He always had such enthusiasm and drive. I was in my early twenties, and Scott was in his late twenties, maybe, at that time. But he seemed like he was forty-five or something. He had this very grown-up air of dispensing wisdom about him and seemed more like a complete person who knew who he was gonna be."

Today, Dikkers goes around the country making speeches about how he created *The Onion*'s style of comedy. This is, shall we say, disputed by many of the old staff. Hanson said, "To hear him tell it, he was the guy who trained us all and developed our comedic voices and told us how to make jokes. And he did constantly lecture us about how to make jokes, but we just made our own jokes. I don't feel that Scott trained me, or Krewson, or Rich Dahm, or any of those people how to be funny. He always had his sights on bigger things. I mean, he would micromanage the editor until he thought that the editor was capable of doing the job, and then he'd go off and do another project." Hanson did say this for him: "Everybody else was kind of a cynical slacker outsider figure, and he was the one guy who was, like, motivating everybody to do shit."

Vebber said, "Scott Dikkers was the overseer who wrangled the talent and moved it into a specific direction. But when I think of *The Onion*, it's Todd Hanson, John Krewson, Rich Dahm. They are the voice of that paper." Vebber called the trio *The Onion*'s "soul." Dahm said, "One of the best things about *The Onion* in those early days was the experimental nature of it. You could try different things, see if they worked. We'd play with form—it wasn't all news parody. Sometimes we'd do a fake magazine cover or put a love letter on the front page. We got to try things out. Some of those things bombed, but at least we were taking chances."

Vebber said they identified five standard varieties of *Onion* jokes, though he could remember only four of them. The first was "misplaced focus," as in "Nation's Popsicle Makers Concerned as Earth Hurtles Toward the Sun." Another was "celebration of boring"—what Tim Keck called "making small things big"—as in "PEN STOLEN FROM DORM STUDY AREA." Vebber said, "To this day, I think the funniest stuff is stuff that's taking the form of something that exists, but actively making fun of it while you're taking the form of it." He said it was kind of a revolutionary thing to have a newspaper, but "what we're using it for is just stupidity." The third variety of jokes was the "stupid non sequitur," and the fourth was "jokes that idiots think are funny expanded until they actually become funny," like "Dan Quayle Poops on Floor." No one could remember what the fifth category was. Vebber and Dahm thought it might be "parody of existing news format," which of course is what *The Onion* became in its entirety a few years later and included things like "Table Boy: The Boy Raised by Tables." In a separate category of its own was what the staff called "Fuck you, Reader" stories, which came from the voice of *The Onion* as an awesome powerful entity that idiot readers didn't even deserve to look at—a voice that would continue throughout *The Onion*'s history.

Vebber also said he brought a more sinister and cynical tone to the silliness. "And definitely more metahumor and antihumor," he said. He also began one of *The Onion*'s most popular features: Drunk of the Week. He got two jumpsuits, adorned them with *The Onion*'s logo, and he and a photographer (usually John Krewson) would go out at bar time on Friday night looking for some especially ridiculously wasted person and interview them. (Vebber said the bit became so popular that people would come running over as soon as they saw the jumpsuits.) To his credit—literally—Vebber's work also helped him graduate from UW–Madison: he was allowed to substitute his *Onion* editorial experience for the university's required English courses.

Sean LaFleur, a Madison student with a double major in English and journalism who became an *Onion* writer, remembers playing with the increase in stupid trend pieces in newspapers like *USA Today*. Throughout the 1980s, real news had been moving away from straight reporting and toward more commentary and opinion. Not only does it fill up space, but commentary also doesn't require the big budget of both money and time that investigative reporting requires, doesn't get you in nearly as much trouble, and generates emotional responses, like outrage or sentimentality, that make readers feel engaged. Trend stories also might appear next to real news stories, which gave them legitimacy. A TV example is the "Cola Wars," a completely PR-manufactured 1980s fight between Coke and Pepsi that was in the news for weeks. *The Onion*'s version of the trend piece was a repeated joke where the headline would start with "Everybody's Doing" whatever it was. The first was a Dahm headline: "Everybody's Eatin' Bread!" LaFleur said, "That to me was a work-of-art masterpiece."

Vebber said the staff had a lot of conversations about what happens after antihumor. They felt it was up to them, he said, to figure out the direction comedy would be going. Still, if comedy was now at the point where every joke is making fun of jokes, "we were legitimately baffled." LaFleur remembers his brain being "on fire" during these conversations. (He also said it was sad the local newspapers they used to make fun of were mostly gone now.)

Ambrose, for his part, said, "There is nothing less funny than a discussion about what is funny. Ben Karlin and Scott Dikkers had long conversations about comedy. They would attempt to describe comedy as a physical entity, like a bucket where you don't know where the edge is. They were the least funny of any of us but the most interested in the mechanics of comedy." When I asked Vebber what the soundtrack to that period of *The Onion* would be, he said, "Everything by Devo, everything by the Residents, everything by the Wedding Present."

By this point I had left, moving to Seattle to edit the *Stranger* in the summer of 1992. I was only marginally involved with *The Onion* at that point anyway. I loved hanging out with Dahm and Hanson, and Dahm tried a few times to get me to write things, but mostly I was way too inhibited and *The Onion* also just wasn't my scene. I did contribute one last piece of short fiction under a pseudonym, a story about a young woman named Christine hanging out in an art studio with Satan. I was listening to the Cowboy Junkies' first album—*Whites Off Earth Now!!*—a lot and especially liked their cover of the Robert Johnson blues song "Me and the Devil." According to some scholars, the "devil" in Johnson's songs may actually have been references to the African trickster Legba, an

the ONION

| Free Campus Weekly | 24–30 October 1989 | Volume 16 • Number 9 |

Wipes Away Dirt-n-Grime!

This new enemy in The War on Drugs has both narcotics experts and cold specialists searching for answers.

Part two in a special three-part series on The War on Drugs

by Dr. Bernard Friedman

Vap•O•Rub: The Silent Killer

A 14-year-old "Blue Ice" dealer wearing Reeboks and a trenchcoat sidles up to a group of younger kids on the school playground and sells them each a small turquoise-hued vial of Vic's Vap-O-Rub. One child leaves the playground and applies it to his chest in a toilet stall. In class, the teacher notices the youth staring into space, in a state of detached pleasure, oblivious to the day's curriculum. The teacher fears reprisals from the menacing Vap-O-Rub dealers in school, and doesn't dare say a word. A tear forms in her eye as the aroma of the mentholated ointment fills the room.

On the street it's called "Blue Ice," "Rub," "Chest Candy," and an assortment of other names by the dealers, who range from 10-year-old elementary-school dropouts to dubious, wayward entrepreneurs. The Rub dealers ply the streets with Uzi-toting crack dealers, sometimes becoming involved in sud-

See Vic's on page 4

UW Snapshots

If these statistics can't say anything nice, they don't say anything at all.

Don't Organize, *Acronymize*!

Onion Operatives rated the most ill-conceived acronyms for student organizations.

62%
ASSAIL!—Art Students Steadfastly Against any Politically Incorrect Thing.

21%
DUMBER—Dedicated Journalism Undergraduates for the Elimination of Basic English Requirements.

17%
AGRI-STUDS—Agriculture Students for Bestiality.

Onion Operatives belong to Friendly Undercover College Kids You *Onion*-reading Underclassmen Adore Like Lackeys.

Rich Dahm's first cover story. October 24–30, 1989.

intermediary between God and humanity who "facilitates communication, speech, and understanding." At the time, though, I didn't know anything about this. I was just responding to how the song made me feel.

Dahm remained the editor for four years: "another college education." He left in 1994 to move to Minneapolis to be with his new girlfriend, shortly after *The Onion* moved to a new office at 122 State Street on the top floor of the building, with much more room than the prior tiny two-room office. It was a significant bump in space and status that Dahm's many hours of hard work and his gift for hiring had helped create. If Dahm had not come along when he did, it's unlikely *The Onion* would have survived much past the year 1990. Zielinski said, "I thought Rich was the captain of the ship for its most important moment." Dahm would soon move to Los Angeles to start a TV writing and producing career.

Ever humble, Dahm said he looked up to Dikkers in those years. Dikkers was always very confident in his writing voice and what he thought was funny, "and at the time I wasn't particularly confident. I was always asking, 'Is this good? I'm not sure. I don't know.'" Dikkers helped him to develop confidence "because I didn't have that." In Dahm's first year as editor, there were a lot of crazy non sequitur stories. "But as the paper evolved, Scott wanted to see more things that had a point of view. And I fought him on that a lot, because I like the silly. But thirty-plus years later, I much prefer the things that have a point of view. . . . Dikkers definitely was the one who helped me realize you gotta have that and not just words that sound silly on the page."

Dahm, I think, is not giving himself enough credit. Because absurdity and metahumor are totally valid genres and were a big thing culturally at this time. As just one example, see the NBC TV show *Late Night with David Letterman*. Letterman, an Indiana native, was the man one journalist said "drove fringe comedy to the mainstream." Absurdity and fringe-style comedy were showing up in other places, too. In print, examples include comics like *The Far Side* and Matt Groening's *Life in Hell*. The fact that *Zippy the Pinhead* was a syndicated comic strip appearing in local newspapers all over the country is actually kind of amazing. Then there was the stuff that Gen X had just grown up with. The 1970s psychedelic counterculture produced a lot of surreal humor, and there were fewer barriers between what was considered "adult" and "kid" material then. Popular television shows like *Charlie's Angels* and *The Love Boat* were actually stepping over the line into camp and training people to appreciate it—even if the legions of sixth graders watching didn't quite get the reference. (See Susan Sontag's classic 1964 essay "Notes on Camp.")

With Vebber at his side, Dahm also maintained the essential *Onion* quality: it was all delivered straight. From the very first issue in 1988, *The Onion* had never—not once—pointed to itself as comedy. Part of the fun of reading it was being taken down a bizarre and hilarious path into an alternative universe where the world and its public communication apparatus had gone insane. It wasn't just jokes. Something more was happening. Dahm said he did have a feeling *The Onion* could be big someday, "but I wasn't willing to wait around for that day to come. I'd already put in four years, which is nothing in the span of a lifetime, but I was in my midtwenties, and I was making bupkes and I wanted to, you know, maybe one day buy a house and have a family. At the rates *The Onion* was paying then—and I was one of the better-paid employees—I just didn't see it as a place where that could happen."

Hanson told me Dahm was "a wonderful human being" who did not toot his own horn. As a matter of fact, he said, Dahm is shy. He told me about a joke he used to play. "I would call attention to Rich in front of large crowds of people when we were in public," Hanson said. "If I was going to meet Rich on, say, Library Mall and I would see him coming from sixty feet away, I would point at him and I would sing him this song really loud, and everyone would turn and look to see who I was pointing at" (singing), "Richard Dahm, fighting for freedom!" And then "he would always blush and feel embarrassed because everybody would turn and look at him."

Chapter 6

The *Onion* was now a downtown Madison advertising and editorial powerhouse. Its primary competitors were the two student newspapers, the *Daily Cardinal* and the *Badger Herald*. And the staff seemed to have relished the battle from both an advertising and an editorial perspective.

It was not much of a contest. Jay Rath said *The Onion* was "killing ad revenue for the *Cardinal* especially, and also for the *Herald*." The student papers were "trying to do real news, real service to the campus and community. And *The Onion* was just coming up with fantasy stuff." Writer Heather Donohue said, "Scott Dikkers explained to me once that *The Onion* was a vehicle to sell ad space. And one year for Halloween [Halloween was a massive holiday in Madison, with a huge party packing State Street every year], I went as an *Onion* coupon. I had a T-shirt from [the State Street record store] B-Side with a line drawing by P. S. Mueller, and I took black tape and made it so it looked like I was a perforated coupon."

Pete Haise's work ethic was one reason *The Onion* was doing so well, despite the fact that he had to cope with continual mockery from the writing staff who, he said, "would get on my case a lot for being too business-y and too sales oriented." Back when he and Scott Dikkers "used to work a lot more together on the promotional and the marketing materials every year, putting the media kit together and doing things like that," Haise asked Dikkers for a mission statement. "That, of course, got scoffs and laughs." Haise told me that "virtually everything I ever said in front of one of our writers, or a writers meeting or a writers' group or a couple of writers at a time, was mocked and laughed at." But in a "great way," he added. Haise also said he was ridiculed in the paper many times. Once, his "I do not give a rat's ass about that" response to a staffer's objection inspired one of the next issues' skyboxes: "Area CEO Doesn't Give a Rat's Ass." Haise said he didn't care about the ridicule. It was fun.

Haise's work ethic was also found in the ad reps he hired. One standout was Mark Banker, whose competitiveness and organizational skills helped take *The Onion* to new levels. Banker—the son of an actual banker—was a natural salesman and fundraiser who understood that relationships, risk taking, and dogged determination were how you made this work. And, also, love for the product.

Banker had been a fan for a couple of years. He was a freshman at UW–Madison when he first saw a copy with the headline "Devo to Play Halftime" and got halfway through the story before he realized it was a joke. "I was like, man, that's really funny. They went to the trouble of writing this as a real story and presenting this as a real thing," he said.

Banker's dream had been to work in entertainment. But because he couldn't see how you could do that and also make a decent living, he'd decided to focus on journalism and advertising, which could let him be inside the entertainment world while not exposing him to the financial risks. "You get to be creative," he said. "But you're also not going to be living in a box. It was very important to me to not live in a box. I just desperately didn't want to live in a box. And I came from a family that was very against living in boxes."

Then, in 1993, Banker, who had been selling ads for another small local publication, ran into a friend who was an *Onion* ad rep. She introduced him to Haise. Soon, Banker told me, he was being interviewed for a job. The final part of the audition was for Banker to write Haise a letter about why he wanted to work for *The Onion*. Banker said, "I went away and wrote from the heart. 'I love this paper. I love the comedy. It opened my eyes to a different approach to comedy, and I would do anything to be a part of it.'" He got the job.

Within a few weeks Banker was in charge of a lucrative, multiyear contract with a major apartment-management company that brought tens of thousands of dollars to the newspaper that he loved. "They became one of our core advertisers," Banker said. "I think they were on page 7 for the three years I was there. And that definitely helped." (In later years, *Onion* writers would mock the ever-present full-page apartment-building ad as evidence of Haise's lack of vision, but the page was a big reason *The Onion* stayed alive long enough for them to be able to complain about it.)

Friday was ad-deadline day. One Friday, Banker said, about three months after he started, Haise didn't show up at the office—and he had all the big advertisers in his book. Nobody could reach him. The other ad reps asked Banker to take care of Haise's accounts. Eventually, Banker said, Haise called him back to say that he'd been out late drinking. "What I need you to do is handle all of my ad clients today." Banker did it, enlisting Todd Hanson to draw last-minute illustrations for a big back-page ad while finalizing everything else. "It felt like it took three weeks," he said, "but it all happened on one day." Not long afterward, Haise asked Banker if he wanted to become advertising manager, saying, "You're a little better at organization and time management and things like that than I am." Banker said, "I'm a twenty-year-old kid in college full-time. I don't know if I can do that." Haise said, "Sure you can do it."

Young Banker took the job very seriously. He wanted the place to run with "maximum efficiency." This meant "putting together systems to organize everybody" so that a situation like that Friday would not happen again. He also took Haise's approach to heart:

> Pete was just one of the hardest-working people you'll ever meet and just hustled all the time, seven days a week, always working on an idea, always trying to push things forward. That spirit and that energy is a big part of what kept *The Onion* afloat in ways where it otherwise would have collapsed. It was all chewing gum and toothpicks, you know; everything was kind of held together in a very sort of fragile way. But it was on his shoulders. He was holding it together, was getting people paid.

> He just made stuff happen. And I very much admired that. The guy was tireless, and would just keep hustling. And that aspect of him, I tried to emulate and follow. . . . I looked up to him and learned a great deal from him, you know, as a young punk coming into an arena where I had never really been.

Haise said he operated according to principles he named with an acronym: SKEED. It stood for "Street smarts, knowhow, energy, endurance, and dedication." Banker set out to win any advertiser he saw in the *Cardinal* or the *Herald* that was not yet in *The Onion*. He made many friends at all the bars, restaurants, and other businesses. Much of what Banker went on to do—he is now an

the ONION

Includes the hit single "Smells Like Shattered Brains"

| Madison's Moral Compass | volume 25 ∅ number 12 | 12–18 April 1994 |

NEWS IN BRIEF

Clinton to appoint dentist to Supreme Court

WASHINGTON, D.C.—Responding to special interest lobbies concerned about ugly tartar buildup, President Clinton announced today that he would appoint renowned dentist Neil Burke to the Supreme Court seat vacated by retiring Justice Harry Blackmun. "Though Burke has never served as a judge in a court of equity and knows nothing about the American legal system, his commitment to upholding the laws of good oral hygiene cannot be disputed," Clinton said.

Dryer sheets recalled for being too snuggly

PETWAMPSE, Ala.—Citizens here are being ordered to return boxes of defective Snuggle dryer sheets that have caused loads of wash to become dangerously snuggly. City health officials became alarmed after masses of residents were discovered huddled in a corner at a laundromat violently fondling a bath towel.

Capital cities to be moved

WASHINGTON, D.C.—Calling it an important reform in American education, Congress voted Monday to force states to relocate their capitals to their most famous city, in order to facilitate easier memorization by grade school students. Cities such as Boston and Indianapolis will be unaffected by the action, but California, for example, will be forced to dig up and move Sacramento, brick by brick, to Los Angeles. "No longer will our students face the shame of embarrassing surveys," said Rep. Roy Rowland (D-Georgia).

Mother of suicide victim sues Judas Priest

SEATTLE—Wendy O'Conner has brought a lawsuit against the rock band Judas Priest, claiming that backwards messages in the band's music caused the suicide of her son, Kurt Cobain. "There were no Judas Priest albums around," O'Conner said, "but I could tell from all the electric guitars in my son's house that he was into heavy metal."

DYSFUNCTIONAL FAMILY BROUGHT TOGETHER BY LIQUOR

A True Story

by Brent P. Welby, Alcoholic

I DIDN'T NEED TO PAY SOME QUACK PSYCHOLOGIST TO TELL ME MY family was dysfunctional. My wife was sleeping in another room because I stunk so bad from my job at the sausage plant, my son would bring home a different hooker every night, and my daughter used our garage as a chop shop for stolen cars. We were messed up.

I tried everything: group therapy, the Unification Church, miniature golf outings, you name it. Nothing worked.

Then, one day after breakfast, everything changed. My daughter was screaming something about a fix. My wife had kicked me in the balls because I said her soiled nightgown offended me. As usual, I cursed like a Marine as I stomped to the door, headed for work.

But when I turned to grab my hat, I saw my son at the top of the stairs. He looked at me with his big eyes, said, "Daddy, you forgot your bottle," and held out a fifth of Beam.

The boy was talking sense. I hadn't had a drink in years. How could I have been so blind as to turn my back on my roots? My family had been on the sauce since before they came to this country. I knew then that hard alcohol was just what our family needed. I ran upstairs, took a pull, hugged the boy, hugged my wife, took another belt or two, threw the bottle in my coat and peeled to work in a blaze of drunken glory. I vowed on that morning that from then on, things would be different.

We've started drinking as a family once a week, like we did when Pappy was alive. Quarters, Three-man, Oblivion Bound—name the drinking game, we'll play it. If we're having

see FAMILY on page 4

A more nihilist version of The Onion *from April 1994 with a couple of pretty rough Kurt Cobain jokes. Note early version of the "News in Brief" section.*

executive producer at DreamWorks Animation—"all started at *The Onion*, and it all started with Pete. So there will always be a warm place in my heart for Pete. I just love him and his long hair."

But it wasn't always easy. Haise described the unique challenge of selling *The Onion* to new advertisers. For one, it was hard to tell them in what, exactly, their ad would be running. *The Onion* wasn't a newspaper; it was just a parody of one. (Haise called it a "magazine" to ad clients to help them understand the concept.) A lot of advertisers also didn't understand the jokes. On top of this, Haise said he couldn't join the national alternative-newsweekly organization because *The Onion* wasn't a real newspaper. He couldn't join the magazine group because it was printed on newsprint. (Most magazines were sold anyway—not given away for free—so their model wasn't right from that perspective either.) *The Onion* was in a category all by itself.

Clearly, they overcame these problems. The pages packed with ads proved it. As Dikkers put it in a 1993 Associated Press news story, "Students would rather read about Jesus at a kegger than the latest meeting of the Board of Regents. Our paper is successful because everybody reads us. We give the people what they want. Advertisers realize that."

One unorthodox way *The Onion* got advertisers was by copying ads they saw in other papers, such as the Madison alternative-ish weekly newspaper *Isthmus*, "this giant boomer-something juggernaut that hoovered up all the local advertisers, and we were trying to claw at them from below," said graphic designer Andrew Welyczko, who was hired by Jun Ueno in 1993.

Welyczko grew up in Madison. His dad worked for Ohio Medical Products, and his mom worked at a drugstore. As with Tim Keck and Rich Dahm, his parents had also fled Stalin's World War II–era genocidal removals. "I was the kid with the strange last name and the parents who have accents," he said. With probably the most knowledge of page layout of anybody yet hired, Welyczko held many design roles, eventually becoming lead designer and taking charge of the production of the satellite newspapers in different cities.

Copying ads "was a totally valid thing" at the time, Welyczko said. "And then you call the advertiser and say, 'Look what we did. We ran an ad for free for you. How'd you like to buy the next one?'" This was "the Wild West of alternative newsweeklies in the early '90s." (Haise said this was an exaggeration. Advertisers always knew they were getting the first week free.) For potential

NOW WITH EXTRA-LARGE PRINT (conveniently reduced for maximum news coverage)

the ONION

Madison's Only Newspaper.   volume 26 Ø number 14   15–28 November 1994

An Important Message from the Alpha Male

Attention Apes! Your leader speaks! Hear him!

RRRAAARRR! GRRAAAA! AARRRRGGG!
From all corners of the jungle my voice is heard!
From across the wooded lowlands where we make our home, my mighty ape call reverberates, striking fear into lesser, weaker gorillas! Hear me, my minions! I am the BIGGEST! I am the STRONGEST! No one is bigger and more fearsome than me!

To those foolish few who would challenge my position, I say this: RRAAAARRR! If you defy me I will run toward you, yelling and screaming, beating my chest in a terrifying display! You will run in fear of my superior girth and muscle! You will cower in terror, because I am the biggest and strongest of apes!

The best fruits and nuts and the choicest morsels of food must go to me! The finest and most sexually attractive of our females must be mine and mine alone to breed! Those who attempt to breed with my elite harem of females will soon learn their place, for if I smell them on my females I will roar and stamp my feet and thrash my powerful muscular arms and shake the trees! And it will be SCARY! And they will RUN!

Of all the apes, who can roar louder than me, the Alpha Male? None! Who can climb higher or run faster or beat

see MESSAGE on page 4

The whole concept of "alpha male" is actually a myth based on an old study of wolves in captivity. In the wild, as a 2023 Scientific American *article put it, wolf packs are just families. Among primates, primatologist Frans de Waal emphasized that the so-called "alpha male" is not a bully but someone with empathy and insight.*

advertisers who didn't take *The Onion* seriously, it was a way for them to say, "Look, your ad that you didn't ask for, we put it in, and it worked." People saw the unauthorized advertisement and came into their business.

The Onion also took note of what their competitors *weren't* doing. According to Hanson, the *Cardinal* had shot itself in the foot by not taking ads from anyone whose business or imagery could be found offensive in some way. Haise, on the other hand, took ads from basically anybody. *The Onion* also had classified ads, as well as a couple of pages of phone-sex and chat-room ads with their borderline-pornographic photos that kept many a '90s alt weekly in business. Possibly the only ad ever shot down by editorial at that time was for an anti-abortion group one of the reps had tried to sneak into the paper.

It wasn't just advertisers and readers who were happy to have an alternative to the *Cardinal*. It was also the writers. Hanson told me the cartoonists from the *Cardinal* who moved over to *The Onion* had gotten tired of having their work changed because it didn't toe the line. "The current on-campus, so-called PC uptightness was foreshadowed in our generation, was definitely happening in Madison on the campus at the time, and was really prevalent at the *Daily Cardinal*," he said, which had "an environment of such incredible self-seriousness." As a 1994 *Wisconsin Badger* yearbook story put it, the *Cardinal's* "increasingly alienating editorial stances" and staff "purges" didn't help, either.

Welyczko, the child of parents who had fled a far more violent political purge, had once wanted to work at the *Cardinal* himself. Then he went to an introductory meeting. "And being a white male at sort of the beginning at the cusp of the rise of some people's awareness of cultural sensitivity and racial sensitivity, I really did not feel welcome at the *Cardinal*. The *Cardinal* had a very specific agenda. And you know, in retrospect, it was the right agenda. And I'm glad they were doing it. But I didn't feel like I had a role." Instead, he went to the *Badger Herald*, which despite its Young Republican reputation turned out to be full of many good people, and learned his trade there.

Thus, by the time people got to *The Onion*, Hanson said, "we were really looking for an antidote to all that self-serious humorlessness of the progressive Left. Not because we no longer believed in the same things, but just because we had a sense of humor about life." The *Cardinal* people "seemed so humorless. All of us had all of our cartooning and comics really scrutinized by the politically correct people. There were constant controversies, and we'd have to change things and make sure we didn't offend this group or that group, so I think we were really looking forward to being in an environment where we could be offensive. I think that was a real key thing, at least for that early era."

Onion writers also disdained the hypocrisy they saw among former *Cardinal* staff. The *Cardinal*, Joe Garden said, was filled with radicals "who later all became investment bankers." Stephen Thompson, *The Onion*'s copy editor, also came from the *Cardinal*. He said, "There was, like, a poster of Vladimir Lenin on the wall, [but then] most of those people eventually went back and got their MBAs. You know, the typical Marxist-to-MBA trajectory." Along with the *Cardinal*'s strident politics and failing ad revenue, its amateurish quality at this time—typos, misspellings, layout, and so on—was also a joke around the office, so much so they decided to create a parody issue called the *Tardinal*, filled with poorly composed, typo-filled, comically overdone college leftist stories to exactly imitate the *Cardinal* at that time. (Everyone agreed that the parody issue's name would not fly today.) *The Onion* distributed the issue around campus, Haise happy to pay for it all.

Haise and his team's ad sales success was now creating a much larger newspaper. But, Haise said, Dikkers refused to come up with any more content. To fill the extra space, Dikkers's idea was to just print reruns. Instead, they made a whole new section: an expanded A.V. Club. Stephen Thompson stepped up to become editor of the "straight" half of *The Onion*.

Thompson grew up in Iola, Wisconsin, a town of thirteen hundred people not far from Waupaca. And he had an excellent upbringing for his *Onion* roles. "I was raised by magazine editors," he told me. "My parents edited the *Comics Buyer's Guide*, which was a weekly newspaper turned magazine about comic books." That "provided the blueprint for my own career as a professional enthusiast." In the summer between high school and college, Thompson did an internship at another local publishing company, proofreading advertisements, when the editor of their flagship magazine quit. "And so for the rest of my summer between high school and college, while I was still seventeen, I became the editor of *Camping & RV Magazine*." Thompson came to *The Onion* via Dan Vebber, who invited him to write *Onion* music reviews. "That ended up launching my career," he said.

Thompson published artist profiles as well as many reviews, both feature and bite-size, in the A.V. Club, and it soon had as much if not more material than *The Onion*'s satire section. It was also well written; people said it was better

the **ONION's** a.v. club

Madison's only entertainment guide | VOLUME 31 | NUMBER 21 | JUNE 18–JULY 8, 1997 |

inside: shitty boat movie, living it up, a savage weasel and more...

XTC

by keith phipps

The Onion talks to frontman Andy Partridge about his music, his lousy old record deal, and where the hell he's been for the past five years

Since making its debut in 1977 alongside The Sex Pistols, The Clash, Wire and other influential acts, Andy Partridge's band XTC has labored in relative obscurity, surfacing with some regularity to produce masterful English pop music that's adored by the group's cult following but ignored by the public as a whole. Following the release of 1992's Nonsuch, this pattern changed, and the generally prolific band seemed to disappear. Singer/songwriter Andy Partridge recently spoke to The Onion about why, and about subjects ranging from deafness and prostate trouble to his band's brand-new retrospective and long-awaited studio releases.

The Onion: Your last album came out in 1992. What have you been up to since then, and why haven't we heard from you?

Andy Partridge: Because we've been on strike. Because we had the shittiest record deal on planet earth. I mean, you hear about those old blues artists who sign away their estate for five dollars and a bottle of beer... Hey, I'm still waiting for that bottle of beer! You know, we had the crappiest record deal. I'll tell you how crap our record deal was: Although we made Virgin Records [the band's label in England] somewhere in the region of 35 million pounds profit, we were still in debt to them after 15 years on the label.

O: You must have been running up a big catering bill in the meantime.

AP: Well, we had a very corrupt manager to start with, but I'm not supposed to talk about that because he made me sign a very uncorrupt manager's gagging clause. The sort of gagging clause that really nice people who don't have anything to hide make you sign. We had a very corrupt manager who kept taking money and putting us continually in the hole. We didn't know. He was setting himself up nicely. And of course, we got shot of him and inherited this debt. And, as I said, they were doing fine out of us and we were still in the red. I mean, things were getting really bad just before we did Nonsuch. Dave [Gregory, guitar] and Colin [Moulding, bass] were collecting Hertz rental cars, you know, for money. One of the best things we've ever put out as a single, "Wrapped in Grey," they withdrew after something like 3,000 copies. They got cold feet and said, "Oh no, this isn't a single," and withdrew it. And that murdered it. That really incensed me, because not only were they not promoting us; they weren't paying us and they were, you know, actively stopping our records from getting played on the radio and stuff. That

See XTC on next page

A.V. Club from June 18–July 8, 1997, featuring an interview by Keith Phipps with Andy Partridge from the extremely excellent 1970s–1990s artsy, brainy, postpunk-pop British band XTC. Highly recommend them.

than *Rolling Stone*. Thompson realized early on that repurposing *Onion* satire writers would not work, so he hired real entertainment writers. (Joe Garden had been turning in reviews of movies he hadn't even seen.) The A.V. Club became instrumental in maintaining *The Onion*'s health as a business because it provided more pages for all the ads Haise and his team were selling. It was also a place for advertisers who didn't want to be seen next to op-eds like "It's Not a Crack House, It's a Crack Home" (December 3, 1996).

By 1994, according to Madison's *Capital Times*, *The Onion* was plowing over its competitors and bringing in $300,000–$400,000 per year, hitting $1 million in total ad sales since it started in 1988. Banker said, "I thought *The Onion* was one of the funniest things not just in print but consistently." And if you believe in something, it makes it very easy to sell. The poor *Daily Cardinal*, a UW–Madison institution for generations, actually went out of business for several months in 1997 after shrinking down to almost nothing.

As *The Onion* got bolder, with both editorial and advertising doing basically whatever they felt like, they started to have run-ins with people who didn't appreciate them as much as their readers did. Luckily, the universe was about to send another angel.

One day, a well-spoken and slightly intimidating older man paid them a visit. His name was Ken Artis, and he was a copyright attorney for Ginger Rogers. He had recently been informed that her image had been used without permission in an advertisement for Dotty Dumpling's Dowry, a local hamburger place, and needed to go through all their back issues to locate the ad. Luckily, he ended up finding nothing—which he was happy about, because it turned out he was a huge fan.

Though Artis was in his midforties, he had graduated from law school only a few years earlier. In his prior life, he had lived in New Jersey and worked as a ghostwriter for the comic strip *Lil' Abner*. After graduating from law school, he had gotten into licensing law—and acquired Ginger Rogers as a client on a hunch after driving past a Wisconsin highway billboard displaying a giant picture of her with Fred Astaire. Ginger Rogers *never* licensed her image. "I went after these people and really took them, which was fun," Artis said. He and Rogers stayed friends until her death.

Seeing that *The Onion* couldn't afford his fee—and also seeing they had no idea what they were doing from a legal perspective—he offered to help them pro bono. A man who had literally walked in off the street had become their lawyer.

And just in time. Not long afterward, for *The Onion*'s "Fine Dining" issue—an excuse to drum up advertising from local restaurants—Dikkers and another writer had interviewed a local meat wholesaler without telling him it was an interview. In the conversation, the meat man told them all the local restaurants where he sold grade-C and grade-D meat. The story ran on the front page. When the man saw it, he called *The Onion* "absolutely in a rage," Artis told me. The man told Haise and Dikkers he was going to sue. He seemed deadly serious, so they called Artis for help. "What do we do? What do we do?" Artis simply picked up the phone and gave the meat man a call. "And I said, 'I just read this really great article about something that you said, and I just was so glad to read it, you can't even imagine, because that's the sort of thing people want to know before they go into a restaurant. And not only that, but I want to come down there and buy from you.'" Artis gave him a big order for steaks and other expensive cuts, $150 worth of meat, "and *The Onion* bought it for me. So that was the beginning of a beautiful friendship." They never heard from the meat man again. More important, Artis had had a blast. As Dikkers put it, "He's not just a lawyer. He's like an undercover agent for *The Onion*." Haise said it was like he'd been sent from God.

Every Sunday night, no matter what he was doing ("I could have been out on a date with Julia Roberts," he told me), Artis came in to review the paper for any questionable material before it went to the printer. "And I didn't charge them anything for quite a long time," he said. "Because you don't deal with genius that often." Dikkers said Artis "just loved coming to the office and reading the paper. He would laugh and laugh." Haise eventually worked out a deal to pay him seventy-five dollars a week. Artis stayed with *The Onion* for many years.

Whenever someone threatened a lawsuit, Dikkers said, "We would call him, and he would just make it go away." Artis's gifts of persuasion do seem to be rather remarkable. On his Facebook page—if I have the right Ken Artis—he describes himself as a "hypnotist." (Dikkers described it as "influence without power.") Artis said he also posed for many photos because he was the only man they knew in his forties with a suit and tie. Over the years, his body stood in for Bill Clinton, O. J. Simpson, and George Bush. Another time he had to put on his suit and run away from a ninja brandishing a sword down State Street, which nobody—it being State Street—seemed to notice.

- -

Vebber left in 1994 to take a job at *Film Threat* in Los Angeles. The transition to the next editor, however, was difficult. *The Onion*'s tradition was that the assistant editor was understood to be in training to become the editor, and Vebber's assistant editor was Kelly Ambrose. Unfortunately, Ambrose did not last long. Dikkers said, "I loved Kelly. I thought he was one of the funniest people I've ever met. I was very impressed that he could go on a three-day bender and then stumble in on Sunday and slap together the entire newspaper and have it actually be pretty funny. That was impressive." But, he said, "I couldn't really stand for that. Not with these changes I had in mind." Dikkers was done with the silly format and wanted to do something different, and he couldn't do that with Ambrose as editor. He lasted "maybe only for an issue or two after Dan left. And that's when I had to let him go and replace him with Ben [Karlin]. And Kelly was really upset about it. But I knew that Ben had the competence to help me turn *The Onion* into this real serious newspaper parody." As a parting shot, Ambrose, who had been making ironic handmade comedy greeting cards with another *Onion* writer, Andy Selsberg, gave Karlin a card that said on the front, "So you finally got my job . . . ," and on the inside, "you fucking prick." Not a gentle transition.

Ben Karlin, another Rich Dahm hire, was the first nonmidwesterner to have a significant role. He had grown up in Needham, Massachusetts, a suburb of Boston. He was also ambitious, assertive, and direct—qualities most midwesterners get stomped out of them by middle school. This seemed to have rubbed a lot of the staff the wrong way. Dahm said, "Scott, however, liked Ben's enthusiasm right away and thought he had a future at the paper. A story that really boosted Ben's stock was 'UW Cuts Funding for Co-Ed Naked Sports.' Ben wrote the story, and he was still pretty new to the paper, but for the cover we needed someone to bare their ass for a photo of a naked basketball game. And Ben volunteered. He wasn't completely naked—some Photoshopping was done—but he proved right away that he was a team player, in more ways than one."

Once Karlin was in place as editor, Dikkers went off to write and film two pilot episodes of a comedy sketch show called *Comedy Castaways*, which he then branded as an *Onion* project. Hanson, who both wrote and acted in the show along with Brian Stack and others who went on to interesting comedy careers (Hanson had also spent time at the Ark Improv), said Dikkers had told them the goal was to get a TV show by going outside the system and doing it themselves. "That's back when I was just really grateful to Scott for taking me under his wing and making me feel included," he said. "I was on welfare. I had ripped the ligaments in my knee and couldn't work and lost my job as a dishwasher." (*The Onion*'s writers were being paid such a pittance that they needed to have jobs elsewhere; *Onion* writing was more or less volunteer work.) However, Dikkers's plan to make a show on his own outside the normal network and pilot system and then have it get picked up for broadcast because people would be impressed by his independence and gumption "is not how it works," as Hanson put it. Dikkers seemed to believe he could self-publish a TV show. In the end, Dikkers paid $1,200 to have the two episodes broadcast on a local Madison TV station, two thousand miles from Los Angeles. That was the end of *Comedy Castaways*. Dikkers also made a radio comedy-skit CD in his personal recording studio branded with *The Onion*'s name called "Not For Broadcast." Rath told me the working title for that project was "The Offensive Tape." (It was filled with sophomoric jokes.) Not much came of that either, though it did get a few decent reviews.

Banker said, "A lot of the money that was coming in, I was out there hustling for it. I felt some ownership as far as where the money was going," while underlining that he thought both Dikkers and Haise were "wonderful." Still, instead of putting the money into unrelated side projects, "maybe this money should be going back into the newspaper. We should be upgrading our equipment; we should be paying people more; we should be getting better resources. . . . Make everybody's life here a little easier," Banker said.

Dan Vebber said he personally just didn't see *The Onion*'s potential. They were happy to write "for the idiots in Madison. Just working in our little office and drinking our Zimas and cracking each other up." (The staff used to drink the alcoholic beverage Zima ironically in the office due to its painful Gen X–targeted marketing campaign.) This was despite the fact that they'd received letters from the *Harvard Lampoon* saying, "You guys are doing what we used to do, and you're doing it better." Like legions of talented midwesterners before them with no connection to the entertainment or publishing world except as consumers of it, there was little idea that you could turn a talent for writing funny things into a bigger career.

The ONION

"Unrated director's cut featuring 18 minutes of never before seen footage!" *(including nipples)*

A Newspaper for the American Family   volume 27 number 19   20 June–10 July 1995

Computers are Back!

The Early '80s Sensation is Making a Startling Comeback

REMEMBER COMPUTERS? WELL DON'T look now, but that early '80s craze—the electronic computing machine, or "computer"—is back. Everywhere you look today, there are computers, from the home to the office to the public library. There are special computer stores that sell computers and computer accessories. There are computer magazines that report the latest computer news. There are even computer courses that teach people how to most effectively use a computer!

The first wave of computer-mania peaked in 1983, when nationwide sales reached $5.5 billion. That year, computers penetrated every aspect of American life: the workplace, the home, and everywhere in between. TIME magazine even declared the computer 1983's "Man of the Year."

By early 1984, however, the computer craze had died, largely due to the landmark film TRON, with its frightening Orwellian vision of a future in which the helpless Everyman (Bruce Boxleitner) is enslaved by the monolithic, all-powerful God/Machine. TRON, along with the Styx hit "Mr. Roboto," sparked a nationwide agrarian revolt in which all electronics were destroyed, plunging the United States into a new Dark Ages. From 1984 right up until early this year, when the computer made its big comeback, all things in the U.S. were done by hand.

But now computers have returned, and as millions of Americans are

finding out, you can do a great many things with them. You can play with the computer's mouse. You can put disks in them. And you can turn them on and off. Virtually all computers also have keyboards that can be typed on.

"They're just, like, a lot of fun," says General Motors CEO Jack Kram, who recently purchased a computer for his corporation. Many other U.S. corporations are purchasing computers as well. Most often, they are placed on employees' desks, where they can easily be looked at and enjoyed. Quaker Oats CEO Gordon Wells, whose corporation owns a number of computers, described them as "extremely neat."

see COMPUTERS on page 8

Computer Fun Facts

BETCHA DIDN'T KNOW...

- Computer disks aren't really disk-shaped—they're square!
- There's a movie special effects company in California that plans one day to use their computer to create movie special effects!
- The computer's "hard drive" contains complex circuitry and a water rat. When shocked, the rat performs all the computer's simple math functions.
- Many people buy computers not to do calculations on them, but to eat them. They're quite delicious.
- A computer "screen" is a lot like your TV screen, but can only display numbers 1–78.
- President Bill Clinton is not a real human being—he's a state-of-the-art interactive holographic program generated by government computers.
- Imagination plays a big part in using a computer. Imagine what 12 times 16 equals. Then, type in the problem and witness the result!

Computers: They'll change your life.

Hanson and Garden told me they used to call their relationship to television, movies, and music "the other side of the screen." The Wisconsinites were on the side with the people who consumed these things. But the people who *made* it were on the other side. And it didn't even occur to them that you could go from one side to the other. Karlin, however, had a different perspective. In Vebber's opinion, everything that "really got *The Onion* famous and really got *The Onion* out there, Ben was behind." Vebber said, "Obviously, Dikkers at some level shepherded all this. But you know, Ben was the guy who did it."

Karlin held the position of editor for a year. His sudden entry after Ambrose's firing was something of a trial by fire, as he wasn't yet skilled with PageMaker and QuarkXPress, which could crash randomly and delete all your work. Plus, there was the ruthless weekly deadline. Karlin said, "I probably had my first and only panic attack of my life those first few weeks editing the paper. It was just a really big job."

Karlin also had a vision that Haise and Dikkers didn't seem to share. He said, "I was really interested in expanding *The Onion*. I didn't see why we couldn't open an *Onion* in every college campus across America that had a medium-sized town to support it." To him, it was obvious: "Just franchise the damn thing. . . . We've got unique comedy content that we know will be attractive to any college student in America." The contents would come from Madison, but they'd hire local ad reps to sell ads and local editors to do the entertainment listings. But *The Onion*'s owners didn't seem to get it on the scale that Karlin imagined. "It takes a specific kind of person to have a certain kind of vision and fearlessness and belief and wherewithal," he said. "You look at the indefatigable spirits out there that do crazy, pioneering things, they almost all have that quality. And I don't think it's an insult to say that neither Pete nor Scott really had that quality."

Vebber said Karlin later became one of his closest friends, but in Madison they couldn't stand each other. Dahm agreed that "in the beginning, none of the other writers liked Ben. No one except me and Scott. I liked that he brought a different flavor to the mix." Vebber said, "It was specifically because he was a smarmy salesman. That was his gift. And I just was so repulsed by it. Because I wasn't seeing it as something that can help me. I was just seeing it as something that annoyed me." What he didn't realize was that at the time, "I was thinking small, and he was thinking big."

Chapter 7

In the summer of 1995, before the fall semester started, Ben Karlin worked with Scott Dikkers to redesign the newspaper's look and feel. It would be in color and adopt a *USA Today*–style all-news-satire format, maturing away from the days of absurdity and free association. (Most of the staff responsible for that early style had now made their exits.) *The Onion* had been doing news-style stories since the beginning, of course, and in the year prior had already been reshaping itself to look more consistently like a straight newspaper, albeit with flexibility in the front-page design. The color redesign, however, standardized everything. Color did mean an increase in printing costs, but, as Mark Banker said, "it's going to make this publication feel more legitimate and it's going to make it feel more impressive."

USA Today had been bringing a more "glib, colorful quality" to the news (as Karlin put it) for more than a decade and in the mid-'90s was at peak popularity— probably in part due to all the local papers that it had helped put out of business. By 1991, *USA Today*, criticized as a "McPaper" even as its circulation increased, had more readers than any other daily newspaper in the United States and was expanding overseas. Other newspapers were adding color as well. Banker pointed out the trend had even been discussed in his UW journalism classes.

Most importantly, the color redesign included a stricter framework upon which to build *The Onion*'s jokes. Now, only "hard news" following AP style was allowed on the front page. More than one story was possible now too. No more "An Important Message from the Alpha Male. Attention Apes! Your Leader Speaks! Hear Him!" (November 15–28, 1994) taking up the entire cover. Inside, however, the features and columns inspired by the local and small-town midwestern newspapers *The Onion* staff had grown up with would continue, though with

ne ONION ®

America's Number One News Source   volume 27 Ø number 20   11–24 July 1995

1000 Years of Peace Begins With This Issue!

Stock Market Soars

You'll never see a penny of it

THE DOW JONES INDUSTRIAL AVERAGE ROCKETED ABOVE 5300 points this week, an all-time high which created vast wealth for a handful of billionaire investors. You, however, along with the overwhelming majority of the world's population, will never see a penny of it.

The floor of the New York Stock Exchange was abuzz after the 5300 mark was broken. Floor trader Clarence Hlaey was especially excited. "I made the CEOs of some big companies even richer today," he said with a wide smile. "And it will be widely reported and celebrated, despite the fact that it has virtually no bearing on the lives of most humans."

Stock Exchange Board Chairman Ernest Toihdbjle added, "Approximately 100 billion dollars changed hands today. It went from one small group of billionaires to a different small group of billionaires. It was very exciting." He added that it had almost nothing to do with you.

Analysts point out that while you'll never see a penny of this new wealth, you are in some way a part of the wealth's creation. According to billionaire Lamar Nicholson, none of this capital could have been generated without America's economic foundation of wage slaves and working poor, which enables compa-

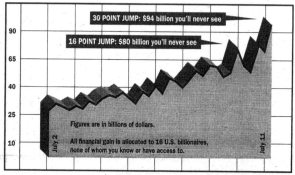

> 30 POINT JUMP: $94 billion you'll never see

> 16 POINT JUMP: $80 billion you'll never see

Figures are in billions of dollars.

All financial gain is allocated to 16 U.S. billionaires, none of whom you know or have access to.

July 2   July 11

> ### "Approximately 100 billion dollars was traded... It went from one small group of billionaires to another small group of billionaires. It was very exciting."
>
> —Chairman Ernest Toihdbjle

nies to earn profits. "God bless all you working Americans!," Nicholson said. "When I think about what I pay you in proportion to the lifestyle I lead, I am overcome with laughter."

Of course, the market surge will take its toll on the economic infrastructure. You and other members of the working poor must make up the net loss to the overall economy caused by the market surge. "Wealth has to come from somewhere," Toihdbjle said. "And at some point on the social ladder, someone has to put a hand in a machine and make something." He quickly commented that his soft, fleshy pink hands have never handled anything but money.

President Clinton announced a plan to pay for the tremendous creation of wealth, proposing that all Americans between the ages of 3 and 83 be sold into white slavery in the Third World. "Those of you who are not white," Clinton said, "will be sold into regular slavery."

To stay in America, the government will now require a $40 million slavery-exemption fee. The capital generated by selling you into slavery and collect-

The floor of the New York Stock Exchange whirred with the excitement of trading and other financial transactions which you neither benefit from nor understand

see STOCKS on page 4

(right): New color design test issue. No, you can't see the color in this black-and-white reproduction, but you can see the design changes: new font, no more coupon section, sidebar and skybox with one-liners, weather report, and table of contents.

the ONION®

VOL. 28 ISSUE 1   NUMBER ONE IN NEWS   8 AUGUST 1995

NEWS

CLINTON ATTACKED BY TIGER

story, page 8

WEATHER

A PLAGUE OF LOCUSTS will be visited upon the U.S. today.

Crops devoured by locusts

Human civilization devoured by locusts

Locusts develop autonomous theocracy

INSIDE

STOCK MARKET SOARS
You'll never see a penny of it

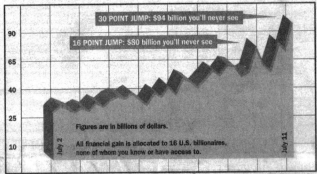

30 POINT JUMP: $94 billion you'll never see

16 POINT JUMP: $80 billion you'll never see

90

65

40

25

10

July 2

July 11

Figures are in billions of dollars.

All financial gain is allocated to 16 U.S. billionaires, none of whom you know or have access to.

The Dow Jones Industrial Average rocketed above 5300 points this week, an all-time high which created vast wealth for a handful of billionaire investors. You, however, along with the overwhelming majority of the world's population, will never see a penny of it.

The floor of the New York Stock Exchange was abuzz after the 5300 mark was broken. Floor trader Clarence Hluey was especially excited. "I made the CEOs of some big companies even richer today," he said with a wide smile. "And it will be widely reported and celebrated, despite the fact that it has virtually no bearing on the lives of most humans."

Stock Exchange Board Chairman Ernest Toihdbjle added, "Approximately 100 billion dollars changed

The floor of the New York Stock Exchange whirred with the excitement of trading and other financial transactions which you neither benefit from nor understand

hands today. It went from one small group of billionaires to a different small group of billionaires. It was very exciting." He added that it had almost nothing to do with you.

Analysts point out that while you'll

never see a penny of this new wealth, you are in some way a part of the wealth's creation. According to billionaire Lamar Nicholson, none of this capital could have been generated

see SOCK MARKET on page 4

ASTRONOMER FINDS CENTER OF UNIVERSE
"It Is My Beautiful 8-year-old Son," He says.

Astronomer James Shirifkin startled the scientific and space exploration communities yesterday when he announced that the gravitational center of the known universe was his 8-year-old son Brian.

"The universe revolves around him. He's so precious," Shirifkin said at a

The Universe (left) and it's center (inset), 8-year-old Brian Shrifkin.

meeting of the American Federation of Space Science convention being held in Atlanta this week.

According to Shirifkin, "My son is the most beautiful thing in the universe. He was born of pure love between my wife Jean and I." He also added that his son is a straight-A student at the Hillburough public school he attends in Hillburough, Mass.

Passersby were amazed by the unusually large amounts of blood. Pass-

see UNIVERSE on page 12

a more consistent tone. They added color on the front, the back, and a couple of pages inside and—marking the end of an era—removed the front-page coupon section. Drunk of the Week also ended, as well as the masthead traditionally filled with fake, absurdist job titles that changed each week, replaced by a consistent masthead that actually listed real roles at the paper.

Also importantly, the new front-page layout created space for many more jokes, with a left-hand column for one-liners and graphics such as charts, weather reports, and so on, which were now standard instead of occasional. A header called a "skybox" would add even more space. The new format meant that *The Onion* lost its "jazzy quality," as Karlin put it. But it also allowed a new, deeper direction. Staff time and energy also did not have to be spent every week coming up with yet another new front-page design and style. The strips of one-liners built into the redesign also provided a home for the many extra headlines produced by *The Onion*'s joke-writing process. Before, most issues had only one joke on the front page. Now there could be a dozen, all interacting with each other.

The new standardized design, Dikkers said, also gave *The Onion* a built-in "straight man" for their jokes: the look and feel of a real newspaper. "After Dan," Dikkers said, "I knew that we had to change what *The Onion* was because it was too much like the wacky funny newspaper." *The Onion* "had to look like a real daily paper with stock reports, a weather map. The headlines should all be laid out the same. They should all look like serious news."

The editorial staff also continued to analyze headlines and stories in their meetings in great detail, further refining and deepening their editing and rewriting methods. Dikkers said, "When you're actually fixing a story or working on a story, we're not, like, busting guts. We're just talking intellectually about why this works better here. What could go here that would make this work better. How do you bring out the humor of this by moving this stuff around." Their cooperative, collective editing and refining process was becoming a midwestern American literary art form.

Randy Jones—the font aficionado and electronic musician with a 1970s computer scientist dad—had already worked with Dikkers to make the prior wacky *Onion* masthead look more serious in 1993. Then, in 1995, new designer Scott Templeton—*another* font aficionado and electronic musician with a 1970s computer scientist dad—updated the masthead again into a version where it would stay. (Templeton joked, "And this is a completely original masthead that I would like to get credit for, so that everybody in the world knows that I designed the

Onion font.") Jones told me that whoever had updated the masthead after him did an excellent job, making exactly the changes he would have made himself.

For Mark Banker, the color redesign was about making *The Onion* into a more serious business. Again, for him, this included improving writer pay. "It was just mortifying to me that the writers were making five bucks for a story meeting and fifteen bucks a story," he said. "I was like, 'We've got to find a way to make enough money to pay people to do this work. These are some of the best writers in comedy, and they're making forty bucks a week.'"

Banker, in fact, joined the writing staff a few months into his tenure as ad rep. Observing from the advertising side, he had "desperately" wanted to be one of the writers. One day, Dikkers said, "Hey, so I hear you telling jokes around here. You're funny." Dikkers invited him to come to the next story meeting.

Banker really admired Dikkers, who "knew what made an *Onion* story funny, and he had a system in place. And just a brilliant mind." Banker remembered coming to the office late at night when nobody was around because it was a quiet place to work and finding Dikkers there too. This gave young Banker a chance to talk shop about comedy with him, a thrilling experience. He also remembered one particular night when they ordered pizza and Dikkers requested a pizza without cheese. "And that was the craziest thing I'd ever heard," Banker said. "It was like somebody told me, 'I'm from another planet.'" Banker said this was "maybe the beginning of me realizing that Scott was a very unique guy and just did things his own way."

This was all taking place in *The Onion*'s new State Street office. If the trope that your physical space is a representation of how you feel about yourself is true, the Madison *Onion* office was an absolute garbage pit. But it was also an insanely multilayered and brainy one that brought high culture and low together in a thousand ways and in hundreds of tiny details. A 1997 Minneapolis *City Paper* profile of *The Onion* described it like this: "Start with the furniture: an orange bean bag that looks like it might start hemorrhaging polyurethane pellets any minute; a futon with its footless frame suspended across stacks of *Onion* back issues; a freestanding car seat with high-pile velour-analog covering, possibly from a minivan of Dodge or Chrysler make. The walls are covered with posters and magazine photos, mostly ironic—or 'ironic,' even, somewhere past camp and irony."

Assistant editor Robert Siegel said, "It smelled like a locker room. If a normal human being walked in there, they'd immediately want to crack open the windows. Every now and then somebody would come in and be like, 'This place is disgusting.'" Siegel also said there were cans of Jolt or Surge everywhere, Gen X–marketed drinks that the staff consumed ironically. (I am reminded of the headline "Ironic Porn Purchase Leads to Unironic Ejaculation," December 1, 1999.) Thompson said he remembered a news-crew cameraman following the periphery of the room "to just scan how scuzzy and filthy and how much, like, encrusted dust and crust had formed on the carpet by the baseboards and old ketchup packets and the soy-sauce packets from a million takeout orders." In his own office, Thompson installed a mini fridge and a TV, to which he hooked up an Atari 2600. Eventually, he brought in some actual arcade machines—weird, off-brand ones—so his office was "part comedy newspaper, part Dave & Buster's." The A.V. Club office was also stacked with "billions" of promotional CDs and other heaps of entertainment-industry publicity detritus.

Every surface had weird toys, ironic objects, handwritten notes, drawings, and obscure pop culture items, especially, I think, from stuff that had flopped or failed or only ever found some weird, bizarre niche, like a *King Ralph* plate. Each item had a meaning. Chad Nackers, who would later become an essential member of the design team and eventually *The Onion*'s editor, remembered: "It was this super-eclectic kind of Gen X playground, basically. And you had just so much stuff on the walls. My favorite was a spread from *Cat Fancy*. This adorable little kitten. And somebody had cut out a penis and glued it onto the page. So it looked like the cat was batting the penis around. I just could not walk past that thing without laughing." Hanson said that above his desk he had a little cardboard chalkboard cut from a Trix cereal box that you could actually write on with chalk. There he wrote a bit of situationist graffito, circa Paris 1968: "Down with a world in which the guarantee that we will not die of starvation has been purchased with the guarantee that we will die of boredom."

Hanson thought it was "a funny juxtaposition of the corporate imagery with a situationist slogan. I had that on my wall for the longest time."

The first color issue with the redesign came out August 8–21, 1995. The front-page headline was "Mount Rushmore Adorned with New Neon Sign." Banker

New Miracle Drug Makes Sex Pleasurable
Excruciating Pain No Longer Part of Mating Process
Story, page 5

CARPETING: IT'S IN THE HOUSE!
Story, page 14

WOULD YOU LIKE A DELICIOUS BANANA?
See page 12

the ONION®

VOLUME 28 ISSUE 1 | NUMBER ONE IN NEWS | 8–21 AUGUST 1995

NEWS

WORLD SCREWED UP BY STUPID GUY NAMED CHAD

Story, page 8

THE DOW

Trading on the floor was active, as 4387 million dollars inshares changed hands.
NOTE: You make $5.50 per hour

+12.75

WEATHER

Crops devoured by locusts

Human civilization devoured by locusts

Locusts develop autonomous theocracy

INSIDE

NEWS IN BRIEF......................2
WHAT DO YOU THINK?...............5
HOROSCOPES.........................5
JIM'S JOURNAL.......................6
PATHETIC GEEK STORIES.............8
DECLINE AND FALL CALENDAR.......12
CULTURAL IDIOCY QUIZ..............17
DRUNK OF THE WEEK................18
A-V CLUB.............................19
MOVIE LISTINGS....................21
CALENDAR...........................24
CLASSIFIEDS........................26

Mount Rushmore Adorned With New Neon Sign

Mount Rushmore's low-profile design was given a significant up-lift by the attractive new neon sign recently constructed upon it. During the sign's construction, an estimated 50 workers fell to their deaths.

BLACK HILLS, S.D.—In an effort to attract more tourism to the Black Hills National Park area of South Dakota, tourism department officials have added an eye-catching neon sign to the famed monument at Mount Rushmore.

The sign, which is roughly the same size as the monument, should bolster visitor attendance to Mount Rushmore by clearly drawing attention to the mountain to tourists who might have otherwise missed it.

"Mount Rushmore, before, was too subtle a display to effectively compete in today's Northwestern tourism marketplace," Park Director Melvin Prego said. Prego explained that severe competition from such area landmarks as Wall Drug, the Corn Palace and the gift shop shaped like a huge cement dinosaur had contributed to the decision to "revamp" Mount Rushmore's image with state-of-the-art neon sign advertising, a proven sales-boosting technique.

Much debate over the sign involved its wording, with suggestions varying from a modest "Snacks Available" to a bolder, arrow-shaped neon box with the words, "Look at this, These heads are huge!" One of the more radical plans called for the addition of neon glasses, mustaches and arrows through the heads of Presidents Jefferson and Washington, but was rejected when fake glasses were deemed "too undignified for two former presidents who had no known need for eyesight-supporting devices."

The Department of Tourism eventually agreed upon one sign, "Keys While

see Rushmore on page 4

This Attractive, Colorful Redesign Is For Our Advertisers, Not You

A Message from Onion Publisher T. Herman Zweibel

(photo, cir. 1911)

[Editor's note: Periodically and without warning, ONION Publisher Emeritus T. Herman Zweibel defies his state-imposed retirement and writes a column for THE ONION, the newspaper founded by his great grandfather. As per his instructions, these columns are printed in their entirety and without copy-editing.]

Welcome to THE ONION'S new design!

As great-grandson of THE ONION'S founder, it is my great pleasure and privilege to debut this major redesigning of America's Finest News Source.™ It was a long time in coming, and we believe it propels THE ONION into the next millenium with a strong, unified vision of the future.

I have a long, glass tube inserted in my urethra. It is very painful, especially during urination. So I apologize if I ramble.

Though I haven't been an active part of THE ONION board since 1960, when I fell ill with Parkinson's disease brought on by my advancing years, I try to stay abreast of the newspaper business from the confines of the lonely white bed in the medical wing of my impenetrable 4000-acre estate.

see Zweibel on page 6

The first color issue, reproduced here in black and white.

provided the headline, and Hanson wrote the story. Siegel said the moment they turned to color felt like *The Wizard of Oz*.

The redesign had gotten a big leg up with a new hire: graphics editor Mike Loew. Loew grew up in Appleton, Wisconsin, and went to college in Madison, "the big city." Looking at his grades and test scores, his high school counselor had encouraged him to apply to Ivy League schools, but his dad, who worked selling bank vaults and security systems, had recently lost his job—and Madison cost only $2,000 a year.

Loew was another former *Cardinal* cartoonist and graphics editor. He had also done a stint as an *Onion* writer a year or two earlier. Within a few weeks of Karlin bringing him back, Dikkers asked him if he wanted to be graphics editor. Loew said he trained with Dikkers for about three days in the new design, and then he was on his own: Dikkers disappeared again, this time for months. "It was a sink-or-swim situation for me," Loew said, who was a few years younger than everyone. Along with Karlin and the rest of the staff, Loew helped finalize *The Onion*'s new look.

One of Loew's first cover images was his most famous: Jesus dunking a basketball for "Christ Returns to NBA" (April 3, 1996). Back then, there were no online stock photos, so they did most of *The Onion*'s photography themselves. Loew found someone who'd taken photos at a UW basketball game for the action shot. Dikkers then found a Madison hippie who looked like Jesus and took his picture, and then Loew Photoshopped the crown of thorns on his head. It was one of their most popular issues yet. "Forward Stacey Augmon, just one of many Hawks players who claims to have a personal relationship with Christ, said, 'He's taught me so much, like how to love your enemies as yourself, to pray for those who hurt you, and when to pass up the three in favor of a higher percentage shot.'"

Mike stayed up all night working on the NBA issue and then went home to crash. When he came back that afternoon, everyone gave him a round of applause. He was twenty-one years old. "I guess I'm doing okay," he thought.

The color version took the publication to the next level visually and comedically. There was nothing else like it anywhere. People had made newspaper parodies many times before, of course—the idea probably goes back to the invention of the newspaper itself—but usually just as one-offs or short print runs. But this was different. Word started getting out "in the way things trickled out before the internet," Siegel said. "People took the paper home and shared it with their cool younger brother, you know? It was viral the way things were viral before the

Owls Are Assholes
See Commentary, page 22

Philip Morris Lawyers
Deny Cigarettes Are
Cylindrical
See Law, page 4

Clinton Found Alive
See National, page 9

⌀ the ONION®

II

VOLUME 42 ISSUE 28   AMERICA'S FINEST NEWS SOURCE   13-19 JULY 1996

NEWS

Local Oafs To Spawn

CHRIST RETURNS TO NBA

After a two-year hiatus, Jesus Christ returned to the NBA last night, taking the court with His former team, the Atlanta Hawks. Christ, who quit the sport in May 1994 to focus on spreading His message of universal love and compassion, made His triumphant return last night against the Bulls, just in time for Easter Sunday.

The return of Christ, who averaged 18.2 points and 7.3 assists per game during His 10-year NBA career, has excited success-hungry Hawks fans, who are calling Him the team's "Savior."

Said Atlanta resident and **see CHRIST on page 11**

Christ's Career Highlights

College: Texas A&M
- School's second all-time leading scorer
- Junior year, led Aggies to NCAA's Sweet 16
Pro: Drafted third overall by Atlanta in 1986
- January 12, 1986—Scored 35 points in one quarter after Nets forward Buck Williams used his name in vain after a missed dunk
- February 22, 1990—During time out at All-Star game in Chicago, turned water into Gatorade
- December 31, 1991—Destroyed concession stands in lobby of Dallas's Reunion Arena, shouting, "This is a house of basketball!"
- March 4, 1992—Appeared on cover of Sports Illustrated for the seventh time, once again with the headline, "It's a Miracle!"

Right: Jesus Christ returned to action last night against the Chicago Bulls, chipping in 13 points and 4 assists, and wowing fans with His trademark "Ascension Dunk."

Mike Loew's acclaimed cover Photoshop for 'Christ Returns to NBA.' The cover also includes one of Tim Harrod's first jokes, a one-liner satirizing the Philip Morris hearings about whether the company knowingly provided false information to the public and regulators about nicotine's addictiveness and the manipulation of cigarette nicotine content to more effectively hook smokers.

internet. Passed around and shared. We could feel there was something kind of bubbling." Comedy people in particular sought it out. For instance, to the staff's delighted shock, Bob Odenkirk was seen reading a copy of *The Onion* on an episode of *Mr. Show*, probably the highest-regarded fringe-comedy program on TV at the time. Other underground heroes like members of Sonic Youth also had subscriptions. In the more mainstream world, MTV flew to Madison and did a segment on them.

- -

Dikkers had taken this *Onion* hiatus to realize his life ambition and shoot his first full-length feature film. The movie, *Spaceman*, was a comedy about a man abducted from Earth as a young boy and raised in space to be a killing machine. Upon returning to "infiltrate Earth society," he takes menial jobs while trying to become a hit man, while distant memories of his childhood on Earth begin to surface. A review in *Cineaste* remarked on how isolated the main character seemed during one of the film's serious scenes, where his calls for help into space went unheard. The experience was extremely stressful for Dikkers, to the point of mental breakdown—he had attempted to do much of the work by himself—and did not return to *The Onion* or communicate with the staff for months. Loew said when Dikkers suddenly reappeared one day, it looked like he'd been through an *Apocalypse Now* experience.

Meanwhile, though Pete Haise continued to be a hard worker—*The Onion* was *packed* with ads—he was starting some big side projects of his own, too. Much to the writing staff's shock and amusement (and also anger and disgust), Haise decided to move seventy-five miles away, back home to Milwaukee, to open not one but *two* submarine-sandwich shops, called PJ's Subs and Clubs. (Before Haise moved, he promoted Mark Banker to assistant publisher to hold down the fort in Madison.) He also opened an *Onion* outlet to distribute the new color publication in Milwaukee. The writing staff, however, was experiencing this moment as a time of potential major growth for *The Onion*. And Haise was spending his time opening sandwich shops?

Regarding his decision to open an outlet in Milwaukee—*The Onion's* first branch office—Haise told me, "I wouldn't necessarily call Milwaukee a city of consequence, but it sure felt like that. . . . I didn't have to reincorporate because it was in the same state. And we had a city that I was familiar enough with to be able to play off the colleges in the downtown . . . to kind of test a, quote-unquote, real market." He also underlined that he never *worked* at the sub shops. He just owned them, and they paid him a lot better than *The Onion* did. (Dikkers had made him commit to never taking a commission for any ads he sold, and Haise told me he sold more than half the ads "for many, many years.") Haise also said his sub shops actually *helped*—they bought ads every week for ten years, and inspired other Milwaukee advertisers to do the same.

Haise also told me that he needed to be very careful with *The Onion's* money. Among other things, they operated on a cash-flow basis. "Do you have any idea how hard it is to run a company knowing you would never get a loan in a million years?" he said. "We were just a way over-the-top liability risk. We could have been sued out of existence at any time. We were nothing but a house of cards." He did a lot of "corporate and financial gymnastics, and a lot of moving and shaking, to keep us alive. We could have been dead many times." But also, "as much as I guided *The Onion*, it really seemed to have an energy and a mind of its own that just kept itself alive and going."

The Madison writing staff, however, really only remember the sub shops, which gave them the message that Haise was just not taking things seriously. A couple of them said he even worked on the shops from the Madison *Onion* office, using the phone to get the bread supplier from a prosperous Madison sub shop called Big Mike's and storing cases of drinks there to bring to Milwaukee later. Editor Ben Karlin said, "It was hard to tell where PJ's Subs and Clubs ended and where *The Onion* began and vice versa in Milwaukee. There were many jokes in the writers' room about one of them being a front for the other, but we just couldn't tell which one." (Haise strongly disputed this portrayal. *The Onion*'s books were open to anyone who wanted to see them.)

For Karlin, it was immensely frustrating. "I just felt like *The Onion* was kind of on a little bit of a rocket ship," he said. "And that the business owners should be 100 percent focused on a growth and expansion plan and not opening sub shops." For Haise, perhaps, like being a single parent, constant moment-to-moment tasks and crises and distractions made it difficult to step back and see the bigger picture, much less make a plan to act on it. The absence of commission on his ad sales also may have limited his salary. It seems plausible that the *Onion* just wasn't going to give Haise the lifestyle he wanted. Who knew how long it would last anyway? A sub shop was a much more reliable business.

Or, as Stephen Thompson put it, maybe it was just a difference in life goals. In the writers' room, he said, the sub shop had become code for "The business side of this paper has no idea what it's doing." At the time, Thompson "absolutely accepted it as stone-cold fact," but now, looking back, maybe Haise just wanted to run a sub shop and be a reasonably prosperous local businessman, which *The Onion* didn't pay him enough to do. "I think everybody tries to build a world that is the size they're most comfortable with," Thompson said. "You see this in people's home lives. You see this in people's marriages; you see this in the jobs people pursue." And for Haise, Thompson said, "that footprint was the size of two cities in southern Wisconsin. And opening a sub shop in Milwaukee made perfect sense to him." It was "a move toward being this diversified all-purpose Milwaukee business mogul. And eventually, there'll be a chain of sub shops, and then maybe he invests in bars. And they all advertise in *The Onion*. And the rest of us were like, 'Why the fuck are you opening a sub shop?'"

Meanwhile, Karlin still envisioned every major college campus in the United States having *The Onion*. "Back then," he said, "there was still a viable print-distribution model, because there were still pretty robust alternative week-lies." He thought the sky was the limit. "And I didn't quite understand why this other stuff was happening simultaneously." Karlin said Dikkers was "so instrumental in shaping the voice of *The Onion*. I learned so much from Scott creatively. But I just don't think he was a visionary leader." Siegel said, "Everything just felt so small-time and half-assed," like *The Onion* was just "one of Pete's hustles, rather than 'you're sitting on a potential media empire here.'" Haise was instead excited about things like getting a primo advertising placement with some Milwaukee beer festival.

Writer Chris Karwowski joined the *Onion* staff around this time. Karwowski was from a suburb of Chicago called Mundelein. His family was Irish and Eastern European, Polish Lithuanian. "Sounds very polite, but it took a couple of years of therapy for me to really tap into emotions other than anger and confusion. But like, everyone's very nice."

Karwowski had been an *Onion* fan for some time. He'd gone to college near Champaign, Illinois, where Haise had also published an edition for a while, so he would either grab copies himself or beg friends to get them for him. "But something happened when it went color. I was just like, 'This is the greatest thing I've ever seen.' And I went from fan to superfan." Then some friends moved to Madison and told him he should come too; he would love it. They were right. "I lived right across the lake in a cheap apartment, a huge apartment for $800 that I split with a roommate. I would just, like, fall asleep after work on the three-season porch every summer. It was very delightful and inexpensive," he said. "I didn't have to make plans there. I would just go to bars, and I would run into people that I knew."

He met Hanson through a guy who played in a Madison band that recorded on the label Alternative Tentacles, home of the Dead Kennedys. (Madison had a great independent music scene at this time, with local bands like Killdozer rounding out *Onion* staff playlists and local recording venue Smart Studios recording or producing bands like L7, Walt Mink, Smashing Pumpkins, and Nirvana.) When he heard the guy knew someone at *The Onion*, Karwowski got excited. His friend said, "They don't get paid as much as you might think. And it's not the happiest place." Still, Karwowski connected with Hanson, who seemed "mystified. Like, 'Why are you calling me?'" Eventually, Karwowski got the go-ahead to send in headlines, which he sent in a manila envelope via postal mail to *The Onion*'s office. Siegel gave him good marks, though he suggested that Karwowski get an email account.

Meanwhile, Karwowski got a job at a sandwich shop called Radical Rye (which happened to be owned by Karl Armstrong, one of the four people who had bombed Sterling Hall—the physics building on campus where Maria Schneider's dad and John Krewson said his mom had worked—during Madison's Vietnam War protests). Radical Rye was also close to *The Onion*'s State Street office, and he would see staff going back and forth all the time. Sometimes they would even come in and buy sandwiches from him. "But I was so shy," Karwowski said. "I wouldn't say, 'Hi, I'm a contributor!'"

Karwowski had no idea that he was in fact a member of a very select club: hardly anyone outside *The Onion* writers' room regulars was allowed to submit headlines. "I thought they were just taking all these ideas from all these people in town," he said. "Sure, my ideas show up relatively frequently, but you know, working at a sandwich restaurant doesn't boost your self-esteem." Then one of his coworkers drew a little sign for their tip jar that read "Chris Karwowski does backflips for tips." A writer saw it and reported back to the office, and Karwowski was invited to attend meetings. They hadn't realized he lived in Madison. "I think they actually really liked the fact that I didn't bug them," he said. "I think they were very suspicious of social climbers or people who were ambitious."

Another new staffer around this time was eighteen-year-old Joe Pickett, from the town of Stoughton, who did distribution and some writing. Of delivering papers, he said: "I remember that smell, the ink. . . . If I smelled it, it would take me right back there. I love that smell." Pickett would later cofound the Found Footage Festival, a funny traveling show of '80s-era VHS-tape clips discovered in yard sales and thrift shops. Pickett told me one of the biggest differences between the '80s and now is that then, people were super awkward on camera because it was still an unusual thing to experience.

The Onion's new look wasn't the only thing coming up in 1995. There was also this new thing called the "internet." (To be precise, the internet itself wasn't new—it had been around since the 1960s, a Cold War government creation to facilitate communication in case of nuclear war. What *was* new was getting access to the internet as an ordinary person via something called the World Wide Web, an application that operated on the internet and could connect your personal computer with anyone else's on the planet.) At first, people could only use text online.

But by 1996, applications like Netscape Navigator (created by a Wisconsinite) were starting to allow people to create websites—a new visual way to use the World Wide Web.

And it turned out a decent number of them were using this vast Cold War–era technology to post content from *The Onion*—without attribution. People were also typing *Onion* articles into emails and sending them to each other, again without saying where the hilarious story came from. A radio host in Chicago started reading *Onion* articles on the air as if they were his own.

One week in 1996, *The Onion*'s lead story was "Clinton to Deploy Vowels to Bosnia," written by Siegel. An excerpt:

> Before an emergency joint session of Congress yesterday, President Clinton announced US plans to deploy over 75,000 vowels to the war-torn region of Bosnia. The deployment, the largest of its kind in American history, will provide the region with the critically needed letters A, E, I, O, U, and Y, and is hoped to render countless Bosnian words more pronounceable.

> "For six years, we have stood by while names like Ygrjvslhv and Tzlynhr and Glrm have been horribly butchered by millions around the world," Clinton said. "Today, the United States must finally stand up and say 'Enough.' It is time the people of Bosnia finally had some vowels in their incomprehensible words. The US is proud to lead the crusade in this noble endeavor."

Not long after, Tom and Ray Magliozzi, the hosts of the popular NPR radio show *Car Talk*, read the whole thing on the air while laughing so hard they could barely speak. *The Onion* was not given attribution. The story appeared other places too. Then the staff learned that a new website called "The Melvin" was posting all of *The Onion*'s content, word for word. Joe Garden remembered watching the site slowly load, pixel by pixel, via the office phone-line internet connection. Clearly, the situation was getting out of control. Siegel said of the Melvin website discovery, "That was kind of an obvious light bulb moment. Like, 'Hey, why don't we do that ourselves?'"

In 1996, pretty much the only staff who had gone online were computer-savvy people using pre-web-browser bulletin boards, like layout lead Andrew Welyczko, ad rep Mark Banker, and new designers Scott Templeton and Jack

Szwergold. Bulletin boards were text-only interfaces where people could go to exchange information, tell jokes, and just chat and socialize.

At the time, most people—including almost everyone on staff—still did not own a personal computer. One, they were very expensive, and two, why would you ever need one? Computers were for scientists who wanted to analyze high volumes of data, NASA to send stuff into space, business owners to keep track of inventory, whatever that bulletin-board thing was, and maybe playing games. You could also now, of course, do things like desktop publishing, photographic manipulation, and accounting spreadsheets. And okay, email was sort of fun and useful if you had a way to send and receive it. Other than these work-type applications, though, why would ordinary life—socializing, shopping, talking to friends, turning your oven on—ever require a *computer*?

As Thompson put it, there was an "enormous amount of skepticism" around the internet at this time. "The early days of the internet were very much like, 'That is where nerds go,'" he said. Nonnerds preferred to communicate face-to-face. Fortunately, "we had on staff a nerd in the person of Jack Szwergold, who was really pushing, saying, 'We should have a presence on the internet. And I will personally undertake whatever the learning curve is to figure out how to post the paper online.'" There was "quite a bit of pushback," however, from Haise and others, who said, "Nobody's making money on the internet." At the time, that was basically true—other than computer makers, website-browser developers, and random-sounding website names for weird new companies generated in California that had lit the fuse of the nascent dot-com boom. But an existing small local business in Madison, Wisconsin? How? Thompson emphasized that "lots of people had that kind of mentality. It was not exclusive to Pete."

But the hype about the internet in the '90s invited skepticism. At times it felt like everyone in America was at a time-share-buying presentation. A communication revolution was now under way that would change everything for the better. Societies would finally create true democracy because everyone could now express their individual voice. Work would become more efficient, and people could be far more productive. Free time would expand. Children would have better ways of learning. Blah, blah, blah. And all you had to do to join this revolution was spend thousands of dollars on a personal computer and several thousand more on software and a printer and all kinds of other weird new things you then had to constantly upgrade and replace! (This was at a time

The Onion's first website server, paid for via an advertising trade.

when a telephone or typewriter could last your entire life and the phone bill was maybe twenty bucks a month.) You could also now create your own publication just by making a website and putting it up. No money needed. No stuffy, uptight editors or fact-checkers, either. A few people did raise the alarm about privacy, as well as the physical and mental-health impacts of even more screen time than people were already getting with 24/7 cable television and VHS movie rentals. But these voices were mostly drowned out by the boosters—and especially by the rapidly expanding dot-com financial bubble.

Still, for existing print publications, the question was thornier. What could going online do that the hard copy couldn't and vice versa? How would the new format affect readers and reading? What about advertising? Would it be worth the cost to find out? "Newspapers didn't really know what the hell to do with the web. And I think *The Onion* was exactly the same way," Welyczko said. Ueno agreed that Haise was skeptical at first. "Profitability in the early days was tough because you had to offset the cost of actually serving up the content, which was massive for the time," he said, "versus the revenues coming in—and not a lot of companies were selling on the internet. It didn't seem like a viable business model."

But Szwergold, who knew some HTML, told them: "I'll do it. Nobody else has to do anything." And because of that, Thompson said, "we got on the internet a year or two earlier than we probably would have otherwise." Haise and Banker traded a new Madison server company called IntraNet a quarter-page ad in exchange for hosting *The Onion*'s website. And Szwergold set about coding *The Onion*'s first web pages from scratch (no website builders like WordPress existed then).

A native Brooklynite, and the son of Holocaust survivors, Szwergold saw himself as the "black sheep" of his family. His parents passed away in 1993, and in 1995 he quit his job to take some time off and figure things out. In the process he decided to move to Madison, which he had visited a few years earlier and really liked. It was the kind of place "that doesn't really exist anymore. It was a very slacker town," he said, in the "wonderful world of the early 1990s," where life was still inexpensive and tons of interesting creative stuff was happening outside the mainstream that you could participate in without needing a lot of money. (If I could name the single biggest difference between then and now, it would be that in the '90s, it was still possible to live almost entirely outside big mainstream corporate influence and still be connected to the broader world. All you had to do was get rid of your TV, read independent and alternative media, listen to alternative music and public or community radio, work and spend your money at local independent small businesses, and cultivate a circle of friends doing the same thing. You could take it even further and live and shop in Madison's co-op houses and grocery stores. Madison had many people doing exactly this.) After meeting people through a connection with Maria Schneider, Szwergold got a job doing graphic design. His other income option at the time, he told me, was being a paid test subject for medical research at the university. He chose *The Onion*.

Dikkers said Haise objected to buying the domain name theonion.com because it cost $400 and he didn't want to spend the money. Dikkers told me, "You have to realize that my drive at *The Onion* back then was to get it exposed to as many eyeballs as possible. We sent free subscriptions out to agents in Hollywood and to other publications. Any chance we got, we were on the radio. So when this idea of the internet came along, for me, it was kind of a no-brainer. It was like, 'Yeah, another way to distribute *The Onion*? Absolutely.'" Karlin said, "Scott, to his credit, was like, 'This is the future of publishing; this is probably the future of everything.' And he worked really diligently to try to figure it out. Andrew Welyczko was also very involved. They worked really hard to figure out how to get it online relatively early compared to the internet writ large."

Haise remembered this situation a little differently. "It would be ridiculous for the CEO of a growing media company to not want to be on the internet and show your wares," he said. Plus, you couldn't just snap your fingers and have a fully functional, well-maintained website when people didn't even know how one was supposed to—or could—look or function. "Part of the delay was, what do you *do*?" Haise said. "There were so many caveats as to what it had to be or what it should be in terms of interactivity. How often it needed to be out there and updated and how much money and people. How many bodies and minds needed to be there to manage it. It took a while to do it."

"At the beginning, it was really almost more like a technical thing than anything else because of the speeds involved," Karlin said. "Everything was so slow. Everything was through the dial-up—there was no Wi-Fi or anything like that. I was principally just concerned with, 'Are we gonna be able to get the contents more or less in the form that we're laying it out in on the website?' The idea of purpose-built websites that use the internet as its own medium, that was kind of a second- or third-generation thing. At the beginning, it was just like, 'Let's just take this thing and put it on the web.' That was the initial push. That's all our imaginations could contain at that point."

The universe must have wanted it to happen. One day, out of the blue, two brothers—recent UW–Madison graduates Dave and Jeff Haupt—approached Haise about opening a branch in Boulder, Colorado. *The Onion* would provide the content, and they would sell local ads and publish local entertainment listings. Jeff Haupt told me that the idea came from Dave, who had worked at a shop that was an *Onion* advertiser on State Street. One day, Dave saw an *Onion* advertising-rate card there, looked at how many ads were in the publication, did the math, and thought, "I bet this thing does pretty well." They made their pitch to Haise. Jeff then joined Karlin on some distribution runs—the post-advertising part of running an *Onion* office—to see how it was done. Then he and Dave moved to Boulder and started the most successful branch office yet. They added another office in Denver a little while later.

For the Madison *Onion*, it was a windfall from heaven. Not a huge one, but enough to make Haise okay with finally pulling the trigger on the website. According to a *Denver Post* article, Haise licensed them the right to the *Onion* name for ten years for a onetime $25,000 fee.

Despite the Haupt brothers' success, they occasionally caused friction in Madison by refusing to publish certain articles, like the not-funny-just-shocking "Christ Kills Hooker" (which I hope was actually a meta joke about offensive jokes). They also refused to print "Columbine Jocks Safely Resume Bullying" (September 8, 1999) after the Columbine High School shootings—which happened in Colorado. And Jeff Haupt could see that leadership at *The Onion's* headquarters was perhaps not as focused on the bigger picture as it could have been. Still, Haupt said the editorial side was so hardcore and perfectionist, "maybe even somewhat to a fault," that it propped up the business side in a way, "because it was just so well done."

"There were a lot of *Onion* miracles out there that helped us along the way," Haise said, "that I would never try and take credit for, but they just fucking happened and kept us going."

Szwergold spent a month creating the "very static" website, mostly at home on his Macintosh Performa. He'd then take the file back to the office, where a higher-speed modem was available, and see how it looked after uploading it. The site went live in May 1996. "It was weird," Szwergold said. Either it was "going to be a big thing, or it was going to be seen as nothing." The site was updated once a week when the newspaper came out.

While all this internet stuff was happening, out in the still sort of new world of cable television, another important media entity was also being created in 1996: Fox News. The brainchild of Republican media consultant Roger Ailes, who had done pivotal work in the successful Nixon, Reagan, and George H. W. Bush presidential campaigns, Fox News was created to pump highly emotional and dramatic versions of conservative opinion directly into people's living rooms, setting up a scenario where any compromise or cooperation with Democrats would be seen as weak—a long-term strategy to elect Republicans and keep them in power.

In a weird way, Fox was also a parallel-universe *Onion*: it was also using the news format to say things that were not actually news. (There are no rules that must be followed in order to use the name "news." If there were, Fox News would actually be called Fox Propaganda. The problem, of course, is that when you make something look like news, act like news, and call it news, many people believe it

The Onion will return July 9, 1997.

Ø the ONION°

Number One In News   Established 1871

Alzheimer's Sufferers Demand Cure For Pancakes
WASHINGTON, DC--Alzheimer's sufferers from across the nation marched on random buildings throughout Washington, D.C., Washington State, and Iowa City, IA, Mo
demanding that Congress prioritize finding a cure for pancakes, the nation's third-leading breakfast food.
See June 18 Issue

Clinton Makes Federal Budget Proposal More Dynamic With Color Charts From Kinko's
WASHINGTON, DC--President Clinton wowed Congress with a revised balanced-budget proposal Monday, utilizing eye-catching, easy-to-read color charts printed at K
to win over Republican opponents.
See June 4 Issue

Area Bowl Cashed
TEMPE, AZ--Disappointment, frustration and disbelief were just a few of the highly charged emotional reactions to Monday's discovery that a bowl belonging to area
residents Mike Cudahy and "Thatches" Moynihan was cashed.
See May 21 Issue

Trouser Downsizing Threatens Raver Industry
NEW YORK--As trouser downsizing continues throughout the troubled economy and budget cuts threaten employees' pants security, many workers in legwear-based fiel

The Onion's website circa 1997, via the Internet Archive.

actually *is* news.) In a 2012 article in *Cinema Journal*, communications scholar Jeffrey P. Jones wrote, "Using the genre of news as cover, Fox confidently creates and dramatizes all sorts of contestable and debatable ideas about public life using the codes and conventions of established journalistic practice."

Ailes had made a couple of prior failed attempts to get conservative-news TV going but only finally succeeded with Fox, which had not only charismatic "anchors" but also a focused, niche approach in which right-wing tropes, ideology, and supposed threats to that ideology would be ritualistically performed, seven days a week—along with an almost holy war against "liberals" and whatever Fox said liberals did and stood for. It made for dramatic and gripping television. It also made viewers into participants in Fox's outraged, paranoid drama, a sort of proto-immersive theater experience. Fox is the most successful cable news channel in the United States.

Back at *The Onion*, the team worked to understand how the website functioned and what it meant to have one. As Haise put it, "It was such a weird, barren terrain to cover where you didn't even know what things were called. . . . 'What's a hit? What's a page view?' Well, that's when somebody stops, at least for a little bit. 'What's an interstitial?' It's something between the page views." What they did know, Haise said, "is that we had a shitload of traffic. Every Tuesday, they would just choke out on bandwidth." Siegel said, "We put it online, and that kind of opened the floodgates almost immediately."

There were hardly any humor sites on the internet in 1996. *The Onion*, nurtured and developed for years in the freedom and sublimated aggression of Gen X alternative-culture obscurity, appeared there fully formed with some of the best humor writing ever created. And it wasn't coming from New York or LA. It came from Wisconsin. *The Onion* was deeply midwestern, which gave everything in it a different feel from the usual ego-heavy coastal fare. Maria Schneider said, "A lot of it had to do with being from flyover country. Everybody ignores us." Comedy writers from Harvard, she said, were often very gifted. But midwesterners "avoid things that seem overly clever, or proud of itself, or obscure." Showing off of any kind, as well as ambition and desire for money, status, and power—the engines driving both the professional entertainment industry and the Ivy League—are antithetical to the midwestern mindset. Here, being visibly ambitious would get you ostracized. It simply wasn't done.

The Onion also parodied the writing and people you would find in midwestern small-town newspapers. "I don't think you have that in the *Harvard Lampoon* as much," Schneider said. Midwestern Area Men and Area Women lived in an entirely different world from aspirational coastal elites. It was not a world that had seen much media representation.

Within weeks, the website had annihilated any competition and was one of the most popular on the entire World Wide Web, getting hundreds of thousands of hits per week from all over the world. Without trying, they had moved to the other side of the screen. A "glowing review" in the *New Yorker* two months after the site went live lit the fuse, followed by "dozens of plugs" in other publications, "from *Esquire* to *Elle*," according to reporter Tom Alesia in an article for Madison's *Wisconsin State Journal*.

"After kind of toiling in semiobscurity for at that point eight years, we just felt like we went supernova," Siegel said. "We had access to the whole world." A flood of national media wanted to do stories. Anderson Cooper, early in his CNN career, came into the office and interviewed the staff. In 1998, the *Washington Post* also did a big feature about *The Onion*, saying, "What the *National Lampoon* was to the '70s—consistently, brutally hilarious—*The Onion* may be for the new millennium. In a world of 24-hour news channels, myriad online sources, the merging of fact and fiction, and corporate media synergy, *The Onion* is an antidote to hype and, oddly enough, a voice of reason."

Siegel said the most common questions they got from media interviewers were about where they got their ideas, if they ever worried about offending people, or if any topics were off-limits. In response, "we probably said, trying to be all badass and edgy, 'There is no line' or 'The only line is between funny and not funny.'" An *Onion* joke was not offensive "as long as it's defensible." A few coastal journalists couldn't hide their shock at the fact that something so brilliant was coming from Wisconsin, or their patronizing attitudes toward the staff. Joe Garden recalls one reporter from New York pointing at his pants in shock: "You're still wearing pleats!"

Haise said this was the "golden age" of *The Onion*. "We had put in such time underground . . . And as we started to find our voice and rise, that's where you're kind of at your best at anything in a career. Whether it's an athlete or some band." *The Onion*'s poor little server company, whose other clientele was probably small local businesses or personal websites about fishing or teaching political science, could not handle the traffic. Banker offered the owner a free upgrade from the weekly quarter-page to a half-page ad as compensation. They did have a contract, after all.

Now that the site was up, it was time to figure out how to make money from it. But how did one go about selling advertisements on a virtual entity that could hyperlink into infinity? Was visiting a website like reading a newspaper or like watching television? And was it something you looked at or something that looked at you? It turned out that user activities—clicking, lingering on a page for a long or short period of time—could be something concrete that you could base ad rates on. It slowly started to dawn that you could do a lot more than just post the equivalent of a print ad on a website and hope maybe somebody looked at it. You could also get data: which people visited and from where, which specific pages they looked at, how long they looked, and so on, a new kind of consumer information that was much more granular than how many *Onion* coupons were used that week—and maybe a lot more valuable. The thing for sale was not an ad so much as the opportunity to access the individual user's attention.

At first, thinking in a hybrid analog-digital way, Banker proposed a strip of ads at the bottom of the page "that never goes away"—kind of like the *Onion* coupon days of old. The writers, however, objected. It would interfere with reading their work. Banker said, "'Look, I get it. Artistic integrity. I believe in that, but it's a lot easier to have artistic integrity when you have a roof over your head. And I guarantee you, we're going to be able to sell more ads, and bigger ads, on this website than we can sell in the paper.'"

As it became clear that digital advertising had many more display possibilities than analog advertising, Haise began arguing with the editorial staff about how much the ads could interfere with editorial content. The writers objected to anything that moved or flashed or drew attention to itself. In addition, as it also became clear that digital advertising was all about consumer data gathering, Haise said the staff wouldn't let him sell certain ad buys because they asked for certain information, "which we all know now is the absolute mack daddy of everything is data collection, geodata collection, and everything else." But the editorial staff would not allow advertisers to find out a user's "age or where they lived or anything like that." They "wouldn't let me do anything."

Despite these arguments, Banker started killing it with online advertising sales, especially national advertisers, who were trying desperately to find ways to get themselves online. He called Sony and told them he wanted them on *The Onion*'s website. Sony was thrilled and asked how much it would cost. Banker, making up a number on the spot, said, "$15,000?" Sony said, "Great!" Banker said, "And I was like, 'It can't be that easy.'" (Banker would leave for LA not long after the website started, but the ease of selling it clearly made an impression on him.)

Once other big names started seeing those website ads, it started snowballing. The dot-com boom was moving into full swing—well on its way to becoming a bubble—and everyone was in a stampede to get online as soon as possible. (In Bill Kovarik's book *Revolutions in Communication*, he writes that by 1998 there were twenty-six million website pages. By 2000, there were a billion.) Haise did note that "there was this irrational demand on how these ads were going to perform online," as if internet advertising would somehow be more compelling than print ads—most of which, after all, were simply ignored by readers. As it soon became clear that the same thing was happening online, methods by which people visiting websites would be *forced* to see and interact with ads in the form of stupid, irritating pop-ups and so on would soon come into play, as well as new ways to target individual users.

All this aside, the sudden rush of advertising money generated by the website allowed the core group of writers to finally be hired on with actual salaries in

1997—enough so they could quit their day jobs and devote themselves solely to *The Onion*. Banker had achieved his goal. The money was modest, not much more than a full-time minimum-wage rate, but it was more than they had been making before. In Madison, it was enough.

Now that they were a real staff, they also needed titles. Maria Schneider became features editor, Krewson was assistant editor, and Hanson became head writer, a title that he said he made up himself after a punch line on *The Larry Sanders Show*.

By 1998, the website was "becoming one of the more profitable things we do," Dikkers said in the *Wisconsin State Journal*. "It's a new medium, and it's confusing for people to realize the power of something like this." Siegel recalled that when he had gone back to Long Island to his five-year high school reunion prewebsite, he had told people he was the editor of a satirical weekly publication based in Madison, Wisconsin, and "they all looked at me with tremendous pity." But when he went to his ten-year reunion—postwebsite—it was an entirely different story.

The growing attention wasn't always positive. A story about a dying teen's last wish to "pork Janet Jackson" produced the threat of a real lawsuit from Jackson's legal team. This threat was a much bigger deal than the angry meat man. Luckily, Ken Artis was on the case. The call had come from a big Rodeo Drive law firm. "I mean, they've got clients like Clint Eastwood, who successfully sued the *National Enquirer*. These are big, heavy hitters," Artis said.

Artis decided to use a bit of conversational jiu-jitsu. He called Janet Jackson's lawyer back and instead of resisting him, "I fell over. If he's pushing me, he has to fall because there's no resistance." By the end of the phone call, they had settled on a letter of apology in the paper. "And we became great friends, and I had sent to them a comp subscription to *The Onion*," Artis told me. The lawyer also said if he was ever in California, he should stop in. Artis had plans to be there soon anyway, so he did. Twenty attorneys all showed up in a conference room to meet him. Artis told me, "They thought that we were at the apex of creativity and humor and satire."

For a brief period, *The Onion* also began to have discussions with the legendary *Chicago Reader*—"a publishing behemoth," as Karlin put it, and the second-largest alt weekly in the country—about potentially buying them and moving their operations to Chicago, before expanding into other markets. Haise, Karlin, and Banker went down to Chicago for a meeting.

Unfortunately, the deal didn't happen. Michael Lenehan, executive editor at the *Reader* at that time, told me that *The Onion* was "really bright and shiny. It was very attractive." He also appreciated the snarky humor, and he saw it as a way for the *Reader*, founded in 1971 and whose audience was aging along with it, to appeal to a younger crowd. (He also saw Karlin as the "creative engine" of *The Onion* at that time.) However, he said the *Reader* would not have provided financial support. Shared distribution maybe, by tucking an *Onion* inside every *Reader*, but not much else. Lenehan said one of his partners to this day thinks it was "the stupidest thing we ever did to pass that up. But I don't think he's right." Looking back on it now, Lenehan said as brilliant as *The Onion* was, "they could never figure out how to monetize it." (He also said the *Reader*, despite its "rock-solid" foundation, was also trying to figure out how to go online at that time. "And it was not at all clear that there was any future in that. But at the same time, it was clear that the print thing was shriveling up.")

Karlin was very disappointed. The *Reader* deal falling through was the last straw, and he put in his notice. Haise and Dikkers offered him an ownership stake to stay, but he turned it down. He said, "I think there was a certain kind of terminal velocity that the paper was going to grow, but I didn't think it was going to grow at the pace and in the way that I wanted it to grow. And I was a twenty-five-year-old that was way too brash and eager to do other things." He'd been in Madison almost eight years. "It seemed like the kind of creative opportunities that I might want to take advantage of might be compromised by continuing to wait out and be more conservative with my life in Madison, and I just didn't want to do that." He moved to Los Angeles. Banker left around this time and landed in LA as well. Rich Dahm moved there also.

Before he left, however, Karlin made a hire who went on to become another writers' room legend: Carol Kolb. Painfully shy and crying easily as a child, Kolb kept her deadpan comedy fearlessness under wraps for years with a series of anonymous, situationist-style public art projects (which, of course, as Dikkers mentioned to me, is exactly what *The Onion*, especially as a physical newspaper, was) beginning in high school. She grew up in Spencer, a central Wisconsin town of about eighteen hundred people near the larger town of Marshfield. Her dad worked in the Land O'Lakes cheese factory, and her mom was a homemaker; they "definitely did not go to college." When her mom found out she'd gotten into Madison, she suggested she stay closer to home and try a Marshfield community college instead. Kolb went to Madison anyway, becoming an English major with a minor in Latin. (Among her *Onion* accomplishments, Kolb is the one who translated the motto, "You Are Dumb," into Latin—"Tu stultus es"—in 1995 as part of the redesign.)

Despite her shyness, in high school Kolb and a friend would do oddball performances in public places like shopping malls that bystanders wouldn't realize were comedy; they changed the school newspaper into "a weird comedy project," too. Once in Madison, Kolb did things like run an entity called the Madison Museum of Bathroom Tissue out of her apartment. Friends brought her rolls of toilet paper from their travels around the world, marked with their locations in black Sharpie—the joke being that all toilet paper looks pretty much the same—until the walls were covered in them, stacked to the ceiling. Though the whole thing was a joke, the museum was listed seriously in tourist guides, and Kolb wrote brochures and recorded an audio tour. Now and then someone would come there to see it, and she would give them the spiel.

"She was just kind of pranking the world," Hanson said. They began dating. He said the reason he originally fell in love with her "is because I had seen these flyers that she was putting up that were parodies of existing flyers on the kiosks of Madison." When you got closer, you'd realize the words or pictures were different, weird, and funny. The flyers were also what got her connected to *The Onion*. "Because I was desperate for attention," she said, "I'd always have a little phone number at the bottom. 'For more information, call.'" And one day Joe Garden called and asked her to bring a copy down to Badger Liquor.

Karlin said he had to beg her to come to headline meetings. She didn't want to be known as "Todd's girlfriend." Eventually, though, she joined, and it was clear very quickly that she was an amazing talent. Karwowski said, "She dissects comedy better than anyone I've ever met." Kolb quickly became Siegel's assistant editor. Her specialty tended toward slice-of-life stories. One of her personal favorites, she told me, was when she wrote the advice column from the point of view of minimalist short-story writer Raymond Carver ("Ask Raymond Carver," May 15, 2002). Some staffers told me that Kolb (the human-interest-story specialist) and Hanson (the hard-news specialist) together should be considered the soul of *The Onion*.

The Onion also hired another important new contributor around this time: Tim Harrod. He first approached *The Onion* by email in 1996 after his brother gave him a subscription for Christmas. "I was living with my parents in Michigan at the time because my career in other forms of comedy was stagnant, and I was having my own bouts with depression. It was really terrible. And *The Onion* was this weird light shining in the darkness."

He sent an email to Dikkers with the subject heading "Area Loser Seeks Writing Job." Dikkers said it made him smile, and Harrod was allowed to submit headlines remotely. These included "Philip Morris Lawyers Deny Cigarettes Are Cylindrical," about the 1996 Philip Morris hearings, and "Area Homosexual Saves Four from Fire" (June 27, 1998). Harrod showed his aptitude by adding his own subhead: "Heroic Neighbor Praised, Gay."

Harrod finally moved to Madison in 1999. It was a big step up from his parents' basement. On top of that, "I suddenly was in a small way a celebrity. I was writing for this ascendant very funny thing and working with comparably talented people and just being accepted into a group. Everything about that is exciting, especially when you've been living kind of the opposite."

With Karlin's departure, assistant editor Siegel took the reins as editor in 1996 (more on that in the next chapter). After arriving in LA, Karlin came up with the idea for himself, Banker, Dan Vebber, Rich Dahm, and Sean LaFleur to market themselves as a five-man *Onion*-trained entertainment writing team; everyone but LaFleur was already in Los Angeles. If Karlin couldn't make *The Onion* into a successful national business, then maybe he could at least use it to help himself and the others get good jobs in entertainment. They received a very warm welcome and were asked to meetings with people like the head of HBO almost immediately. Soon they had written and produced a pilot for a character-driven comedy news show for Fox called *Deadline Now*. Unfortunately, it didn't get picked up for production, though it was apparently the top viewer-rated pilot at Fox that year. Still, it led to other things. Among other projects, Karlin was tapped to be the head writer for Jon Stewart's *Daily Show* in 1999. Six years later, Karlin cocreated *The Colbert Report* with Stewart and *Daily Show* correspondent Stephen Colbert, and hired Dahm as co-executive producer and head writer.

Back in Madison, Dikkers said he was also fielding inquiries from major entertainment executives during this time. However, most were rejected out of hand. One of the most notable was sometime around 1999, when Jerry Bruckheimer (yes, that Jerry Bruckheimer—producer of over-the-top high-budget Hollywood films like *Armageddon*, directed by Michael Bay and released in 1998) partnered with *SNL* cofounder Alan Zweibel to pitch an *Onion* television show to him. But Dikkers, as he wrote on his website, "without having to think too long about it" said no. Bruckheimer was a bad fit for *The Onion*. Dikkers also didn't think *The Onion* was ready to make a TV show—even though he would have been thrilled to work with Alan Zweibel.

The Onion did agree to provide material for the *Dana Carvey Show*, which aired briefly in the spring of 1996. Stephen Colbert made some of his first TV appearances there and in one segment played a TV newscaster reading *Onion* stories pretty much verbatim from the newspaper. Unfortunately, the *Onion* segments never aired. Dikkers also voiced a segment for an animated thing on MTV called *Virtual Bill*, a Bill Clinton parody.

In March 1999, the writers were invited to the HBO Comedy Festival in Aspen, Colorado, the "*Onion*'s first big road trip," as Harrod put it. "That was an incredibly fun time," he said. "It was heartbreaking to leave. We saw a lot of shows and met a lot of celebrities who we'd always admired and stuff. Ben Stiller and Janeane Garofalo." He remembered during one show laughing so hard that he had to "reflexively stop laughing and keep from passing out because of the thin air at that altitude. It was David Cross who made me laugh that hard." The *Onion* crew seems to have been welcomed with open arms by their comedy brothers and sisters. The photos from that adventure show how excited they were to be there, and how young.

Another adventure was when "Weird Al" Yankovic stopped by (Stephen Thompson brought him in). "He was performing basically across the street from *The Onion* on his 2000 tour, 'Touring with Scissors,'" Harrod remembered. "And he just dropped by the office one day." They snapped some photos together.

This was fun, but for Siegel and the other writing staff, the situation was also very frustrating. "We felt we were this burgeoning media empire," Siegel said. "And then we were also just this completely half-assed, rinky-dink operation in Madison, Wisconsin." They were getting written up in the *New Yorker*, journalists were coming by regularly, and major Hollywood people were calling them, but the buzz in the office was that Gumby's Pizza was going from a half-page to a full-page ad. Still, the "most incredibly talented staff of writers," as Haise put it, was now assembled. Under Siegel's leadership, they would keep working and refine *The Onion*'s voice even further.

Chapter 8

Robert Siegel grew up on Long Island and went to college at the University of Michigan–Ann Arbor, where he majored in history. He moved to Madison with his girlfriend, who was pursuing a PhD in medieval English. And while she was studying Chaucer, he needed something to do.

Siegel's two primary interests were comedy and journalism, but at that time there wasn't really a way to combine them. "So in retrospect, it was kind of kismet that I landed where I did," he said. Siegel first thought he'd try being a newspaper writer. "And Madison turned out to be a really perfect place for that, because it was a medium-sized city where they had a newspaper and they had a public radio station. I just started knocking on doors." Unlike in New York, in Madison people would easily open them. He also volunteered at WORT, the local community radio station, as well as on Michael Feldman's hit comedy show *Whad'Ya Know?* that was produced at Wisconsin Public Radio. "Just throwing as much shit at the wall as I could," he said.

One day in 1994 he went into the Espresso Royale café on State Street and saw a newly distributed pile of *Onion*s in the doorway. He picked one up and flipped through it. "And it was one of these fairly revelatory mind-blowing moments where you're like, 'I don't know what this is, but I have to be a part of this.'" Siegel called *The Onion*'s office, and Joe Garden, the friendliest man in Madison, answered. Garden invited him to a writers' meeting and gave him the address.

When Siegel got there, the address was a church. In attendance were Garden, Kelly Ambrose, Andy Selsberg, John Krewson, Maria Schneider, Todd Hanson, Ben Karlin, and Dan Vebber. Siegel sat and watched, amazed. It was his first time meeting the staff of *The Onion*. "I'm suddenly amongst what I think are the eight funniest, most talented people I've ever met, pitching one hysterical headline after another. If you've never been exposed to this before, it felt like something from outer space." He'd been in pitch sessions before at his college newspaper. But this was a "weird alternate-universe journalism where you make up funny stories that never happened. It was thrilling. I just wanted to be part of it from that first moment. And these people were . . . I'd never really been around people like that. These artsy, weird, misfit midwestern slackers."

Siegel felt sort of "cut from the same cloth" as Karlin, who was also Jewish. But the rest of the crew:

> I'd never met anyone like them. Even at Michigan, there's so much New York, Chicago, Jewish suburbs at Michigan. That was still sort of the circle I was moving in. So it really wasn't until I got to Madison that I met what felt like true artists who, you know, read *Infinite Jest* and listen to Pavement. It was all total probably '90s slacker cliché, but to me, it was just the coolest thing. You know, Todd Hanson. "Oh my God, this guy's just incredible." They all fit the image you have of troubled, damaged, fucked-up artists in the tradition of Michael O'Donoghue and Belushi.

> I wasn't a comedy historian, but I knew enough about it that I felt like I was somehow stepping into some sort of tradition from *National Lampoon* and Second City. Todd and John and Joe, they all lived in these dumps and didn't have their lives together. And I loved them.

At the time, to support himself, Siegel was working at the gift shop at the Madison Children's Museum. Now he would spend all day writing headlines in between ringing up toys and books. "It was a really fantastic, exotic, bohemian, thrilling life for me," he said. "I'm sure my parents were probably worried." Siegel said when his first headline got published (he thought it was something like "Family Like Gang to Area Man"), he went to the Memorial Union to watch people read the new issue, hoping they would "maybe chuckle slightly." He said "it was an incredible, thrilling feeling."

After Karlin left for Los Angeles, Siegel was next in line for the big job. He says there wasn't much competition. "I wasn't like a scheming, ambitious person, but I was sort of the only one that wanted to take on the responsibility of it." At a place like the *Lampoon*, he said, "I'm sure the fight to be the next editor was vicious.

But, when Karlin left, we all just kind of looked at each other, and it was like, 'Do you want to do it?' 'No, do you?' And I didn't want to be greedy, but I was like, 'I'll do it!'" The move to editor from assistant editor paid an extra $75 a week, making Siegel's weekly salary about $400. "It was like a fortune," he said. Haise said Siegel was "fucking amazing.... That's my partner in *The Onion* for the next seven years."

Multiple writers told me that Siegel was the one who completed *The Onion*'s transition to the all-AP-style format and its mature-news satire voice. *The Onion*, of course, had been printing news-parody stories since the first issue and "hard news"–style stories since "Dead Guy Found." What finally went away with the color change in Karlin's editorial year were the *Weekly World News*–type stories and any hint of silliness—in presentation, anyway—on the front page. With Siegel, the deadpan seriousness went even further. Siegel told me:

> I felt *The Onion* needed a standardized structure, a format, that we could plug things into. The AP thing became that. I felt that it would give the paper more of an identity. If we were too many things, the danger is that we'd be noth-ing. Kind of like a stand-up comedian who doesn't have a signature style, an identifiable voice to call their own. That bland, rigid AP generic juxtaposition between the outrageousness of what we're "reporting" and the staid, bland for-mality of how we're saying it, that's a lot of what makes it funny. The rigidity and soullessness give it a certain charge, a comedic tension. (Which is also why *The Onion* has no bylines—it's meant to feel like it's been spat out of some giant, faceless, monolithic news machine.) I felt that was really important.

Assisted by his equally OCD-for-AP-style copy editor, Stephen Thompson ("We definitely bonded over that," Siegel told me), Siegel thus orchestrated one of the best creativity-meets-structure matches in American literary history. "Basically," Siegel said, "you need a rigid container to put the crazy stuff into."

He took it very seriously. By his own admission, Siegel "lived and died" on every issue. "Every headline, every article," he said, "I got crazy with the writing and the rewriting and the craft thing. It was like my art. I was tortured." There were weeks where he thought, "This is brilliant. This is fucking great. This is us at our best." Then there were other weeks when he thought the lead story was mediocre or derivative, "and it would just kill me." But then the paper goes out, "and the reaction is not all that different from the weeks where you thought the other extreme."

What is "AP style," anyway? Every publication of any kind adheres to some kind of style manual that provides rules for how the text is presented. Associated Press (AP) style is what most newspapers use—it tells you not just stuff like what the proper abbreviations and spellings are, but how to structure and detail stories as well. Its use creates a specific framework, freeing the writers to focus entirely on the jokes in the same way that a real journalist uses the form to focus entirely on the facts. Using AP style also freed the writers from having to become highly developed individual stylists—and allowed the method to be passed down as writers came and went, again just like in a real newspaper.

The approach also encompassed more abstract things like the temporal reality the story existed in. Thompson gave an example of a writer wanting to do a piece about passing a law in Congress. "There's this tendency, if you're a comedy writer, to write about it being proposed, it being debated, it being passed, it being implemented, and it having had a certain effect, and the temptation is to have all five of those things take place in a single news story that is running on one specific day." Except that in real life, that's not how it happens. Those things would happen on many days. So, if the goal was to parody a daily newspaper, the story would need to be about only one of those things—the "event" that modern news always reports on as an answer to the emblematic "What happened?" question. Such boundaries force an artist to focus, go deeper, and frequently improve the work.

Thompson continued, "Anything you're satirizing, you have to be able to do as well as the thing you're making fun of. It was really important that *The Onion* really look and read like a newspaper. And so I always refer to myself as the verisimilitude cop." He was there to make sure you weren't taken out of the reality of the story by factual errors. "So proper names had to be spelled properly. The secretary of such-and-such had to be in the party that was in power, and just all these little things that if we got them wrong, it would jangle you; it would clank against something if we got it wrong."

I was not good at writing jokes. I was not somebody who could sit there with a notepad and scribble out fifty headlines. You could count the number of headlines that I pitched and got into the paper on one hand. But I like to think that

I made every comedy story 5 to 7 percent funnier just by virtue of really locking in the verisimilitude. It's the job that I miss the most.

I was an obsessive employee of *The Onion*. I lived and breathed *The Onion*. I worked seven days a week. I completely burned myself out and ruined my life in so many ways. But the one job at *The Onion* that I still wish I had is copy editor. I was really damn good at it.

AP style also relied on the concept of objectivity: the neutral, factual "view from nowhere" basis attributed to news. According to scholar Candis Callison (also the Canada research chair in Indigenous journalism, media, and public discourse at the University of British Columbia and an old friend from grad school), the whole modern idea of "news" came into being in the early twentieth century at the same time that the concept of scientific objectivity was becoming a primary intellectual goal, not just in science but in other areas of life as well. *The Onion*, in other words, was taking a fundamental, largely unquestioned Euro-American sociocultural belief in a transcendent "objective" truth and reality—as well as the belief that it was possible to see the world from this imaginary objective location—embodied in AP style as the basis for what would become some of the best American humor ever written.

On top of all this, when Thompson wasn't copy editing each week's issue and editing the A.V. Club, he was also coaching *The Onion*'s softball team, which at this stage was apparently terrible. Thompson described them in an essay called "Here's to the Losers," which is available online. The team, Thompson wrote, was not some group of "sporty ringers sponsored by *The Onion* as the paper's way of reaching out to Madison, Wisconsin's softball-playing community. These would be writers and editors, designers and interns, sales reps, and momentary romantic companions. A reasonably skilled player would no doubt find his or her way onto the field every now and then, but, much of the time, my charges were playing for the rare opportunity to be exposed to natural light." The *Onion* team did win a few times (such as by forfeit) and also beat Madison alt-weekly competitor *Isthmus*, aimed at the "coveted 49–64 demographic," once or twice. Most of the time, though, they went home defeated, to try again another day. It was okay. When winning wasn't everything, playing was more fun.

In response to his obsessiveness, Siegel remembered Dikkers advising him to not worry about perfection so much. You just didn't need to work that hard, he said. Most readers couldn't tell the difference between good and bad anyway, and in any case forgot about all of it the moment they tossed the paper in the recycling bin. Siegel did appreciate his advice. "Scott was always sort of in and out," Siegel said. "But he was always kind of a presence and guiding light. I think if you talk to people about the later years, they'll probably have maybe not fond memories of Scott." But for Siegel, he was a "mentor and father figure. I had nothing but a wonderful relationship with him."

Still, Thompson said, despite Dikkers's advice to take it easy, "Rob was a very, very meticulous editor. I can still picture the dark circles under Rob's eyes as he sat in his dank, little, miserable office, hunched over a computer for a fourteen-, sixteen-hour day." He was also known for attention to minute details like changing the names of the people in the writers' stories so they would sound more authentic. At one point, Krewson just started naming everyone in his stories "Rob Siegel" since he knew they'd all be changed anyway. (Graphics editor Mike Loew said that for some reason all the names would get changed to people who sounded like they were from Long Island, with Jewish and Italian names. All the Hank Schwartzes and Ingrid Olsons were edited out. On the other hand, Thompson said he recalled Siegel poring over stacks of old Wisconsin high school yearbooks for names, choosing a first name from one person and a last name from another.) Siegel also admitted to being a big rewriter, which the staff wasn't always excited about.

Some of the classics from this era revolve around the Clinton-Gore administration, including "Clinton Denies Lewinsky Allegations: We Did Not Have Sex, We Made Love" (February 3, 1998) and "Clinton Calls for National Week Off to Get National Shit Together" (July 23, 1997). Headlines reflecting the lived reality of masses of Americans include "Clinton Written Up by Total Bitch Supervisor" (December 18, 2007) and "Clinton to Get Teeth Cleaning, Glasses Before Coverage Runs Out" (August 2, 2000). Some of these were definitely emailed around within the Clinton administration, as a Freedom of Information Act request showed. In what I hope was not another case of *The Onion* predicting the future—I'm writing this sentence in July 2024—on November 15, 2000, when nobody knew yet if Bush or Gore would become president after the disastrous "hanging-chad" November 8 election, *The Onion* published "Clinton Declares Self

the ONION®

VOLUME 36 ISSUE 41   AMERICA'S FINEST NEWS SOURCE™   16–22 NOVEMBER 2000

Nation Plunges Into Chaos

Pro-Bush Rebels Seize Power In West; D.C. In Flames

Tipper's Thumb Delivered To Gore Campaign Headquarters

see ELECTION page 2A

Naderite Loyalists Nuke Dam

see ELECTION page 4A

Bob Dole: 'Bob Dole's Been Shot'

see ELECTION page 7A

McVeigh Urges Calm

see ELECTION page 8A

STATshot

A look at the numbers that shape your world.

What Are We Hoarding?

1. Ammunition
2. Bibles
3. Hostages
4. Beefaroni
5. Throwin' rocks
6. Fertile women
7. Strawberry Quik
8. Palm VIIs

INSIDE the ONION

Above: Riot police advance through downtown Miami, where clashes between Gore and Bush factions left 23 dead Monday night. see COVER STORY page 6

Clinton Declares Self President For Life

WASHINGTON, DC—Denouncing the American electoral process as "immoral and corrupt,"President Clinton announced Tuesday that he will not step down on Jan. 20, 2001, declaring himself "President For Life."

Proclaiming Nov. 14 a new national holiday as "Day One of Americlintonian Year Zero," Clinton issued a directive of total martial law over "all territories formerly see CLINTON page 8

Right: Clinton greets his subjects from a White House balcony.

NBC News Reverses Earlier Report Of Gore's Death

NEW YORK—Three hours after placing Al Gore in the "dead" column, NBC News retracted its projection Tuesday, changing the vice-president's status to "too close to call."

"I'm sorry, but it now appears that we reported Mr. Gore's death prematurely," NBC News anchor Tom Brokaw announced on air at approximately 2:15 a.m. EST. "The latest readings show his red-blood count down to 3.1. At this point, it could go either way."

Gore, shot Monday by a Republican see NBC page 12

Communication With Florida Cut Off

TALLAHASSEE, FL—Federal officials confirmed Tuesday that all forms of communication with Florida, the bloody battleground for 25 electoral votes, have been cut off.

Across the state, Atlantic Bell phone lines and relays have been severed. The efforts of Georgia-based emergency crews hoping to reconnect lines have been hampered by piles of burning vehicles choking all roads leading into the state.

In addition to the loss of phone contact, Internet, television, and radio communica- see FLORIDA page 11

Bush Executes 253 New Mexico Democrats

Retakes State's Five Electoral Votes

ALBUQUERQUE, NM— New Mexico's five electoral votes swung back into the Bush column Monday when George W. Bush executed 253 Las Cruces-area Democrats. With their deaths, the Al Gore-backing Democrats were declared ineligible, wiping out the Democratic candidate's narrow 252-vote victory margin in New Mexico and giving Bush the state by just one vote. "We express great sorrow

for the families of the condemned," said Karl Rove, Bush's senior strategist. "We must keep in mind, however, that these are not innocent people we're talking about here. These individuals were guilty of a variety of crimes, from vagrancy to jaywalking to reckless endangerment of see NEW MEXICO page 10

Right: The bodies of Democrats are taken by Bush 2000 coroners.

Hopefully not an example of The Onion *predicting the future.*

President for Life." "Dressed in full military regalia and flanked by members of his elite Demopublican Guard, Clinton told reporters, 'Let all peoples of the land know this: The era of bipartisan inaction and paralysis has ended. The Age of the Great Cleansing Fire begins today.'"

There were, of course, many nonpolitical articles. Hanson's trademark "Study: Depression Hits Losers Hardest" (March 5, 1997) genre of story would make regular appearances. Most of these, Hanson said, were just based on his actual life. The story reads:

> Losers, sad excuses for human beings who have no reason to feel good about themselves or their failed, miserable lives, are approximately 25 times as likely to suffer the emotionally crippling effects of depression as any other group researched, the study claims.

> Worse yet, the prospects for successful treatment of depression among the loser populace are "poor at best," the study found. The reason: Most losers are such hopeless lost causes that they can never get a life, no matter how hard they try, and are "doomed to repeat their mistakes forever, living out their pathetic existence as little more than human garbage."

The straight news-style stories were mostly on the front page. Inside were also opinion columns written by every kind of person imaginable as well as a few animals ("I Can't Stand My Filthy Hippie Owner," by Thunder the Ferret from April 15, 1998); advice columns (the "Ask a . . ." genre, which include "Ask a Coffin Salesman," "Ask a Conspiracy Theorist," "Ask a Gut-Shot Policeman," "Ask a Bee," and many more); stories about relationships ("Woman Angered When Veiled Anger Expressed as Mock Anger Is Interpreted as Real Anger" [August 11, 1999]); various stoner jokes ("Area Stoner Has Mind-Blowing Out-of-Cheetos Experience" [April 29, 1998] or the classic "Everyone Involved in Pizza's Preparation, Delivery, Purchase Extremely High" [October 7, 1998]; and on and on. News stories would cover scientific discoveries, technology, the workplace, the way Americans spent their leisure time, and anything else you'd find in a newspaper. Hanson told me that the group developed a process that was almost mathematical in its joke-writing precision. "There'd be the straight-line words that were strict journalistic syntax, and then there'd be departures that wouldn't be in AP style that would be the joke words. That's how you would construct the rhythm and timing of the gags in the prose."

The op-ed columns—where the staff could finally stretch out a bit, just like in a real local newspaper—by Jean Teasdale or Herbert Kornfeld were written by Maria Schneider, Jim Anchower and Jackie Harvey by Joe Garden, T. Herman Zweibel by John Krewson or Maria Schneider, and Smoove B by several people: Chris Karwowski, Siegel, Tim Harrod, and occasionally Dikkers. The horoscope was mostly by John Krewson. Schneider also drew the comic "Pathetic Geek Stories," which illustrated mortifying true personal stories sent by readers. There also remained a streak of the old absurdist, silly, conceptual art jazz from the Keck, Dahm, and Vebber years, which would appear in, say, columns written by a pie (one of my all-time favorites, "You Want a Piece of Me?" written by Krewson, May 26, 1999) or from the point of view of a raccoon ("Raccoon Leaders Call for Loosening of Garbage-Can Lids," May 31, 2000).

The coverage of the George W. Bush administration became some of *The Onion*'s best work, such as the classic postinauguration headline on January 17, 2001: "Bush: 'Our Long National Nightmare of Peace and Prosperity Is Finally Over.'" Part of the story is an official quote: "Under Bush, we can all look forward to military aggression, deregulation of dangerous, greedy industries, and the defunding of vital domestic social-service programs upon which millions depend. Mercifully, we can now say goodbye to the awful nightmare that was Clinton's America."

Siegel worked very closely with Loew, whose job as graphics editor was to design, shoot, and Photoshop all the images as well as create all the charts, diagrams, maps, and so on. They ended up working eight and a half years together. "I love Rob Siegel," Loew said. "I always felt like Rob and I worked so well together. . . . He could really count on me, and Rob had trouble getting other people to turn in their work on time." Krewson was so bad that Siegel actually suspended his pay several times due to all his "the dog ate my homework" stories, but others had issues too. At one point, after the writers were finally salaried, Loew told me Siegel said, "Never before has so much been paid for so little."

Loew did say that Siegel could be a "control guy." He remembered him standing right at his shoulder when he was Photoshopping for a while, trying to direct every move. "Make that a little more green. Make that a little bigger. Can you grab that arm and just move it a little bit, like twenty degrees to the left?" He finally had to ask Siegel politely to step away.

Unfortunately this was a prophetic headline.

By 1997, however, Loew was becoming overwhelmed. So he asked an old friend named Chad Nackers to help. Nackers also grew up in Appleton, "home of McCarthy"—as in the famous life-ruining anticommunist. His parents were "fairly blue collar" and "very much not Republican." His dad ran a produce business—farm work—and Nackers helped all through high school, working twelve- to fourteen-hour days picking corn, laying irrigation pipe, and so on until by college he could do everything from planting to selling the produce to grocery stores. "It definitely gave me a very grounded understanding of blue-collar stuff and also the work ethic of you just keep on pushing and going," Nackers said. His parents were very supportive of his creative endeavors, which included drawing and writing and making videos with his friends, including Mike Loew, whom he met in their seventh grade art class. He went to college at UW–La Crosse and majored in mass communications and minored in photography. Now, Loew needed a reliable photographer for shoots—so he called Nackers.

They shot on 35mm film, adding the wait for processing and printing and then scanning the prints into the computer to the job. Much of the work was going up and down State Street to recruit people to be in the photos—no stock photography. Neither of them had a car, so if they needed to do something off-site, they'd end up on the bus for hours. Nackers said he got ten dollars per photo that ran in the paper. "I was basically living off of ramen and peanut butter," he said. He did well, though, and was soon hired as associate graphics editor.

Most of the time it was Loew, Nackers, and Siegel in the office. The writers would come around regularly for meetings, and the ad sales team would be in and out, but the usual everyday in-office staff were the editors and the production team. "We were the ones who stayed till three in the morning to put the paper to bed," Loew said.

Nackers said some of the most challenging images they had to make were fake products because they really had to get the font right. "The classic one was Responsibilityuns instead of Funyuns," he said. These days, there are probably programs that just "turn things into fonts," but back then they had to dig through the Font Book, find one that looked pretty close, and then change it by hand to make a match. The two of them got to be a "well-oiled machine," though altering so many things by hand in the early days of Photoshop could be challenging. The writers—most of whom were also cartoonists—would have their own ideas for images also, some of which were very ambitious. As with the stories, the goal was to make the photos look as straight and as much like real photojournalism as possible.

All this care and attention took place because *The Onion* was in print. Nackers said when the website first started, nobody cared about the internet—they thought it was fleeting and not very interesting. But print was forever. "Anytime we had some little error in print, it just always felt devastating."

the ONION

VOLUME 36 ISSUE 12   AMERICA'S FINEST NEWS SOURCE   6-12 APRIL, 2000

Inflatable Chair's Novelty Wears Off
see LIVING page 2D

U.S. Population At 13,462

'We Don't Think Everybody Sent In Their Census Forms,' Say Officials

Population Per Square Mile   United States Census 2000

- 250 or more
- 100–249.9
- 50–99.9
- 25–49.9
- 10–24.9
- 6–9.9
- Less than 5

1990 U.S. Population: 248,734,129
2000 U.S. Population: 13,462

Guy At House Party Must Be At Least 32
see CAMPUS page 11E

Call Ignored In The Order It Was Received
see LOCAL page 8B

Brand-New Wife Breaks Down
see LIFESTYLE page 2C

STATshot
A look at the numbers that shape your world.

What Is Robin Williams Nicknaming His Genitalia?

1. The Ol' Robby Rob Rob
2. The Pork From Ork
3. Mr. Doubtfire
4. Garp Jr.
5. The One-Eyed Sailor Man
6. Robin Willy-Yums

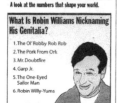

WASHINGTON, DC—With the April 1 deadline for returning Census 2000 forms finally passed, the Bureau of the Census announced Monday that the U.S. population stands at 13,462. "We at the Census Bureau are shocked by the incredible decrease in the population that apparently took place in the 10 years since the last Census in 1990,"Census Bureau director Kenneth Prewitt said. "A 1999 projection estimated the U.S. population at 274 mil- see CENSUS page 7

Census 20[0]
is in your han[d]

Above: Census Bureau director Kenneth Prewitt.

Above: The unpopular product.

Funyuns Still Outselling Responsibilityuns

DALLAS—Funyuns, the world leader in artificial onion-ring-flavored and -shaped snack-food items, continues to enjoy an "overwhelming sales lead" over competing brand Responsibilityuns, the trade publication *Impulse Purchase Quarterly* reported Monday.

Responsibilityuns, launched last May in a bold attempt to challenge Funyuns' dominance of the faux-onion-ring snack market, have done "little to no damage" to its rival's sales through the first quarter of 2000.

"I just don't understand what went wrong," said James Connell, CEO of Delayed Gratification Foods, the Dallas-based maker of the sober, salted snack. "Everybody knows that responsibility and self-reliance are virtues which, with patience and persistence, bring rewards see RESPONSIBILITYUNS page 10

Attempt To Impress Becky Lundegaard Undermined By Interloper

HAMPTON, VA—An attempt by Brian Shuman, 12, to impress fellow seventh-grader Becky Lundegaard, 13, met with spectacular failure Monday, when his school supplies and shoulder bag were forcibly seized, his sweater vest yanked over his head, and his face pressed into a row of lockers, witnesses reported.

According to the unpopular Shuman, known primarily among classmates at Hampton Middle School for his scholastic achievements and awkward social manner, he was "deliberately undermined by the uncalled-for actions of an interloping usurper intent on humiliating me in a derogatory manner in front of Miss see INTERLOPER page 11

Right: Brian Shuman, the foiled would-be suitor of Becky Lundegaard (inset).

One of the more challenging images to create, changing the Funyuns font into the fake product.

The dedication to a very high standard of quality was felt by everybody. And that could cause conflicts. Thompson said Siegel "clashed constantly with the writers." There were "routinely screaming matches," of which Thompson said he was sometimes a part. Loew said Siegel and Hanson in particular fought like "cats and dogs over every single thing." Hanson said, "Rob would often, in my opinion, err on the side of making it too straight and not having enough of the joke words. And I would always, in Rob's opinion, err on the other side." They especially fought over changes that Siegel made to Hanson's stories, which, since Siegel didn't like conflict, he sometimes did in the middle of the night.

Hanson told me, "I think that people took the decision-making process at *The Onion* really seriously. Because it was their life, you know? Like, more so than anything else. That was their identity. And so when they would debate which was the funniest way to do something, the debates could get really heated." He gave me an example:

There was this joke, "Aliens Mourn as Final *Cheers* Episode Reaches Alpha Centauri" [May 5, 1999]. And we're like, "Oh, that's really funny. Let's run it." And then we [he and Tim Harrod] researched it a little bit. And we're like, "Wait a minute. Alpha Centauri is six light-years away. And this was four years ago. So we need to find a different star that's *four* light-years away." We found the correct star, which is called Barnard's Star. And we're like, "Just change it to Barnard's Star."

And Rob Siegel wouldn't change it. He's like, "It doesn't matter." And we're like, "Any scientist who would get the joke is going to know that it's two years off. Nobody else will get the joke. The only people who will get the joke are going to know that you did it wrong." And he would not change it back. And we begged him and begged him.

It was very frustrating. Because we solved it. And then he wouldn't use it. He's like, "Barnard's Star doesn't sound like a star. Alpha Centauri sounds like a star." And we're like, "Do you know anything about astronomy? Most stars don't have names like Alpha Centauri!" It was so fucking frustrating.

Hanson actually started getting a little angry again when he told me this story. I said, "You can see that this is funny, though, right?" and he answered, "Yeah. I guess."

Loew remembered another battle over the story "Taco Bell Launches New 'Morning After' Burrito" (March 12, 1997). He and Siegel were finishing it up in the middle of the night, and Mike was working on the images, one of which was a diagram explaining how the different layers of the burrito worked ("Hot sauce breaks down uterine lining," and so on). Hanson had written the story, and he had called the burrito the "Contraceptimelt." Loew, however, came up with "Mexicarriagemelt," and Siegel agreed to change it.

Then, however, Hanson came in, found out the name had been changed, and went ballistic. "He really lit into me," Loew said. They changed the name back. (Indeed, a morning-after burrito, if it worked in the same way as the morning-after pill, would prohibit implantation of a fertilized egg in the uterine lining, which from a medical perspective is when pregnancy actually begins; a miscarriage happens only after someone is pregnant. So calling it a "Mexicarriagemelt" would actually be inaccurate.)

Hanson, Thompson said, "saw *The Onion* as very subversive and underground. And that it should be speaking truth to power but also stretching the form of comedy, to push the boundaries of art. And that's very different from doing a rigorously disciplined newspaper parody." Hanson, another staffer told me, just had a lot of issues with authority. No matter who was in charge, he would fight with them. Dikkers told me, "Todd Hanson was the only person who ever had an opinion that went counter to my or any editor's and felt the need to express it." However, "he would always lose because he was a writer. He wasn't an editor."

Siegel told me he had wanted to fire Hanson many times. "We had a very tempestuous love-hate sort of relationship," he said. "He's the greatest, but he drove me absolutely crazy." He would get to the point of firing him and then not do it. "I just didn't want that blood on my hands. . . . I didn't feel confident that he would be okay." Hanson would go on "sabbaticals," sometimes, Siegel said, to get himself together. "As crazy as he made people, everyone loved him and didn't want to see him suffer or hurting or in a terrible place in his life. So we always tried to take care of him." At one point, Hanson said, Siegel did demote him to staff writer "after I had a nervous breakdown and almost ended up in the hospital and couldn't really, you know, meet my requirements." He would not become head writer again until 2005.

Thompson himself had a long-standing conflict with Hanson, centered on the content of the A.V. Club, which Todd didn't think was cool enough for *The Onion*. "Todd's way of needling people certainly could cross over into bullying," Thompson said. "And I had an inferiority complex, very much maneuvered by

Todd, that the A.V. Club wasn't as cool as the comedy section." Thompson made sure to add, "I love the guy to the ends of the earth. And I'm not sitting here holding a grudge against him. But there were definitely points where he would just kind of work your nerves or find insecurities."

Hanson admitted, "I suppose I had a problem controlling my temper. Me and Carol used to yell at each other. And I don't know if I did it worse than other people. But I certainly did an unfair amount of it." He said he was just "emphatic about wanting to get the jokes right. You know what I mean? It just struck me as incredibly important that we not screw up the joke. And so I would emphasize, and I would speak in a loud voice." Hanson often used to say he saw *The Onion* as his family, which made these dramas feel "unbelievably, epically important."

Thompson said he remembered Hanson and Schneider also having some battles. Schneider said that now, many years later, "I think about stuff that happened, things that people said to each other. That it was a pretty intense atmosphere." Part of it, she said, was because of "the darkness of the humor we dealt with and the personal issues that various people were dealing with." Still, "I think about it later and go, 'None of that shit had to be said. And it was perfectly ridiculous. Just because you don't identify with being a frat dude, you think of yourself as a nerd or a bit of a loser, a misfit, doesn't mean you can't be a dick.'" Today, she said, "it does affect my perception of them. I always have that little imperfect kind of sourness, kind of bitterness feeling towards them, and I wish I didn't have it, but it's there."

Kolb and Hanson fought in the office as a couple as well. In one infamous incident, during a headline pitch meeting, Hanson apparently would not stop baiting her. Hanson said, "She said something like, 'Don't say one more thing.' And I was being a smart-ass, and I said one more thing." Whereupon she took a round container of Morton salt sitting on a side table and poured the whole thing over his head.

The thing about Hanson is that outside the fights and the depressive episodes, you will never find a more brilliant and hilarious conversationalist. He can spin hours of original insightful commentary on nearly any subject just off the top of his head. (For example, Todd Hanson postponed one of our interviews for this book because he was watching reruns of *Columbo* with his mom. When he called back, he spent the next ten minutes meticulously and spontaneously explaining why the show was so good—an insightful, organized, funny, and fascinating summary that could have easily been a winning pitch for a magazine essay or even the start of a PhD dissertation proposal in media studies. My editor, alas, refused to allow me to print the twelve-hundred-word transcript.)

Hanson is also a compelling performer. You can find a couple of story-tellings he did for the *Moth* in New York online that give a glimpse into his charisma. Old *Onion* media appearances also demonstrate this. He would have made a brilliant arts-culture-intellectual-stuff talk-show host. Alas, as Hanson admits in one of his *Moth* performances, he is often his own worst enemy. Being too much in your head almost always ends up leading into a corner or down a very dark hole. (That's why I do a lot of yoga now.) I hold out hope that he will still find a way.

"We all wrestled with anxiety and depression, and a lot of us compensated with alcohol and self-medication," Joe Garden said. And depression often manifests as irritability and anger. Some of it, Garden said, was also cultural. "That's another midwestern thing about it. It's like, 'Well, I don't have a problem. I'm just going to chin up and tough it out.' Which is bullshit. That just led to a lot of people just making themselves worse."

A couple of staff also described themselves as ADHD to me. Even if they were joking, ADHD is a real disability that can have profound impacts on all kinds of things—especially relationships and the ability to plan and see the bigger picture. The screwups that inevitably occur no matter how hard people try then torpedo self-esteem. Despite popular efforts to call it a "superpower," ADHD's role in many people's personal and professional lives is more like a perpetually exploding bomb.

Dikkers was one of the people who told me he had ADHD. He also told me he was once "offhandedly" diagnosed as "high-functioning bipolar" by a therapist. I had asked him how being at *The Onion* felt to him, and—after telling me that he was a *T* and not an *E* on the Myers-Briggs scale—he said that whenever he was doing anything *Onion*-related, he often felt "ecstatic." He'd once had surgery to correct a deviated septum, he said, which required an application of cocaine to numb the area. "I had never done drugs. I had never done cocaine," he said. "And when I was on it, I immediately recognized the feeling, because I feel that manic excited feeling, that confident feeling, so much that it saddened me that other people had to take a drug to get this feeling. It was a very familiar feeling to me." I asked him if the bipolar thing might have had something to do with all his coming and going from *The Onion*, and he said, "If we really wanted to get more armchair psychiatry about it, I would say the coming and going has a lot to do with self-sabotage, probably. When things are going well, something inside me says, 'You don't deserve this.' And so I stop doing it, and I start something else from scratch."

The office wasn't all arguments. Siegel said the fact that they were all comedy nerds gave them common cause. They would gather around to watch *The Simpsons* in the office and "revered" *Mr. Show*. "When the *South Park* 'Spirit of Christmas' bootleg tape came along, we all went nuts over that." There were also conversations about, say, the merits of the new Beck album or if *The Phantom Menace* was going to be any good. "After a long day of comedy writing, we'd all go to a bar in Madison and just hang out and continue to talk comedy." Siegel said he had fond memories of everybody. They might all drive each other crazy sometimes, "but you still love each other. You just know each other too well."

Hanson always said he thought *The Onion* writing staff was like a "garage band" that never expected to become famous. I asked Thompson what band he thought it was. "I think in Todd's mind, it's the band Boss Hog. Or it's like the Jon Spencer Blues Explosion, and he's Jon Spencer. And they're the coolest band of 1995, and there are these uncool market forces that they're up against. And they're constantly having these long, drawn-out philosophical conversations about selling out."

Siegel said he "really discovered my people and my place in the world" in Madison. The *Onion* staff were the people who sent him on his path. They were "hugely important formative relationships." Still, something often nagged at him: the world outside the office. Even if readers loved the work, they didn't know it was you who made it. The upside was that "no one had an ego. It was really about the paper." The downside was that he never really knew how much their work was reaching people. Were his obsessive fourteen-hour days perfecting *The Onion*'s voice bringing anything of value into the world at all?

Chapter 9

Civic (or public) journalism was having a renewal in the 1990s. The idea goes back at least to the 1920s and John Dewey's belief that the media should do more than just provide facts. It should also educate people how to be citizens in a democracy and play a conscious role in the community, rather than merely "covering" its news. (Scholar Jay Rosen made a famous speech at a journalism conference in 1989 that is sometimes said to have sparked this new phase of the movement.) At a time when potentially 70 percent of what you saw in the news, print or otherwise, was actually a regurgitated press release, and when even reported news and the editorial pages contained plenty of PR-generated spin, funded by corporations and organizations paying people to express certain opinions, the movement was sorely needed. (See, for instance, Edward S. Herman and Noam Chomsky's classic 1988 book, *Manufacturing Consent: The Political Economy of the Mass Media*, which shows that contrary to the popular idea of journalists as the voice of the people, most professional journalism was simply promoting the worldview of dominant, privileged groups and institutions.)

The 1990s alt-weekly movement was a part of the new civic journalism, especially since many mainstream newspapers didn't want—or know how—to change their models, such as the requirement to discuss "both sides" of an issue if you were going to be objective, a method that not only is overly dualistic but has also been exploited by questionable actors for decades to cast doubt on settled problems, such as the dangers of smoking and the causes of climate change.

As the former editor of the alt weekly the *Stranger* for a short but important time in the early '90s, I had a couple of different principles behind my work: We were not objective, and we didn't pretend to be. Objectivity was a made-up thing that worked primarily to sustain an increasingly useless, even dangerous, status quo. We were also, however, factual and accurate as much as possible. Thinking objectivity had problems did *not* mean that our writers didn't do research and support their work with interviews and digging.

The Onion was doing this as well—just with satire, which was also gaining prevalence at the time. Carol Kolb said:

You asked why news satire became so popular in the '90s and the aughts. And I believe it is because at that point, news was still an authority figure, and was held in more esteem until then. I think that curtain hadn't been pulled away yet so much. And as it started to become more and more commercialized and people started to notice, it started to cheapen. People started to get more savvy and notice little things, and they stopped taking news sources as so much of an authority.

So there was this desire to, like, take them down. It was one of the last remaining institutions that people hadn't really been questioning. And then they started to question it. And I think part of the reason is that it started to get more dispersed and less reliable and more influenced by commercialism. The news was not a sacred cow, but an esteemed cow. It was time for it to tumble, you know what I mean? It was time to examine the news.

Amber Day, a scholar of news satire, told me that a "satiric Renaissance" was going on in the 1990s and 2000s, with many new and biting forms. "There's nothing new about satire; it's been around forever. But there was clearly something about the way it was developing at that moment, and it led me to look at satire as a reaction to flaws in political debate." This satire included not only *The Onion*, *The Daily Show*, and *The Colbert Report*, but also people like filmmaker Michael Moore and street-theater/culture-jamming performance-protest groups like Billionaires for Bush and the Yes Men. Day continued:

The PR machine had gotten so good, right? The PR machine around everybody—around corporations, around politicians. People had figured out how to play the system. How to perform, how to be very media savvy. The PR industry had exploded at the same time it felt like the press had not quite figured out how to keep up. Obviously, there were still journalists doing amazing work. But news—particularly cable news, where people were getting a lot of their news—was doing a particularly poor job of being able to cut through some of the staging of our public discourse. And was in fact aiding and abetting that staging, rather than actually giving people a look into how it was being produced.

So I use the metaphor of "pulling back the curtain" for what satire at the time was doing. It was saying, "Hey, look at the fact that these talking points are being repeated on thirty different television stations at the same time." And nobody else was pointing that out. Nobody was saying: "Where do you think those talking points came from?" Instead, the press was just happily repeating those talking points. And that's where satire was coming in. It was filling this void.

All this is to say, with Siegel at the helm, *The Onion* took the final decisive step toward the thing that would elevate its AP-style comedy into something much deeper: point of view. *The Onion* now wrote jokes that had a point beyond just getting a laugh. Siegel, whether he realized it or not, started channeling turn-of-the-twentieth-century Wisconsin progressive hero and former governor "Fighting Bob" La Follette. Just in *Onion* style.

Siegel remembers a moment when this started to happen. They were planning on doing a joke on the front page that was at first going to show both an anti-abortion and a pro-choice bumper sticker, with the joke being about how (in)effective bumper stickers were at solving societal problems. Siegel said the staff instinct was to show both stickers. But then he looked at it again and thought, "Why don't we just make fun of pro-lifers?" He realized it was time to "just fucking pick a side here." The final joke showed a photo of a bumper sticker that said "Abortion stops a beating heart" with a caption that said "Bumper Sticker Ends Abortion Debate." Siegel said:

I don't know that anybody else thinks of that as some watershed moment. But for me it was a point where I'm like, "Let's use this platform to say things, and let's have opinions. Actual stances on things." That moment was for me the birth of looking at *The Onion* as political satire. There's nothing stopping us from speaking our minds through this device, this strange format we've created.

Once we did that, it was like, "Oh, this opens up the entire world." . . . Suddenly we had this lens, that way of processing and reacting. At that point, the paper became something that *could* last forever, because it became a medium through which one can tell jokes about and engage in the world.

Satire, in other words, is one of the few rhetorical methods that effectively seeks out and destroys spin. This is why people started saying that *The Onion* was the only source of truth in journalism.

The idea of civic journalism also resonates well with another important concept from the 1920s: the Wisconsin Idea. First coined in 1904 by UW president Charles Van Hise, the Wisconsin Idea says that "education should influence people's lives beyond the boundaries of the classroom." But that is really just a very general encapsulation. In a deeper sense, the Wisconsin Idea means that research and ideas coming out of the university, the public, and local, state, and national politics should all deeply interconnect in a spirit of enlightened cooperation. Chad Alan Goldberg, a UW–Madison sociology professor who published *Education for Democracy: Renewing the Wisconsin Idea* in 2020, said Wisconsin was "a pioneer in social political reforms that would catch fire, and would be implemented in other states, and eventually at the national level."

State Street, with Madison's capitol building on one end and the university on the other, was a physical manifestation of the Wisconsin Idea. In the 1990s, *The Onion*'s office was in between the two. (True, it was across the street from a porn shop that also sat between the campus and the capitol, but still.) But during a period of massive corporate media conglomeration alongside the neoliberal shredding of the social safety net, public education, and the very idea of mutual interconnection, whether the staff realized it or not, I think that *The Onion*—by using their midwestern foundations in public education, mutuality, and critical thinking—became one of the most important and influential embodiments of the Wisconsin Idea in the current era. They just did it through satire.

The world was also heading into an accelerated stint through the postmodern condition, where meanings constantly shifted and broke apart, nothing seemed solid or eternal anymore, and past "progress" often seemed like a lie, especially around things like technology, politics, and the environment. Journalism was supposed to be the first draft of history. But now, as the cable and digital ages dawned and "news" ballooned from being experienced in specific, bracketed moments into something consumed (and produced) twenty-four hours a day, that draft was sprawling into something with no shape or structure. As scholar Colin Harrison wrote in *American Culture in the 1990s* (2010), not even time or memory felt like it had inherent stability anymore. *The Onion* provided levity in this "twilight" era while also shining a light on how these shifts were affecting everyday life.

That said, there *was* disagreement about the level of actual political activism (for lack of a better term) going on at *The Onion*. For once, Hanson was on the same side as Siegel:

> The great thing is that we actually maintained the advocacy-journalism mission of the *Daily Cardinal* in our *Onion* work, in the things we satirized. We satirized things from a progressive point of view. We weren't ripping apart the progressives; we were backing them up. We were ripping apart the things we disagreed with, which were by and large Republican.
>
> Some people will deny this and say, "*The Onion* was never political," which is fucking totally a lie. Like, that's just bullshit. Because *The Onion* was like, you'd make fun of racism. You wouldn't make fun of antiracism. You know what I mean? You wouldn't mock feminism; you'd mock sexism.
>
> I never felt that we stopped being the kind of progressive people we were at the *Daily Cardinal*. We just learned to have a real cynical attitude towards that kind of self-righteous pretension. Especially since a lot of those holier-than-thou, politically correct people went on to completely give up all their principles once they graduated from college. Who just completely embraced capitalism in every way. The kind of people who'd want to curb you for not being politically correct enough, and then they would go on to work for Wall Street. I mean, it's just sick; it's just ugly and gross. And so in a weird way, we were the least hypocritical, even though we were supposedly politically incorrect.
>
> I'm not exactly an activist and never have been, other than the *Onion* work I've done. I kind of considered it a form of activism because we were satirizing things about American society and the world that deserved to be satirized. That sounds really self-righteous, but that was my attitude.

On the other hand, Maria Schneider said she thought many readers liked the absurd and everyday stories the best. One of her favorites was a headline on the front page with no accompanying article over a photo of a woman looking at a shirt: "Top Cute," written by Carol Kolb (May 17, 2000). "I've been interviewed on the radio before a couple times by people who just wanted to talk about nothing but the political headlines. And I just thought, 'I want to talk about "Top Cute."'"

The 1990s staff were also taking a literary approach to their writing, deliberately choosing topics and framings that would make their work last longer than the current news cycle. Though the staff did sometimes write about politicians as characters—developing personae and then telling stories about them based on those personae—until the social media age set in, *The Onion* was not focused on making jokes about current real news. Schneider said, "I think we just wanted to make headlines, make stories that people would laugh at fifteen to twenty years later, whenever civilization ends." Schneider, however, did seem to agree with Hanson and Siegel's take on *The Onion*'s ultimate political point of view. She said, "I think you can be a Marxist and not be a MARXIST, you know? You can agree with Marxist general points about the trajectory of history and how economies evolve. You can have a general agreement or understanding of that without wearing the Che Guevara T-shirt."

Comedy often being sublimated aggression, a lot of rage was also expressed in the 1990s *Onion*. And you don't get angry about something unless you really care about it. Carol Kolb said, "*The Onion* absolutely is political. It has a liberal agenda. A progressive agenda." At the same time, however, Kolb recognized, "We were preaching to the choir. And I think that is something that maybe you don't want to admit to yourself because you feel a little self-important or something when you're in the fake-news biz. You feel like you're changing things, but the reality is you're just preaching to the choir. The correct liberal choir."

They did try to be egalitarian, though. "We used to say, 'We make fun of the rich'—but we also made fun of the poor," Kolb said. "We would make jokes about dumb poor people spending their money on the wrong thing or being uncouth or eating at fucking fast-food restaurants and all that. But our sympathies were definitely still with those poor people we were making fun of. They were not with the rich people that we were making fun of." She added, "We did definitely try to make fun of the Left as well. Because who doesn't, you know?" (See "Area Liberal Worried His Asian Dry Cleaner Doesn't Like Him," December 5, 2001.)

Scholar Amber Day said, "I would argue that good satire is never cynical. It's quite the opposite. I think that a cynical form of humor would just say, 'Yep, politicians are all a bunch of jerks. What do you expect?' It actually can really be demotivating. As opposed to good satire, which really has this hopefulness to it. 'We actually deserve better.' 'This is wrong.'"

Scott Dikkers disagreed that *The Onion*'s intent was to be political. He said goal number one of *The Onion* has always been to be entertaining and funny. But to be funny, "it helps to have really good subtext. And in order to have good subtext, you have to have some kind of opinion." Common-sense progressive opinions resonate "with just about any kind of reader." So in that sense, Dikkers said, *The Onion* was political. "But it was never the intent. The intent was always to entertain."

John Krewson said, in a 2012 WGBH presentation, "What we try to make fun of is lack of human compassion, lack of imagination, willful stupidity, apathy, knee-jerk meanness, and an unwillingness to be flexible mentally or spiritually, which is a very broad and high falutin way of saying we try to make fun of jerks. If one party has a lot more cold-hearted jerks than the other, then they're gonna be in for more of the stick." They did try to hand it out evenly. "But sometimes it's just too hard to do. It's not like we haven't made fun of Democrats. When the Democrats were flailing to try to find direction, we would make fun of that."

But the thing was, "American politics tends to fall into the classic crime-novel thing where it's not so much good versus evil as strong versus weak. And it's a lot more fun to make fun of the strong than it is to pick on the weak." Republicans had been dealing from a place of strength for a long time, and their policies had hurt a lot of people. "I think that comedy is great at lifting the spirits of people who already believe a certain way but think that it's hopeless. And now they think that, 'Well, it's hopeless, but at least this comedy source also thinks it's hopeless! So I'm not the only one.'"

Ultimately, what's most resonant for me is the compassion that lies under much of *The Onion*'s best work. In this period, *The Onion* was one of the few national publications to stick up for the economic underdog and argue for the worth and value of ordinary people—the great mass of Area Men and Area Women stuck in a system they didn't create or choose. By the late 1990s and early 2000s, many local papers—however mediocre many of them might have been—were gone, and (aside from the personal Facebook feeds that would appear a few years later) media sources were moving toward the almost entirely national and global perspective they have today. *The Onion* remembered the regular people and ordinary communities this new world was treating as irrelevant. Their work *did* matter.

At the same time, the mid-1990s staff had noticed something. However valuable those ordinary people were, they were also often incredibly stupid. And the more straight *The Onion* played it, the more "bone dry" the tone, the more they fooled readers into thinking *Onion* stories were real. "And that part of it felt like a high, you know?" Siegel said. "This is a direction we need to go."

I came up with five primary reasons people think *Onion* stories are real.

1. The story is in print. I suspect this affects especially people who grew up during a time when what you saw in print was usually edited at minimum and fact-checked and verified if it appeared in something calling itself "news"—and when anything created by amateurs was very obviously created by amateurs. Back then, personal communication and personal opinions were also delivered either in person, speaking on the phone, or via handwritten paper letters through the US Mail; you'd rarely see such things "in print." Younger generations, who have always used typed text for everything, do not have as much trouble with thinking print means "true." (It's more like the opposite. They think everything is bullshit and truth does not exist.)

2. The story provides an answer to a deep need. One example is "New Smokable Nicotine Sticks: Can They Help Smokers Quit?" published on July 22, 1998. After the story was published, people who were desperate to quit smoking called *The Onion* asking where they could buy them.

3. *The Onion* confirms a belief they already have. One example was "*Harry Potter* Books Spark Rise in Satanism Among Children" (July 27–August 2, 2000). The public response to this was apparently completely ridiculous. Americans—we are *so stuck* in the 1980s—just love imagining that Satanism is secretly happening all over the place. Hanson tells a story in his 2011 appearance on Marc Maron's podcast about a group of parishioners at his dad's church who were freaking out about the

Auto Industry Agrees To Install Brakes In SUVs

see BUSINESS page 5C

Standard Deviation Not Enough For Perverted Statistician

see LIFESTYLE page 2D

Kenyan Grandmother Dominates Walkathon

see SPORTS page 1E

Dishwasher Trained

see WORKPLACE page 5B

Remaining Unregistered Internet Domain Names

▸www.fullyclothed.net
▸www.godlovesyouwithallhisfuckingheart.com
▸www.ludditeworld.com
▸www.pissguzzlinggrannies.edu
▸www.tomskerrittisgod.com
▸www.gayrepublicanmetalheadwiccans.org
▸www.njkfjkhrjhojfkjhwqfkf.com

⌀ the ONION®

VOLUME 36 ISSUE 25   AMERICA'S FINEST NEWS SOURCE™   27 JULY–2 AUGUST 2000

Harry Potter Books Spark Rise In Satanism Among Children

LOCK HAVEN, PA—Ashley Daniels is as close as you can get to your typical 9-year-old American girl. A third-grader at Lock Haven Elementary School, she loves rollerblading, her pet hamsters Benny and Oreo, Britney Spears, and, of course, Harry Potter. Having breezed through the most recent *Potter* opus in just four days, Ashley is among the millions of children who have made *Harry Potter And The Goblet Of Fire* the fastest-selling book in publishing history.

And, like many of her school friends, Ashley was captivated enough by the strange occult doings at the Hogwarts

School Of Witchcraft And Wizardry to pursue the Left-Hand Path, determined to become as adept at the black arts as Harry and his pals.

"I used to believe in what they taught us at Sunday School," said Ashley, conjuring up an ancient spell to summon Cerebus, the three-headed hound of hell. "But the *Harry Potter* books showed me that magic is real, something I can learn and use right now, and that the Bible is nothing but bor-

see POTTER page 10

Right: Three young *Harry Potter* fans in Winter Park, FL, recite an ancient Satanic incantation.

Bush Reluctantly Accepts Donation From Parents

DEL MAR, CA—Despite strong personal reservations, Republican presidential contender George W. Bush confirmed Monday that he has "reluctantly" agreed to accept a $2 million donation from his parents "to help with some of

Left: Presidential hopeful George W. Bush is flanked by his mom and dad, who holds a check for him.

the mounting expenses involved in running for office."

"I didn't want to do it, as I have always prided myself on paying my own way," Bush told reporters during a campaign stop near San Diego. "Unfortunately, the increasing difficulty of competing with the Gore campaign's unlimited taxpayer war chest has forced me to

see BUSH page 7

Ad-Agency Print Buyer Can't Believe They Want To Add A Perf This Late In The Game

LINCOLN, NE—Milt Olberding, a print buyer with L&G Advertising, expressed disbelief Tuesday that Capital City Chrysler owner William "Biff" Brignola wants to add a perforated insert to his ad this late in the game.

"A perf? At this point?" said Olberding, 33, upon learning of the change from L&G Advertising account manager Phil Essene. "We were about to put this whole thing to bed. Why didn't Brignola mention this last week when I was giving him quotes for coated?"

Essene, who helped design the full-page Capital City ad slated to run in a 32-page "Great Savings" sales flyer that will be mailed to all Lincoln-area households Monday, said he was "just as blown away" as Olberding.

"I was all set to seal up the Cap City ad and send out a proof, when I get this fax from Brignola asking about a BRM," Essene said. "Talk about a complete 180. I was, like, 'What? Now you want a 4 1/4 corner perf? Do you have any idea what that entails? Hello!'"

According to Olberding, the insertion of the business-reply-mail postcard will not only necessitate the perforation changes, but a switch to heavier paper, as well.

"I was going to go with Blue Lake, but I don't even think they do perfs on card stock," Olberding said. "Brignola had better be prepared to pay for 110-pound weight, because I'm not pulling the Great

see BUYER page 11

Right: L&G Advertising print buyer Milt Olberding.

The Harry Potter *article that set off another round of that ever-popular American fear: Satanism.*

story. His dad finally told them that in fact it was a fictional piece of satire written by his son and colleagues at *The Onion*, which was met with stunned silence and then (probably) everyone trying desperately to figure out how to spin their beliefs to make them continue to be correct instead of admitting they were losing it over a piece of fiction.

4. The story taps into some deep irrational fear. This might include "'98 Homosexual-Recruitment Drive Nearing Goal" (July 29, 1998), which Siegel said went up on a lot of antigay hate-group sites, saying, "See, look at what the gays are doing." A more recent example is when the *Onion* offshoot site ClickHole published "'90s Kids Rejoice! The Spider Eggs They Used to Fill Beanie Babies Are Finally Hatching!" (November 5, 2014). Readers apparently freaked out and started binding their Beanie Babies in plastic wrap and asking *The Onion* for proper methods of disposal.

5. Finally, the inability to discern multilayered-ness or irony. That is, it's not so much that people think it's real; they just don't get the joke at all. This is sort of the "innocence" defense. These are maybe the same people who don't understand poetry unless it's rhyming or in a Hallmark card. In a weird way, the problem here is a sort of unsullied purity around what language and rhetoric is and how it is used. Growing up in a house detached from all advertising and marketing, where everyone in your family was open, honest, and real all the time, where language was never used to manipulate, wallpaper, or cajole, might produce such an innocent. In our culture, however, it's more likely to be a product of trauma-induced dissociation or a learning disability. Or just, you know, being kind of dumb. Which is okay. We're all kind of dumb.

In this way, *The Onion*'s motto, "You Are Dumb," is both about lack of analytical ability and the very human tendency to not understand what you don't understand, particularly around our own emotional and developmental blind spots. Both of these, though, I think are subordinate to the larger thing we are stupid about, which is tolerating an economic and political system dedicated to taking advantage of our dumbness and a culture that exploits and violates rather than protects and cares for.

I wanted to briefly mention one other *Onion*-related phenomenon that started happening in the Siegel years: its ability to predict the future. (It's not actually that hard to predict the future of either individual people or a society. Simply look at what they did in the past; clearly ascertain why they did that without clouding your mind with fantasy, wishful thinking, or ideology—a good understanding of human psychology and motivation helps too; and then just exaggerate or extrapolate what you find. Presto: you've predicted the future.)

A big one for *The Onion* was the US invasion of Iraq in March 2003. The *Onion* staff, more clearheaded than real news opinionators at the time, were highly accurate in their prediction that George W. Bush would push the United States into war under false pretenses ("Bush on Economy: 'Saddam Must Be Overthrown,'" October 16, 2002). It's hard to believe now, but at the time nearly all of the media's talking heads were totally credulous about the whole "weapons of mass destruction" thing—the lie told by the Bush administration to gin up support for an invasion—resulting in a massive "debate" that went on in the media for months that was basically little more than a well-orchestrated PR stunt. *The Onion*, however, didn't fall for it, running headline after headline like "Bush on North Korea: We Must Invade Iraq" (January 15, 2003).

The Onion has also long predicted technological futures and the predictably stupid human ways we will experience them. One example is "Area Man Consults Internet Whenever Possible," from January 26, 2000. In the story, the man carries out what is now a common occurrence: using expensive technology to go through a time-consuming, confusing, multistage process to get ordinary information that results in far too many options, distractions, and digressions— while doing it the old-fashioned way with a phone call or quick look in the dictionary is much faster, more direct, and almost free (and, these days, more likely to be accurate as well).

On a more pedestrian level, we have a commentary titled "Fuck Everything, We're Doing Five Blades," by the CEO of Gillette, from February 18, 2004. The commentary is a macho rant about producing a disposable razor with five blades, which at the time didn't exist. There was, however, a ridiculous hypermasculine one-upmanship going on at the time with bigger and better multibladed razors that so far had made it to three blades. A couple of years later, Gillette came out with a five-blade razor.

With Siegel's leadership and a phenomenally talented team of writers, *The Onion* was now in peak form. A bunch of twentysomething Generation X nobodies out in flyover country had invented something that would become one of the most culturally influential American publications of all time.

Chapter 10

One of *The Onion*'s best and most influential projects took place alongside all the activity I've been describing in these past few chapters. Sometime around 1996, an occasional remote contributor named David Javerbaum—a friend of Ben Karlin's in New York who used to write for the *Harvard Lampoon*—came up with an idea. The end of the century was approaching. What if they wrote a book of *Onion* newspaper front pages for the whole twentieth century, the way that the *New York Times* had done in the past, and published it in recognition of the end of the millennium? Siegel, who as a kid had enjoyed reading these collections, thought it was a great idea. Dikkers did too. They also had a great set of writers for something like this; John Krewson and Maria Schneider had already shown a knack for writing in vintage news styles. They started mocking up a few pages. The title would be *Our Dumb Century*.

However, they had no literary agent. Luckily for them, a recent UW–Madison graduate named Daniel Greenberg—another East Coast kid—had decided to enter the business. He had moved back to New York and needed clients. Having enjoyed *Jim's Journal*, Greenberg approached Dikkers to see if he needed an agent for the comic. Dikkers already had an agent, but asked if Greenberg would be interested in representing *The Onion*.

At this point, Greenberg said, he had been aware of *The Onion* but wasn't a huge fan of the silly phase that they'd been in when he'd been a student. "Earth Nearly Hit by Flaming Space Hat" (November 3–9, 1992) wasn't exactly his idea of work that had the potential to reach a large audience. So he said no. Not long after, though, he was talking with his girlfriend, who worked at *PC Magazine*. Greenberg himself didn't have access to the internet yet, and he had missed the development of both the updated, all-news-satire style as well as the website. And when she heard he'd declined to represent *The Onion*, she said he needed to call them back right away and say yes instead. Every week her whole office went online when *The Onion*'s website updated—and it was *really* funny.

The Onion went on to make Greenberg's career. Greenberg remembered how impressed he was when he first saw the *Our Dumb Century* proposal, which sold to Hyperion, a division of Disney, for about $150,000. "At the time, a lot of money," Greenberg said. The acquiring editor was David Cashion, "a great guy." A couple of years passed as the staff worked on the manuscript.

Graphic designer Scott Templeton acted as art director on the project and was essential to the creation of the flabbergastingly good faux-vintage newspaper pages. He designed the first fifty years of front pages, while Andrew Welyczko designed the second fifty years.

Templeton grew up in a suburb of Milwaukee and discovered *The Onion* when the UW sent him a copy with his admissions package. He loved it. After he graduated in 1993, an ex-girlfriend sent him an *Onion* job ad: they were looking for a graphic designer. Thinking of himself more as an artist who did computer stuff, he didn't really believe he would get the job, "but it sure would be cool if I did, so I gave it a whirl." There were sixteen candidates, and he won.

At first, Templeton was put to work designing ads. "When I first got there, I was this super-enthusiastic, young, kind of naive, fresh-out-of-college guy who was just all gung ho for *The Onion*, and I think some of the people there just immediately saw me as a mark." He was soon roped into address-labeling the pile of print subscriptions. (He remembers Douglas Adams, author of *The Hitchhiker's Guide to the Galaxy*, being on the list.) He also got up at five in the morning to do distribution with Joe Garden.

When the *Our Dumb Century* contract was signed, Templeton got to work with all his creative powers to make the historic pages as accurate as possible. "If we had existed back then, we wouldn't look like the *New York Times*. So I chose typefaces and things out of local papers." He also developed processes with which he could make the pages look like they had been set in hot metal type, with authentic uneven gaps between letters, as well as make the pages look old. Templeton was even conscious of the historical transition from typeset ink to digital in the more modern era. Before digital, the pages have some ink blotches here and there, which decreased slowly as the book moved toward the present; the later ones are "crystal clear."

Templeton also designed three new fonts for the book. One was called "Glorious Coal," after an article on the subject from 1900. He said hot metal type "was very wonky back in the day. So I made sure to make it very wonky. And it was a challenge because I was laying it out on a computer." He had to "override the computer's instincts and tell it, 'No, please make this look awful. Please make this look like it was laid out by some greasy-faced, hot fellow in a printing press area.'" The process, which garnered him much-deserved staff admiration, "was a magical time for me." Dikkers paid him extra for the work, Templeton said. The money helped him buy his first house.

An excerpt from the 1900 page, the first one in the book:

A NEW CENTURY DAWNS! NATION'S SKIES FILLED WITH BEAUTIFUL, BLACK SMOKE.

Will man-made grime reach the very vault of heaven?

Look up, citizens, for all across the sky floats glorious proof of our incomparably robust manufacturing power! Indeed, there can be no more apt portent for our fair Republic's ever-growing industrial might than the very sky above us, thick and endowed with the beautiful black smoke of industry.

. . . Watch the other nations turn green with envy as the American landscape reminds them of our greatness at every turn, from the loco-motive smoke which clogs our skies to the boiling lead which seeps into our soil. Huzzah!

Each writer worked on all the sections, though there were also three section editors: Maria Schneider (1900–1939), John Krewson (1940–1969), and Robert Siegel (1970–1999). Schneider told me she remembered thinking: "I was *made* for this." Siegel said, "Maria Schneider was extraordinary." It was like she "somehow had the soul of someone from 1914." Siegel also said, "I think we didn't realize how big an undertaking it was." The project, carried out on top of their regular weekly *Onion* work, consumed their entire lives for at least a year.

Dikkers told me, "I rewrote and considerably lengthened stories on just about every page in addition to drafting my own. The other writers gave editorial notes and punch-up on all the stories, including mine. We all contributed headline

THE LAKE COUNTY TIMES

VOL. 1, NO. 55.— NIGHT EDITION.   HAMMOND, INDIANA TUESDAY, AUGUST 21, 1906.   ONE CENT PER COPY.

MEN WHO THINK IN BILLIONS ARE BUILDING THE TOWN OF GARY

Morgan's Brain the Birthplace, and the New Steel Town on the Sand Dunes of Northern Indiana the Cradle and Nursery of the Greatest Industrial Combine in the History of the World. More Territory than is Contained in States; More Money than Kingdoms Hold.

By THE GADFLY

J. PIERPONT MORGAN
The Greatest Concentrator of Capital and Physical Energy in the World

JUDGE ELBERT H. GARY
The Illinois Farm Lad, Lawyer and Judge, for Whom is Named the Steel City on the Dunes

LAST MOMENT FLASHES

A real newspaper from 1906—the Lake County Times, *which was the predecessor to the* Hammond Times *where Tim Keck's mom published her reporting. Dig out your copy of* Our Dumb Century *and compare them. J. P. Morgan was one of the tech bros of his day, a wildly wealthy banker who helped drive Gilded Age industrial consolidations that normalized enormous quantities of pollution and the destruction of entire ecosystems.*

---

ideas, sidebar jokes, and (some of us) drawings. Even headlines got punched up and retooled. . . . It was a joy to be working with what felt like a team of comedy geniuses every day." Dikkers added, "One thing I remember fondly was when I was done with it and ready to turn it in to the publisher, they pushed for one final pass to pick out the weakest half-dozen or so jokes in the book and work on better material."

Dikkers's comments didn't quite add up with what other staffers told me about the process, though they agreed that a huge amount of writing and revision took place—especially after Dikkers was "done with it." Contrary to Dikkers's rosy assessment, the process was, it seems, extremely frustrating—and most of that frustration came from Dikkers's management style. Hanson told me that Dikkers would remove good jokes and replace them with bad ones, dumb things down that made the content worse instead of better, had them write tons of text he then changed his mind about, and so on—a process that dragged the whole thing out for a very long time.

Garden, who was now living in Chicago—he did not contribute—said, "The process of writing Our Dumb Century really just knocked the shit out of everybody." He visited the office occasionally, "and Todd would be in the stairwell of the building on State Street and have like a cigarette-overflowing ashtray." (Hanson had dragged a desk out onto the stairwell landing so he could smoke and write at the same time.) The workload was "triple." Garden said, "Todd and John Krewson and Maria and everybody's like, 'I just don't have a break.'"

The office was not far from the downtown branch of the Madison Public Library, and the writers would check out piles of books for research. Familiarizing yourself with an entire century of history is no small task, even with three history degrees on the staff (Siegel, Schneider, and Thompson). Kolb said, "I know it's not like walking in ten feet of snow or shoveling coal or something. But it was a different process than today."

Unlike the design staff, the writers were doing all this additional work for free. Then, Dikkers—as fitted his longstanding pattern—at some point mid-project just disappeared. And in his absence, Siegel took over.

"Rob Siegel was extremely instrumental in making that book," Carol Kolb said. "I would say that Rob Siegel was the shepherd of that project." Schneider said Dikkers "seemed to kind of abandon" Our Dumb Century. Still, "it probably was a bit of a blessing in disguise that Rob took over." Hanson said he remembered Siegel waiting until Dikkers left the office and then going in and undoing all the editing changes Dikkers had made that day.

Siegel did say that Dikkers was instrumental in making the project go. "I could say with confidence that it wouldn't have happened without him," Siegel said. But he doesn't remember Dikkers being deep in the trenches. "I think that was a period when he was a little more away," Siegel said, diplomatically.

(Dikkers "definitely" did write some headlines, Siegel said. Dikkers told me his favorite personal contributions included "Earth-Quake Marks Least Gay Day in San Francisco History," "Martin Luther King: 'I Had a Really Weird Dream Last Night,'" and the "three-article runner on *It's a Wonderful Life*.") David Javerbaum contributed the classic headline "World's Largest Metaphor Hits Ice-Berg," about the *Titanic*. "Titanic, Representation of Man's Hubris, Sinks in North Atlantic. 1,500 Dead in Symbolic Tragedy."

Hanson said at the time, they just thought "Wow, this must just be how books get written." But looking back on it, he said, "I realized that a lot of it had to do with Dikkers's incompetence as a manager. Because every other book that he was in charge of, everyone walked away from it going, 'I'm never working with that man again.'" A couple of writers said they also thought Dikkers might even have doctored the author page of the book right before publication to minimize other people's contributions and increase the appearance of his own. His name is indeed listed first on the list of writers, which is not in alphabetical order.

In 1997, the staff finally finished their draft of *Our Dumb Century*. Greenberg took a look and could hardly believe his eyes. "I just remember flipping through it and saying, 'Oh my God, this is so much more than what anyone thought this book could be,'" he said. "It was jokes upon jokes upon jokes, and they were so consistently funny, and you can read the big headlines and laugh, and you can read the tiny headlines and laugh, and you can read every single article and they're all equally funny. And I remember thinking, 'This is going to be a big best seller.'" Greenberg took the manuscript home with him on the subway:

And I bump into the previous editor-in-chief of Hyperion, who had left to take a new job, and I say, "Holy shit, Brian. I have the *Onion* book with me." And we take a long trip back to Brooklyn. And I say, "It's amazing. *Look* at this!"

So we're flipping through it. And he sees a Mickey Mouse joke. And he sees an Oprah joke, as he's flipping. That's my memory. And he's like, "Uh-oh. This is going to be a problem with Hyperion, because it's Disney."

Disney's purchase of Hyperion was part of the long, slow, and (by now) nearly complete monopolization of all media in the hands of a very small number of ever-larger companies that has been going on since the 1980s. (For a primer written in the same era on this topic, see Ben Bagdikian's *The New Media Monopoly*, published in 1983 and revised in 2004.) And indeed, Disney had problems with the manuscript. Three jokes were flagged: a Hitler joke, a Mickey Mouse joke, and an Oprah joke. (They had a publishing partnership with Oprah at the time.) *The Onion* agreed to cut them. It was only three out of thousands of jokes. Done.

Except it wasn't done. Editor David Cashion said his boss asked him about the legal review, and when he learned there were still a couple sections left, he said it needed to be done *now* and gave it to a senior Hyperion lawyer, who in turn sent it to Disney's lawyers. Soon afterward, Cashion called Greenberg and said, "Fuck. I'm about to send this manuscript back to you." A messenger delivered it to Greenberg's office. Greenberg opened it up and saw that "a third of the book is X-ed out" in red pen. Cashion said, "*The Onion* serves as a way to take the piss out of bigotry and racism by pointing it out, pointing out how bad it is. That's the whole point of using these stereotypes and clichés. But that kind of thing is, it's edgy." So "anything that was about Black people, Hispanic, Asian, Jewish—all got red ink."

As a side note, Cashion said, "I'm gay. And maybe I'm a little sensitive to this, but I did note that they did not cross out any of the gay sections. That seemed to be okay." (Cashion said Disney has since had a better record on gay rights.)

In a subsequent conference call with the Disney lawyer—Greenberg described it as a "hostage situation" for Cashion—Cashion explained that they couldn't publish the manuscript the way it had been submitted. *The Onion* refused to make the changes, and the deal with Hyperion was over.

Greenberg said to Dikkers and Haise, "We are in the catbird seat right now." In the two years that it took to write the book, *The Onion* had gotten much bigger. Their online audience was now a quarter-million people a week. They also had the complete manuscript rather than a two-page sample. Greenberg said they would do an auction, and "everybody was going to fight tooth and nail for it." Which is exactly what happened. *The Onion* signed with Crown for $450,000—three times their Hyperion advance. *Our Dumb Century* had already brought *The Onion* nearly a half-million dollars, and it hadn't even been published yet. Haise told me the money allowed him to open the Chicago office, which was very successful.

Templeton said, "The writers were so excited that we got an even better deal. And it was like, 'Wow, we did it. We screwed Disney!'"

As soon as *Our Dumb Century* was released, it hit number one on the *New York Times* best-seller list. Reviews called it brilliant. Greenberg said the publisher just kept "printing and printing and printing copies," and even so it kept selling out. *Our Dumb Century* ultimately sold five hundred thousand copies.

Chad Nackers said some staffers had an identity crisis about it. "I remember Todd Hanson was terrified by the prospect of having a number-one bestseller. He was like, 'What's it going to do? Is it going to change everything?'" Nackers said mainly it "changed the fact that people knew what *The Onion* was. It made it legitimate for those East Coast people who assume everything comes from there."

Unfortunately, the writing staff each netted only a small additional stipend for their work. Hanson said it was $1,300, which was "the largest check that I'd ever received from *The Onion* at the time." Mike Loew said, "We got a glass of champagne from our editors in New York, our publishers. They were toasting our success. And we're kind of like, 'We're glad it's successful for somebody!'" Loew did say, "I was not ripped off as hard as the writers." He got "an extra 100 bucks a week or something here and there" for the project. "We never probably did get the money we deserved on it," Siegel said. "I was so obsessed with making *The Onion* bigger that I probably would have done it for free. Might have been what I wound up doing it for."

When *Our Dumb Century* won the 1999 Thurber Prize for American Humor, "one of the highest recognitions of the art of humor writing in the United States," it came with a small cash prize. According to the writers, Haise apparently passed around just a few dollars and put the rest in *The Onion*'s bank account. The Madison office did receive a tin of cookies to celebrate on the day the book hit the *New York Times* best-seller list. Unfortunately, they were actually cookies from a Brewers game-promotion thing Haise had succeeded in arranging, which happened to be on the same day.

Siegel said it was all more of the "schizophrenic feeling" of "Now we're number one on the *New York Times* best-seller list. We're being profiled in every major publication under the sun." They'd been invited to the New Yorker Festival and the Aspen Comedy Festival. They were getting Webby Awards. National media were coming to Madison to profile them. Yet they were still in the same dumpy office on State Street. "Nothing had changed whatsoever."

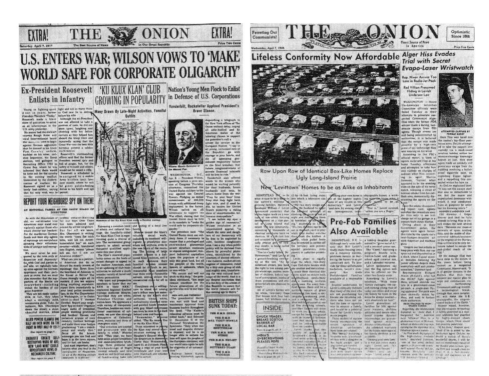

Some of the crossed-out
Our Dumb Century *manuscript pages.*

Schneider said, "*Our Dumb Century* was sort of 'teaching history without cramming it down your throat.'" She thought "the midwestern sensibility kind of plays into that. I mean, I'm sure we're not the only region in the country where people kind of avoid pretension and preciousness." But in the Midwest it was important both "not to be an ignoramus" but also "not to cudgel people with your knowledge."

The release party for *Our Dumb Century* was held in the apartment below Kolb's place (the one with the Madison Museum of Bathroom Tissue). Nackers said the stoner dudes who lived there made it into an "über-eclectic apartment filled with TVs playing laserdiscs of weird '80s movies and outdated video games. It was sort of a giant ArtPlace. They called it the Down Below Lounge." A punk band played. Garden around this time had been expanding his performance repertoire into a bit of burlesque and had been seen around town dancing onstage sans clothing at concerts and events. People recalled him doing things like attaching a guitar string to a certain important body part and playing the string like a harp during a rock show while a guy in the audience

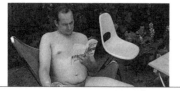
Joe Garden was the go-to Naked Guy whenever The Onion *needed one for a photo shoot. At one point, they apparently were almost fined by the US Post Office for sending obscene materials through the mail via their subscriptions.*

tripping on mushrooms stared up at him in awe. Nackers said, "And I believe Joe Garden was dancing naked at the party."

(Garden seems to have gone nudist in the office periodically for years. He did feel bad about the time he sat on Loew's office drum-kit seat. "It was a different time," Kolb said. She told me Garden would also sometimes put an *Onion* sticker over his penis and dance around the room.)

Easter eggs abound in *Our Dumb Century*. Go take a look at the lower left-hand side of the page for 1900 for a really good one that was just for the hometown Madison audience who'd been reading *The Onion* since 1988: a coupon.

Chapter 11

T he *Onion* was definitely famous now. And they were one of the earliest publications on the web. So why not see if there was a way for *The Onion* to make them all rich? It was the 1990s dot-com boom. Mike Loew remembered, "You've got all these websites selling for outlandish amounts of money that just appeared, and suddenly they're worth $800 million or something. So we're like, 'Holy cow, this internet thing could really be something here.'" Maybe they could do an IPO (initial public offering). Maybe the whole staff could get a stake. (If you want to be 1990s about it, be sure to pronounce the "double-you, double-you, double-you" in www.theonion.com.)

Looking at existing websites selling for zillions of dollars, Stephen Thompson said, "You'd be like, 'They don't make anything. It's a URL. How is it worth that much? We must be worth five times that, right?'" Thompson took out a bank loan and bought a 1 percent stake in the business.

And I was like, "Am I an internet millionaire?" But then the process of trying to sell *The Onion* was, you know where you stand in this machine about the size of a phone booth? And it's sending up a cloud of dollar bills and the person in the machine is trying to just catch as many dollar bills as possible? And the prize that you win or whatever is to catch as much money as you can?

It was like being in one of those machines with your hands tied behind your back. There was just money swirling all around us. And we were trying to catch it, and none of it, *none of it,* landed in our hands.

Thompson told me the guy they'd hired to broker the sale would come back to them with a list of all the venture-capital firms he'd tried to sell *The Onion* to, "all the internet companies, all the investors." And every week he'd come back and say, "'Well, we got a no from this one, and a no from this one, and a no from this one.'

"And we would just be like, 'What? Why? Why are we valueless?'" Thompson said. Meanwhile, "Pets.com, with its stupid sock puppet, is flushing away millions and millions and millions of dollars." Because *The Onion* actually produced something. Often at a profit.

That may have been *The Onion*'s problem, actually. *The Onion* was still a product, not a brand. And brands were the ones getting all those millions. (The classic work on how the ramping up of corporate branding in the 1990s affected both the economy and the culture is Naomi Klein's 1999 book *No Logo*. The book is still very relevant today.) Andrew Welyczko said *The Onion* was successful "because it was a well-run college-town newspaper with the master of hustle as its owner, Pete Haise, who could turn ten minutes in any downtown Madison bar into a yearlong ad contract." Yet such concrete, real-world, in-person skills and accomplishments had little value to the digital mentality that seemed determined to make the whole world virtual.

Siegel, who had bought 5 percent of *The Onion* from Dikkers for $10,000 when he had been raising money to shoot *Spaceman*, said the list of suitors had included AOL, Viacom, and a place called BigWords.com. He said he'd gone to San Francisco for *The Onion*'s 1999 Webby Award and visited some of the dot-com offices. "And I was like, 'What the fuck?'" These places were less than a year old. But they had more money "and more everything" than *The Onion* had. Meanwhile, *The Onion* was not some smoke-and-mirrors bullshit entity. "We have a goddamn content archive, for God's sake," he said. "*We're not pretend*, and yet we just can't sell out."

Thompson said the editorial staff used to talk a lot about how the business side never came close to the comedy side in vision or quality. What they needed was the business equivalent of *The Onion*'s comedy genius—something I heard again and again from the writing staff, from all generations, when I was writing this book, so often that it qualifies as *Onion* lore. "And what we didn't understand," Thompson said, "is that that doesn't exist." With the hindsight created after being canned during *The Onion*'s final takeover by corporate management in 2004 (and watching it devolve even more after that), Thompson said:

"Looking back, *The Onion*'s best ownership, *The Onion*'s best business mind, was a Milwaukee sub-shop owner, because he paid the staff salaries and left us alone."

Eventually, they got good news. The up-and-coming cable channel Comedy Central was interested in buying *The Onion*. Very interested. *The Onion* hired Adam Richman to put together a business proposal. A draft of Richman's more than forty-page proposal paints a picture of *The Onion* circa 1999, which it calls "THE WORLD'S MOST POPULAR HUMOR PUBLICATION": "Starting with a single newspaper in Madison, Wisconsin only a few years ago, the Company has since utilized its comedy style to successfully expand the newspaper operations and branch out into other entertainment media. *The Onion* now provides humor through a variety of media, including newspapers, television, radio, books, branch merchandising and the Internet, which has become the Company's prominent business in terms of growth and exposure."

The proposal stated that the award-winning website received more than four million page views per week from five hundred thousand weekly visitors, and the print version, distributed in Madison, Milwaukee, Boulder, and Chicago as well as sold at Barnes & Noble and Borders, had approximately five hundred thousand readers per week. Subscriptions were somewhere around eight to ten thousand a year, all done in-house. (Subscriptions seemed to be a sore spot for the staffer making handwritten comments on the proposal I saw, who couldn't restrain themselves from using their pen to vent in the margins: "The fact that we do subscriptions in-house is proof that we have NO CLUE how to build our subscription database. Our database is run by an INTERN in MILWAUKEE!")

Other details show that Onion Radio News was on fifty different stations through Westwood One. Online, *The Onion*'s archive contained eleven years of material—thirty-five hundred stories from four hundred editions of the paper. The staff also increased from six employees to sixty between 1990 and 1998. Typical reader demographics were well-educated males between the ages of eighteen and thirty-five who worked in tech, at universities, and for the US government. In the first six months of 1999, Onion, Inc., had revenues of $1,593,938, "an increase of 84% over the first six months of 1998." Between 1996 and 1998, revenues increased by 252 percent, from $882,939 in 1996 to $2,228,741 in 1998— almost entirely due to website ad sales, with a compound annual growth rate of 316 percent. *The Onion* was now "a comedy institution, creating cutting-edge humor content and products enjoyed by millions around the world." The proposal notes that "at thousands of businesses across the country, Wednesday is 'Onion Day,' a weekly tradition where employees briefly put aside their work and log onto theonion.com to read the just-posted new issue."

The proposal also noted that *The Onion* intended to launch a "major national humor magazine" in the next year called *The Onion Newsmagazine*. (This never happened.) In addition, an *Our Dumb Century* year-end TV special written and produced by Dikkers was also being shopped around (this didn't happen either). On the staff list, Dikkers was identified as "Vice President/Creative Consultant," with a note: "Scott Dikkers has primarily had a consulting role as opposed to a management or writing role for the last two years; 1997 was the last year that Scott was involved in any daily capacity in the newspaper."

This draft of the proposal wasn't final, but aside from the impressive reader and revenue numbers, overall it felt, as my grad school advisor used to say, "pretty thin." Several pages of future plans read like pure fantasy (or just throwing spaghetti at the wall), listing everything from live skit comedy shows to feature films to comedy CDs to PalmPilot content to a revamped website, where people could talk on discussion boards that would link to other comedy sites (the latter idea being ridiculed by the *Onion* staffer making written comments on the draft). The A.V. Club was not even mentioned, even though it was more than half the paper by then. A lack of cohesion and focus was evident.

While the proposal was being completed, the editorial staff, directed by Dikkers, also had what Todd Hanson called "secret meetings" outside Haise's view, where they put together two agreements to be part of the proposed sale. One was for the writers to obtain stock-appreciation rights, which would pay out the difference in share price over a specific period of time. This agreement apparently would have given them all a sizable cash bonus when *The Onion* was sold. (Hanson told me he thought it would have been about $100,000; Mike Loew thought it was potentially multiples of that.) The other agreement was to sign away their rights to their work in the paper and make them work-for-hire staff, which Hanson understood as an exchange for the stock-appreciation rights. Loew remembers Dikkers handing the papers around for them all to sign.

To make the sale, rights needed to be established. When the staff was hired, there may not have been any formal employment contract that specified their status—so the agreement made sense on that level. (Joe Garden, however, apparently refused to sign away either Jim Anchower or Jackie Harvey, the characters for whom he wrote columns.) And it wasn't as if the writers got any royalties or anything now. Still, Hanson said he objected to being formally contracted into a work-for-hire employee. "Wait a minute," he thought. "We're giving up the one thing in order to get the other thing. But what if the sale doesn't go through? Then we will have given up our rights for nothing." It was exactly like what happened to the creators of Superman. So they added a clause in a last-minute meeting, saying, "In the event that the sale doesn't go through, this is void."

The Comedy Central deal, Dikkers told me, was for $12 million. "And I think they were ready to bite and they were going to do it," he said. Haise added a few more details. He said that when Comedy Central made their initial offer, he came back with a counteroffer. He'd had a conversation with Larry Divney, Comedy Central's CEO, at the Comedy Central Christmas party, and Divney had told Haise he thought the company was worth $35 or $40 million. Haise making a counteroffer based on his "calculations, conversations, and discussions" was reasonable.

He mentioned the number $20 million, though I don't know if that was in fact the counter he proposed. Nor could I verify if Dikkers's $12 million quote was correct, either. In any case, the goal would have been for Comedy Central to say something like, "We could go up to $15 million and no more," whereupon Haise would say "Sold!" and everyone would ride off into the sunset with newly packed bank accounts, albeit with no rights to *The Onion*'s work.

Unfortunately, during the thirty days when they were waiting to hear back around April 2000, the dot-com bubble burst. (The peak of the bubble was March 10, 2000, the crash began the next day, and by April 6 almost a trillion dollars in dot-com value was wiped off the map.) "All these big websites that had been fueled by pretend internet money for billions of dollars like bluemountain.com, the greeting-card company," Dikkers said, "so many websites and companies like that were just gone. They just vanished like a vapor." And, unfortunately, as a result, Comedy Central got cold feet and didn't want to buy. (At least, Dikkers said, *The Onion* "was primarily a print business. That's how we made most of our money. The website was just like a side thing for us. So we rode that crash out easy.") Haise seemed to have the phrase memorized: "We are no longer authorized to close a deal with *The Onion* on the purchase of their company." Andrew

Welyczko said he also thought "some kind of turnover or something happened to Comedy Central and they were no longer in a position to pursue." Regardless, as Haise put it, "That deal just went away."

Dikkers was furious and called Haise "the worst CEO in the world." Dikkers also told the writers that Haise's incompetence was to blame for the deal going south. Several writers told me they'd heard that Haise's counteroffer was way too high and that's what tanked the deal. By that point, it was easy for them to believe Haise was not competent to handle their rising star. (The thing is, though, Haise and Dikkers were equally responsible for ownership. As Joe Garden said, "It's interesting that Scott would immediately throw Pete under the bus like that.")

Haise knew he'd been made the scapegoat of the failed sale. But he would have been derelict in his duty if he hadn't counteroffered. And he had no power over the dot-com bubble bursting. "It seems so unfair to pigeonhole me as the guy who fucked the deal up," he said. "It's ridiculous." Indeed, it does seem a little . . . amateurish to think that a large entertainment corporation like Comedy Central, if they had really wanted *The Onion*, would storm away in a huff just because of a counteroffer.

Chicago ad manager Matt McDonagh remarked on "the level of distrust that I would see when we'd go to Madison and see the editorial team and just how much they kind of hated Pete. And you know, was it always fair? I don't know. Probably in some ways, yes. But he was also probably an easy person to hate because they were still working out of a shitty office in Madison. They weren't in New York." McDonagh added, "Was he doing his best? I think he was. He was trying." McDonagh also said that it was probably a good thing the deal died. "I think a lot of people probably thought that was the end-all-be-all for *The Onion*. . . . But I've worked enough with Comedy Central. Would that have been an amazing place for *The Onion*? Not at all. *The Onion* didn't fit anywhere. People would have been miserable in any of those skyscrapers." (The question of whether the writers now had the rights to their work back was apparently never resolved.)

Haise said that in the aftermath, Dikkers made an unexpected announcement. "The next meeting we have, he starts the meeting without me. I'm coming from Milwaukee or Chicago or New York at that time, I can't even remember . . . And Scott says he's quitting and wants to sell his shares. 'Pete can't run this company.'" So, since Haise had already been in the process of raising real money for the first time anyway, he found somebody to buy Dikkers's shares.

Dikkers told me his decision to sell had to do with taxes. The gist of his story was something about owing a lot of taxes on the difference between the $3,000 he'd paid for *The Onion* and its current value. Before, he said, they'd always used the company's bank account to pay their taxes on any gains, but now he was worried that couldn't happen. Given that a major tax bill would be triggered only if you sold, selling your investment in order to not pay taxes on it doesn't make a lot of sense, but who knows? It was hard to get the details.

The man Haise found to buy Dikkers's shares was wealthy New York investor David Schafer. Schafer was managing the Schafer Value Fund, which in turn was marketed by the multibillion-dollar Milwaukee-based Strong Capital Management. Schafer connected with *The Onion* via a man named Steve Hannah, who was friends with (and a client of) Brady Williamson, the Madison lawyer working with Haise to sell Dikkers's shares. Williamson called Hannah up one day out of the blue and asked if he knew anybody who wanted to buy *The Onion*.

Hannah would have made sense to Williamson as a person to ask this question. Steve Hannah was raised in New Jersey and spent a lot of time in New York City. One of his first jobs was for Walter Cronkite at CBS News. He then fell in love with and married a woman from Wisconsin, a place he also fell in love with, on a visit, and began a Wisconsin journalism career.

Hannah went to work at the *Milwaukee Journal* as a farm and state reporter, even though he knew "absolutely nothing about agriculture." Over eighteen years he eventually rose to the position of executive editor. He left when the *Milwaukee Journal* and *Milwaukee Sentinel* merged in the late 1990s and started a media consulting business—also known as public relations. Strong Capital Management, based in Milwaukee, was his client for ten years until the firm was sold to Wells Fargo in 2003. (Hannah didn't mention that Strong was shut down due to being caught making frequent trades in violation of their fiduciary duties during the 2003 mutual-fund scandal.) "I did a variety of projects for Strong, but the centerpiece was helping manage the firm's media relations with the likes of *Forbes*, *Fortune*, *Money* magazine, the *Wall Street Journal*, and all sorts of other national media," Hannah said. "I spent most of my Strong time in New York." He also wrote a syndicated newspaper column called "State of Mind" and— after his *Onion* adventures—published a book with University of Wisconsin Press called *Dairylandia* about his observations of Wisconsin culture and people.

After hearing from Williamson, Hannah called David Schafer, whom he'd met and become close personal friends with after Strong tasked Hannah with recruiting Schafer to the firm. Hannah asked Schafer if he'd be interested in buying *The Onion*. Schafer reportedly said, "Is it a produce company?" As the story goes, after Schafer's son told his dad he would finally be cool if he bought *The Onion*, Schafer agreed to take a look. "David bought in his lifetime probably five hundred companies at that point," Hannah said.

They had a meeting at Hannah's house with one of Haise's "minions," as Hannah put it, to discuss a potential deal. Schafer asked Hannah what he thought, and Hannah said, "Boy, it sounds like a lot of work." Schafer was intrigued, though, and he said he was going to go for it. Hannah remembers him saying, "We can grow the business, and we can work on fixing the business model. But I don't think that in our wildest dreams we could ever create a product as unique as *The Onion*." He then asked Hannah if he wanted to be CEO. He did not. Schafer told him to let him know if that ever changed. (I don't know what Dikkers got for his shares, but I suspect it was around $1 million.)

Hannah did agree to advise Schafer, however. He said, "When you run a newspaper like the *Journal* as managing editor, and then executive editor, you're involved in editorial things, but you're really running a business. There's multi-million-dollar budgets, and people to hire, and people to fire, and decisions to make, and all kinds of legal consequences for what you do."

The deal was done, and Dikkers was out. Haise's business partner was now David Schafer. And the writers then sat down in a meeting with Haise and told him that if *The Onion* didn't move to New York, they would all quit. Kolb said it wasn't a threat; it was more like "you know if you don't do this, you're gonna lose all of us." The Comedy Central idea had given them, as Chad Nackers recalled, "a little taste of 'Maybe we could be working with other comedians or having peers,'" as well as opportunities to pitch TV shows and movies and things like that. Haise had not, the writers felt, shown anything like the degree of understanding needed for them to move *The Onion* to the next level. So they would do it themselves.

For Loew, the whole thing was Siegel's idea. He said, "We can prolong this youth that we have. Look at us. We're twenty-six, twenty-seven years old." In Madison they were "kind of like old men." But in New York, they could keep the youth going. Siegel told me it also just felt like there was this "invisible ceiling" over their heads in Madison. "Maybe if we just moved to New York, all these things that aren't happening, maybe they'll happen."

Haise, though apprehensive, agreed to take the plunge. He was feeling, I think, mortified about the dead Comedy Central deal, which had crushed many dreams besides his own. The writers, he said, were "fucking heartbroken." But they'd just had a profitable year. The high quality of the writers' work had taken *The Onion* this far, after all. Why couldn't it take them to New York? (The Comedy Central proposal mentioned several times how *The Onion*'s humor writing method ensured high quality and longevity because it was a group effort that could be taught to new staffers and passed down, rather than something that had to rely on the output of any individual star.)

Still, he knew the move was going to cost a fortune. He decided to go for it anyway. "We'll keep doing what we do," he said. "Let's roll." They could do it themselves, he said. "We don't need Comedy Central." Haise said he told them: "I'll take us there." He said to me, "You can hear the song playing in the background in that scene in the movie. 'I'll take you there.' *I'll* fucking take us to New York." (As we were talking, Haise sang the line from the 1972 gospel song "I'll Take You There," by the Staple Singers.) Haise's philosophy was "steady, profitable growth." This was a much bigger jump than Madison to Milwaukee for sure. But he was ready to try.

When Tim Harrod heard the news, he thought, "It was just a couple years ago I was in my parents' basement. And now, on our talent and our moxie, we're all moving to New York." Siegel said, "It just really felt like *The Muppet Movie*, or *Muppets Take Manhattan*. This wacky band of Muppets got on a bus and headed to the Big Apple." (The band of Muppets did not include Andrew Welyczko's layout team and the A.V. Club; they stayed behind in Madison. As did Siegel's PhD student girlfriend; they broke up before the move.)

Haise said he "fucking doubled, tripled people's salary" so they could get by in the big city. (He also said that when Schafer saw what he had been paying himself—$1,000/week—Schafer was so embarrassed he doubled Haise's salary as well.) Getting at least one benefit from the dot-com bust, Haise also found office space in Chelsea at an amazing price. They bought out the "dirt cheap" lease of an "early online weirdo furniture shop" that had just gone under. The lease had almost ten years left on it and the rate was $13 per square foot—when everything else in New York started at $35–$40. Siegel said when they first toured the space, some of the furniture was still in there, like "a giant spoon that was a chair."

Haise then got his own people to renovate the space for the staff and lay phone lines—as in people from Milwaukee, who apparently drove there from Wisconsin in a van. This met no end of ridicule by the staff when they arrived. They also discovered—alongside the oddly placed outlets and the coating of toxic dust that covered everything after Haise's crew decided to sand all the white paint off the brick pillars—that whoever Haise had arranged to pack their office boxes had somehow mixed their stuff in with a bunch of random other items, like wooden jewelry. Chris Karwowski said at one point the workers' van stopped working, "and they just left it outside of our building and walked away." Harrod recalled, "To install the phone system, he hired a guy [who] showed up one day with a few tools and a portable TV and then watched the TV for a while and then left for the day. Would come back later and do a little bit of work and watch some TV. It was the strangest thing." On the other hand, at least the guy was useful for the staff in one way: they bought weed from him. (His offer of a free sample bag of cocaine wasn't as popular; that's how they get you hooked.)

Haise said he used the "absolute cheapest" way of doing everything. "I slept in Rob's apartment before Rob even moved there. I slept on the floors of that office," he said. But his usual home base in New York was the Gramercy Park Hotel, which he chose because the price was right and they could have meetings there. Along with arranging the office renovation, Haise hired local ad reps and office staff and figured out New York printing and distribution. He got the utility bills paid and computers hooked up, all the details taken care of so that the creative staff could get what they had wanted for so long.

He knew he was taking a risk. It was already making him uneasy. "When we're going to be able to start a new venture, I've got to have the ad sales to justify it," he told me, and despite the prior year being profitable, I am not sure they were quite there for the New York move. But he did it anyway. Dikkers had abandoned them when things got tough—cashing in for a lot of money on *their* years of hard work. Haise, however—in spite of the writers' complaining, judging, and ridicule, in spite of them thinking he was uncool, out of touch, and a terrible businessman who only cared about sub-sandwich shops—stayed by their sides.

The early 2001 move was written up in both the New York and the hometown Madison press. One of the best was an article in *Penthouse*, by a reporter who visited the office not long after they arrived. "Over the past ten years *The Onion* has quietly become the Next Big Thing in comedy. Its success is the tale of the Little Independent That Could. In a media world where a handful of corporations owns all the major news and entertainment outlets, these satirists have managed to expand without being bought out or cushioning their sensibility to appeal to the masses." The writer also noted that Garden removed his clothes for the occasion: "'In honor of *Penthouse*,' Joe Garden said of his pasty bare chest and flaccid penis."

By the spring of 2001, in between writing the paper every week for the other *Onion* offices, they were exploring the city, hanging out with members of the Upright Citizens Brigade, and meeting comedy idols who, to their shock, also wanted to meet them, as Haise and his staff did the legwork to prepare for the first New York print edition that fall. Mostly, though, Siegel said, they had pretty much the same lives they had back in Madison. They did get a Miramax first-look deal, though that didn't end up going anywhere. Former editor Rich Dahm, who was still contributing headlines, writing, and punch-up from Los Angeles, had his story "Canadian Girlfriend Unsubstantiated" optioned, and Hanson's story "10th Circle Added to Rapidly Growing Hell" was optioned as well.

Siegel said they had "a little toast of the town" moment, "although none of us were really equipped to recognize it." Siegel said his wife now teases him that he didn't understand he could have "stepped through the door into some kind of glamorous world of cool literati people." They were at least invited to join the New York media softball league, where they played against the *New Yorker* and *High Times* and so on.

The *Onion* team was not very good compared to the New York elite. "They all seemed to have guys that played lacrosse for Princeton. Like athletic, strapping college men. And we didn't. We had a lot of smokers," Siegel said. During the *Paris Review* game, Siegel apparently hit a line drive at pitcher George Plimpton and almost killed him. (Plimpton signed the ball, and Siegel still has it.) The *High Times* team was the best in the league; they smoked in the dugout while smoking one team after another on the field. Siegel said they gave out samples, and "all they talked about was weed."

Haise was now running an entirely new *Onion* office in New York, on top of the Madison, Chicago, and Milwaukee offices. Welyczko described how outposts worked in this era. "There was a core set of *Onion* offices that were all owned and operated by *The Onion* itself—not franchises. Each one of these offices was operated largely the same, with a local manager, one local designer (these were the people who made up my team), a local sales staff, and a local A.V. Club writer. Some of these offices also had some business staff and a national sales rep or two." These were opened slowly across the mid- to late 1990s. "It was all very Pete Haise. Seat of pants, get on the ground, and hustle," Welyczko said.

Now, though, they were in New York—not with just a local A.V. Club writer but the entire core Madison editorial staff. The Haise hustle had brought them to the biggest city in America—the town whose very name meant "success." The pain of the Comedy Central breakdown, Dikkers selling his shares, making all the arrangements, renovating the office, spending money like it was going out of style—by end of the summer it was all finally finished. Loew described how excited he was to be in New York City:

Here I am in Manhattan, and you know, it's tons of beautiful people, and graffiti, and garbage everywhere, and it's exciting, and there's people spilling out everywhere, and drinks, and Todd Hanson turns around, you know, like smoking a cigarette: "We're in New York City, man. Isn't this the best ever?"

Yeah, it is! We were super jazzed. I was super excited. It was a beautiful thing to move to the city with my group of friends. Most of us settled in the Park Slope area. We called it Little Wisconsin. A little joke. Krewson lived down the block from me; Chad was just two blocks down. It was awesome. I was excited to be working for *The Onion* in New York City.

"And our first issue was to be September 16, 2001," Haise said. "*The Onion*'s first issue in New York City. And it was never to be published. They walked right into 9/11."

Chapter 12

On the night of Monday, September 10, the staff attended a They Might Be Giants album-release party (for *Mink Car*) after a concert at the Bowery Ballroom, which seems to have doubled as a party to celebrate *The Onion*'s first issue in New York. (Joe Garden introduced the band, and much whiskey flowed.) It was pouring rain. Maria Schneider, who left her umbrella at home, remembers getting totally drenched on the way there. In *MEL Magazine*'s oral history of the 9/11 issue, John Krewson said, "We didn't know it then, of course, but it was the end of the 1990s. It was our last party of the 1990s, and the 2000s were about to really fucking begin."

It would seem that a number of the staff partied pretty hard that night. Getting up early the next morning was not a top priority. For those who were up, as Krewson said, "I will say what everyone else says. It was a beautiful fucking day."

Karwowski, who was sharing a Park Slope apartment with Garden, remembers Garden banging on his door yelling, "Karwowski, a plane has run into one of the World Trade Center buildings. There might be another one. America might be attacked—get down here."

Siegel lived in Manhattan on Fifteenth Street. "Like so many other New Yorkers," Siegel said, "we woke up and a friend called and said, 'Turn on the TV.'" He and his now-wife, voice actor Jen Cohn, sat together in shock, watching the events play out. "We were newly in love," Cohn said. "We had started dating in May. And we had just, maybe a month earlier, declared we were in love and exclusive. So 'my new boyfriend, my new girlfriend.' We were there."

Siegel was not hungover, but he was sick—he had missed the big party the night before because of it. Cohn, taking care of him, had brought him a big pot of chicken soup from her nearby apartment, "which came in tremendously handy."

Some of Jen's friends came over, "a gaggle of New York City girls," as Cohn put it, and they all sat together in front of the TV eating chicken soup. Siegel, however, was already starting to worry about the big issue. He did not want to mess up their first print edition in New York. Carol Kolb and Todd Hanson were living together at that time, and they didn't have a TV. "We didn't have access to the news," Kolb said, so they went down to a neighbor's apartment. "I was watching the TV, and then I just remember being like, 'I can't be with these people that I don't really know.'"

The first plane had hit the World Trade Center at 8:46 a.m. At that point, most people thought it was some sort of terrible accident—a small plane flying too low. Mike Loew had left his apartment and gone down into the Seventh Avenue F train stop in Park Slope to head to the Chelsea office, believing this was all that had happened. It was bad for sure, but he needed to get to work. When he got to the turnstile, he saw a piece of masking tape over the Metrocard slot. Thinking it was just kids goofing off, he pulled off the tape, swiped his card, and went in.

The underground part of the Seventh Avenue station stretches almost three blocks, and Loew had entered at one end of that wide space. He waited for a while. But something was wrong. It was peak travel time, and not a soul was in sight. It was also dead silent. No subway cars screeching, no talking, no sounds of walking except for his own. Nobody playing music on the platform. It was a "last man on earth" feeling, Loew said.

He walked all the way to the other side and came up the stairs. There he finally saw another person: an MTA worker. He told Loew what had happened. It wasn't a small plane; it was a 767. And there were two planes, not just one. (The second plane had hit at 9:03 a.m.) And a third plane had just hit the Pentagon too. At this point, Loew said, "My mind is melting."

The MTA worker then told him twelve planes were still in the air right now. So where were they coming next? Loew went out of the station into a little bodega with a TV on and people gathered around. He watched the towers burning on the screen, he said. Then he went back outside, looked up, and saw that the smoke from the tower fires, and the debris carried by that smoke, was there in the real sky above him.

I was feeling all the paper fall on me. And the ashes. I just saw bits of paper falling down. I picked up a piece of paper. And there were all these people's names on it. It was all a lot of Indian names, you know, Indian language. And I just wondered how these people did that day.

I went to Chad's house because he lived a block away. He was up in a third-story brownstone apartment. And he had a back balcony that had a view of Manhattan. So I was able to look out the window and watch Manhattan burn. And it was just the same exact shot that we saw on the television set.

I saw this little girl chasing the bits of paper. Kind of like they're like falling leaves or something in the air, you know?

Siegel was on the phone with Hanson. "We were already like, what are we gonna do? What are we gonna say? How do we handle this?" Hanson "was the guy who would have the strongest, loudest opinions. And I wanted to make sure I was on the same page with him first." Chad Nackers was one of the next people Siegel spoke with. And as Siegel and Nackers talked, the first tower went down. Not long after, Nackers said, a huge wall of smoke came down Park Slope's Fifth Avenue.

A few staffers and friends who lived in the neighborhood had congregated at Krewson's place and gone up to his roof to see what they could see. "The air was blowing towards us," Karwowski said. "So you could pick burned, charred pieces of paper out of the sky." It was such a strange thing to hold in your hand. "Like, this is from there." Loew had friends who worked downtown near the towers whom he hadn't heard from yet. "You just had that feeling of, like, how many of my friends are dead?" he said.

Back in Madison, Welyczko, Templeton, and Thompson were experiencing their own grief and shock. The morning of September 11 had been spent watching the little color TV Welyczko had found on the street and brought up to the office. Had any of their friends died in the catastrophe? Cell service was down (only a few people had a cell phone anyway), and in the first hours after the attacks, so many landline phone calls were being made to New York that the system couldn't handle the traffic.

Nackers remembered Siegel calling him on September 12, saying, "Comedy doesn't sleep," and he and Loew should go into the city and start working. They stopped along the way to buy props for a photo. Signs for missing people were everywhere. When Nackers and Loew finally arrived at the office on the far

West Side at Twentieth Street, about a mile and a half from the site, they had a clear view of the smoke, which just kept on coming even though it was the next day. "It was just a big black rainbow in the sky," Loew said. "And the smell was just viciously evil, like burned hair and metal, like you had thrown a bunch of computers and swept up the barbershop and put that on top for the bonfire." They also saw "the entirety of Tenth Avenue lined with ambulances and police cars and emergency vehicles and fire trucks as far as the eye could see." But the ambulances stood still and empty. The destruction was so rapid and total that everyone had perished.

It soon became clear that no work could happen that day. Nackers said they "kind of talked Siegel down" from doing a paper that week—they had at first decided to do an issue of reruns—and then he and Loew went back home to Brooklyn. Welyczko, waiting in Madison, soon heard the news. "The decision was made not to publish. There was no way we could put out our funny paper after this had happened," he said. Tim Harrod said Hanson called to tell him about the cancellation. Hanson also said, "Remember what a big deal Oklahoma City was? Well, think how crazy this is going to be. The country is going to become super right-wing."

The staff then took a weird "dreamlike" week off, as Harrod put it. One day he went into a bar and realized that urban legends were already starting to form. One story was about a guy in the towers who had somehow slid to safety on a piece of debris, as if it was a sled on a snowy hillside. On another walk "in the still of the night," Harrod talked to a guy who said he'd been in the towers but escaped because he was Italian.

The next Monday they were all back in the office. Pete Haise, communicating from Wisconsin, was a big reason for that. Skipping even one issue meant losing a lot of money at a time when they could ill afford it. *The Onion* still had "a lot of buckets to choose from," Haise said. The website was still bringing in money. "But one of our biggest buckets [the print edition] just got completely erased."

"I need to print," Haise said. "We need to be in business. We had taken a week, and I was like, all right, everybody's got to take a week. This is insanity, right? Everyone's crying on TV." But, financially, no more time could be taken. Haise reasoned, correctly, that *The Onion* was not just potentially offensive headlines. They had the A.V. Club. They had classifieds. They had other features that weren't necessarily problematic. "We can do this differently," Haise told Siegel.

"I didn't want to be an asshole," Haise said. "I didn't want to be insensitive. That wasn't the idea. But I was like, 'Dude, you know where we're at.'"

So Siegel replied, "Yes, we can."

"That's all I really had to do with it, that it had to be done," Haise said. And what they did from there "was nothing short of absolutely brilliant."

Cohn said Siegel "immediately went to work cooking up what the tone should be." Siegel said, "There were times in the history of the paper where we would do a rerun issue," he said. "But you couldn't do a rerun issue that week. Readers would say, 'What the fuck is this?'" Loew remembered that the front-page headline planned for the canceled week had been "some story about Cheetos." But Siegel told him, "We can't put that out right now. That's gonna look so wrong if we don't deal with what just happened."

Even so, at first, they thought they would not run anything related to the World Trade Center destruction at all, "because everyone's traumatized as fuck," Hanson said in *MEL Magazine*. "Our normal, irreverent, edgy, cynical, dark humor wasn't going to be emotionally appropriate with this situation." That plan, however, did not last long, and soon they had decided to devote an entire issue to the attacks. Krewson remembered he and Garden saying, "I don't know, man; that sounds horrible. Sounds like we'll just be dancing on a bunch of graves." Siegel said:

Of course we're not going to do *that*. We knew we weren't gonna make jokes at anyone's expense, in a situation like that, where there's so much emotion. And pain. You just have to kind of almost just rephrase the pain slightly, and it comes out as laughter. It's cathartic laughter; it's a different form of laughter. I don't think we did anything in that first issue other than just express what people were feeling. But sometimes, at the root of humor is just truth.

There is a specific form of *Onion* joke, Siegel said, "where you just state reality very plainly." The pieces in that issue did so, but they were more than just jokes. They were also stories told to comfort the afflicted, and, in that mode, they were something human beings had been doing to help each other for thousands of years. Kolb said, "We didn't mean to do the full issue as a 9/11 issue. But clearly, this is all that is on our minds. Why would we not write about this? We were never like, 'You can't write about serious things.'" And then, she said, "we started writing, and we just had so much that we wanted to say, all this stuff that we wanted to print, that we did do that whole issue on 9/11." Krewson remembered Siegel encouraging the team: "I believe that you guys can do this. You just have to get in the right groove. I mean, we did a whole book of history of the twentieth century. We can do this. It's just one event. We're just expanding on it. We just have to get the right idea."

Like they had done hundreds of times, the editorial staff came together for their headline meeting to pitch their jokes. There were no fights that day. Siegel said, "That core group of writers had been together for almost ten years. So we're all so on the same page. [Nobody] would pitch a joke that went too far or wasn't in the right spirit. I don't remember anybody being like, 'No, that's offensive,' or 'That's the wrong message right now.' Or 'We'll get killed for that.' We were all very much on the same page in the meeting."

Loew, however, recalled in *MEL Magazine* that it was also terrifying, "because we're these kids from Wisconsin coming into New York City, and we're going to drop this silly comedy paper about this horrific tragedy. So we knew we had to get it right—it was like threading the eye of the needle."

Harrod helped get everyone out of their shock and hesitation at the start of the meeting by suggesting a headline that Hanson had thrown out after the Columbine school shooting in 1999. Newsweek had published a big front-cover headline that just said "WHY?" afterward, and Hanson had suggested that the next time there was a huge national tragedy they should just print a big "WHY?" on *The Onion*'s front page over a picture of a chicken crossing the road. So, Harrod suggested it. "It was a dumb idea and it didn't fit," he said, "but I threw that out just to lubricate the machine and get the ice broken. And everybody said no, and I didn't disagree. And we were off and running about real ideas." Siegel remembered, "We knew exactly what we were doing."

Cohn said it was "amazing" to watch Siegel go. She remembered him putting in massively long days that week, "pulling and editing and pulling and rewriting." She had been a fan of *The Onion* before they started dating. And then, a few months later, a "massive, global event, this seismic event happens, and he's my new boyfriend." She said he was "on fire."

Welyczko now had to design the special issue. For inspiration, he asked himself, "How is *USA Today* going to cover this? How was a sort of a very jingoistic version of *USA Today* going to respond to 9/11?" He and Siegel came up with an American flag "Special Report" banner for the front page, which also had four lead stories instead of the usual two or three. They would "overuse" red, white, and blue and patriotic symbols "like how network television covers elections, how it's just vomiting flags and red, white, and blue everywhere." Nackers and Loew created the "Holy Fucking Shit: Attack on America" logo; the catchphrase was written by Siegel.

The design team was making the special issue on top of also laying out the A.V. Club section of the paper like they did every week, as well as many ads. (That edition of the A.V. Club featured an interview with Laurie Anderson discussing her new show based on the Herman Melville novel *Moby-Dick*. In the piece, interviewer Keith Phipps notes that "*Moby-Dick* is about a quest that destroys the people questing.")

Harrod said Hanson was the "superstar" of that issue, having written "God Angrily Clarifies No-Kill Rule" and "American Life Turns into Bad Jerry Bruckheimer Movie," both of which "ended on poignant rather than funny notes" and were "masterful." The former ended with God crying, "and it wasn't maudlin or contrived. It just worked. It just fit perfectly. Which is a real testament to anyone's talent who can do that." In a 2021 documentary directed by Nick Fituri Scown and Julie Seabaugh called *Too Soon: Comedy After 9/11*, Hanson—the son of a minister—said, "These murders had been committed for religious reasons, because someone thought God wanted it done. And I was 100 percent sure that anyone who knew anything about religion would agree the purpose of God is to get us to not kill each other. And it just struck me as so sad that it was going to create Islamophobia" as well as "all this long-term cultural antagonism that was already bad. But it was going to become much, much worse. And it just seemed so tragic." Hanson was actually crying when he wrote the story.

Krewson wrote "Hijackers Surprised to Find Selves in Hell," which allowed him to use his creative storytelling abilities to imagine a wide array of terrible punishments, and Kolb wrote "Not Knowing What Else to Do, Woman Bakes American-Flag Cake," based on an actual event attended by Kolb. In the *Too Soon* documentary, Hanson said the cake piece was "very beautiful and very sincere," things you "normally don't think of when you think of *The Onion*." Karwowski got a one-liner headline joke on the front page—"Jerry Falwell: Is That Guy a

Ø the ONION

VOLUME 37 ISSUE 34   AMERICA'S FINEST NEWS SOURCE   27 SEPTEMBER-3 OCTOBER 2001

SPECIAL REPORT

Hugging Up 76,000 Percent
see NATION page 10A

Jerry Falwell: Is That Guy A Dick Or What?
see PEOPLE page 3C

Rest Of Country Temporarily Feels Deep Affection For New York
see NATION page 8A

Massive Attack On Pentagon Page 14 News
see NATION page 14A

STATshot
A look at the numbers that shape your world.

How Have We Spent The Past Two Weeks?
1. Crying
2. Staring at hands
3. Feeling guilty about renting video
4. Calling loved one
5. Thinking about donating blood
6. Watching TV for nine hours, finally getting up, going to corner store for Cheez Doodles, eating Cheez Doodles, realizing Cheez Doodles aren't helping, throwing Cheez Doodles away

Above: Flanked by Condoleezza Rice and Donald Rumsfeld, President Bush pledges to "exact revenge, just as soon as we know who we're exacting revenge against and where they are."

U.S. Vows To Defeat Whoever It Is We're At War With

WASHINGTON, DC—In a televised address to the American people Tuesday, a determined President Bush vowed that the U.S. would defeat "whoever exactly it is we're at war with here."

"America's enemy, be it Osama bin Laden, Saddam Hussein, the Taliban, a multinational coalition of terrorist organizations, any of a rogue's gallery of violent Islamic fringe groups, or an entirely different, non-Islamic aggressor we've never even heard of... be warned,"

Attack On America

Bush said during an 11-minute speech from the Oval Office. "The United States is preparing to strike, directly and decisively, against you, whoever you are, just as soon as we have a rough idea of your identity and a reasonably decent estimate as to where your base is located."

Added Bush: "That is, assuming you have a base."

Bush is acting with the full support of Congress, which on Sept. 14 authorized him to use any necessary
see WAR page 6

Hijackers Surprised To Find Selves In Hell

'We Expected Eternal Paradise For This,' Say Suicide Bombers

JAHANNEM, OUTER DARKNESS—The hijackers who carried out the Sept. 11 attacks on the World Trade Center and Pentagon expressed confusion and surprise Monday to find themselves in the lowest plane of Na'ar, Islam's Hell.

"I was promised I would spend eternity in Paradise,

being fed honeyed cakes by 67 virgins in a tree-lined garden, if only I would fly the airplane into one of the Twin Towers," said Mohammed Atta, one of the hijackers of American Airlines Flight 11, between
see HIJACKERS page 12

Right: Mohammed Atta (top) and Ahmed al-Haznawi.

American Life Turns Into Bad Jerry Bruckheimer Movie

Above: An actual scene from real life.

NEW YORK—In the two weeks since terrorists crashed hijacked planes into the World Trade Center and Pentagon, American life has come to resemble a bad Jerry Bruckheimer-produced action/disaster movie, shellshocked citizens reported Tuesday.

"Terrorist hijackings, buildings blowing up, thousands of people dying—these are
see MOVIE page 13

Not Knowing What Else To Do, Woman Bakes American-Flag Cake

TOPEKA, KS—Feeling helpless in the wake of the horrible Sept. 11 terrorist attacks that killed thousands, Christine Pearson baked a cake and decorated it like an American flag Monday.

"I had to do something to force myself away from the TV," said Pearson, 33, carefully laying rows of strawberry slices on the white-fudge-frosting-covered cake. "All of those
see CAKE page 12

Above: Pearson

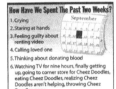

The 9/11 issue.

Dick or What?"—because of Falwell saying that America had been attacked due to its openness to homosexuality, which "released God's protection of our lands." Falwell, Karwowski said, was supposedly the "leader of a love-based religion." Yet when Falwell was faced with "people who need reassurance," he decided to use that moment to make a cruel, divisive diatribe.

In the *Too Soon* documentary, Hanson said, "*Onion* writers have always been very sincere in what they're trying to say. Even if they use sarcasm as the way of conveying their message, the message is not sarcastic." There were some rejected headlines during that first meeting. One of them was "America Stronger than Ever, Says Quadragon Officials," which Hanson said would have been exactly the kind of thing *The Onion* would have written in a different context. "We were not cracking jokes in the traditional sense," Harrod added. "We were engaging the real feelings that had come out during the foregoing week." He and Krewson collaborated on "U.S. Vows to Defeat Whoever It Is We're at War With." The very effective graphic for that article showed the entire world as "possible locations of terrorists." (This included the United States. The Oklahoma City bombing had taken place a few years earlier, in 1995.) Maria Schneider felt the closest the issue got to making fun of anyone was "President Urges Calm, Restraint Among Nation's Ballad Singers."

The issue also featured a funny chart of TV listings. Karwowski remembers that at Krewson's house on the day of the attacks, they had been flipping through all the cable channels. "And it was news, news, news, news, *Golden Girls*, news, news. Whoever was running *Golden Girls* was like, 'Nope, we're good,' and that actually made it in the paper."

Some of the noneditorial staff back in Wisconsin got wind of what they were doing and were appalled, telling the writers that if they went ahead with the issue, they would quit. Karwowski remembered saying, "Well, why don't you wait until we're done?" Nackers said they were much more careful about that issue than they had been with any other, asking noneditorial staff like the office manager what they thought. Garden said, "Rob was like, 'People are reading us; people are looking to us. We can make important points.'"

Kolb said they had never cared about offending anyone before. But this was different. "We didn't want to make people feel worse. We only wanted to make people feel better."

We were never a patriotic paper. But we definitely did not do anything that we felt was blatantly antipatriotic or too political because we just didn't feel it was the time for that sort of thing. We had some stories that we didn't run that were more about "This is fucking your fault, Republicans, for going to war in this area this many years ago," but we stayed away from that sort of thing because we didn't want to be divisive. We wanted to be whatever the opposite of divisive is.

Garden was one of the people most concerned about the impact. "I was just like, 'This is gonna ruin us. We're just going to be doomed. We just got here to New York, and now we're gonna be chased out of New York by a torch-carrying mob.'" Welyczko said, "Pete Haise was incredibly nervous and didn't want us to fuck anything up, and didn't want us to make anyone mad, and was really scared of us publishing this issue."

But Welyczko also remembered reading the stories as he was laying out the issue and having an overwhelming feeling of, "Oh my God, I can't believe I get to work with these people" and being "so in awe of what they were producing, of just how razor spot-on it was." With that awe was also worry: "Oh my God, I hope people get it. I hope people get it. Just not being able to fathom how people would react to this and being a little scared, but just putting my faith in these incredible people and what they were producing. Their immense talent to navigate what was going on emotionally and factually."

Welyczko said it had easily been a hundred-hour week. But they were "all really excited and really proud of it. So proud of what we had done. But so tired. So just drained and then just kind of waiting for the shoe to drop."

"Our format was a really great asset," Siegel said. "We weren't Letterman, where we had to stand in front of an audience and make jokes." *The Onion* could hide behind the monolithic journalism voice. The issue was online by September 26 and hit the streets on September 27.

The very first response they got was a fax filled with the words "Not funny, not funny, not funny, not funny" in a giant font. "I remember it being passed around," Harrod said. "And when it got to Krewson he went like, 'Hmm, interesting,' and then violently crumpled it and threw it on the floor." The first response, however, was basically the only negative comment. Because then the positive ones started rolling in.

There were thousands of them, emails and faxes. Loew said, "We got a stack of emails this high from all these people just saying like, 'I just lost my fiancé,' 'I just lost my brother,' you know, all this stuff. And 'I've been lost in grief. But your issue made me laugh again for the first time, which I thought I would never do.'" Siegel said it was "one of those moments where it felt like we were actually doing something useful." It felt really, really good.

"People were blown away," Cohn said. "It was many people's first laugh. It was certainly the first publicly distributed laugh. And it just struck such a chord

From: ▓▓▓▓▓▓ ▓▓▓▓▓▓
To: <editorial@theonion.com>
Date: Wednesday, September 26, 2001 2:14 AM
Subject: Best Wishes

Hello Onion Staff,
Last week I saw the Towers burning while riding the Q train over the
Manhattan Bridge. I saw the second one fall when I was standing out in front
of the New School on 5th Avenue. I always read you guys and was wondering
how it would be possible to handle this. I always get much indignant lefty
relief and laughter from reading you, but all my usual smartass defense
mechanisms have failed me these past two weeks and I wondered how you guys
would handle this. I feel like I am sounding prosaic and corny - I just
wanted you to know that I was moved by reading your paper this week. It made
me cry, especially the "Bad Jerry Bruckheimer movie columns and the "Hugging
Up" caption. You prove me right that many skeptics are the deepest lovers of
people and that sarcasm is most cutting when it's informed by anger at the
abuse and exploitation of sentiment, not a lack of sentiment on the part of
the sarcastic person. Anyway thank you.
All the best,
▓▓▓▓▓▓
Brooklyn, NY

From: ▓▓▓▓▓▓ ▓▓▓▓▓▓
To: <editorial@theonion.com>
Date: Wednesday, September 26, 2001 11:24 AM
Subject: latest issue

When I opened the Onion for my weekly update, I wasn't sure what to expect. Maybe I hoped you wouldn't
address recent events at all - I've laughed at so many of your stories, even when they seemed wildly inappropriate
and maybe in poor taste. I wasn't ready to laugh about this.
I read every article in your latest issue. And I was amazed at how you found the absolute perfect mixture of
comedy and empathy. Each article was a humorous look at how we are coping, a funny response to recent events
that made me smile and even made me tear up a little. I don't know how you did it, but you managed to be
sensitive and caring while entertaining - and without sacrificing the traditional tone of your humor. What an
achievment. So I just wanted to thank you for this masterful, sensitive and funny issue of the Onion. It was just what
I needed.
Sincerely, ▓▓▓▓▓▓

From: ▓▓▓▓▓
To: <editorial@theo▓▓▓
Date: Wednesday, September 2▓, ▓▓
Subject: Intel Community Thanks You!

Dear Onion,
I am a linguist with military intel. We have been working 80+ hours a
week even before this latest round of attacks on America. The Onion is read
aloud and passed around before our daily briefs. We loved the Onion even
before the new issue. We wondered aloud the day after the attacks about the
next issue. Thank you for not caving in and pussing out in the face of this
tragedy. This was the best issue ever. Laughter is needed here and you've
provided it in abundance. I just wanted to thank you for keeping the faith
in style. As an American, I apologize for all the humorless fuckers who
have probably called the latest issue tasteless and inappropriate. They
should move to Afghanistan where laughter is outlawed right along with
toilet paper, soccer, pissing while standing and flying kites.
Unfortunately, even your best attempts to exaggerate the knee-jerk demand
for bloody revenge do not come close to the truth. We want to exact all
that and more. And we will.

Thanks for the laughs
▓▓▓▓▓▓ ▓▓▓▓▓▓

To: <editorial@theonion.com>
Date: Wednesday, September 26, 2001 5:15 AM
Subject: Excellence in journalism

Not long after the second tower collapsed, I suddenly found myself feeling
sorry for, of all people, comedians. With everything the President has to
say all of a sudden being met with the total agreement and thunderous
applause of even those Americans who didn't vote for him last year, this is
a terrible time to have to depend on making people laugh in order to put
food on the table. After all, what is there that we can make fun of
without finding ourselves accused of being Un-American?

I don't know how you guys did it, but when (if) the dust settles, the Onion
deserves recognition as having produced the first genuinely funny,
intelligent satire from this entire fiasco. I don't know if there's an
industry award that can be given out for that, but you deserve it. Kudos.

A sample of the thousands of messages The Onion *received from readers after the 9/11 issue came out.*

From: ▓▓▓▓▓
To: <infomat@theonion.com>
Date: Tuesday, September 25, 2001 10:16 PM
Subject: Regarding the America under Attack issue

jesus and mary.

more than one person asked me, last week, if i thought you guys were going to make fun of the attacks. I replied that i thought you might hold off for a few months, and then do a story that poked at them obliquely, if at all.

I want to extend my humble and shamefaced apologies for not ascribing to you the collective wrought-iron testicles and awe-inspiring empathy that you so masterfully command. i find myself unable to express, to my satisfaction, the depth of my appreciation for what you have created.

I will say that I will preserve the hard copy of this issue, as I have preserved nothing else from these god-awful times.

Thank you.

▓▓▓

From: ▓▓▓▓▓ ▓▓▓▓▓▓▓▓
To: <editorial@theonion.com>
Date: Wednesday, September 26, 2001 5:15 AM
Subject: You have earned my profound respect.

This is not hate mail,

Satire always has, at it's core, a kernel of truth. Because of this, satire is more difficult to write than farce. The more horrifying the truth, the more difficult it is to spin it into satire.

While the Onion occasionally wanders into farce. Satire is what has made it great. The kernel of horrible truth has made it great.

Now, when truth is needed more than ever. When bringing the truth to light is more dangerous than ever. You have impressed me.

I was a fan before. I enjoyed your magazine. I envied the consistent skill with which you plied your craft. (I know how difficult it is to write humorously week after week.) But now you have my respect.

As you deal with the repercussions of your recent issue, (I hope they are not as bad as I assume they will be) I want you to know that myself, and many of the intelligent, levelheaded but silent people who comprise your readership appreciate and respect what you have done.

Christ, did that sound like a fucking long-winded Hallmark card or what?

▓▓▓

From: ▓▓▓
Reply-To: ▓▓▓
To: <editorial@theonion.com>
Date: Tuesday, September 25, 2001 11:00 PM
Subject: Midnight Praise

Guys,
I've read The Onion online for I don't know how many years now and have always managed to laugh my ass off. Right now, it's 11:45 p.m. on Sept. 25 and I'm three-quarters of the way through your "Holy Fucking Shit" edition online and am amazed. In fact, while I can't exactly justify what I'm about to say seeing as I have no part in it, I'm fucking proud of you guys. I think you found the right mix of reverence and humor and managed to pull it off--this from a generation supposedly to cynical to give a shit.

And what prompted me to write this is the "God Angrily Clarifies 'Don't Kill' Rule" piece. As an atheist, the last two weeks have driven me wild with confusion and rage at all these people turning to this idea of God...the same God whose name was invoked in the destruction. I still feel that way, but something about your article seemed to redeem, if not my fellow man, the basic concepts of religion in the first place.

I don't know what it says about the world we live in that you guys and Letterman are the people who've made the most sense to me in the past couple of weeks, but you're doing something right. From the New Yorker to the New York Times, from CNN to CBS News (and lucky me, all I get here in Brooklyn without cable is CBS2: When Pablo fuckin Guzman is your most reliable source of news on a network that quotes Nostradamus, well...), I've seen relatively decent NEWS coverage (nothing stellar) but the commentary has been so insipid... Eh, but what does that matter? I've got a kitten crying outside my window, a ride on the F tomorrow, but three more article in The Onion to read.

A million thanks for doing your peeps proud. This is me waving a flag for The Onion.

If you ever make it out to Park Slope, give me a holler; I know a Dominican place that makes pork chops so good, it'll make you want to slap your momma.

▓▓▓
Brooklyn (yo!)

of truth in so many people." Kolb said, "It was so meaningful to us that people understood what we were doing. And that we'd helped them feel better." Others in the world of comedy also took notice. In the *Too Soon* documentary, David Cross said, "No other type of comedy, whether it was sketch comedy or stand-ups or anything that broached the subject, came close to *The Onion*, just hitting every level, hitting every tone." "Weird Al" Yankovic told me:

When the nation was reeling in pain and shock after 9/11, *The Onion* took on the seemingly impossible task of putting out an issue directly addressing the tragedy. Even though the humor was shockingly dark, it was also oddly healing. During a period where people were wondering if we'd ever be able to laugh at anything again, *The Onion* took those first baby steps, and I honestly think that helped a lot of people believe we were not going to live in fear. We were going to be okay.

Readership doubled in response to the issue. In the end, Welyczko said, "It was a masterstroke. I mean, I think it's even more so than *Our Dumb Century*. It's the greatest thing *The Onion* ever did. The 9/11 issue. Absolutely masterful. There is not one misstep within it editorially. The things that were funny were genuinely funny that anyone could laugh at, even people who had experienced the tragedy on the ground." They had floated between satire and commentary "in a way that I think was very nuanced and I think very respectful. And I think reflected very much the reaction of comedy to tragedy." People would get bent out of shape all the time about *Onion* stories, he said, "legitimately or not legitimately, but somebody was always pissed off at us about something. And I think that was one issue that everyone was like, not only is it funny without being milquetoast, but it's perfect. The voice was perfect." Karwowski said, "I think it was one of the first times people realized we're not, you know, just sarcastic monsters." People would say, "You guys make fun of everything." But that wasn't true. "We're very careful about who we attack," he said. "We're always trying to punch up."

Writer Mike Sacks said in the *MEL Magazine* oral history:

If you look at it now, it's very gentle. It wasn't the typical *The Onion* necessarily, but they kind of crept back into it in the perfect way. Comedy fans especially needed a first take on it. We needed someone to say, "It's okay." Not to make fun of the situation, but to make fun of our anguish and our confusion. It was a real fine line. There really was no margin for error. They really had to stick the landing, and they stuck it.

Some even felt it was Pulitzer-worthy. *Philadelphia Daily News* editor Zach Stalberg voted to make it a finalist.

What stands out for me today is the way *The Onion* expressed grief and outrage about the attacks while also providing a deeper historical context within the jokes. In the "News in Brief" section, for instance, one of the five short items is called "Bush Sr. Apologies to Son for Funding Bin Laden in '80s." The story read: "'I'm sorry, son,' Bush told President George W. Bush. 'We thought it was a good idea at the time because he was part of a group fighting communism in Central Asia. We called them 'freedom fighters' back then. I know it sounds weird. You sort of had to be there.'"

The issue also included a "Parent Corner" article written by Joe Garden called "Talking to Your Child About the WTC Attack," which went into detail about the roots of present-day Islamic fundamentalism. Garden's brother—a religion professor who specialized in medieval Islamic history—happened to be visiting him in Brooklyn at the time, and since his flight was canceled, he stayed in New York another week and helped him write the story.

Siegel said, "I definitely spent a lot of the two weeks following it doing interviews about 'the death of irony' and 'will we ever laugh again?' Which both struck me as ridiculous, stupid questions." I asked Siegel how he responded. "The obvious," he said. "Humor is a coping mechanism. Humor is a way of processing terrible things. Most comedians, they do it as a means of self-therapy, to handle and to manage their pain. That's what humor is. I mean, certainly what satire is. It's a way of making sense of horrible things and making them less scary and taking control over them."

September 11 inspired a lot of people to reassess their lives. And their relationships. A few months after the 9/11 issue, Kolb and Hanson's relationship ended. They had been together for seven years. "We should have broken up long before," Kolb said.

Still, Hanson would be right on the money with his prediction that the United States would soon go into reactionary, jingoistic, and opportunistic mode. And as Kolb told me:

The city was for months so horrible and dark and just terrible. It was so terrifying. And it really honestly felt like everything in the world was going to change. And then you know what? It didn't. I mean, we went to war, and that was huge and stupid, and there was definitely a lot more of certain types of racism. There was more fear. But I thought that people would put their lives in perspective and life would not be as dumb and meaningless. I thought, "This is so huge that we are all going to live better; we're going to be better people." I thought there would be some major shift in all of society. And then I just realized, "Oh." That wasn't going to happen. It just went back to normal after like a year.

It is safe to say that if *The Onion* had been owned by a big corporation in 2001—if the Comedy Central deal had gone through, for instance—the 9/11 issue would never have happened. Their lawyers would not have allowed it. Pete Haise, the Milwaukee sub-shop owner, did.

Chapter 13

They had now been in New York for a couple of years. And despite the boost to the website's traffic from the 9/11 issue, the publicity, and the acclaim, *The Onion* office was hemorrhaging cash. Pete Haise's hustle was finally meeting a reality that it just couldn't handle. They were now in the red to the tune of $100,000 a month while competing in one of the biggest media markets on the planet. More full-page apartment-complex ads, modestly priced movie options on *Onion* articles, and the occasional book advance were not going to get them out of this. At one of the events the group attended when they first arrived, Siegel met fellow former Madisonian David Zucker, of *Airplane!* fame, who asked them if they wanted to make a film, which eventually became *The Onion Movie*. But the process had turned into a nightmare, and the film—which went straight to DVD—would not be released for years.

Jeff Haupt, who was successfully corunning the Boulder/Denver branch and would later oversee *The Onion*'s print franchise operations in multiple cities, told me he wouldn't even know where to begin in New York. "It's so overwhelming. You're trying to operate in probably the hardest market ever." And Haupt said the people who Pete Haise had running the office in Madison and Milwaukee were "woefully underprepared." The held-together-with-toothpicks-and-gum model was finally collapsing.

A basic problem, Andrew Welyczko said, was the lack of "even the most basic sort of institutional financial controls or structure, or any kind of business structure." *The Onion* "was always this very creativity-forward organization. It was about the writers first and foremost. Maybe the second level was people like myself or Jun Ueno, or other designers or photographers, or people serving the needs of the creative content. And then the salespeople who are just trying to generate money." Everything else, he said, was Haise. "He was accounts payable, accounts receivable, the president, the CEO, HR—it was all him. And it was no way to run a business." Welyczko added, "*The Onion* was remarkably financially successful as a small local business. It punched above its weight in terms of influence and recognition, and at its core it was profitable and paid its bills . . . *right up* until the time it opened the New York office. That was the tipping point where *The Onion*, the company, tried to jump up to the status of *The Onion*, nationally revered media outlet, and failed miserably."

In January 2003, one of the first casualties of their tanking economic situation was designer Scott Templeton. The Madison office had moved a few years earlier from its State Street location to a tidier office on the twelfth floor of 131 West Wilson Street. Templeton had just returned from vacation when Welyczko gave him the bad news. The Milwaukee business office had decided that the design staff needed to cut a position, and "faced with this Sophie's choice," Welyczko had told publisher Chris Cranmer that Templeton would be most likely to land on his feet if he was let go. Templeton was blindsided by the layoff, an abrupt end to eight and a half years at *The Onion*.

Remaining staff had already had their salaries cut or frozen. Hanson said he went from $90,000 a year to $75,000. John Krewson said the promise was that their pay would eventually go up to those levels again—but it never happened. New York was supposed to have been an expansion of their fortunes. It was becoming the opposite.

But laying off staff and salary cuts were not enough. Not long afterward that year, Haise realized he just couldn't do it anymore. He said he had been loaning the company his own money to stay afloat, and now "I had nothing. I had just gotten married, and *The Onion* was on a beeline straight down." The stress was so bad it was making him actively sick, and he was breaking out in hives from his neck to his knees. So in April 2003, Haise decided to sell his ownership shares to David Schafer, who then became majority owner. According to legal documents describing the process, Haise received $1.7 million. "And that was the end for me of a hell of a crazy, crazy ride," Haise said. "It was my time. I'm only built to go so far. I'm not a corporate guy." (Some of the writers told me they thought Haise had been forced out by Schafer due to incompetence. Steve Hannah told me this was not the case. Schafer just wanted to have a controlling interest in the business. "Pete was never forced out.") A January 2004 *Greater*

Milwaukee Today article about Haise leaving quotes him saying: "I had no problem letting go of *The Onion*. It was a transition, but I was very OK about the decision." He remained a minority shareholder.

Haise told me *The Onion* had just grown far bigger than he ever thought possible. "We never imagined people over twenty-five or twenty-nine would ever read it. We never imagined we could make a living doing it. We never imagined so many things," he said. According to a 2014 *Wautatosa Now* article, Haise became a stay-at-home dad for several years while his wife, Susan, got her own business off the ground, a regional franchise called Neroli Salon & Spa. He then opened up a custom framing shop/art gallery with a nice upstairs bar that people could rent out for local events and joined a local organization that helped new small businesspeople get their projects off the ground.

If a frame shop seems odd after *The Onion*, Haise said in the article, "I thought, 'This is civilized. It's creative. It's fun. It's crafty. It's people-oriented, which kind of fits strangely and oddly with publishing, (where) you're laying out pages and playing with space. It's quite similar." The article notes, "After the 15-year roller coaster ride that was *The Onion*, Haise said he's happy to take it slow. 'I went through chaos running what was an exciting and adventurous kind of afterschool club that became this huge phenomenon nationally,' said Haise." Though he has since gone on to other business ventures, Haise lives in the area to this day.

Owner and investor David Schafer's task was now to create a high-level institutional and business structure at *The Onion* for the first time, which was not a task for the weak of heart. He convinced Steve Hannah to finally come on board as CEO to do the job.

Hannah signed on in 2004. It was the first time in the fifteen years of its existence that the self-creating, self-propelling *Onion* had had a person who could conceivably be called a "boss," and as far as I know, aside from Schafer and lawyer Ken Artis, also the first time someone born before 1965 had ever played any major role in operations, aside from perhaps a few phone calls with Tim Keck's mom in 1988. Hannah was—Lord help us—a baby boomer, in his midfifties. He enjoyed *The Onion*. But his worldview seems to have been on a different planet from the editorial staff.

Hannah's entry marked the beginning of a significant shift in *The Onion's* organizational and editorial style. It was the professionalization of *The Onion*:

the transformation of a unique—maybe even eccentric or insular—long-tenured editorial group with extremely high standards for comedy, deep distrust in anything corporate or business-y, and a total indifference to Type A careerism, all funded by Haise hustle, into a multiplatform, mostly digital national media company staffed largely by young, highly educated professionals who could have done well in a variety of organizations, run by men with very different administrative methods.

Welyczko said everyone was really freaked out at first about the new management, though the writers were glad Haise was no longer running things. However, Hannah came in open and friendly, "wanting to talk to people and get opinions and ideas and very, very gracious," a "sort of grandfatherly person." He was also "very public about not wanting to interfere with the creative process."

Hannah then started "pushing buttons and pulling levers" to create basic business structures, including, in 2005, bringing in a young man named Mike McAvoy as controller. McAvoy was twenty-five and had previously worked as a financial analyst at a bank and a for-profit college helping them with their IPO. He did not yet have any experience working in publishing or with creative people, though he told me some of his best friends had always been artists.

McAvoy was born in 1980 and grew up in Waukesha with three siblings, a dentist dad (who was originally from Brooklyn, New York), and a mom who kept the dentist office's books. As a kid, he would help stuff envelopes with invoices and found the mechanics of running a business fascinating. He started reading The Onion in high school—Pete Haise's mid-'90s Milwaukee expansion—and thought it was "pretty cool and very underground." He had three majors at the University of St. Thomas in St. Paul, Minnesota: Spanish, finance, and accounting—not because he wanted to be in finance, but because "I was always taught that it's the language of business" and essential to know if you wanted to succeed in that world.

In 2004, the Minneapolis Onion outpost opened, and McAvoy met Steve Hannah through Hannah's son, who was doing Onion distribution and knew one of McAvoy's roommates. Hannah met and hired him in February 2005. Hannah, McAvoy said, liked people who "have a high upside." (Todd Hanson told me McAvoy spoke only in business jargon. This was mostly accurate, though he was always willing to translate.) "Steve loves the story, you know," McAvoy said. If he "met someone at a shoe store," he'd want to bring them on.

McAvoy, though, said he was the most credentialed finance person *The Onion* had ever had, which I don't doubt. Like so many others, he had never imagined actually working for *The Onion*, and here he was—a "dream job" worth the pay cut from the for-profit college.

McAvoy seemed to find the multilayered, interconnecting, and constantly changing logic problems and mathematical puzzles of finance, accounting, and profit-making fascinating; he was probably quite good at it. He would stay at *The Onion* for more than fourteen years, rising steadily through the ranks: controller, 2005–2006; chief financial officer, 2007–2008; chief operating officer, 2008–2015; president, 2013–2019; and CEO, 2015–2019. (During this time, he said *The Onion* did much better than most other media companies, and they did it without a private equity [PE] firm or some rich guy pumping money into the operation. Schafer had provided a $500,000 bridge loan for working capital when he bought Dikkers's shares, but other than that he did not put any of his money into *The Onion*. It always operated on a cash-flow basis, which was "unheard of" and made *The Onion*'s operation unique. McAvoy said, "There's things, obviously, that we wish we could have done better, but to be able to protect the integrity of the editorial product forever was pretty special, given the rest of the media world.")

It was good that McAvoy enjoyed crunching numbers, because when he started in 2005, two years after Haise's departure, *The Onion*'s financial operations were "a train wreck." He had his work cut out for him. "Nobody knew where the money was," he said. Nobody knew what was in *The Onion*'s bank account or what people's salaries were. Taxes were wonky, and financial procedures were nonsensical. The person who signed the checks was in a different city from the person who cut the checks, so the Milwaukee manager would print a bunch of them from QuickBooks and put the bag of paper checks on the Badger Bus (a popular local transport service taking people to airports and so on) down to Chicago via courier service to get them signed—twenty-two dollars per trip, McAvoy recalled—after which the checks would be sent back to Milwaukee. (Why they didn't just open a FedEx account was a mystery.) McAvoy said many checks were never delivered or cashed; at one point, he found about fifty of them sitting in a former manager's desk. Others got lost while traveling. McAvoy said he also found traces of Haise's sub shop mixed in with *The Onion* early on, though he didn't think this was due to anything other than a haphazard approach to organization. He also sought out inefficiencies and found *The Onion* was paying twice as much for printing in Madison as they should have been. The perk of fifty-yard-line seats at Badger games that apparently came with the overpricing was absurd. How could that possibly make up for such an obvious waste of money?

Hannah, McAvoy said, was entrepreneurial, but his experience was more along the lines of managing a newsroom budget—a smaller lens than being in charge of all revenue and expenses for an entire company. He didn't get the bigger picture. McAvoy believed he did—and set to work making the numbers clean, functional, and appropriate to their stations.

Many very smart people have come through *The Onion*, but it seems safe to say that this was the first time a very smart person like this had arrived. Indeed, Welyczko told me that the only thing McAvoy cared about was the numbers. Other young staff were experts in Photoshop or writing certain breeds of joke; McAvoy had advanced skills in Excel spreadsheet making. Multiple former staffers also indicated that though McAvoy might have been excellent with finance, he perhaps had some work to do on his bedside manner and his understanding of the interpersonal context of his financial decisions. Haupt put it this way: "Mike was a very intelligent guy. He was a great accountant. And it sort of ended right there." (I told McAvoy that people had, um, commented on his interest in financial projections. He said of course he was interested. "To me, the entire job was balancing creative and business. Without having a successful business, you can't finance the creative side, and if you don't understand and appreciate the creative editorial side, you won't have a business. So we were always threading a needle, and I think if we didn't, there's no way it would still be what it is today.")

A few years earlier, Hannah had also recommended his nephew Sean Mills ("It's like a theme going on here," Haupt said) to Schafer. Mills did have appropriate experience in digital media and brought needed knowledge and skills to the table, however. In 1999, he had founded Agile Interactive in San Francisco; its focus was buying and selling online advertising. Agile was sold to DoubleClick in 2001, and Mills's technology, according to his LinkedIn page, "quickly became the industry standard for the online advertising industry." Mills was hired as director of the national sales team from 2001–2003 and then moved up to president from 2003–2011. He seems to have been a dedicated and insightful proponent of *The Onion*'s work. Still, *The Onion*'s primary source of revenue was now moving into a very different world from the tangible, brick-and-mortar space where Haise had cocktails with business owners and readers held paper coupons in their hands.

At first, the Madison staff—designers, ad reps, and so on—found the professionalism a refreshing change. They were now in a new "bougie" office space in a renovated warehouse building where Hannah, McAvoy, and the rest of the new and growing *Onion* business staff were headquartered. No more piles of trash and Gen X kitsch. Now it was white walls, high ceilings, and trendy exposed ductwork. The A.V. Club had moved to the Chicago satellite office already due to the staff needing to be in a bigger metro area to do their jobs well, though Stephen Thompson had stayed in Madison.

Hannah spent the first six months or so saying and doing all the right things, Welyczko said. A "honeymoon period." Then the honeymoon was over. "Steve put his people in place, he put a structure in place," Welyczko said, "and once he had that structure, now that *The Onion* had proper HR and proper accounting, and had people who were tracking A to B to C in terms of how the business worked, he then leaned into those people and wasn't interested in the rest of us anymore." Hannah was finished talking about the past and became focused on where he was taking *The Onion* in the future. And the friendliness dropped away. Welyczko said:

> That sounds really dramatic [but] it really was. . . . *The Onion* was now much better funded; it was no longer in danger of going out of business. The constant conflict between Pete Haise and the creative staff wasn't there anymore. But it felt like things had gone so overboard in creating this corporate structure, this business structure behind the scenes, that it no longer felt like *The Onion*. . .
>
> Pete Haise knew what *The Onion* was; he was just in way over his head in understanding how to navigate. But I never doubted for a second that Pete knew and loved *The Onion*. And I think a lot of people started to wonder about Steve Hannah. Did *he* understand *The Onion*? He certainly understood how to run a business and how to put things in a format that made sense to him and to David Schafer. But it all started to feel like we were

working for an accounting firm. All the little freedoms we used to take for granted started to go away.

According to Welyczko, Hannah also started criticizing what people were wearing. "I don't remember there ever being a memo about a dress code. But he was very abrupt with people who he felt were dressed inappropriately." Meanwhile, all the other satellite offices—along with New York, now Chicago, Denver, Boulder, Los Angeles, San Francisco, and Minneapolis—tooled along, though Welyczko, a shareholder, said the large-market papers "never sustained any kind of financial success." Denver/Boulder under the Haupts, however, "did extremely well for a while, as did Milwaukee and the Twin Cities." McAvoy put it this way: Each office was only as good as their local manager, and most of them were not great. Print was good for marketing, but as a business it was variable, expensive, inefficient, very time consuming, and very labor intensive. What really kept *The Onion* running financially was digital.

Hannah needed help and advice, so he turned to an old Wisconsin friend with an MBA from Stanford named Bill Wernecke, whom he'd known for thirty years and who had run a family lumberyard business in a small town north of Milwaukee called Cedarburg for decades—managing and moving from place to place a material, real-world product. Wernecke did not have a publishing background, true, but he worked hard to understand it. And many of *The Onion*'s problems weren't about publishing anyway. The piles of uncashed checks were only the beginning. Wernecke told me Hannah was getting financial statements sixty to ninety days after the end of each month and asked him what was actually a "reasonable and customary" time to wait for those. "And I said, about five days after the end of the month." Other issues included the accounts-receivable person living in Minneapolis, while the accounts-payable person was in Madison. "They had people spread out all over, and they weren't coordinated at all."

The staffers I spoke with (except McAvoy) all had high praise for Wernecke. People liked him a lot and respected his calm, researched, common-sense advice. Welyczko said Wernecke "was that rare bird in that he was a boomer who didn't try to be with the kids. He was so unhip that the dial went all the way around

AMERICA'S FINEST SPORTS NEWS SOURCE

NASCAR Cancels Remainder Of Season Following David Foster Wallace's Death

LOUDON, NH—Shock, grief, and the overwhelming sense of loss that has swept the stock car racing community following the death by apparent suicide of writer David Foster Wallace has moved NASCAR to cancel the remainder of its 2008 season in respect for the acclaimed but troubled author of *Infinite Jest, A Supposedly Fun Thing I'll Never Do Again*, and *Brief Interviews With Hideous Men*.

In deference to the memory of Wallace, whose writing on alienation, sadness, and corporate sponsorship made him the author of the century in stock car racing circles and whom NASCAR chairman Brian France called "perhaps the greatest American writer to emerge in recent memory, and definitely our most human," officials would not comment on how points, and therefore this year's championship, would be determined.

At least for the moment, drivers found it hard to think about the Sprint Cup.

"All race long on Sunday, I was dealing with the unreality presented me by his absence," said #16 3M Ford Fusion driver Greg Biffle, who won Sunday's Sylvania 300 at New Hampshire Motor Speedway, the first race in the Chase For The Cup, and would therefore have had the lead in the championship. "I first read *Infinite Jest* in 1998 when my gas-can man gave me a copy when I was a rookie in the Craftsman Truck Series, and I was immediately struck dumb by the combination of effortlessness and earnestness of his prose. Here was a writer who loved great, sprawling, brilliantly punctuated sentences that spread in a kind of textual kudzu across the page, yet in every phrase you got a sense of his yearning to relate and convey the importance of every least little thing. It's no exaggeration to say that when I won Rookie of the Year that season it was David Foster Wallace that helped me keep that achievement, and therefore my life, in perspective."

"I'm flooded with feelings of—for lack of a better concept—incongruity," said Jimmie Johnson, driver of the #48 Lowe's Chevrolet who is known throughout racing for his habit of handing out copies of Wallace's novels to his fans. "David Foster Wallace could comprehend and articulate the sadness in a luxury cruise, a state fair, a presidential campaign, anything. But empathy, humanity, and compassion so strong as to be almost incoherent ran through that same sadness like connective tissue through muscle, affirming the value of the everyday, championing the banal yet true, acknowledging the ironic as it refused to give in to irony."

"And now he's gone," Johnson added. "He's taken himself away. We can't possibly race now."

David Foster Wallace's work came to stock car racing in the mid-1990s, just as the sport began experiencing almost geometric yearly growth. But the literary atmosphere of the sport was moribund, mired in the once-flamboyant but decidedly aging mid-1960s stylings of Tom Wolfe, whose bombastic essays—notably "The Last American Hero Is Junior Johnson. Yes!"—served as the romantic, quasi-elegiac be-all and end-all for NASCAR fans and series participants alike. When a new generation of young drivers like Jeff Gordon arrived on the scene, sporting new sponsorship deals on their fireproof coveralls and dog-eared copies of *Broom Of The System* under their arms, a seed crystal was dropped into the supersaturated literary solution of American motorsports.

"Suddenly DFW was everywhere," said #88 Amp Energy Chevrolet driver Dale Earnhardt Jr., whose enthusiasm for Wallace is apparent in both his deep solemnity and the *Infinite Jest*-inspired Great Concavity tattoo on his left shoulder. "My Dad was against him, actually, in part because he was a contrarian and in part because he was a Pynchon fan from way back. But that was okay. It got people reading *V* and *Gravity's Rainbow*, and hell, nothing wrong with that. But to think we'll never see another novel from him... I can't get my mind around it."

"David himself said that what he knew about racing you could write with a dry Sharpie marker on the lip of a Coke bottle," said NASCAR president Mike Helton, who announced the season cancellation late Monday after prompting from drivers and team owners in a statement that also tentatively suggested naming the 2009 Sprint series the Racing Season Of The Depends Adult Undergarment in referential and reverential tribute to Wallace's work. "But that doesn't matter to us as readers, as human beings."

"Racing and literature are both part of American life, and I think David Foster Wallace would agree with me that one wouldn't want to make too much of that, or to pretend that it's any sort of equitable balance," he added. "That would be grotesque. But the truth is that whatever cultural deity, entity, energy, or random social flux produced stock car racing also produced the works of David Foster Wallace. And just look them. Look at that."

Wernecke cited this story written by John Krewson as his favorite, though he referred to it as "NASCAR's Tribute to David Foster Wallace." I think I like Wernecke's title better. (Krewson started The Onion's *sports section.)*

to him being cool again." Wernecke told me that what he liked about business was being able to "help people solve problems or do something to make people's lives better."

Regarding *The Onion*, Wernecke said he always found it "really funny. I thought it was really off the wall. Sometimes outrageous. Some of the humor I couldn't believe it could get away with." Wernecke also thought Hannah's entry immediately raised *The Onion*'s editorial standards and that it was much funnier and more consistent after he signed on. (Hannah told me he actually did very little with the editorial side. The start of his reign, however, coincided with the start of Carol Kolb's stint as editor-in-chief.) Wernecke also said the NASCAR story (see reproduction on previous page) was emblematic of one of the company's basic business challenges: the jokes operated at a level that required a lot of highly educated background knowledge—something that most people, including advertisers, did not have.

Wernecke and Hannah started having monthly meetings, joining McAvoy in helping Hannah untangle the mess. Hannah also hired him to write a report on their advertising sales-management system, which was so loose that Wernecke had to recommend elementary things like writing job descriptions.

As time passed and things moved beyond this very basic level, Welyczko said he felt Wernecke was "torn between his open-mindedness and his kindness, his ability to relate to all of us Gen Xers" and what Hannah began directing him to do—and that he was continually put in an untenable position where he was not going to succeed. "Lots of things were set up to fail at that phase," Welyczko said. Wernecke was stuck as the bearer of bad news, having to relay that Hannah and McAvoy weren't interested in pursuing his ideas. Welyczko said, "For all of his faults, at least you could always try and talk to [Pete Haise] and he would always listen. . . . And it just got to this point where it felt like the suits were running the asylum, and they had no interest in what any of us thought would be a pathway forward in anything."

Then the hammer dropped. "I was told either I move to Chicago or I quit," Welyczko said. Hannah and McAvoy had decided to shut down the Madison office and consolidate more efficiently in Chicago. Welyczko saw the writing on the wall. He and his staff designed the print editions in all the outposts, most of which were not doing well. If he went to Chicago, he felt he would soon be put in charge of shutting down the newspaper he had loved for so long and firing his staff, one by one. Templeton wouldn't be the last. "And I loved my staff so much," he said. "My staff was the most stable, the most loyal, the most highly performing of everyone at *The Onion*." So Welyczko quit. Another long *Onion* career was over, though he remained a shareholder and continued observing from the sidelines.

A new franchising operation, Onion Nation, LLC, came into being after Welyczko left. Local newspapers—the *Washington Post*, for instance—would be the operational home for new print editions, allowing older brands to associate themselves with *The Onion* and hopefully pick up a younger audience while using their existing print infrastructure to make and distribute the papers. Jeff

Haupt eventually established nine new *Onion* printing contracts worth $4.5 million. Wernecke developed a franchise plan for Onion, Inc., to follow, "quite a major project and quite difficult." Unfortunately, though Haupt was on board with Wernecke's recommendations to provide a lot of support for the franchises, Hannah and McAvoy did not take his advice. So, Wernecke said, "I thought it best that if they're going to do it that way, that they should have someone else running that." His association with *The Onion* ended, and he went on to open a boutique wealth-management company called Pegasus Partners, "an independent, employee-owned firm that offers comprehensive wealth management services for individuals, families, and foundations."

McAvoy had a different take. He said Wernecke was brought in mostly because he was Steve Hannah's "buddy." Wernecke was a smart guy, McAvoy said, but he was "not a great brand fit." And *The Onion* tried a franchise in Indianapolis following Wernecke's advice that "failed miserably." He had been tasked with getting the local *Onions* "stable" and couldn't do it, McAvoy said, because—if I understood McAvoy correctly—the local print bosses never had the chops to do so. The problem wasn't a lack of financial support from *The Onion*; it was the incompetence of the local print operators. Anyone good, McAvoy said, had already "graduate[d] to digital media." Working with local print guys was like "managing copier salespeople." They were living in the past. Wernecke, he said, was "let go" as a result. (Still, in McAvoy's opinion, the franchise experiment extended *The Onion*'s run in print longer than it would have otherwise. "The fact that we were able to do any of them with the way print looked at that time was honestly pretty brilliant," he said.)

Welyczko's shareholder updates revealed that none of the franchises succeeded. "The decline of the alt-weekly industry at the hands of the internet was already in full effect," he said, "and I think the general opinion among some of us ex-*Onion* people who were still in touch with one another was that Onion Nation was a stupid idea and destined to fail. Some of us believed, conspiratorially, that it was an excuse for Hannah et al. to declare that context and tradition be damned, newsprint was dead, and *The Onion* should be digital only."

I saw one franchising slide deck that had been passed around via email in 2010 to potential participants. For each five-year deal, franchisees were expected to come up with $100,000–$250,000 up front, then $5,000–$6,000/week for the duration of the contract, while providing sales, printing, distribution, ad design, production layout, and "all other operations" outside the content and some advertising. The proposed franchisee in Madison commented, "Can't imagine how we'd make money if these terms aren't highly negotiable." Wernecke said, "I think you characterize it as a disaster. Really unsuccessful." He thought that not a single one of the franchises made it through their three-year contracts.

Back in New York, however, creative freedom still (mostly) reigned. Siegel remained as editor until 2003, as *The Onion* continued to produce hilarious—and prophetic—satire about the Bush administration's "sales pitch" for war in Iraq, among many other subjects (examples include: March 13, 2002: "Military Promises 'Huge Numbers' for Gulf War II: The Vengeance"; and September 11, 2002: "Bush Won't Stop Asking Cheney If We Can Invade Yet"). As scholar Theodore Hamm put it in his 2008 book *The New Blue Media*, "While serious liberal news organizations such as the *New York Times* helped disseminate the White House's specious rationale for war, *The Onion*'s lampoons turned out to be far more accurate."

Tim Harrod left in February 2003 after being asked to write for *The Onion Movie* without any guarantee of payment. "No contract meant we'd get whatever they saw fit to give us. Rob liberally declared 'Everyone's going to get paid' but faltered when pressed on important matters like amounts," he said. It was by now an old *Onion* writer story. (Harrod was also tired of being the only one who ever showed up for meetings on time.)

It was probably just as well. *The Onion Movie*—which would finally be released straight to DVD in 2008—ended up as a mostly tasteless, 1970s-style interconnected-storyline series of ensemble comedy sketches that borrows the plot of the famous 1976 film *Network*, complete with a version of the "I'm mad as hell" speech, with some '90s-style meta elements in the mix. The shock/offensiveness/sophomoric content is high. Steven Seagal punches men in the crotch multiple times throughout. Siegel and Hanson are listed as the film's writers.

Hanson told me, "We wanted to make either an excellent film or just not make one. And in the process of making it, it became very clear that we weren't making an excellent film." They wanted it to be a really smart satirical commentary on corporate control over the news and everything else, but none of that came through. Hanson said a huge problem was that though they gave the producers tons of sketches, pitched both high and low, the only ones that got approved were the dumb ones. They had emergency meetings where they tried to get some smart jokes back in and save the film. It didn't work. "Even when we had an intelligent take, only the lowest-common-denominator *part* of that joke would make it into the film," Hanson said.

The whole experience was something they all wanted to forget. (Except for Pete Haise. Promised an executive producer credit on the film, when the DVD finally came out, his name was nowhere to be found. In 2014—six years after the DVD was released—he sued David Schafer, Steve Hannah, and *The Onion* for the right to be considered a producer on the film. The case was eventually dismissed, though Haise told me he won. Andy Dhuey told me he guessed Haise received a modest settlement. The lawsuit documents were where I learned Haise had received $1.7 million when he sold his shares to Schafer in 2003.)

In 2003, Siegel sold his shares as well and ended his own time at *The Onion*, turning his $10,000 investment into $250,000. Not a bad return at all, but a far cry from the internet millionaire he had once hoped to become. On his last day, Siegel said, Hanson picked a fight with him over some "petty, bullshit, nit-picky thing." It was a huge blowout. Siegel was hurt and really angry. "I wanted to fire him," he said. "I couldn't fucking believe he was doing it on my last day. I thought, 'Well, what better way to end it?'" But his better judgment won, and he told himself, "Be the bigger man and walk away." Siegel went on to a highly regarded, award-winning film and TV writing and directing career, using his *Onion* profits to fund his first movie, *Big Fan*, starring Patton Oswalt. (It went to Sundance in 2009 and got great reviews.) He also wrote the screenplay for the Oscar-nominated, award-winning 2008 film *The Wrestler* and created the 2022 miniseries *Pam and Tommy*, about 1990s icons Pamela Anderson and Tommy Lee.

According to an August 2003 CNN article, *The Onion* now had revenues of about $7 million a year and a modest profit, replacing "fallen dotcom advertisers with such blue chips as DreamWorks, HBO, Nike, and Volkswagen." *The Onion* also continued to turn down offers, such as a regular spot on Jay Leno's *Tonight Show*. Their agent, David Miner, said in the article that most of his job was to say no to potential deals. The "looming fear" was that "the brand could languish if the commentary doesn't stay relevant and funny." Noting the "failure of *Spy Magazine* and *National Lampoon*," the article points out that "humor publications have historically had trouble staying hot for long periods." However, *The Onion* so far was rolling with the punches, helped by their adherence to "their cheapskate alt-weekly roots while other sites adopted go-go dotcom thinking." They also continued to refuse any compromise in editorial quality.

Stephen Thompson told me, "I feel like I mostly just wanted two things from management post-Pete. I wanted the place run by someone innovative, with a willingness to look beyond display advertising when they were thinking about *The Onion*'s growth. And I wanted them to pursue a talent pool that extended beyond our personal networks. I wanted—and this is gonna sound crazy—a leadership team that wasn't just 'Here's a guy I know.' Maybe they could even do a formal job search for people with relevant experience in business!" Instead, Thompson said, they "graduated from Pete's buddies—Milwaukee barflies who sold weed and wore jean jackets and had nicknames like 'the Grizz'—to David Schafer's buddies, and buddies' nephews, and that sort of thing." They weren't all bad, Thompson said, but *The Onion* ended up with "the same limited imagination, just with a fresh whiff of ruthlessness."

Thompson's time at *The Onion*, however, was limited. In December 2004, the new management decided to fire him. Thompson had met with new boss Hannah a few weeks earlier to discuss how things were going, which he had thought went well. During the meeting he tried to explain how difficult his job had become. "I was proofing every word of editorial that went into every single edition of the print paper, including stuff like concert listings in Minneapolis and Denver. I guess he thought I'd complained too much or was some kind of malcontent; who knows?" On December 3, Thompson said he got a phone call at his *Onion* desk to meet management in a nearby coffee shop. There, he said, they fired him, not even allowing him to go back inside and get his stuff. The reason, he was told, was "philosophical differences." (Movers delivered his belongings to his house that weekend.) Thompson heard later that they had even changed the locks. In hindsight, he said, "I guess I was sort of like the first person to get bitten in a zombie movie."

Chapter 14

Along with Carol Kolb becoming editor-in-chief in 2003 after Siegel left, other major editorial changes also started happening: one, many unpaid interns; and two—directly related to the first—the first staffers from the millennial generation. One of these was Peter Koechley, who had originally been *The Onion*'s first (and maybe only) intern back in Madison when he was still in high school. He said, "I was one of the first super Type A overachiever types to get into the mix, which I feel bad about on a lot of levels because there were a lot of us who followed." He was hired as a writer after graduating from Columbia, "an absolute dream job." Koechley said he was a business-minded person who was also good with words; he was friendly with the money side when some writers were less so. He also said he was the new college grad who said things like "I have some ideas for how to optimize the workflow" and how they could "scale," which I'm sure went over very well with the older Gen X staff. (Koechley said he understood now that these things had been "off culture.") He became managing editor.

The Onion now had a new hiring process involving conventional advertisements in Mediabistro and so on, rather than by admiring funny signs hung up in the windows of a local liquor store. (The Gen X staff used to have other funny/actually-sort-of-serious requirements for a writer to be accepted: The Rules for Writers. Any new staffer needed to have 1) worked a minimum-wage job; 2) cleaned out a grease trap; and 3) been punched in the face.) The new regime also involved performance reviews. Maria Schneider said they started having them every six months. Even *The Onion*'s office had changed: they were now in an expensive new space on Broadway in SoHo.

One of the first New York interns was Mike DiCenzo, age twenty-two, who got the job by contacting the office and asking if they needed any interns. (The 9/11 issue had been one of his first *Onion* exposures when he was a freshman at Boston University.) Proofreading once a week soon led to daily intern work. "They were just doing it all themselves, because I think they just didn't realize people would do work for free," he said. Other early interns were John Howell Harris (editorial), who went on to become a highly regarded *Onion* writer and later wrote for comedy TV shows like *Rick & Morty* and *Mythic Quest*, and Aziz Ansari (business) before he became a famous comedian and actor, starring in *Parks and Recreation* and creating and starring in *Master of None*. Megan Ganz, another highly regarded *Onion* writer, also came in around this time as one of the first writing fellows (staff reviewing the big stack of applications remember her being head and shoulders above everyone else); she later wrote and produced for *Modern Family* and *Community* and cocreated *Mythic Quest*, "the best workplace comedy on TV." A *This American Life* episode about the *Onion* writers' room features Ganz in action.

Among the new young staffers, Dan Guterman was also very highly regarded. (John Krewson said he passed their "Rules for Writers" test because he used to be a busking street musician.) Guterman lived in Rio de Janeiro until he was six, when his family moved to Montreal. In about 1998, when he was in high school, he discovered *The Onion*. "At the time, I was feeling pretty depressed, and fairly alone, and I was working hard to try to develop what would eventually become my voice—and finding *The Onion* was like finding an old friend." He picked out Tim Harrod from the masthead and sent him an email asking if he could submit headlines. He was seventeen. It didn't take long before he was a staff writer. Guterman's headlines include "Bassist Unaware Rock Band Christian" and "Heinz Factory Explosion Looks Worse than It Is." He also wrote the horoscopes for a while.

The Madison crew found these new young people coming into *The Onion* very different from themselves. (I'll tell you about several more of them shortly.) One, the new kids saw the job as a deliberate first step toward careers in comedy and media, with ambition and drive and organization to take on such careers, which was definitely not the case with most of the Madisonians. Some of the new kids also had family and experiences and connections that gave them a framework of knowledge and support for a professional career; they were not first-generation public university kids from rural Wisconsin whose parents were housewives and cheese-factory workers. They were graduates of Harvard and Brown and Columbia, children of doctors and lawyers and CEOs. And they were "very smart and funny and savvy about the idea that they could just do this for a living," Kolb said. Nackers said he thought, "Man, these kids are organized. They know what they want to do. They want to be comedians. And they have a plan."

The new staff had also grown up as *Onion* fans. "And to see them so excited about a thing that came from Gen X and be like, 'This is so cool, and I want to work towards this,' was very interesting," Nackers told me. Ambition to become part of a group of antiambitious people. Todd Hanson said, "It's just very, very different from the whole worldview that we all had back then."

As editor-in-chief, Kolb told me that her goal was to maintain *The Onion*'s quality rather than make any big changes. She did, however, institute some new processes that made the old schedule and the writers' room more humane.

Dan Guterman said it was tradition that prospective *Onion* headlines could be delivered only in a flat monotone. By doing this, "it strips away all showmanship—all salesmanship—from a joke, leaving it to live or die on its own merit." Headline meetings "could last anywhere from several hours to half a day, with hundreds of headlines read aloud in a flat monotone. From those hundreds we'd winnow the list down to about eighty. And from those eighty, we'd ultimately pick just twelve," Guterman said. However, from around 2004, "we all had to stop using 'the Voice,'" as he put it. Writers had been killing headlines they didn't like by repeating them in a sarcastic voice.

Guterman and many others said they loved the writers' room. "We stuck around each other so much, in fact, that we developed a kind of hive mind, with different writers finishing each other's sentences and entire articles flowing out seamlessly between the staff."

Kolb's assistant editor was fiction writer Amie Barrodale, whom Kolb met when Barrodale was working at a little shop in Park Slope created by writer Dave Eggers and the magazine *McSweeney's*; the shop sold quirky, unrelated things like dog toothpaste and *American Window Cleaner Magazine* as a sort of retail performance-art project. Kolb and Barrodale created a great partnership. Barrodale later wrote a *Paris Review* article about how Kolb—with Krewson's help—had pranked the business team over *The Onion*'s Hurricane Katrina coverage. The ad team had warned her not to do anything offensive, which they were not planning to do, so Kolb and team created a fake, horrifically-in-bad-taste front page and left it in the printer for the ad staff to find.

Barrodale wrote that Kolb was "the funniest person I have ever known." Guterman said, "There is nobody like Carol Kolb. She's just insanely, preternaturally funny. And never, ever sweaty." Kolb was also very dark. Headlines from Kolb's era include "Holocaust Museum Cashier Has Yet Another Depressing Day."

Editorial definitely crossed a line in 2004. Krewson was angry that "Weird Al" Yankovic had seemingly copied the horoscopes he'd been writing for a long time and made them into a song. (Weird Al had been an *Onion* fan and friend for years.) Yankovic's parents had just died in a tragic carbon-monoxide accident in their home, and Krewson took tasteless revenge with "Weird Al Honors Parents' Memory with 'Tears in Heaven' Parody." Schneider found the choice "pretty fucking mean." Garden said he might have supported it at the time, but now, "as I've gotten older, I've gained more empathy. My fuck-you attitude has gone in the direction toward people that I feel more deserving, like billionaires and politicians and health insurance companies." Stephen Thompson at least gave Al a heads-up. (Thompson was not happy about the article.) Tim Harrod said Yankovic's response was, "Okay, that's not gonna be my favorite *Onion* story, but I get it that you guys do that."

When I talked to Krewson for this book, he felt bad about it. "One of the big regrets of my life is that I got mad about Weird Al obviously doing something very tributary to us. It was obviously meant to be adulatory. Because when I went in the office everyone was like, 'This is so great!' And I'm like, 'Where's our money? What are we getting from it?'" Looking back on it now with more perspective, Krewson said, "What was I really mad about? Like, was I actually mad at Weird Al? I don't think that I was. What the hell was going on with me? It was wrong."

I had an email interview with Weird Al where I passed along Krewson's regrets. Al said he had given *The Onion* a special thank-you in the liner notes for that album. Still, he said, "I feel really bad that John was angry with me for a period of time. I realize that sometimes there's a fine line between loving homage and abject plagiarism, but I absolutely guarantee you, my intention was the former. I'm glad we're cool now, and I hope John knows I don't harbor any ill will at all about the article he wrote about my parents."

Carol Kolb's time as editor-in-chief was brief. She told me that in 2005 she decided "This place has given me headaches. I gotta get out of here." She'd been working with the same people for a long time. "I love them all, but you just want to kill them after a certain point." As Karwowski put it, "Comedy writers are not the most manageable types." She went off to pursue a TV writing career.

With Kolb gone, Hannah turned to a former *Onion* editor to take the reins: Scott Dikkers. He was back. (Dikkers had moved to New York at the same time as *The Onion*.) Dikkers told me that on his return, things weren't really that different. Every time he would leave *The Onion*, he said, "it always tends to kind of ossify. [The writers] treat it like a museum piece. Like, 'Oh, we must preserve the way *The Onion* is.' And every time I would come back, I would feel like it needs a real serious shakeup."

People respected his vision, though, he said. "I remember this especially happening between 2000 and 2005 [after Dikkers sold his shares and left], where the writers would talk about, 'Well, Scott would do it like this. This is what Scott would have wanted,' and stuff like that." I asked him how he knew people were saying that if he wasn't there, and he said, "Because people were telling me." Dikkers did go back to the old days in one way: he named Hanson head writer again. (Hanson remained head writer until his title was changed to story editor a couple of years later.) Dikkers said Hannah, Mills, and Schafer felt the same as he did about the current supposed flaccidity of *The Onion*. "*The Onion* needs a hot-beef injection, they called it," he said. The new generation of writers would definitely take the institution into new territory.

Looking to build the writing team, Dikkers asked intern Mike DiCenzo to try writing stories and was very happy with the results. Unlike some of the older writers, he'd come in with beautiful complete drafts. Krewson then started "Onion Sports" with DiCenzo's help, soon joined by Nackers and later DiCenzo's college friend Seth Reiss. It became one of the most popular parts of the paper. (Krewson, DiCenzo said, was one of the most brilliant writers he'd ever met.) DiCenzo recalled that when he was finally hired as a real staffer, Krewson, Hanson, Karwowski, and Garden lifted him up on their shoulders and carried him around the office singing—a wonderful day. (DiCenzo went on to write for Jimmy Fallon and *Saturday Night Live*. He told me that when people found out you'd been an *Onion* writer, they knew you would be good.)

Dikkers found the writers' room unreceptive to his attempts to inject hot beef. It seems one of his new ideas was to start putting bylines on the stories—not real bylines, but funny fake names. This seems to have been met by incredulity. Schneider recalled saying in the meeting, "Nope, not necessary." She didn't think it had anything to do with trying to take *The Onion* in a new creative direction. "I think he just wanted to fuck with people's heads." Schneider also remembered him wanting to bring back a more 1990s style of headline that wasn't really what they were doing anymore, "something I think even in the early '90s *Onion* would have been kind of like, 'Well, they're a little off this week.'" One writer remembered Dikkers actually not getting some of the newer writers' jokes.

Dikkers, used to being an owner, not an employee, was also having difficulty with *The Onion*'s management. He thought *The Onion* "really could have used a young, dynamic, forward-thinking management team that worked hand in hand with our talent agents to really leverage what we had and make it great. And also, think long-term. Invest in talent; invest in projects. I think they were too concerned with 'How do we profit from this?'" According to Garden, Dikkers then went through a phase of trying to get the writers to rally around him and against management. Garden said the writers' attitude was basically, "Pass." Garden said, "I didn't get the sense from that conversation that we were backing ourselves. I got the sense that we were backing him."

One day, out of the blue, Dikkers came into the writers' room and told them that they would now be writing a book ("It wasn't a discussion," DiCenzo recalled), the atlas *Our Dumb World*, which—in typical *Onion* moderation—was meant to be about the entire planet. Soon DiCenzo was working on that too. Like *Our Dumb Century*, *Our Dumb World* was another massive pile of extra work for the writers, with similar exhausting traumatic effects on the creative team and similar issues with Dikkers as manager. Nobody for a long time seemed to know what the book was supposed to be or how to create it. (Eventually, the staff realized they could have a theme for each country, which gave them an organizing principle, but figuring this out took at least a year.)

Graphics editor and *Our Dumb World* art director Mike Loew said creating the atlas was a totally "fucked-up organizational process, tons of wasted work, spinning our wheels." Dikkers was in charge and just wasn't cutting it. "The atlas fucking killed me," Loew said. He said when the book finally went to press, the staff actually wrote a letter to Dikkers listing their grievances. Chet Clem, a young man from Massachusetts who had been recently hired as editorial coordinator after an internship and did a ton of work trying to manage the production of the book, said the process was "an enormous undertaking" made even more difficult "by being extraordinarily inefficient and disorganized." There were also a lot of questions, he said, about "Are we getting paid for this?" In spite of this, like *Our Dumb Century*, *Our Dumb World*, which was published in 2007, was also brilliant, with one reviewer calling it "possibly the funniest book ever written."

Unfortunately, Loew became a casualty of the atlas. When *Our Dumb World* was finally done, exhausted from doing two jobs at once, Loew at last was able to take his summer vacation. Right before he left to go home to Wisconsin, though, managing editor Koechley asked to meet him for breakfast. Loew said he was a guy "who seems like he read a lot of business books where it's like, 'Here's how you maximize profits,' and I just felt like it was always constantly more and more work, for no more pay. And he liked to fire people a lot."

At the breakfast, Koechley said, "How about you come back from your two-week break and you think about a new role for yourself at *The Onion?*" Loew was blindsided. Koechley said he thought Loew was burned out. It was true, but still. Koechley continued: "Maybe you want to jump onto the video side. Maybe you want to get into 3D graphics and work on stuff with video, with VFX [visual effects]. Maybe you want to create a whole new role for yourself. Or," Koechley said, "maybe it's time for you to leave and go work on the Mike Loew brand."

Loew, in shock, went on his vacation and realized he didn't want to work for Peter Koechley anymore. He also didn't like the direction that *The Onion* was headed in. None of the young interns would even say hello passing in the halls. The old family feeling was going away. "And I was like, 'All right, I guess I'm gonna leave.' I *am* pretty burned out. I've been doing this a long time. Maybe it's time to spread my wings and fly." The staff threw Loew a big going-away party where everyone sang his praises. Loew had played a central, pivotal role at *The Onion* since the early 1990s. His work had been crucial for its success.

Then, a week later, Loew attended the launch party for *Our Dumb World* at the Explorers Club in Manhattan—and during the party Koechley made the announcement that he was leaving to work for MoveOn.org. Loew couldn't believe it. Koechley had to have known he was about to take another job when he suggested Loew go work on his "brand." "They wanted to replace me with two young guys, and they probably would get two guys for the price of me, you know?" Loew said. "And Peter wanted to maximize the bottom line right before he leaves." He'd been stabbed in the back by an ambitious millennial—one from

Madison, no less. Clem agreed that Loew had been "pretty unceremoniously forced out."

Loew immediately tried to buttonhole Koechley at the party, but Koechley dodged him in the crowd. In the end, however, Loew thought, "Well, Jesus, maybe it is time for me to do something by Mike Loew." He wrote books, did prop art for Siegel on a film, designed for a number of interesting places, and eventually became assistant art director for *MAD* magazine. Still, it seemed pretty obvious to Loew that the company was "pretty excited to get my salary off the books."

Loew was indeed replaced by former intern Nick Gallo, who had been working as a contractor on *Our Dumb World*, and another designer named Michael Faisca. Since Nackers was now a writer, Gallo and Faisca became the new Loew and Nackers. Gallo was sad to see Mike go, but was very happy to be hired at *The Onion*—his first real job—even if the pay was substandard. The work was fun and intense. Every week he had a list of fifty things to do, from casting to shooting to buying props off Amazon. (The props were all stored in Gallo's office, including a box of giant dildos and other sex toys for use in shoots.)

Clem told me Loew's departure made him start wondering what was really going on. Were people—especially the Gen X group, with their higher salaries, recalcitrant attitudes, and outside-target-demographic ages—now being pushed out? There had been rumors that Viacom was going to buy *The Onion* in 2005, but that had fallen through because the price wasn't high enough for management, and now it seemed obvious there was a push to make *The Onion* bigger solely for the sake of pushing up its sale price, not because *The Onion* itself wanted to get bigger. Clem said during his time at *The Onion*, they went from a staff of thirty-six people to more than seventy in less than two years. Meanwhile, there was no transparency around the business side's goals.

For Clem, a bigger question was whether there would ever be a real ownership opportunity for the people who created *The Onion*. Piles of money were going to end up in the already-stuffed bank account of some guy they barely knew, while staffers who had been there since the early '90s and had created the thing got little or nothing. Clem said, frustrated with what could have been, "You literally could have had an all-hands meeting and just said, 'This is where we are; this is what we're trying to do as a company. Does anybody have any questions?' And you would have neutered some of the rumor mill, and you would have made people feel like they were a part of something," as opposed to being a ball-bearing maker in a ball-bearing factory. When I asked him why he thought communication from management was so bad, he said, "What's the old saying? 'Never attribute to malice that which can be adequately explained as incompetence.'"

Aside from the issues with *Our Dumb World*, Dikkers's behavior in other contexts also raised eyebrows. Dikkers's second wife had given birth to their son around this time. One day, Dikkers told me, he went into president Sean Mills's office and informed him that he would now be coming in only three days a week. (Mills, Dikkers said, had "a big, luxurious office, like a real boss's office. . . . I always liked being in a tiny office or sharing an office with other people in the thick of it.") Mills, he said, "panicked. He's like, 'Wh-what?'" Dikkers said that was the dynamic then. "I ran the show. I was going to tell him what I was going to do. It wasn't going to be the other way around." And then for a long time, Dikkers said, he worked three days a week. Plus, "I had delegated a lot of the stuff, and I was really just sitting at a desk looking at things saying, 'Yes. No. Yes. No.' So I didn't have to be there eight hours a day."

Joe Randazzo also joined the editorial staff during this period. Randazzo was born in New York and lived in an Italian Irish Catholic neighborhood until he was eight, when his parents moved to New Hampshire. There he had a "pretty normal lower-middle-class upbringing." He also discovered nature, while keeping a strong connection to New York. Today, as a divorced forty-five-year-old dad of three, he said he thinks back on his own childhood and the stuff we all do just out of reflex. "Where does that come from? Why am I acting this way?" As the oldest kid in his family, growing up Randazzo felt "a lot of responsibility for making sure everything was okay" with the younger ones, using comedy and jokes to mitigate conflict.

Randazzo majored in broadcast journalism at Emerson College and worked at the Boston NPR affiliate WBUR before moving back to New York. He connected with *The Onion* via an improv class that had Kolb and Barrodale in it. Randazzo was hired as assistant editor to Dikkers—the first editor to come from outside. "I had a little bit of a hill to climb, I think," he said. "The core *Onion* people are inherently mistrustful and loyal and are like, 'We need to maintain this integrity and keep doing things the way we've been doing them.'"

Randazzo won them over, though. Guterman said Randazzo also "got me, and a lot of other people, for that matter, to loosen up and enjoy ourselves." Guterman would later become Randazzo's head writer.

Randazzo, born in 1978, was between the older Gen X group (most of whom had been born around 1967–1970) and the recent-college-grad millennials in age. I asked him what made the older staff Gen X. "Everybody was lazy," he said. "Everybody was like, 'I worked at a pizza shop. I didn't even fucking go to college. We didn't even want to be famous. This is stupid.'" The problem, though, with saying business was for squares was that they were not "savvy enough to stand up for themselves" when business made decisions that affected them. There was also suspicion around the young new staff because they had ambition. To Randazzo, in the middle, it was more like "Why can't we do things with quality *and* organization?"

Randazzo said Dikkers could be a "genius" line editor, though he didn't think he had a very sophisticated taste level. "But I think *The Onion* needed a lot of that, because he would rip a lot of the bullshit out and just be like, 'Simplify this. Dumb this down.'"

One day, out of the blue, Dikkers brought Randazzo into his office. He was leaving, Dikkers said. And he wanted Randazzo to be the new editor-in-chief. Randazzo was taken by surprise but also thrilled and said yes. Dikkers made the announcement, and everyone congratulated Randazzo.

Dikkers told me he felt at that point that he had put things in place the way he wanted them. He also wasn't happy with management and was disgruntled about the insurance. (Their health insurance was indeed horrifically bad. The company was called Beech Street, which was apparently not even health insurance but rather a Delta Dental–type discount thing. Almost no providers accepted it. Nackers said, "We were all like, 'What the fuck is going on with this stuff?'" He remembered having to go way out to southern Brooklyn to find a provider who accepted it. Upon coming up out of the subway, before him was a dumpster full of chicken feathers and a worker spraying blood off the sidewalk. Then he had to wander around with a paper map trying to locate the office. The online reviews for Beech Street are terrifying. Eventually, they did get a better plan.)

Dikkers also told me he left because "I get bored. You know, I have ADD." He decided to start an animation company, leaving the editor-in-chief role in good hands. But then, according to Randazzo, Hannah and Mills said, "Not so fast." Dikkers, it seems, had not only made his choice abruptly—people said he gave two weeks' notice and was gone—but also hired Randazzo without consulting anybody. Randazzo then had to go through a formal interviewing and hiring process. He did get the job, but "it was my first kind of taste of bullshit." One thing management did was eliminate the title of "editor-in-chief," who could make editorial decisions for *The Onion* as a whole. Now it was just "editor," who could not.

Randazzo also faced a basic and growing disconnect in worldview between business and editorial that was more than generational. Soon after he was promoted to editor, he went to Chicago and gave a presentation to the business staff on the upcoming year. "Here's all the things you guys can sell," he told them. "Here's what we're going to do around this holiday. Here's what we're gonna do around Back to School, so you can bundle all that shit."

And then taking questions after meeting everybody, giving my presentation, this guy's like, "What keeps you up at night?"

And I said, "Global warming." And everybody started laughing. I was like, "What are you guys laughing about?" They were like, "No, we mean with *business.*"

Randazzo said there were now also constant requests for "questionable integration stuff." Things like going back into old articles and Photoshopping a brand's logo onto some object in an *Onion* article illustration. Clem, who had become something of a liaison between editorial and sales with a focus on editorial advocacy, would have to say, "No, we're not going to bastardize a twenty-year-old comedic institution to satisfy Monster Energy." So increasingly, "editorial just was saying no to everything."

Randazzo said his biggest goal was just to maintain quality—and get *The Onion* into a more frequently updated digital mindset. To him, *The Onion* needed to adjust to the reality of digital media, which, yes, meant doing things a little differently from before (though, no, not by Photoshopping a Domino's logo on 1998's "Everyone Involved in Pizza's Preparation, Delivery, Purchase Extremely High"). The writers' room, he said, was an "almost sacred Talmudic discussion"

The Smallest Ex

⌀ the ONION®

DECEMBER 8, 2011 · VOL. 47 ISSUE 49 · AMERICA'S FINEST NEWS SOURCE · ONION.COM · Copyright © 2011 Onion, Inc. All Rights Reserved | 8450

WATCH THE ONION'S TV SHOW, ONION NEWS NETWORK. ONLY ON IFC. FRIDAYS AT 10/9C.

INSIDE

LOCAL
Burrito Eaten Like Someone In The Room Wasn't Crying *Page 8B*

ENTERTAINMENT
Brief Reprieve From Mariah Carey's Christmas Song Comes To Resounding End *Page 17D*

HIGHLIGHTS

Burglar Makes Sure To Crack Glass On Family Portrait
LOCAL, Page 14B

Equestrian Instinctively Feels Deep, Meaningless Connection With Horse *LOCAL, Page 6B*

SPORTS

Hedo Turkoglu Somehow Comes Out Of Lockout $50 Million Richer *Page 11C*

A.V. CLUB

A.V. CLUB THE BEST MUSIC OF 2011

Report: Global Warming May Be Irreversible By 2006

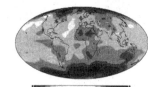

If global warming isn't under control by 2006, scientists say it will achieve unstoppable momentum, destroying the only planet we have.

GENEVA—A new report from the U.N. Intergovernmental Panel on Climate Change warned Monday that global warming is likely to become completely irreversible if no successful effort is made to slow down the trend before 2006.

Unless greenhouse-gas emissions are drastically reduced by then, the report concludes, it will be too late to avoid inflicting a grave environmental catastrophe upon future generations of humans.

"We have absolutely no time to waste," said Dr. William Tumminelli, lead author of the report, which stresses it is utterly crucial the world cut its carbon footprint in half by the year 2000. "If we wait until 1998 or even 1995 to really start doing something about climate change, our planet's rising temperature will already have set in motion a series of devastating and irreparable long-term consequences. We need to have strict international rules

in place well ahead of 2006 or, to be blunt, many of the earth's inhabitants will be doomed."

"The situation could not possibly be more urgent," Tumminelli added.

The report—the most comprehensive study of climate change ever undertaken—estimates the failure to address global warming immediately could result in sea levels rising 6 inches by the end of the 20th century, 2000-2009 being the hottest decade ever re-

see IRREVERSIBLE, page 7

In Major Gaffe, Obama Forgets To Dumb It Down

CINCINNATI—In a serious miscalculation that may prove devastating to his bid for a second term, President Barack Obama neglected Tuesday to simplify a statement to the point where it could readily be grasped by anyone with the vocabulary of an 8-year-old.

"Instead of saying, 'There are many global variables at work here, and unless they all fall into place, we could find ourselves in a recession,' he should have just said, 'Times are hard. We gotta be strong,'" said *Washington Post* political correspondent Brian Meltzer, noting that Obama's statement during a speech on job creation was met with dumbfounded looks and audible gasps from the crowd. "Americans are so used to meaningless homespun homilies, they don't know what to do when they're treated like thinking adults. The president has to understand that if he goes out there throwing around words like 'currency' and 'economy,' he'll end up being branded an elitist."

In an attempt to correct his error, Obama concluded his speech with the words "Jobs good. No jobs bad. God bless America." ⌀

Study Finds Getting Smacked Right In The Mouth With A Goddamn Tree Branch Really Sucks

■ 'But After A Minute, You're Basically Fine,' Researchers Say

BOSTON—According to a study published Monday in *The New England Journal Of Medicine*, getting smacked right across the mouth with a goddamn tree branch really fucking sucks, but after a minute or so, you're pretty much fine.

The study, in which researchers at Boston University documented the reactions of more than 400 unsuspecting volunteers getting smacked right in

the mouth with tree branches, found that regardless of gender, ethnicity, age, or socioeconomic background, a full-on, unexpected smack to the mouth with a stupid goddamn tree branch initially really blows, though the subject is more or less okay once a few minutes have passed.

"We observed volunteers being smacked square in the mouth with birch branches, pine

see TREE BRANCH, page 5

A researcher explains the $6 million goddamn tree branch study to reporters.

Secretary Of Agriculture Attends Diplomatic Meeting With Foreign Cabbage

Vilsack (left) with the cabbage (right).

LJUBLJANA, SLOVENIA—In the latest stop on his goodwill tour to improve U.S. relations with foreign produce, Agriculture Secretary Tom Vilsack attended a meeting Thursday with a fresh head of Slovenian cabbage.

The high-level meeting, which included a private dinner with the leafy-green Slo-

vene dignitary, involved strategic discussions on a range of bilateral and global issues, including the lack of arable land in Slovenia, the recent overhaul of vegetable-canning regulations, and the rise of the new center-left Positive Slovenia political party.

Though no official

see CABBAGE, page 6

Global warming may be irreversible by 2006. (The issue is from 2011.)

about "headlines and word choice and what it means and what's the thesis of the article." In the old weekly format, "it was kind of a precious stone that we were able to hold on to and polish for so long, where we could take two weeks to write a story." But that much care didn't work in the new media environment. Dikkers may have "dumbed stuff down too much and had some questionable choices," Randazzo said. "But I agreed with him that everything doesn't have to be so precious."

The 2008 presidential campaign was starting up, and *The Onion* needed someone to take charge of their election coverage. They also needed someone to take charge of their digital operations, though they hadn't realized it yet. They found both in Baratunde Thurston.

Thurston was born in 1977 and grew up in the Mount Pleasant neighborhood in Washington, DC, with his mom and sister; his father died when he was young. "We were Black people," he said. "Still are." He said he grew up in a tumultuous time, "crack wars, gun violence, drug violence, but also like a real sense of community, very multicultural area. Everybody in your business looking out for each other." He said his mother "was a super politically active person and was always encouraging me to be informed and to be aware and conscious, especially of America's limitations and faults."

Thurston was a huge news fan from a young age—and loved comedy as well. At Sidwell Friends, he wrote for his high school newspaper and worked in the copy room at the *Washington Post*. Thurston then went to college at Harvard and was intensely involved with the *Crimson* for all four years. He said, "I thought that if people just knew stuff, and could understand the things . . . that things would be better." When I asked how he thought about that now, he said, "It's a piece of the puzzle, but it's not enough. Information is not knowledge. And knowledge is not wisdom. Wisdom is not compassion. We need layers of this to build a healthy society. Information is very important, it's necessary, but insufficient to create a healthy society."

Thurston also was an early computer adopter. At the *Crimson*, he helped take the paper online for the first time, learning the same things the *Onion* website staff was also figuring out sixteen hundred miles away in Madison. After college, Thurston worked for several years in "the default Ivy League path that accelerates debt repayment, strategy consulting," where he learned even more about business and technology—specifically, how people were going to make money after the Telecommunications Act of 1996, which had just passed amid many other huge changes going on at that time in the industry. "It opened up a huge can of worms," Thurston said. (Socialist historian Howard Zinn said the act dealt a major blow to community and alternative media. The act also led to even more extreme media consolidation; by 2005 there were only six major media content corporations controlling nearly all the entertainment and information

Americans consumed.) Thurston had also been doing political stand-up and writing satire on his own for years, as well as experimenting with internet distribution via his own newsletter, blog, and podcast.

In 2007, a friend sent Thurston an ad posted on Mediabistro and told him, "You were born to do this job." It was for a politics editor at *The Onion* to direct coverage of the upcoming presidential election. During his interview, upon seeing his experience, the *Onion* people realized they also needed a digital director, Thurston said. Could he do that too? "I entered that job in November of 2007 with two hats, to come up with how we would cover this election, which is clearly a big fucking deal," he said, "and use the internet to help us do it."

Despite being overwhelmingly white (an old office joke was to announce the arrival of a new writer to the editor with "There's a young white man here to see you"), Thurston said *The Onion* was "one of the most diverse places I've ever worked because of weirdness. Just sheer weirdness."

Just like, very specific white guys who somehow managed to capture so much more than their own experience. I was floored at how sensitive that writers' room was to issues of race and class. Because you're just like superficially, "Oh, what a bunch of white dudes," but they would question things. "Are we making fun of homeless people or making fun of the people who don't empathize with homeless people? Let's be clear about the target." It was grad school for satire to sit in that room and watch these people argue.

Thurston helped develop a plan for their web strategy and election coverage, called "War for the White House"—the first coordinated project including all available forms of media: print, podcast, Onion Radio News, Onion News Network (ONN), website, emails, social. Thurston was observant enough to know that "I show up at a magical generative time of new birth and possibility because of the internet and presidency and all that," he said, but it was also "a time of deep exhaustion and hurt and feelings of misuse and abuse. Because *Our Dumb World* had just wrapped, and it had drained the life out of that place." Still, he said of the staff, "despite their initial gruffness and suspicion, they opened pretty quickly." "War for the White House" sent their web traffic through the roof as Barack Obama won the presidency. By now, the print edition was in fourteen cities, with a circulation of 690,000. Online followers were in the millions.

Classics from the Obama era included "Black Guy Asks Nation for Change" (March 19, 2008) and "Black Man Given Nation's Worst Job" (November 4, 2008).

In his new high-stress, low-reward position, Obama will be charged with such tasks as completely overhauling the nation's broken-down economy, repairing the crumbling infrastructure, and generally having to please more than 300 million Americans and cater to their every whim on a daily basis. As part of his duties, the black man will have to spend four to eight years cleaning up the messes other people left behind. The job comes with such intense scrutiny and so certain a guarantee of failure that only one other person even bothered applying for it. Said scholar and activist Mark L. Denton, "It just goes to show you that, in this country, a black man still can't catch a break."

Readers were also introduced to the popular character of "Diamond Joe" Biden, the middle-aged ponytailed dude washing his Trans Am shirtless in the White House driveway. (In the 2020 presidential election, Biden won by fewer than twenty-one thousand votes in Wisconsin, which ultimately tipped the Electoral College balance in his favor. Given how many *Onion* fans there are in the state—and how long political memories are here—I have always wondered if the Diamond Joe portrayal played a real role in unseating Trump. And if *The Onion* had already saved democracy without anybody even noticing.)

Hired in 2009 as editorial manager, Kate Palmer appeared at a perfect moment. Palmer was a navy brat who grew up in Virginia, Texas, and Florida. Her aspiration at first was to become a foreign policy journalist, and after college at the University of Florida she worked at *Foreign Policy* magazine for about six years. The bloom faded, however, so she started looking for something else—and saw a listing for the role of editorial manager of *The Onion*. "I was like, 'Oh my God, this is my dream job.' It's like, it's meant to be. I was obsessed with *The Onion* as a younger person." Palmer's job at *Foreign Policy* had been to change it from a giant bimonthly journal to a daily publication online—just what *The Onion* was trying to do.

The Onion had some advantages in the new media environment. Real journalists, Palmer said, would spend months researching and writing a three-thousand-word piece—but then most people only read the headline (which the journalist often didn't even write). For *The Onion*, though, it was "kind of magical" since everything did flow from the headline. The one-liners on the front page were basically tweets.

This was important because "the local advertising market for the print product had really fallen out." Finding ways to monetize the content digitally was now essential. The platform age had arrived for *The Onion* and all other media: previously nonexistent third parties between publications and their audiences that were rapidly gaining in power. Their existence created a new kind of product: the behavior of the user on those platforms. In other words, the page views and clicks of you and me. Tangible things were still bought and sold sometimes, like those *Onion* photo props, but the main thing for sale was our attention. Our privacy was now being obliterated, and our attention routinely monitored and manipulated, for the benefit of invisible tech giants behind the scenes—all with most of us being entirely clueless about any of it. Most people probably thought the new thing in this picture was simply novel ways to communicate.

The group also included two new and important writers, Seth Reiss and Will Tracy. Reiss grew up in Connellsville, Pennsylvania, a small rural town forty-five minutes south of Pittsburgh. Unlike most of the rest of the staff, his parents were not divorced. Reiss joked, "Anybody now who would be reading this from the Madison days would be like, 'What's his trauma?' . . . Because we have to have trauma." Reiss said Connellsville was "very much filled with Area Men and Area Women." (One of Reiss's headlines was "Restaurant Patrons Entranced by Sizzling Order of Fajitas" from May 31, 2008.) Reiss said he became "obsessed" with *The Onion* online in high school. He called it a very Gen X publication that "points out all the bullshit in life." Reiss said *The Onion* was also the rare comedy institution where the writers truly run it. He told me he felt "protective of that thing, because it doesn't exist in a lot of places." About the Madison crew, he said, "I just remember being so blown away by how smart they were about everything. Film, literature, history, art. . . . I've never been in a room with people like that since." Other Reiss headlines include "Rubber Band Needed" (April 23, 2008), "Everyone in Improv Troupe Balding" (September 8, 2012), and "Meat" (an op-ed by Robert Martin, Boar's Head CEO, April 4, 2013).

Will Tracy grew up in a "happy middle-class family" in Portland, Oregon. His dad worked for the city, and his mom taught art lessons to children. His mom was "a very funny, neurotic, hypochondriacal, anxious person." He and his brother were sort of the same way. "So there was always a lot of funny stuff happening in the house." He went to college at Vassar, and unlike many other *Onion* writers was not an aspiring comedian. If he had any aspirations, it was to make movies. After college he followed his friends to New York and started working in entry-level publishing jobs.

He knew *The Onion* from *Our Dumb Century*, which his mom had handed to him at a bookstore when he was in high school. "I think it's the funniest book, word for word, sentence for sentence, the funniest book ever written," he said. Tracy got an *Onion* internship and then became a freelance headline contributor while working as a fact-checker for *Vanity Fair*. When DiCenzo left for Jimmy Fallon's show, Tracy was asked to join the writing staff.

This next part is sad. Just as things were looking promising for the new crop of writers, one of the original crew hit his lowest. In 2009, Todd Hanson, after many years battling severe, incapacitating depression, attempted suicide by taking a pill overdose in a Brooklyn hotel room.

Before this, Clem said, "I had an alarm clock on my desk at 10:00 a.m. And if Todd wasn't there, I had to figure out if Todd was coming in that day." So when Hanson didn't show, Clem and a couple of others started calling and visiting emergency rooms trying to locate him. (Tracy said his very first day of work as an *Onion* writer was the Monday after it happened.)

Marc Maron interviewed Hanson for his *WTF* podcast about the suicide attempt in July 2011; the episode is one of Maron's best. In the interview, Hanson explains that he woke up from his overdose on his own and was somehow delivered back to his apartment, still very sick from the medicine. As is customary, he was sent to a psychiatric hospital for a while. Kolb visited him every day. Hanson says on the podcast that while he was reading everything he could about depression, he learned that "one of the highest levels of the defense mechanisms is humor." (You can find some of Hanson's articles by searching the website for the character names "Eli Wasserbaum" and "T. Eric Mayhew.")

Tracy said he got to know Hanson much better later on and, like many others, experienced the fun of hanging out and talking with him. On Hanson's depression, however, he said, Todd always had "a really interesting skewed perspective." He was very focused on what was wrong with him, but almost never in a constructive way. "You would spend two hours trying to say, 'Well, what if you try this? Or what if you looked at it this way?' And he had just a well-honed, well-trained answer for everything and why, actually, everything you're saying is bullshit." Tracy did not want to minimize Hanson's struggles, which clearly were real and for which he clearly had compassion. "But I think some other part of him was hanging on to that stuff as scraps or badges of honor that were part of his identity," Tracy said. And by then it had been going on for so long, he couldn't shake it. Tracy also said:

> But I do think that the voice of *The Onion*, a big part of that voice, is Todd. That particular kind of self-lacerating melancholy of *The Onion*. "Study: Depression Hits Losers Hardest," right? That headline is like classic Todd. And that headline is right there in the DNA of *The Onion*. That headline is to me one of the ten formative ones in some way. The perfect encapsulation of his voice and a certain kind of midwestern ennui of that generation of guy. And that's what *The Onion* is. So we always kind of idolized him and always felt he was a genius.

Randazzo, Thurston, and Palmer continued with their mission to get *The Onion* up to speed with new media. They were at the helm of a legendary *Onion* Twitter feed during a time when people were not yet using Twitter much for comedy. Not only is a tweet the same size as a headline, but the writers soon were making Twitter-thread stories that played with the concept of breaking news or that intersected with the website, Facebook page, and video in all kinds of creative ways. (This also led to Thurston's side gig as an advisor to various entities—local and international—on their web strategies, as well as a sought-after speaker for tech and journalism events.)

With all this new, innovative digital effort led by the younger staff, "our traffic is through the fucking roof, our relevance," Thurston said. "We have iPhone apps and iPad apps. Our videos are crushing it on YouTube and on Facebook, our ad rates. I feel like we were getting eighty-dollar CPMs [cost per thousand impressions] at the time. Eighty dollars per one thousand users. Today, it's, like, ten bucks. Maybe less. It was so high. And the gravy train ranneth over."

Helping organize all this was another new young staffer: Brian Janosch. Janosch grew up just south of the Wisconsin border in the northern suburbs of Chicago, in a town called Mundelein—the same town Chris Karwowski came from. He and his friends read *The Onion* online in high school and imitated it for their high school newspaper. He studied journalism at Indiana University, and a copy of *The Onion* would always be sitting around the college paper's newsroom. The "metacommentary about the news industrial complex that's inside of *The Onion*" gave him and his young colleagues a guide toward what not to become. Janosch first did an internship for *Field and Stream*, then was a freelance fact-checker for *Parenting*, then had an editorial assistant job at *Maxim*, and then—through his Karwowski hometown connection—became editorial coordinator at *The Onion*. Janosch wasn't trying to be a headline writer. He wanted to "lay down the tracks in front of the locomotive that was the writers' room." Another of Janosch's central tasks was wrangling interns. By now there were "hundreds and hundreds" of applicants.

By the time Janosch left, "we were a modern online digital-first media enterprise." More important, "The genie came out of the bottle during that time with *The Onion* being what a lot of people know it to be today, which is an institution that is reacting to news on the day that it happens."

This was indeed a fundamental change in *The Onion*. They had never before aspired to respond quickly to current news. Janosch said the first time *The Onion* responded to a news story immediately after it happened was on the day Michael Jackson died, June 25, 2009. Someone quickly wrote a piece and they got it online—whereupon it instantly "blew up" with popularity. The team said, "Oh, shit. Look what we just did." As a side effect, an old *Onion* Michael Jackson article making a joke about him being dead also began getting traction because people were Googling "Michael Jackson death" at the same time. This was "beginning to realize that we could play in a different way," Janosch said, using social media. One story in this vein was "Enraged 500-Foot-Tall Bin Laden Rises from Sea, Destroys New York, Washington," which came out in tweets as if it was happening in that moment.

Janosch also realized *The Onion* now had the potential to do "experience design." One of the most ambitious projects the editorial staff created during this period was the "China Issue" on July 24, 2009. The project was much more than an *Onion* story and was more like a multicomponent prank about, as Palmer put it, a time when "a ton of publications were getting gobbled up by various entities." The joke was that *The Onion* had been purchased by a Chinese fish-products conglomerate, Yu Wan Mei Amalgamated Salvage Fisheries and

Polymer Injection Corp. The staff first "leaked" the news that *The Onion* was going to be sold to the real media—which was reported as fact by *Gawker*—and then made an entire alternate post-takeover *Onion* website (which you can still see on the Internet Archive—go to July 25, 2009) with all of the articles written through the voice of the new owners (including an editorial by the CEO of Yu Wan Mei group, "Why Did No One Inform Us of the Imminent Death of the American Newspaper Industry?"). Also included were "Clear American Sky a Constant Reminder of Industrial Inferiority" and "Area Man Uninterested in Creating a Better Community Even Though This May Benefit Him in the Long Run." They also made a very funny website for Yu Wan Mei Amalgamated Salvage Fisheries and Polymer Injection Corp. itself (which you can also find on the Internet Archive—search for yuwanmei.com), as well as a YouTube promotional video and Facebook page. The whole thing captures the beautiful absurdity of translation from one language to another (apparently there are jokes that work only in Chinese), as well as a cheerily oppressive, modern multiplatform voice joining T. Herman Zweibel's decrepit nineteenth-century analog industrialist rantings. As always, *The Onion*'s attention to detail is incredible, with every tiny component a part of the joke.

Social media also resulted in some audience participation. After *The Onion* ran one of its most famous articles, "Planned Parenthood Opens $8 Billion Abortionplex," in 2011, written by Jason Roeder, not only did pro-life Republican congressman John Fleming of Louisiana repost it on his Facebook page credulously, but readers made a Yelp page for the abortionplex and posted reviews. (This is funny, but it also shows that the wall between business and creative was going down in real life too.)

Janosch said, "Media has become something so much more than just a paper that arrives on the doorstep. It's so entwined with reality." So it was "inevitable" that they would experiment with this as part of *The Onion*'s mission. The numbers, he said, were "astronomical." Indeed, by 2010, *The Onion* had 2.2 million Twitter followers and was the number-three media organization on Twitter overall; they also had almost 700,000 Facebook fans. The website had 7.9 million monthly unique impressions and 40 million page views, and *Onion* articles were constantly pushed to the top on Reddit and Digg. The iPhone app launched in the spring of that year already had 150,000 downloads. But despite the numbers, Janosch said the business side "didn't want to innovate or evolve what we were doing with *The Onion* as a media entity, the way we were evolving the way *The Onion* delivered satire."

In 2010, Mitch Semel, an experienced TV executive who had worked with Comedy Central, David Letterman, Conan O'Brien, Bill Maher, and others, was brought in to try to improve the relationship between business and editorial. Semel had originally been asked to advise the Onion News Network (described in the next chapter), but once he got there, Steve Hannah offered him the position of general manager. Semel said, "There was a need to have creative and business talk better to one another. And I think he'd sussed out that I was an ambassador of sorts. I kind of do the language of each."

The tension between editorial and business was, Samel said "for good reasons heightened, because of the sort of singularity of purpose and also the clarity of the editorial . . . the antiauthoritarian nature of the content that made it so good." But, being in two cities, "games of telephone start bad and get worse." He characterized the sides as "'Those business guys don't get the brand. They don't get the nature of what we're writing and why.' And the businesspeople are like, 'Why does this process take so long? Why do you need so many people?'" Semel said a really interesting thing for him at the time was that the writers "were doing such a good job parodying tensions in the media businesses. We had to be funny about it. But we also had to deal with the actual challenges in the media businesses." Semel added, "Sadly, it seems that the model these days if you want to be in the news business is you either have to go nonprofit or find a billionaire who likes you."

Ben Berkley is the last of the fresh-faced new generation discussed here. Berkley was from Tempe, Arizona, and was born the year *The Onion* was founded: 1988. His mom was a high school teacher, and his dad worked at a local utility provider. "I think everyone at *The Onion* had this very traumatic childhood or some sort of really deep-seated something," he said, "and I never quite felt like that was me." However, he joked, "Luckily, *The Onion* provided enough trauma for me to catch up to them."

Berkley also found out about *The Onion* because of *Our Dumb Century*. When he read it, "it broke my brain a little bit." At Arizona State University he spent most of his time in the newsroom of the daily print student newspaper.

When he graduated with a sociology degree in 2010, he applied for an internship at *The Onion*. Berkley had lived at home all through college, so this was his first time moving out of the house.

He showed up two hours early for his interview. After waiting anxiously at the Starbucks across the street for a while, he "popped up the elevator and arrived in the office, and nobody was there." He walked through the empty space looking for intern wrangler Janosch.

I just kind of assumed I would never encounter a single *Onion* employee in my life, let alone be in their office, let alone be there for a day of work. And it just had that aura to it. That office was just so cool. It's very cinematic in my mind. . . . I can imagine the soft lighting coming through and the hardwood floors, which are just so, so loud.

If you looked at it from a certain angle, you'd kind of be like, "Oh, just a bunch of cubicles." But then, you find little elements of delight throughout. Their front pages hanging on the walls. And everyone's desk has some sort of strange shit going on. . . . The glass conference room was in the corner and had the nicest sunlight and clocks on the walls. . . . I was so tickled by the places they had selected. [The clocks were labeled with various small Wisconsin communities and all set to the same time.] And then you kind of turned the corner back toward the writers' room. There's a cute little kitchen and Joe's Cold Beverages. You'd pass that and be like, "Okay, what is this?"

And then you land in the writers' room, which is just, it just has that mystique to it. You're just like, I don't know. That "holy shit" moment, the first time you're ever in there.

The interns' job was to manage the river of jokes generated in that writers' room and keep track of what made the cut and what didn't. Berkley also did fact-checking, which has long been very important at *The Onion*; as Stephen Thompson said, satire needs to be based on reality. Berkley would meet someone in New York and they'd ask "So what do you do?" and he'd say, "I fact-check *The Onion*." People would laugh, so he'd say, "No, actually, I do."

But it wasn't all work. Like Berkley, everybody talked about Joe's Cold Beverages, which was the mini-bodega that Joe Garden ran out of his office. People would go there to buy Clif bars and chips and gum and soda and that sort of thing. He would occasionally also bring in a little grill and hot pot and serve homemade grilled cheese sandwiches and tomato soup, sending out all-staff emails to tell them about that day's specials. Sometimes people from other offices in the building would come too.

Garden continued with various little body-oriented performances, though the full nudity seemed to have been left in the pre-intern era. Tracy said, "I remember him lifting up his shirt and he would take his belly, and he would form a bagel shape with his belly button as the hole in the middle of the bagel. And that was a constant thing that he would do." Others remembered him wearing those roller-skate sneakers in the office and zooming around. He also had a character called Baby America, which was Garden in an American flag diaper speaking in a Russian accent.

Art director Rick Martin came up with a staff social event known as Whiskey Friday, a mostly mild-mannered staff party. Some writers avoided it when it became a "hashtag Whiskey Friday" thing, but others remember Whiskey Friday fondly. Baratunde Thurston seems to have adopted Whiskey Friday and taken it far beyond what it had been before, inviting people from tech and comedy to come hang out too. He has a short Whiskey Friday video on his YouTube page featuring Garden writing out his *Onion* tweets on postcards with a pen and mailing them to readers.

The Onion also still had its softball team, which was made up of not only current staff—both editorial and business—but also alums. Joe Pickett, who was in New York as distribution manager at the time, told me a story about a near brawl with the *New Yorker*. Krewson, he said, hit a ball into the outfield and tried to make it into an inside-the-park home run. He was rounding third, the *New Yorker* got the ball, and the infield catcher had it as Krewson headed toward home plate. And then Krewson lowered his shoulder "and plows into him." The catcher got up and grabbed Krewson by the shirt and pulled back his fist. "Krewson pulled back his fist, and they both start screaming at each other."

And then both dugouts were just like "deer in headlights." These were people who fought with the pen, not the sword. But they eventually all came "sauntering" out to assist, just like on TV but more literary. "I've been play-ing baseball my entire life," Pickett said, "and I've never had a bench-clearing brawl, except *The Onion* versus the *New Yorker*." (The *New Yorker* actually started in 1925 as a highbrow humor magazine.) Krewson told me he didn't remember this episode, but he did say he liked playing better back in Madison, when peo-ple weren't so serious about winning.

Hanson said he attended a few New York games as a heckler. "I never played because I hate sports. But it was fun to heckle and to try to be creative in that heckling." Hanson remembered one game in particular, also against the *New Yorker*. "I was heckling the *New Yorker* by deconstructing their cartoons," he said. As the batter got ready for the pitch, "I was going, 'He's behind the desk. He says something in business jargon.' And then right before they swing, I go, 'But here's the thing—he's a duck!'"

And on one glorious day in 2008, *The Onion* beat *High Times*. Chet Clem said, "It was always the saga. We could never beat *High Times*." This time, though, *The Onion* had "stacked the team" with alums who were good players alongside the current *Onion* staff team members. (The media leagues always made sure to include the often more muscle-bound members of the distribution, advertising, and business staffs along with the egghead editorial people.) Pickett said, "We had such a great team. I remember every play from that game." Clem described the scene:

It was one of those just hilarious days where everything goes right. I remem-ber the first inning, there was a hard-hit ground ball to DiCenzo, who was playing shortstop. And he dove for it and it hit a rock and went up, and he went and caught it and knocked it down and made the play. I was playing first base because I was an old hockey goalie, so I wasn't afraid to get in front of all these errant balls that were thrown.

Someone hit a pop fly. And it was one of those picturesque beautiful days in Central Park where *everyone's* there, and there are people watching; there are people on towels out and everything. The fly ball hit the foul territory, and I just turned and ran. And I dove and caught the ball in foul territory. And I came down on my shoulder, and I ended up like significantly fucking up my shoulder. Didn't realize it because we were all on such adrenaline because all of a sudden we turned a double play, which *never happens.*

Everything seemed to work that day. And we beat *High Times.* It was like we'd won the World Series. I think the Yankees celebrated less in some of their championships than we did that day.

Pickett said, "I still think about that game. Every time I run into Mike DiCenzo, that's all we talk about is that *High Times* game. It's like 'Do you remember? It was five to six; bases were loaded.' The glory days."

The Onion's creative side was also starting a new digital enterprise: the web video. And here the younger generation would also really shine—once they got past the older generation's well-deserved skepticism.

Chapter 15

While *The Onion*'s editorial side was developing and expanding their digital presence, a new *Onion* enterprise had also started that was digital too—but in a form very different from written text. In 2006, *The Onion*'s business managers were ready to spend money on something to diversify the brand and take advantage of a new kind of media just beginning to bloom: the online video.

Website-based video was suddenly being discussed all over the place. YouTube had started the prior year, and people were starting to upload home-made videos like crazy from their digital cameras. (This was still the flip-phone era—the iPhone wouldn't come out until 2007.) Twitter was also created in 2006 but wouldn't be able to show videos without linking to an external website until 2010; Facebook, founded in 2004, was similar. (Unfortunately, even though such platforms would rapidly become a form of publishing and exert paradigm-shifting influence on both media creators and media consumers, they would exercise few of publishing's norms, standards, or sense of responsibility.)

Professional web video was being made too. For comedy, you could go to College Humor, Funny or Die, Comedy Central, or Adult Swim. Sitcoms like *The Office*, which people still watched on regular TV, would put up supplemental video shorts on their network websites—extra content for fans of the show. Newspaper websites started experimenting with video pieces as well, part of an industry-wide conversation about how to create effective "multimedia" stories. (It mostly seemed to be about *how* to do it, not *whether* to do it.) Meanwhile, on YouTube, all kinds of amateur videos were starting to appear: tutorials, commentary, and vlogs on every possible subject, homemade TV shows, life coaches giving pep talks, psychologists or people pretending to be psychologists.

Credentials were optional, mashing true experts in with people who were just making stuff up. Then there were the endless cute children, kittens and puppies, and home movies clipped to spawn a thousand memes. (Porn is a whole other story, but I'm sure you can imagine what was happening.) Whole new genres began to appear on YouTube, like the idiotic, mesmerizing "unboxing" genre (which thankfully has been parodied; for instance, see TitanicFan97, who has been posting very excited videos of himself unboxing VHS copies of the film *Titanic* for years, adding to a collection that now consists of at least 3,378 tapes), as well as the "video of a guy playing video games" genre thrilling tweens across the planet for more than fifteen years while leaving their parents scratching their heads as to the appeal. (Thurston told me he thought it was about the feeling of personal connection the kids develop with the gamer.)

Still, in 2006 it made sense to ask: Was online video on its way to becoming the new television? If so, *The Onion* should be in on that and at the highest production levels possible (and also sell a lot of ads to play before, during, and after the videos). President Sean Mills was one of the main people promoting the idea and being aggressive about getting to the front of the pack. But to do that, they needed new staff.

The Onion first hired twenty-four-year-old Will Graham, an MFA student in film at Columbia University. Graham was brought in by a friend from college at Columbia, managing editor Peter Koechley (who was also helping the video project get off the ground), to produce and direct. Koechley said he hired Graham because he was smart and capable, even though he did not have a deep comedy background and had not done the usual *Onion* apprenticeship process. Dikkers also helped get things going in the early stages.

By now, of course, there had been numerous prior attempts to put *The Onion*'s distinctive style on screen, none of which had been successful. The older staffers were skeptical about the whole idea of video now. Koechley, however, thought it was a great opportunity. To him it was a hard sell not so much because of the older staff's prior bad experiences, or because he'd brought in a complete outsider with no *Onion* training, but because the operation was getting a little old-fashioned. "It was an online publication with the spirit of an old-style Hearst-like newspaper," he said. Digital "felt like it was a stretch," spiritually and psychologically, even though they'd been online since 1996. They were still exporting the paper from QuarkXPress to copy and paste onto the internet once a week on Wednesday nights, even after content-management systems and daily publishing had clearly become the trend.

The writing staff was also skeptical about the real motivations of the business side in promoting this new enterprise. Why was video suddenly getting all this money when the paper wasn't? "Tons of things get adapted to a new medium and get bastardized in the process or lose their soul," Koechley said. "And we were just coming off the experience of *The Onion Movie*. I was late to that, and didn't play a major role in it, but it was an awful experience from where I sat. I think people were deeply distrustful."

Graham, Dikkers, and a small staff spent months tinkering with different ideas, trying to come up with the right approach. Much of what they made never aired. Some of their early efforts, Graham said, sounded good on paper, "but when you play it out in video form, either there's not enough there, or it just becomes very conceptual, and it becomes really boring, and there's not a visual aspect to it. And then we tried some things that were also too loonball and too broad and too silly." Koechley said they at first purposely tried to *not* do news segments. One early experiment was Osama bin Laden giving a tour of New York City—or at least all the weak spots that would be vulnerable to terrorism—done in a fun, peppy voice. Ellie Kemper (a former *Onion* intern) and comedian Kristen Schaal appeared in it. Koechley also remembered making a "weird public-access show about all of the lost and found items in the nation." They then screened their experiments for the staff, which did not go over well. "What are you guys *doing*?"

Koechley thought his problem was being trained at *The Onion* to be a very logical comedy writer and thinker. *The Onion* was so "rigorous and disciplined in its execution. Not in how we ran the place, but in the actual product that came out." But that hyperlogical space didn't work for video. For the production process, yes. For creative, however, you need to be able to get at the in-between spaces—the emotional, the irrational, the archetypal. Or, as Koechley said, "Video's just goofier and less restrained and less disciplined than print as a medium," even though "they can be really smart and really deep in all the same sort of ways" as *The Onion*.

Finally, Graham said, they eventually gave in and made it news: "a twenty-four-hour news network—something more sinister and scary than Fox, more bombastic, with the swooshiest graphics imaginable and secretly a shadow government," as he described in a 2008 *Guardian* article. The Onion News

HAPPENING NOW
Daniel Medina
EXPERT

IDS NOW TOO LAZY TO IMITATE TELEVISION VIOLENCE   MILITARY /

ONN's "Some Bullshit Happening Somewhere." The Onion demonstrates how cable TV news creates its nonstories and makes them seem urgent and important. Watch it once for the jokes and then again for its structure and technique.

Network had arrived. Graham—like Siegel a decade earlier—also realized "the closer we stuck to the real voice, the more absurd things we could do." He started building a team to create the videos.

What was cable news like at that time? Graham said, "In the 2006 to 2010 years, the cable news ecosystem was really settling into place, and Fox News was becoming a huge deal. Suddenly, this was a twenty-four-hour part of our lives outside of just CNN. *The Onion* made some of the first real jokes about that and pointed out the ridiculousness of what they were doing." Will is right, but his timing can be expanded. By 2007, as Kathryn Cramer Brownell wrote in her 2023 book *24/7 Politics: Cable Television & the Fragmenting of America from Watergate to Fox News*, cable TV had been changing "the very idea of news" into whatever viewers (supposedly) wanted for more than fifteen years. CNN's coverage of the 1991 Gulf War, which introduced exciting music, vivid graphics, and a "you-are-there" reality-show feel, instead of the prior paradigm of a calm, steady network anchor like Walter Cronkite giving you the highlights of a researched report is often marked as a turning point.

Cable grabbed people's attention twenty-four hours a day, seven days a week, and producers learned early on that "controversy and conflict sold well," making the promotion of political division important for the bottom line. Such programming was also much cheaper to create than investigative journalism. Old favorites like sex, music, cute animals, romance, sports, food, and making stuff also found plenty of open airtime. The idea of "breaking" news, which formerly had been reserved for things like presidential assassinations, had also disintegrated in the 24/7 news environment to include basically anything. (ONN's "Some Bullshit Happening Somewhere" is a two-minute master class in how cable structures and creates its nonstories. A reporter is shown delivering an exciting, vivid report "with the use of expensive technology" on a not especially newsworthy event.) Keeping butts in seats also resulted in an intense ramping up of visual and emotional style that was more akin to the day's video games, music videos, and action-adventure films than the prior thirty years of network TV news broadcasts.

Cramer Brownell writes that this evolution of cable was actually in large part due to President Richard Nixon (1969–1974), who hated the network news and how it had portrayed him and his policies. To fight it, Nixon had set up Project BUN (Break Up Networks) and predicted that once their plans to deregulate and promote cable got rolling, cable would rise into ascendance in about ten years. Indeed it did, with cable coming into wide American use in the early 1980s. Though some saw it as a new technology that could flatten hierarchies and facilitate democracy (sound familiar?), modern cable programming was actually created in part so Nixon and friends could get their messages out to the people directly, bypassing the old traditional network news and their "basic assumptions about news, public interest, and civic duty."

Because of this, *The Onion* had selected a very interesting person to create its new cable satire. Will Graham was not just any MFA film student. Like founder Tim Keck, Graham also grew up in a newspaper family, though Keck's childhood probably had a lot more beer and Polish sausage and a lot fewer cashmere sweaters and trips to Martha's Vineyard. Graham was the son of Don Graham, the publisher and CEO of the *Washington Post*, and the grandson of Katharine Graham, who had been publisher of the *Post* during the Watergate scandal. Graham may not have realized it, but he was now carrying on the family heritage around Richard Nixon. He said:

> I grew up in a house that was all about news and surrounded by journalists
> and people who were engaged in the world in a really meaningful way. I think

because of that, I love the smell of news and the sound of news. I grew up around a lot of people who were in love with it. And I always wanted to write and make television and make films and do the things that I'm doing now. But I always felt like there was going to be some kind of moment where I maybe touched on that news world in a fun way.

By 2007, Fox News had become an institution. The phenomenon of young and middle-aged people watching their parents or grandparents get sucked into the Fox News worldview had reached the point where it was becoming common to hear stories about how these family members now ruined every visit home for the holidays, were newly obsessed with made-up crises like Barack Obama's birth certificate or losing access to machine guns, and otherwise expressed weird, paranoid, angry, persecuted, and fearful points of view on a regular basis.

The Daily Show and *The Colbert Report* were also now extremely popular evening shows, with a very different approach than Fox News. Communications scholars and public commentators analyzed both shows with intense fascination. Were people now getting most of their news from news *parody*? (A famous 2004 Pew Research Center study showed Stewart and Colbert had more impact on young people's understanding of politics and current events than the actual news—even though Ben Karlin told me they always thought that was "bullshit.")

For viewers under thirty-five or so, studies showed they were—and that both Stewart and Colbert seemed to be excellent teachers of media literacy. Every night was a little class in how to unpack the way the media and politics worked now—something that the regular news seemed to be unable to do, forever mired in the objective, both-sides, events-focused reporting paradigm that conservatives had been manipulating for decades into serving their political purposes. Stewart and Colbert were so popular that scholars and commentators asked: Was news satire going to save democracy?

If Fox News was a mirror image of Stewart and Colbert, though, the older Fox viewers were getting most of their news and commentary from fake sources now too—just with a different agenda. And though probably a lot more liberals than conservatives watched Stewart and Colbert—conservatives unfamiliar with Colbert's show sometimes thought his parody of a right-wing cable blowhard was the real thing—both made fun of all sides of the political spectrum. Their primary target was not conservatives, but the way the news had abdicated its public-service responsibilities.

In 2007, as ONN was getting going, Fox News took a shot at their own late-night news parody show: *The ½ Hour News Hour*, created by conservative television producer Joel Surnow, a self-proclaimed "right-wing nut job" who hoped the show "would make Michael Moore spontaneously burst into flames." (The show was aimed at Rush Limbaugh fans and featured former *SNL* "Weekend Update" anchor Dennis Miller.) Though 1.4 million people tuned in for the first broadcast, the numbers sank quickly; the show was godawful. Relying on cultural stereo-types, sophomoric jokes, and general offensiveness for its humor, its Stewart-rip-off interviews and commentary were based not on actual political or media events, as Stewart did on *The Daily Show*, but rather on straw-men liberal stereotypes embodied by fictional characters played by actors who threatened to take away your guns, make you believe in global warming, fixate on race and gender, and so on. News-satire scholar Geoffrey Baym wrote in a special 2012 issue of *Cinema Journal* that the show tanked not because conservatives aren't funny, but because it lacked "the outsider stance that motivates satire and empowers parody." *The ½ Hour News Hour* was upholding the paranoid status quo, not exposing its flaws.

When Graham arrived on his first day, no desk was provided to him, so he sat at the office Ping-Pong table. This became ONN's production office. Graham said, "We stayed at the Ping-Pong table until the point that the Ping-Pong table was clearly about to break from everything that was on it." One of the first people Graham hired was editor JJ Adler, whom Graham knew from the Columbia MFA filmmaking program. Adler had grown up in New York as an Orthodox Jew. And her first major foray into the broader world was at *The Onion*. Until that point, Adler said, "I truly had no relationships with anyone outside of the [Orthodox] community, other than fledgling relationships at film school." Everything was new. "I had no frame of reference at all for this, to see people sit around a table and debate philosophically about a joke. It was like, 'What?' I had no idea what I was witnessing."

Adler said Dikkers gave her "a little comedy tutorial, like me, personally." He would tell her, for instance, "People are laughing for the wrong reason at this joke. You have to be really clear on what the intention is." She said it was a positive experience working with him. On the other hand, she could imagine that "if you were trying to get a story through and he was saying no, that would be very annoying." Dikkers, she said, had his own view of things. "And that's it, you know?" Many people told me how confident Dikkers always was in his judgments, even when others did not agree with him. "I don't think I was intimidating," he told me. "But I was definitely so sure of myself that most people probably cowered away from trying to fight me on anything."

Dikkers said he and Graham met constantly during Graham's "training" period, "approving all the ideas that went online. I was approving and punching up all the rough drafts." Dikkers also was there at the editing process to tell Adler which cuts worked, whether two jokes should be switched around, and so on. Graham said Dikkers was "incredibly specific" about how *The Onion* "worked from a satirical perspective, and how those kinds of jokes should operate." As Graham put it, though, "At the end of the day, that's the most subjective thing in the world."

In February 2007, *The Onion* hired Julie Smith, who was in her late twenties and had been working producing both TV and live comedy in New York for years. Smith had grown up in Weymouth, Massachusetts, with loving, supportive parents with a strong work ethic, "a really nice, lovely family childhood." And then she went to college at Fordham University in New York City "to get the hell out of the beautiful place I was raised" and became a journalism major. There she began interning at NBC, MTV, Adult Swim, and many other places, learning professionally how to put a show together—often on a tight budget. She was also well connected to the New York comedy scene, tasked by TV producers to scout out new talent. ONN now had a leader with the ability to take their experiments to the next level—the only staffer to enter the Onion News Network with extensive real-world video production experience. On top of this, Smith could also handle and understand the corporate mindset with ease. She got along well with Mike McAvoy—now chief financial officer—while also getting along with the creative staff. Smith said she'd worked on a lot of "scrappy" productions, but ONN was one of the scrappiest. She said ONN "wasn't just satirizing Fox News. I think it had to also be CNN. . . . It had to be equally thinking about Americans and our actual society and our response to media. And not just the media." Graham said, "I always thought of it like it was a news broadcast that had gotten a concussion and didn't realize it was comedic."

While Smith was settling in, the first ONN piece went up a few weeks later in March 2007, directed by Dikkers. It was about an immigrant who became the CEO of a major company, trading places with the original CEO who became a busboy in a restaurant. Unfortunately, the *New York Magazine* Intelligencer shredded it with a short review titled "New 'Onion' Fake News: Actually Fake, Not So Funny":

> Here's the remarkable thing about the *Onion News Network*, the satire stalwart's first foray into video content: It's the first televisual product to literally fit the wrongheaded moniker "fake news." *The Daily Show* and *The Colbert Report*, which are regularly saddled with that descriptor, don't fake the news; they fake the format. *ONN*—as of this writing, less a network than a Web page with four clips and a Dewar's ad—finally takes that extra step. Its news items are, indeed, mocked-up rather than simply mocked. This means that both the anchors and the subjects are played, hammily, by actors, and the "news footage" is as scripted as the banter around it. Sadly, though, it is not particularly well scripted, nor particularly amusing.

The review went on to say that the video had "a setup so broad it could have come from medieval puppetry" and lacked visual thinking. "As it stands, it's an *Onion* print story, mirthlessly pantomimed." I didn't think the video was nearly as bad as the review did—in fact I enjoyed it—but it did again basically follow the read-out-loud-*Onion*-newspaper-story model that failed in the past. It also felt more like a circa 1995 network news segment than twenty-first-century cable. Dikkers also directed the early ONN videos "Gap Unveils New 'For Kids By Kids' Clothing Line," about child labor, and "Multiple Stab Wounds May Be Harmful to Monkeys," perhaps inspired by his animal rights convictions. The scathing *New York Magazine* review aside, Graham said after they launched, "The immediate response to it was so good," which was "a huge relief for the people from the paper, but also for Sean Mills and Mike McAvoy and the business team." (Dikkers would quit *The Onion* a few months later.)

Over the next year, the ONN staff kept experimenting with new formats and started working on increasing the frequency of releases from once a week to two or three, all trying to duplicate the feel of a monster cable news network. In every round of shooting, they would try a new show to make ONN feel bigger.

They also found ways to shorten the turnaround time. Mitch Semel said, "The dry, quieter tone of *The Onion*, which works so well in print and on the website, wasn't built for web video, let alone for cable TV. They had to, frankly, be bigger and louder." And ONN did start getting bigger and louder—and really good. The newspaper side couldn't deny it: once ONN found its voice, as Todd Hanson put it, it became "peak *Onion*." By June 2010, they would have three million impressions per week and more than a half-million iTunes subscribers.

A primary reason ONN got so good was the choice to bring back Carol Kolb as head writer, who seemed to have stepped easily out of the network-era mindset. She, Graham, and Smith seem to have made a perfect team—an *Onion* news-satire veteran with a taste for situationist-style performance art, paired with talented new blood who grew up with the *Washington Post* in his house and a producer with years of street cred in both downtown cutting-edge comedy and TV production. Graham said of Kolb, "I was probably slightly intimidated. Is this someone who's going to come in with a really different perspective?" There was nothing to fear. Graham said he quickly realized Kolb was one of the world's great people. "She's warm and funny and has a sense of humor that's not like anyone else, and I think you see it all over the ONN videos. [Kolb] had an incredible love of the jokes that were a little more oddball and a little more eccentric. . . . I can't say how much I love her and respect her and how much she deserves credit for all of the things that ONN was."

Graham added, "I think in some ways, possibly because I'm queer, and Carol is a woman, the *Onion* paper always seemed to have this male energy at the core of the creative process. And I think from the beginning, the videos had a kind of very different energy, and a lot of that was because of Carol." Kolb said Graham was—like Smith—great with organizing and talking to the business side.

In an echo of how real cable evolved, when networks were faced with the challenge of filling up airtime quickly and cheaply, ONN created a morning show—*Today Now!*—starring the brilliant Brad Holbrook and Tracy Toth as the chipper, upbeat, note-perfect hosts, Jim Haggerty and Tracy Gill, who interviewed guests like the "Expert Who Wasted Entire Life Studying Anteaters," pop stars, parenting experts, and a chef who cooks a delicious omelet that came to him in a dream. "Make sure you use the whisk because if you use a fork, Robin Williams is gonna come and offer to lend you his whisk, then the two of you need to go up to his grandparents' attic, and there's millions of doors up there." "War for the White House" also offered many opportunities, like "Voting Machines Elect One of Their Own," "Poll Reveals 430 New Demographics That Will Decide Election" (featuring John Krewson as a member of the "Farmhouse Dwelling Self-Publishing Mystery Novelist" demographic and Joe Garden as part of the "Underemployed Mathematicians" group), and "Study Finds Youths Don't Follow Office Politics."

ONN's insanely over-the-top "War for the White House" graphics— explosions, fire, overdramatic music, zooming jets—tell an entire satiric story all by themselves. Adler had hired a very talented VFX person named Billy Cummings, as well as the equally talented Chris Ervine and J. J. Shebesta to handle the graphics. Indeed, the team got so good that a staff friend at CBS said *The Onion*'s visuals were better than their own, and an *Onion* VFX person was actually hired away by Fox News.

ONN also decided to create a *Meet the Press*–style debate show called *In the Know* and brought in "incredibly talented improvisers" to come in and experiment, like Julie Brister and Brian Huskey from Upright Citizens Brigade. "We didn't know what we were doing," Graham said. "We weren't sure that we were going to release any of these." It turned out the shows needed to be scripted rather than improvised. Graham and Koechley went down to Washington to watch *Meet the Press* be filmed, noting the camera angles, lighting, sets, pacing, and everything a filmmaker needed to emulate the show.

Graham kept his illustrious family background—both culturally and newswise—on the down-low. Adler said she didn't know about it for years, and if I hadn't asked him about it when we talked, I am sure he would not have mentioned it. Kolb said Graham was hardworking, down-to-earth, and well educated, and that it took a while for her to realize, "Oh, you're from this newspaper family. And you're now heading up this parody of a news organization. I guess there's probably a connection there." She met his family. "His dad and mom were super smart and cool and funny and great to talk to, and it was just the opposite of the old Madison people. It was just a different world." (It is unclear whether Dikkers knew about Graham's background when training him in fake-news production. Despite having a "weak handshake" and being a "total newbie," Dikkers told me, Graham ended up being a "great leader.") Graham told me, "I grew up really knowing how seriously journalists take what they do. And leaning into that seriousness in the voice was part of the magic tone of ONN."

Unpaid interns were very important to ONN's success. The first was Dan Mirk. When he came to *The Onion*'s office building in a suit and tie to interview for an internship at the paper, he happened to get on the elevator at the same time as Graham. By the time they got to *The Onion*'s floor, Graham had asked Mirk—who had arrived in New York only two weeks earlier—if he wanted to intern for the brand-new Onion News Network instead. Mirk said yes, becoming the first writing intern.

Dan Mirk grew up in Ojai, California, a very beautiful, very small town "that I was very excited to get out of." His family was bookish, "very quiet people who read a lot. We spent so many dinners around the table with everybody, me and my sister and my parents, just all reading books, in silence." Mirk always loved comedy, though he didn't know it could be a career. In college at UC–Santa Cruz, he learned how to write news articles and radio stories, so it was not a stretch to combine those things into an *Onion* news voice. ONN's sensibility was "kind of a little darker" also, which seemed to suit him.

Graham said, "Dan is brilliant, very tall, very skinny. We used to make him do 'wind sock outside a gas station' dances. He is this really strange combination of one of the kindest people that I know, but also one of the sharpest satirical minds." Mirk, he said, really helped to establish ONN's tone and had exactly the right comedy sensibility.

Mirk said that Kolb taught him the *Onion* style of joke making. "You need to be able to clearly identify what is the target that you're making fun of, and all the jokes need to aim toward that target. And it needs to be a target that you actually believe should be attacked," he said. Mirk also said a centrally important idea at *The Onion*—both the newspaper and ONN—was that it was a group effort. "Everything at *The Onion* is done so collectively," Mirk said. Graham also emphasized that ONN was a team. "There's no one person who can say, 'I am the creator of the Onion News Network,' any more than there's one person who can say, 'I created *The Onion*,'" he said. "That's just antithetical to how the place works."

Another new hire, as writer and director, was Lang Fisher—also a friend of Graham's from Columbia. Fisher was born in Charlottesville, Virginia, to physician parents. After college at Columbia, Fisher stayed in New York and started doing improv and stand-up, "sort of trying to get my foot in the door in the comedy world."

She said that this was such a specific time on the internet. The year 2007 was a "sweet spot where people were excited to post and pass these videos around." Instead of rapid-fire Instagram stories or TikTok, people "were going to *Gawker* or Perez Hilton, or the *Huffington Post*, or us, just to read content and see things that were funny. College Humor. It felt like a big moment for comedy videos." Today, website-based videos have gone by the wayside. When I asked Fisher why, she said, "Because your shows are *on* the internet. It's not like if you have a show on Netflix, Netflix is gonna have short comedy videos in addition to your show that you're already streaming." Besides, now "there's *so much* content, right?" Social media is "where people's attentions are. They aren't searching out the NBC website anymore." ONN got really popular before smartphones. "At work, you're taking a break from whatever you're doing, and you're on your desktop computer looking around for funny videos."

It also was a time when people still chose to go to a website and consciously select what they wanted to watch. Individual videos also created an experience that had a beginning, middle, and end. Now, autoplay and that infinite list of enticing thumbnails keep the show going forever, an endless stream of content that is not deliberately chosen by you, but is instead poured onto your screen by algorithms created by billionaires with their own set of priorities.

Elizabeth Koe also joined ONN early on as an intern. She grew up in a small "98 percent Latino" New Jersey city right outside New York with a single mom and is half Japanese. As a teenager, Koe would take the train into Manhattan and go see films at the Angelika. She graduated from Brown University in 2004 and started taking sketch-writing classes at Columbia and the New School and improv classes at Upright Citizens Brigade. But she had no idea how to make that into a job. Then she got an *Onion* internship. "I just remember being in awe of Carol," she said, because "when you walk into the office, there were definitely a lot of dudes there."

Koe's intern job was to compile all the chosen headlines into a list for Kolb, Mirk, and Graham to go through. Koe likened the process to a "funnel," where hundreds poured in, but only a few came out. Headlines that weren't enough to become a whole story would be used for the one-liner jokes running on the little ticker at the bottom of the screen of every ONN video. After several more rounds of cutting and winnowing, the number of scripts actually produced would amount to about a dozen. The process was intended to be democratic as well as rigorous, with a Google spreadsheet where everyone could vote anonymously for their favorites. No more screaming fights.

Kolb said that although ONN had taken a lot of money to produce compared to the paper—millions of dollars, according to Steve Hannah—it was still done on the cheap. "We were very careful about counting our pennies; we were not just given a bunch of cash and didn't have to think about it," she said. Graham said they spent around $3,000–$5,000 per episode. ONN, still, however, had really high production values, or at least appeared to have them. Graham said they found creative ways to create the illusion of a big budget.

As ONN become more solidified and successful, it all began to grow. Fisher said, "It felt like we were a fungus that was slowly taking over all of their space." Mirk recalled that the newcomers really had to earn the trust of the old guard, who needed to be convinced the newbies weren't just going to make bullshit. He said they were understandably very suspicious when suddenly a bunch of twenty-two-year-olds showed up saying, "We're gonna make videos out of *The Onion!*"

The new kids, though, were very respectful of the Gen X crew. Even starstruck. When Mirk was asked to come on as an actual paid writer after his internship, he was ecstatic:

Oh my God, it was the most exciting thing that had ever happened to me. It was just unbelievable. I mean, it was like a dream. I couldn't even believe that I was working at *The Onion* at all to begin with, and then to be a paid as a writer there was like—it's still shocking to me that I was able to do it. It was such a dream. I had been such an enormous fan for such a long time. I thought of *The Onion* as almost like a sacred thing in my life. I felt like when I was in the *Onion* office, I was on hallowed ground, you know? It was very, very important to me. And I just felt like, "I can't even believe this is my real life."

Koe was hired full-time at *The Onion* as well and was just as excited. She said her first job was to find real news footage they could use as background— the sort of thing you would see "if you watched Anderson Cooper live, when you're seeing a feed from Iraq or Afghanistan, you're seeing the footage from China, you're seeing footage from a house fire." She found it in the network news archives and at CNN.

Much of the filming took place in a New York studio normally used for soap operas. The ONN shoots were done in batches of thirty or so at a time that, after postproduction, would then be released onto the website once or twice a week. Fisher said, "We would just shoot there all day, hammering out a million videos. Our anchors would put on a different blazer, and then they would have to read copy really fast, switch it out, and do something else. It was a real grind." Adler, who also directed many videos, said this would all cycle into post while new scripts were worked up, so by the time post was completed on the first group, the next round of scripts was ready to produce.

The work might have been intense, but the group was exploding with creativity. The casting, for instance, was incredible—using not only real former news anchors for ONN's anchors since professional actors could never get the cadence right, but also character actors who were so good that even today they fool people watching the ONN archive. And there were so many of them. ONN made hundreds of videos; almost all of them had characters that appeared in only one episode. Smith said, "We had to be up there with *Law and Order*" with how many actors they went through. Cody Beke and Seth White, who were getting their own careers started, did much of the casting. They hired New York City actors and other people who brought the verisimilitude ONN was looking for. Kolb said it worked great when they got people who couldn't act very well, "because that's what people do when you do a news interview—they're not actors." But experienced pros came through the door too, even though, as Mirk said, "they were certainly not doing union work for us." Smith said they did a special new thing called a "new media" deal with the union to hire them.

The silliness was epic, the darkness very dark. ONN had it down—landmark work in *The Onion*'s history, up there with *Our Dumb Century*. There are Onion News Network videos that made me laugh and then cut so deep they really did make me cry, like "Panda Demands Abortion." On the absurd side, one of my favorites is "Pop Star's Single, 'Booty Wave,' Most Likely Civilization's Downfall." The actress/dancer playing the pop star K'ronikka, Katie Webber, knocked it out of the park with her portrayal of the aggressively idiotic singer, while Fisher and Koe wrote the lyrics for the song. Its music video was shown in the segment, with, um, booty effects by Shebesta. Jim Haggerty asks, "Now tell us, K'ronikka, how did you first decide that you wanted to be the cipher through which the cynicism of a morally bankrupt industry is channeled?" Everyone is so note-perfect, it's uncanny. Much of ONN carries that uncanny feeling, like you've somehow slipped into an alternative news universe that looks, feels, and sounds exactly like the real one but is just . . . off, in a way that is uncomfortable, shocking, and very funny.

ONN examples satirizing the human condition include "Attractive Girls Union Refuses to Talk with Mike Greenman," "Nation's Girlfriends Unveil New Economic Plan: 'Let's Move in Together,'" and "New Law Would Ban Marriages Between People Who Don't Love Each Other." There were also a good number of Iraq War jokes, like "Bring Your Daughter to War Day," and one about the Iraq War mascot being killed in action.

Other ONN segments poked a sharp stick in the eye of how professional news and commentary so often works these days—especially around how much of it is basically just filler around advertising. Graham said one of his favorites was an *In the Know* piece, "Situation in Nigeria Seems Pretty Complex," where members of the guest panel bullshit their way through discussion on a topic they know nothing about. Graham also enjoyed the silly, more local news segments, especially one written by Megan Ganz, "Ninja Parade Slips by Town Unnoticed Once Again." Graham also added, "Without realizing, I kept green-lighting jokes that had horses at the center of them. One of them was a profile of the first openly gay racehorse to compete in a major race. We were shooting it on this farm in New Jersey. And the guy who owned the horse was like, 'You know what? This horse is actually gay.'" Koe said not many of her own ideas made it through the process, but one that did happens to be a classic ONN *Today Now!* episode: "Finding a Masculine Halloween Costume for Your Effeminate Son." Then there's "Missing Teen's Friends Go on TV to Plead for Her Release, Gossip About Ugly Classmates," a *Today Now!* segment that show-cases two of the most amazing cinematic performances I have ever seen, by Courtney Baxter and Jessica Rothe as the missing teen's cliquey, backstabbing friends, somehow expressing both jaw-dropping horribleness and total vulner-ability in the three-minute segment.

ONN also experimented with doing international news videos in dif-ferent languages, made with the same verisimilitude as the English ones. A standout includes the NSFW "Denmark Introduces Harrowing New Tourism Ads Directed by Lars Von Trier," featuring a terrifying run through a forest and a nausea-inducing humiliation scene. It even has the running ticker in Danish. Though the segment is in English, I have to mention "Prague's Kafka International Named Most Alienating Airport" as another ONN classic, with haggard, despairing travelers lost in mazelike terminals posted with nonsensical signs and hand-spinning clocks.

At first it seemed like only *The Onion's* existing audience was watching ONN. But then around once a month, Graham said, "we would have one that just exploded." The first ONN clip to go viral was about the "MacBook Wheel," an expensive, absurdly inefficient new Apple laptop that hid its uselessness under a thick layer of Apple marketing hype. Graham said, "I had never had that experience before. We made this thing, and suddenly my parents, friends, and everyone were talking about it." Also perhaps expressing how Americans really feel about technology, "Sony Releases Stupid Piece of Shit That Doesn't Fucking Work" has 9.6 million views.

ONN won a Peabody Award, which honors "excellence in storytelling that reflects the social issues and the emerging voices of our day" in 2008. Graham said, "At first I thought that we were being pranked" when someone texted him, "ONN just won a Peabody!" The award boosted everyone's confidence. "We also won a bunch of Webby Awards," Mirk said. "They'd be used as pencil holders around the office."

The staff also decided to make a parody of C-SPAN called *O-Span*. For this venture, Koe and another intern went down to Washington, DC, and got someone with press credentials to sneak them into the empty White House press room and congressional hearing room so they could shoot background video to make it look like their actors were in those locations. This was "maybe a crazy amount of work for a comedy video," as Koe put it. (Graham said he remembered "everyone looked a little sort of brain-fried when they got back from that trip.") But this work produced such memorable *O-Span* clips as "Breaking News: Bat Loose in Congress" and "Congress Struggles to Come Up with Cool Name for Drug Law" (which also may be a parody of *The Onion's* headline-submission process).

It didn't take long before TV offers were coming in. Steve Hannah remembered getting calls from Sundance, IFC, Comedy Central, and CBS. And all this interest was "fortuitous, because that was the 2008–2009 Great Recession." In a 2010 shareholder letter, Hannah described the impact. The year 2009 had been the toughest twelve months any of them had ever experienced. In that year, "the bottom dropped out of the national advertising market, in print and online, and that drop was largely responsible for more than a $5 million swing in total revenue, from about $22 million in 2008 to roughly $17 million in 2009. In the end, we finished approximately $3 million in the red." It was also, Hannah wrote, "a time when it became painfully clear to us that running a business so heavily dependent on advertising—both national and local—was no longer viable."

They did two deals: the *Onion News Network* for IFC and *Onion SportsDome*, the *Onion* sports show, for Comedy Central. Hannah said when he told the staff they were doing two shows, there was a lot of pushback, "and I think reasonably so." They had never done a TV show, and now they were being asked to do two at the same time. But Hannah told them, frankly, they had to do it, to make money for *The Onion*. The whole economy "is just for shit at the moment. Have you noticed?"

The shows paid well. "I don't mind saying I think that we were paid $500,000 per episode for the IFC show," Hannah said. For *Onion SportsDome*, the budget was "about $750,000 per episode." This influx of cash "added a lot of money at a really important time for us." But going from making two-minute videos to a full-episode twenty-two-minute show meant their work was going to increase by a factor of ten. Mirk said the IFC show "was very, very hard to make." The hours got really crazy. "We were working through the weekend, every weekend. We were staying there until like 3:00 a.m., or later, many nights." Graham said, "I will take responsibility for that. . . . Being the age and experience that I am now, you would just be like, 'No, we're not going to do that.'"

Graham said the IFC budget was "much more money than we were used to working with, but also shockingly little from the perspective of what TV usually costs," which can run $3 million or $4 million for a single half-hour episode. Adler said it was a challenge to get the production quality she wanted with the IFC budget. A cheap-looking approach wouldn't work because "the whole visual gag is that we're a very well-funded, incredibly massive media company." Adler wanted a big newsroom touchscreen and huge video wall, but they told her it was too expensive. She called around herself and found an affordable version of both.

They shot ten episodes of *Onion News Network* "I think in five days, which is like, psycho," Adler said. And then there was all the postproduction. Her pay for all that work for the full season was $50,000, no residuals. "And that's, like, nuts." Hannah said, "It was an enormous strain on the video staff, and some people were very unhappy." Matt McDonagh said, "Should we have done two TV shows at the same time? Probably not. That was probably a really shitty decision." After the first season of the IFC show, Adler decided to reduce her stress level and go back to the website ONN video production instead—which had kept going on top of the two cable shows—"and had a really fun season there." As a place to park ads—before, after, and during—the videos were too lucrative for Onion, Inc., to stop just because of the TV deals. Adler worked closely with Carol Kolb on these, "just the two of us . . . I really think she's the best ever."

By now there were so many *Onion* interns they made an ONN video starring them all: "Police Slog Through 40,000 Insipid Party Pics to Find Cause of Dorm Fire." To do the shoot, the team hosted an actual party in the office and invited all the interns; the video makes it looks like there were hundreds of them. Adler, directing, said: "There were like a million interns." A ton of beer was provided. "And everyone forgot it was a shoot," she said. "The interns just would not listen. I would be like, 'Hey, I need you to do XYZ,' and they'd be like, 'I'm in the middle of a game of beer pong. No.'"

The joke in the video was that New York police were trying to figure out how a fire had started in an NYU dorm. To do this they had to go through thousands of photos taken by the students during the party. It was 2008, the start of people taking zillions of digital photos and videos of everything, everywhere, all the time—a change in people's everyday behavior significant enough (or stupid enough) for *The Onion* to point it out. In the video, the police investigator says they solved the mystery by reconstructing "every second of the event" using evidence from the "twenty-five iPhones, fifteen BlackBerries, ten video cameras, and forty digital cameras obtained from the students who attended the party." Luckily, no one was hurt because after the fire broke out, "forty-five people had called the fire department, and thirty-eight people had tweeted that they were fleeing a fire, and many sent picture mail warnings to friends as they ran down twelve flights of stairs and then waited for help to arrive."

And just like with the newspaper, people mistook ONN's satire for the real deal. During a 2011 Paley Center for Media panel discussion about the show, Mirk said they did a piece on Olympic gymnast Shawn Johnson, where the joke was that she broke her leg and then the officials "run out onto the mat and put her down." Johnson had to tweet that she was still alive after a public outcry. Another one was caused by a video where the joke was about a horrible child with cancer who went to the Make-a-Wish Foundation and wished for infinite wishes. "So he's like getting jets and he's getting aircraft carriers," Mirk recalled, and bankrupting the Make-a-Wish Foundation. (The real Make-a-Wish Foundation had to post a message on their website saying that children could not wish for unlimited wishes.)

Another one, "Country Music Stars Challenge al-Qaeda with Patriotic New Song 'Bomb New York,'" was about how bombing the city was welcome because New York didn't matter to real Americans. The song features instructions to al-Qaeda on weak areas in New York's infrastructure—perhaps a revision of the early Osama bin Laden tour video that was never released. Koe said, "We definitely got bomb threats at our office after that video came out." *The Onion* also tried a new business model: a paywall. They spent a ton of money on a short film called *The Onion's Future News from the Year 2137*, which sold on iTunes. Unfortunately, as Adler said, "Nobody, not one person, bought it." (It has since been released for free and has more than two million views.)

ONN's amazing output was done by people making modest salaries. Fisher said, "The real truth is that *The Onion* paid very little compared to late-night shows or other TV shows and comedy outlets." Julie Smith said the salaries allowed them to get as many people on board with the productions as possible—and make many more videos. If you hired two people at $40,000 a year instead of one person at $80,000, you could get twice as much work done. This tactic seems to have convinced Mike McAvoy to spend money he might not have otherwise. More videos meant more advertising sales. (Smith said she was aware of the strife with *Onion* corporate out in Chicago, but, to her, McAvoy was just this "nice midwesterner" who "really loved *The Onion*" and wanted to have high-quality content and do the right thing. Her dad was an accountant, so she probably understood how McAvoy's mind worked better than most of the staff.)

McAvoy seems to have trusted her opinion. He was "really, really young," as Smith put it, and I expect he valued the advice of a creative who was not reflexively hostile to his point of view. Smith also said the videos were doing very well with ad sales, which surely helped her make the case that they were building a whole in-house production company and needed to keep hiring people and funding the unit at an adequate level.

Once they had real TV shows, though, the Writers Guild of America (WGA) reached out and suggested that the ONN writers join their union. The primary writer taking up the charge was Jack Kukoda, head writer for *Onion SportsDome*. Staffers told me that management, including Graham and Kolb, said if they unionized, the cost would mean they wouldn't be able to make the shows. Graham said the issue came up in the "chaotic" middle of the season—when all budgets would probably already have been set. "I remember feeling like, 'I wish we could slow everything down for a minute and kind of figure out all the stuff,'" he said. Another issue was what it would mean when the TV shows ended and the staff went back to *The Onion*. Nobody else there was unionized.

Mirk said he was torn. "It was the first time where there was really a split among the staff," he said. The WGA was even planning to hold a picket line outside the *Onion* offices. "It was tricky, you know," Fisher said, "because we were this kind of ragtag group of friends. And then it definitely created a bit of a rift, I think especially between Will and the producers and the writers." A work stop ensued. Eventually, Mirk chose to side with the writers. "And that's actually how I got into the WGA. And I'm eternally grateful for that now," he told me.

Kolb now feels bad, even "embarrassed," that she once opposed the union. "I should have been out there with a picket sign," she said. Graham also said that after fifteen years of experience, he thought "Of course writers should be in the union if they want to. I'm a really proud member of I think now three unions." (My first interview with him took place during the 2023 writers' strike, which was partly against the encroachment of artificial intelligence into the entertainment industry.) The ONN writers unionized, and, according to Mirk, their salaries basically doubled overnight.

Unfortunately, *Onion SportsDome* was canceled after one season, and IFC's *Onion News Network* was canceled after two. "Frankly," Fisher said, "I feel like when we moved it to long form, it just wasn't as enjoyable to watch. . . . Too much information, too many jokes coming at you." At least it got the writers unionized and for many of them started their careers in TV. Smith left to pursue other projects, as did Graham. Marc Lieberman was hired as the new ONN web video producer and VP of business development.

By 2011, however, not only was most video just going up on YouTube instead of on websites, but the vast majority of it didn't have anywhere near the production values of the ONN work. The model had gone for quantity instead of quality, so *Onion* management decided to do that too. In such a world, content is both product and junk at the same time, the media equivalent of a shirt made as cheaply as possible, purchased at a fast-fashion store, worn once, and thrown away.

As Smith said, they had been in a "really lucky funding bubble" along with a sweet spot in "talent and timing." But that spot was now in the rearview mirror. Smith and Graham were also no longer there to protect the staff from upper management's decisions. Corporate let go the entire ONN staff, including head writer Kolb: everyone on the TV shows was not hired back when the shows were canceled. *The Onion* still wanted them to work, though—just as freelancers. As Mirk put it, "*The Onion* fucked us over, like, immediately." They were made into week-to-week employees with no benefits or job security, even though their duties were the same as before.

Production budgets had also been slashed dramatically. Mirk said it was depressing because now everything was an anchor sitting at a green screen to be punched up with Photoshop. Worse, the newly freelance video writers were now being asked to create sponsored content—the first step toward a movement that would soon suck up most of the *Onion* video-making enterprise. Kolb remembered being asked to think of ideas for Jack Link's Beef Jerky. "It was just sort of the beginning of the end, I guess," she said. At least staff members went on to excellent new shows. As just one example, Fisher wrote, directed, and coproduced for *30 Rock*, *Brooklyn Nine-Nine*, and *The Mindy Project*; she also codeveloped and was showrunner for *Never Have I Ever*. Kolb also has a successful TV career.

Mirk said after the *Onion* freelance work dried up, for a while he was just "a freelance writer adrift in New York" whose income was dropping fast. He took any odd jobs he could, at one point writing commercials for rat traps and another for an oil company. "We came up with this whole kind of sketch about giving condoms to rats. It was totally crazy," he said sarcastically. The bit for the oil company was based on the existence of a town called Strong, Arkansas, and the campaign was something about "we're already strong, but this oil makes your car stronger." Mirk said, "It's so boring even talking about it," but to me it is emblematic of how much talent, ability, and enthusiasm our system just dumps in the trash. (Mirk did eventually become a successful TV writer too.)

How much money did ONN make for the company? Using Hannah's figures, a rough guesstimate is that, in only four years, a team made up almost entirely of twentysomethings and interns with little prior experience brought at least $20 million into their bank account. The $3 million 2009 deficit had been wiped clean and then some. Hannah said, "Our revenues were up considerably during those years." McDonagh said the ONN money was actually mostly pass-through revenue. "It's not hugely profitable, but it gets your top line revenue up quite a bit. And that was super important in the eyes of potential investors."

To Onion, Inc.'s credit, Mirk said in the early days at least, "We had a lot of opportunity and leeway to do exactly what we wanted. And we were really supported in doing that, because no one knew what the internet was going to be. . . . [It] was almost like our ignorance over where things were going allowed for this really beautiful time of unfettered creativity."

Today, many of the original ONN segments have millions of views, and the comments on the YouTube page keep coming, which means people are still watching them. (Many of the comments are variations on "Why doesn't *The Onion* make satire like this anymore?") "It's just one of those magical times in your life, when you and a group of people are working on something you really believe in," Mirk said. "And you're young enough that you're able to really devote 100 percent of your energy to that thing." Graham said, "Part of what I loved about doing ONN was people would laugh first, hopefully, and then also maybe think, and they would walk around with it, and they would talk with their friends about it. Sometimes it felt like we were building a campfire that people got to have conversations across, you know? I think there's always going to be a hunger for that."

"Everyone was so aware of how lucky they were even to be working there for free," Adler said. "People were fucking over the moon, you know?" She said they wanted all the clips to feel like "little treasures. We wanted them to be like little jewels, you know, and we really put everything into it."

Chapter 16

O n the newspaper side, toward the end of Ben Berkley's internship Brian Janosch was promoted, so Berkley took a chance and applied for the intern-wrangling position. He got the job.

The writing staff was now working on a third original book, *The Onion Book of Known Knowledge*, which was—carrying on the tradition of hyperdetailed, research-heavy book projects that took nine million years to write and edit—an encyclopedia. At this point, Berkley said, "The book was on track to be a masterpiece, and the two cable shows had come out and they were really great. And we were putting out hit stories and getting love on social, which, in many ways, *The Onion* was really early in the driver's seat, and had a big following before most publications did." Everything, in other words, was going very well. "Which of course is when the hammer drops."

One day in mid-2011, the New York–based editorial staff was called into a meeting by CEO Steve Hannah and Mike McAvoy (now chief operating officer), who had flown in from Chicago. With them was A.V. Club editor Josh Modell to serve as an intermediary between creative and business. Everyone crowded into the writers' room. Several boxes of pizza were delivered that Hannah had ordered for the staff, though he ordered fancy sandwiches from Dean & DeLuca for himself, McAvoy, and Modell. He wore a baseball cap and affected a casually dominant pose, sitting with McAvoy on tall stools above the rest of the group sitting down at the table. Will Tracy said Hannah always came to the office with a funny, "Hey, I'm cool. I'm a cool guy" attitude. "And it was just the wrong attitude." McAvoy described Hannah's jokey demeanor as bizarre. "It couldn't have been more off."

Many staffers had no idea what was going to happen, though editor Joe Randazzo, writers Will Tracy and Seth Reiss, and a few others had been given hints in the weeks prior. Some of them had been felt out by representatives from Onion corporate; others were clued in by other staffers. Management had even done a retreat where Randazzo had been brought into a conversation about possible new cities for *The Onion*'s headquarters. Still, at a "very depressing" lunch some days before the meeting, Tracy said, they decided to keep it under their hats for now to avoid freaking everyone out. They also didn't have all the details. (President Sean Mills had been informed, and in response left to pursue other projects.)

The New York office now had twenty-seven full-time staff. Sixteen of those were editorial. Hannah would come out to visit occasionally, but as Tracy put it, "Once a year, this guy with a beard comes out, and we have to pretend like he's the boss. . . . And I think he didn't want that anymore. I think he wanted to actually be the boss."

A key problem was that the New York editorial staff had been resisting requests to break down the firewall between business and creative that Dikkers and Haise originally set up in 1989. Among other things, the staff was being pressured to allow online ads to be more visible, with pop-ups and roadblocks and animation and so on that interfered with your reading. Dikkers told me his attitude in prior years had been, "Ads are a necessary evil; they pay the bills; let's just try to make them as unintrusive as possible." But now, advertisers "just want to be in your face."

The writers, however, didn't seem to realize the digital advertising model was undergoing major changes: Baratunde Thurston's gravy train was about to fall off a cliff. Bill Wernecke told me, "The cost that we could sell the advertising for was going down a lot. One of the things with internet-based advertising is you can measure the effectiveness. How many people are clicking on it, right? Or how many people are seeing it. And, obviously, if you want to get people to see it more, you want to have more tailored content. But just like with the written content for the newspapers, they did not want to tailor the content based on advertising." Another problem was how advertising was positioned around the content: banners, things that bleed over or move—whatever the technology allowed. And advertisers going in with other media companies "were becoming very aggressive about offering new and different types of advertising adjacencies and doing things differently, so that the advertising was harder to miss or that people had to see it." They were saying, "We want a pop-up in the middle of the story."

Thurston said, "We were like, okay, we want to make money. We also want to maintain our dignity and the primacy of our content." Cheetos, he said, did a homepage takeover, "where you go to the website and the ad would explode Cheeto dust all over the page. It looked like the Cheeto was jizzing all over our content. It was filthy. And the Cheetos people were proud of their work, and we felt sullied by it."

Another new ask was for sponsored content—something that business saw as a necessary reality in the rapidly changing digital media environment but the writers saw as repugnant. Indeed, when I first learned *Onion* writers had been asked to create sponsored content, I thought I hadn't heard right. I literally had to have the person repeat it because the idea violated everything I knew and loved about *The Onion*. As Todd Hanson put it, "Satire is telling the truth to power. Marketing and advertising is literally telling lies on behalf of power."

Related to this was the less gross (because it wasn't hidden) but still distasteful procedure where advertisers would sponsor specific content, like Dewars's sponsoring the first ONN videos—linking brand names with particular *Onion* creations. This wasn't entirely new, but it seems the method began to increase around this time.

To the editorial staff, though, this stuff was like American soldiers bombing the Vietnamese village in order to save it. Why couldn't the corporate office use something else to keep *The Onion* afloat besides homepage takeovers? And were they really expected to turn beloved *Onion* features into "*American Voices*, Brought to You by Pepsi"? Surely, with their creative know-how, they could come up with another way.

A.V. Club editor Josh Modell, however, said that when Onion, Inc., tried to do something different, the editorial staff would refuse because they saw it as sullying *The Onion*'s voice—especially the idea of always playing it straight. There could not be an *Onion*-branded comedy festival, for instance, because that would out *The Onion* as not real—even though everyone knew *The Onion* was comedy. (Eventually, they did relent and an Onion Comedy Festival did happen.)

Ultimately, though, Modell agreed that much of the problem was with the business side. Editorial, he said, would come up with a big idea. But "nobody ever wanted to take a swing—like, a big money swing—and didn't realize those are the things that are going to move the needle and move the whole thing forward." And if the business side did take swings, people said it came from a place of serious disconnect around what the creative team actually did and the time it took to do it.

Several staffers told me McAvoy seemed to be especially deaf to editorial methods and priorities. Yet as time passed, Jeff Haupt said, McAvoy "just kept getting handed more keys, to the point that he was essentially CEO." (McAvoy didn't really dispute this part. Hannah, he told me—the actual CEO—behaved more like a "chairman." He also said, "You're never going to be the favorite person when you're the only person managing the realities of a business.") In the meantime, Haupt said, writers were bringing in all kinds of new ideas for revenue generation, but the answer—in spite of the big success of ONN and *The Onion*'s new digital creativity—was "no, no, no, no, no."

As just one example, in the spring of 2011, Thurston, Palmer, and Randazzo helped organize a retreat in upstate New York to the Mohonk Mountain House, "where Roosevelt used to go. It's a storied place where people go to figure out what happens to the world," Thurston said. There they created a strategic plan for the future of *The Onion*. "New business opportunity, new revenue lines, including everything from merchandise to online community to different relationships with advertisers to new forms of content. Everything that the guys in Chicago never tried." They came up with a sixty-eight-page slide deck outlining forward-reaching projects as well as both short- and long-range plans to remake *The Onion* into a high-quality, smart comedy producer in many formats, not just a news-satire publisher.

Looking at the deck for the first time in more than a decade, Thurston said, "I think we were way smarter than we understood." It was "really rare for the sum of the creative teams to converge on and develop a strategy for the future of the thing." The deck went through nine challenges they needed to solve, including "platform diversity, interactivity, staff morale, efficiency, and cost." Most important, though, the biggest "investor class" at *The Onion*, he said, was the staff itself. "When I look back at this sixty-eight-page document, I'm like, 'This is a declaration of love,' right? And commitment to ensuring the survival and longevity and sustainability of this thing."

Unfortunately, not much seems to have come of their vision. McAvoy said the group had been led by an *Onion* board member, Harvard MBA Greg Foster (now deceased), who had formerly been an executive at Turner Broadcasting. McAvoy said Foster was from a prior generation that did not understand how online advertising worked. In short, people were no longer needed. Digital ads were now something called "programmatic advertising" that ran at just-in-time electronic speeds, fed users ads based on recent individual browser cookie history, and made advertising money into a sort of auction that worked like the high-speed computerized trading now on Wall Street, where thousands of exchanges happened in seconds. In other words, ad sales was now an automated "engineering job," as McAvoy put it, not account management where an ad rep met with clients. "They weren't data people," McAvoy said. "They were journalism people, and that's great," but in the programmatic advertising environment, you wanted someone who organized "through data sets and structures," not with words. The only place humans were needed now was to sell sponsorships around specific *Onion* content, which could be positioned as unique, premium advertising. And the idea became so popular among advertisers hoping to be "cool" that more content was needed to attach that special premium advertising to. Yet the editorial staff, already busy with their new ramping-up-to-digital-speeds schedule, carried out on top of writing original books, found this a very large ask.

Joe Garden remembers a conversation with Kate Palmer at Whiskey Friday. Garden and his wife had recently separated, and he wasn't feeling that great. "I was complaining to her," he said. "I was like, they're just asking more and more and more of us, and we're not getting anything in return. We're not getting paid commensurate to what we're doing." Plus, writing for *The Onion* was no ordinary media gig. It was a way to influence American culture, to say things that needed to be said. To make the world a better place. Not to make as much money for shareholders as possible. Fighting the corporate media system with satire took a great deal of intellect, creativity, and energy. Having to also fight their own business side in real life, which was supposed to be *helping* them, affected morale a lot. Palmer said they pushed for the addition of a breaking news and social media team for a while, "so it wasn't just always on the people who were producing the weekly publication." Business, however, didn't see new staff as necessary.

Palmer said there were people in Chicago who "clearly loved the brand" and were loyal to it, some of them enough to become investors. (The newcomers to the New York editorial staff had been shut out of the opportunity to buy into *The Onion* themselves because the current investors didn't want to split their shares.) "But I think that there was always a lack of understanding or respect about the individuals who are creating this product," she said. "They saw everyone as replaceable."

Hannah saw the situation differently. The staff, he told me, was like a club. "They were mostly small-town Wisconsin kids. They were very suspicious of outsiders, not comfortable with outsiders. And it didn't matter that I had run the biggest newspaper in the state and I've been to every community in the state as a columnist," he said. "I was an outsider, and that made people nervous."

Hannah said the editorial staff were also not accustomed to change. "They had very, very little familiarity with the kind of new people coming in. Certainly, new businesspeople coming in and saying, 'Now we're going to make this thing more profitable. Now we're going to expand the business.'" Hannah said, "There was a naïveté that I had never encountered before, frankly, in all my years." The A.V. Club side was "much more sophisticated when it came to business." But the satire side "really didn't understand business at all. . . . Are they brilliant? Absolutely. But on a scale of one to ten, where does their business acumen run, ten being the highest? Two or three maybe. Tops."

At the pizza-catered meeting, Hannah made his announcement to the staffers gathered in the conference room. The New York office was going to be closed, he said. He knew some people wouldn't be happy about it, but the entire editorial operation was going to be moved to Chicago, and *The Onion* would no longer have a presence in New York. If people wanted to keep their jobs, they would have to move also. If they didn't, well, bon voyage.

The room was stunned. What? Move? Why? Someone yelled out, "You can't do that!" Hannah said that actually, as CEO, yes, he could. He could do whatever he wanted. He told them they would receive raises and nice relocation packages as motivation to come along to Chicago. Their standard of living would rise, the organization would be more cohesive, and the games of telephone would finally stop. It was the best idea for everybody.

The staff were very upset. Josh Modell said Joe Randazzo baited Hannah over and over until Hannah lost his cool. Modell said Hannah was holding a manila folder, and he banged it on the table and said, "I have all these résumés of people who want to write for *The Onion*." Randazzo replied, "Oh, so we're just totally replaceable." The attitude didn't apply only to writers. Berkley said the line from management on staffing editorial operations—the processes that coordinated the flow from the writers to all the different platforms *Onion* stories now appeared in, both print and digital—was literally "We can find someone off the street for that."

McAvoy said the goal was to get people to *want* to come, not to mandate them—but Hannah just "couldn't help himself." His "inflammatory" comments undid all the communication they had previously been attempting. McAvoy said he was in a difficult spot because Hannah was his boss. "I like Steve a lot on certain sides. I could look up to him." But on other sides, "I learned a lot of what *not* to do. And it made my job so much harder." Modell said he ultimately thought the meeting was "hilarious." As somebody who was both "sort of outside and sort of inside, I'm like, everybody was wrong." He did refuse Hannah's request to sit up above everyone, choosing to sit at the table with the writers instead.

Thurston recalled, "One of the shittiest days of my time at *The Onion*. People were sad; people were shocked; people were confused. People were depressed. . . . People have leases. People have friends. People have relationships, maybe pregnancies. Like, there's a whole life. There's the professional questioning of why does this make any sense? And there's a lot of personal challenge with uprooting." Joe Garden added, "We're all just like, 'What the fuck are we going to do? I don't want to move to Chicago. We fought to move here.'"

According to Mitch Semel, one of the reasons Chicago was chosen was because it attracted the "right kinds of businesspeople." In the Midwest, he said, if you go to "any of the good Big Ten schools, you're graduating with a business degree. Chicago is very often the big move you want to make." (More than one writer mentioned the "frat boys" working in the Chicago office.) Joe Garden said Hannah told them proximity to Second City was going to be the big advantage in Chicago. Still angry after all these years, Garden said, "What does he fucking know about comedy? I mean, yeah, some very talented people came out of Second City and Improv Olympic. However, recruiting talent has never been the problem at *The Onion*." The problem was that "we have homes. We have lives here in a city we've lived at for over ten years now. And you want us to move to Chicago in my forties and start over again? No." Palmer said, "There was very little transparency from the business side to those of us who were in editorial, certainly not even to Joe [Randazzo] and to me, and we were supposed to be running things. There was just very little explanation about what the long-term goals were and how a move could potentially help, other than just saying, 'We're gonna cut costs.'"

Maria Schneider said, "I think we were seen as prima donnas." (She had left *The Onion* a few years earlier in 2008, but the observation still applies.) In so many organizations, "You've got the academics and then you've got the frat boys, and it always seems like the frat boys have the money. . . . But they didn't write a *letter* of satire." Garden said, "They didn't want to create value for the company so much as sort of extract value from the company repeatedly." Jun Ueno, doing graphic design in Chicago, said, "I'm sure somebody made money off *The Onion*, but it wasn't the people who worked there. . . . The writers got screwed over so many times. So many times."

"There's no question about it. It was very contentious," Hannah said.

There wasn't really any compelling reason to have a good chunk of the company in New York. I know that people enjoyed being in New York. . . . I could see this magnetic attraction that brought kids from small towns, particularly in the Midwest, to New York. They thought that was fantastic. And of course, they get to go to their high school reunion sometime, and people would say, "So where are you now, Bob?" and they'd say, "Well, I live in Manhattan." That was better than saying, "I live in Richland Center." I mean, suddenly, you are kind of a celebrity.

But, Hannah said, the New York editorial staff had "completely pretty much forgot where they were from." By the time the move came up, "they thought Chicago was a small town somewhere in the Midwest that Carl Sandburg had once wrote a poem about." He was "personally sympathetic to their point of view. . . . But it made no sense for the company whatsoever." Hannah emphasized people's lifestyles would be much better in Chicago. "And I can tell you that that argument had zero effect on people from Wisconsin Rapids and Richland Center and Marshfield, who had no intention of ever going back to the small towns they came from."

Another thing, according to Hannah, was that it was much less expensive to produce video in Chicago, "which was becoming a bigger and bigger part of our operation." Both Chicago and the state of Illinois offered big tax breaks for web video production. Producing it in Chicago also meant they wouldn't have to deal with New York City unions, "which were very difficult."

Thurston said the move to Chicago "wasn't presented as a conversation, or an offer. It was presented as a fait accompli." Steve Hannah apparently had a cottage near the Wisconsin River in southwestern Wisconsin he enjoyed visiting. Will Tracy said, "I think he mentioned his cottage a few times," both before he started telling them the news and afterward, "I think maybe in an effort to ingratiate himself to the midwestern crew, talking about his cottage in Wisconsin." Tracy said he remembered a graphics person, Colin Tierney, saying at the meeting, "I'm not going to do this move. And I'm not going to have health insurance soon. So I don't really want to hear about your fucking cottage."

Always trying to be fair, Thurston said the separation probably caused each office to misunderstand what the other was doing. Still, "There was not a deep well of goodwill going into that decision." There was also something vaguely insulting about it. Even after everything they had accomplished, were they being told that they had failed? Thurston said, "No one goes from New York to Chicago. That's a weird move."

Another issue was the timing of the announcement. The editorial staff was in the process of creating their encyclopedia, *The Onion Book of Known Knowledge*. (The book was published in October 2012.) Dropping a bomb in the middle of this project "just felt dumb," Thurston said. "To do that, and not ask in a moment of celebration or ease." On top of this, he said, the business had just "inked some kind of deal with YouTube" that, though they welcomed the money, "involves a commitment to producing a certain amount that I think was done without full consultation with the creative teams."

The staff did not know the Chicago move had actually been in the works for years. Bill Wernecke told me it was part of an ultimate plan to consolidate all of their operations in one place. He said he knew it would be like walking into a hornet's nest when the announcement was made to the New York staff. New York *had* apparently once been on the list of places that Onion, Inc., had thought about consolidating everyone—as had Madison and Milwaukee. McDonagh believed two major strikes against New York were the TV shows being canceled and a real-estate deal to move the office to the DUMBO neighborhood in Brooklyn falling through. "Once that fell apart, it seemed like the writing was on the wall," he said. Ultimately, however, according to McDonagh, the deciding factor was mostly that Steve Hannah and Mike McAvoy lived in Chicago. (McAvoy disputed this. He said he would have loved to move to New York.)

Hannah said, "Like all CEOs of creative companies that I've ever worked for or witnessed, when I said yes to things that the writers wanted, I was a hero of incredible proportions. When I said no, I was a mean old man." Hannah agreed the staff probably were blindsided. But he said he couldn't think of any way, nor could his advisors think of any way, to make the change "without causing considerable upheaval."

Of the pizza Hannah had ordered for everyone, Berkley said, "Nobody touched a single piece." Afterward, the staff threw it all away. Berkley said he was often one of the last people out every night, and he was also living in New York on a "not very livable" salary. He really wanted to take some of that pizza home with him, but he didn't.

Soon it was clear that pretty much nobody was willing to move to Chicago regardless of the raises and relocation packages. A few people, like Will Tracy, weren't sure what to do. Tracy happened to be in a long-distance relationship with someone in Chicago. He didn't think moving there was the right choice for *The Onion*, but it was hard not to think about what it might mean for his relationship. Saying yes to Chicago would mean betraying his colleagues. Saying no would be telling his girlfriend he wasn't committed. "So ultimately, I kind of threw my lot in with luck," he said. "I'll do whatever the group wants to do."

Thurston remembers knowing he would not go. His book, *How to Be Black*, was about to be released. Maybe he could work remotely, but he wasn't moving to Chicago. He was angry at how one of his most important staffers, Matt Kirsch—a website guru whom he'd poached from respected PBS journalism icon Bill Moyers—had been treated by the corporate office during the fallout and made to justify his position to the suits. "So now these fucking guys from Chicago are coming in and insulting Matt, having no idea how many times he saved their asses. And just like how little he asked for," Thurston said. He felt like a parent. "You can fucking come at me. You don't mess with my kid."

It didn't take long to decide. The New York staff told Hannah they would not come. None of them. Good luck starting a new *Onion* with no writers, no editors, no institutional knowledge, no Gen X, no millennials, no John Krewson, or Todd Hanson, or Joe Randazzo, or any of them. Good luck with that, sir.

To try to change their minds, the business office sent a couple of people from the A.V. Club to New York to talk the staff into coming. I admire their bravery; it was kind of like sending two quaking French pageboys to Agincourt to ask Henry V to give up his position. It wasn't so bad in Chicago, the A.V. Club people said. They were doing great! The businesspeople were nice! Tracy remembered them saying, "You can go right into their office and ask for things, and they'll give them to you!"

But "no one in New York was really receptive to that," Tracy said. So for a while, "it seemed pretty dire for the business side." Hanson said the idea was, "As long as all of us stick together, they can't win, because they have nothing without all of us. But if some of us go over to them, then we can't win." So "everyone agreed, and everyone was all sticking together."

Then the sticking together began evolving into something else. Thurston told me he started thinking bigger. Much bigger. The Matt Kirsch issue, he said was the "moment where I had an internal break around possibility."

He had a good relationship with Steve Hannah, he told me, but they did not see eye to eye on this. If the problem was money, Thurston said, "We are in New York City. There is no shortage of money." If the problem was the business, "We can build a bigger and better business." Thurston was not just spinning fantasies. He'd just spent the past several years interacting regularly with major figures in the New York tech world, "speaking at all these conferences, going to all these parties, and hanging out at New York tech meetups." He also had been a primary contact with the Chicago business office as part of his job as head of digital—an intermediary between editorial and business. So he had a picture of the situation that maybe others did not—as well as knowledge of a world outside *The Onion* where there was a ton of money and people looking for interesting things to invest it in.

One company that especially came to mind was Betaworks, "a venture studio—still is a venture studio—that introduced Bitly, the URL shortener, and Chartbeat, the analytics platform every media outlet was using to measure their success on social media," Thurston said. Betaworks had also created digg.com, "which was the most popular aggregating news site at the time, and so many other tools. I knew them, and the head of them, John Borthwick, personally."

Thurston said, "I was like, I think we could just buy *The Onion*. If it's such a burden to these guys in Chicago, we can relieve them of the burden. 'You don't have to worry about us anymore. We got it. We got it from here.' And that's when I started fomenting rebellion."

The first thing Thurston did was check in with Betaworks. "I didn't want to make promises to people at *The Onion* because they didn't know this world at all. And I didn't want to get people's hopes up." Hypothetically speaking, he asked the Betaworks leadership, "If you knew about a small, independent, well-regarded comedy outlet with tentacles in multiple forms of media and relevance to the digital future that could be for sale, would you be interested?" And Betaworks said, "Hypothetically, we'd be very interested in that."

Thurston then started "making the rounds" and approaching *Onion* people individually. "I got relationships," he said. "Because I worked with all these people. That's the beauty of my job." A little subversive group began meeting at a nearby bar called Botanica on Houston Street as well as an upscale deli called Delicatessen, where Thurston was a regular, to brainstorm ideas—if there's anything *Onion* people can do, it's brainstorm—and make their plans for a possible *Onion* coup.

Thurston gave the plan a code name, Project Allium, and set up private Google and Facebook groups. He remembered, with affection, "We thought we were spies or something. We were operating with a high degree of attempted information security, never using our *Onion* accounts." They would "huddle in the private dining room at Delicatessen and plot. Me and basically the heads of the departments. We have a bunch of meetings. I would take walks with Todd Hanson and talk about the future, as he explained the Puck building [the former home of the nineteenth-century satirical magazine of the same name near the office] and Puck and Shakespeare to me and, like, wax eloquent."

He and the group came up with several basic ideas. One was that *The Onion* really needed to create a new form of revenue that was not fucking pop-up ads. Brian Janosch said having the basis of the business be selling display ads on digital web pages "was deeply dispiriting." Why would anyone move their life for that?

Solutions didn't have to be complicated. As just one simple example, Thurston pointed out the *New York Times* sells twice as many crossword puzzle subscriptions as it does newspaper subscriptions. *The Onion* needed the equivalent of the *New York Times* crossword puzzle. For Thurston, "merch was the low-hanging fruit." *The Onion* still sold T-shirts and mugs like it did in 1988. Surely, there was a way to update that.

There were also many possibilities for non-*Onion*-branded stuff. Founder Tim Keck had helped keep the *Stranger* going by creating an event-ticketing app aimed at small- to medium-size venues that didn't want to hand over piles of fee money to Ticketmaster—and he did this in his forties, proving that you didn't have to be twenty-five to come up with good ideas. Dan Savage told me Keck was very savvy in his understanding of what the *Stranger* was and how it related to its community:

> Most of the other weeklies that went down were on paper profitable but couldn't service their debt. And because we were a smutty, small start-up and because Tim ran it to pay for itself, we never were able to get a loan from anywhere. So we never ended up having any debt, which became a virtue.... The paper [also] became not just reacting to Seattle's culture or documenting it, but also helping to create it. And some of those things that the paper helped to create, like HUMP! [the *Stranger*'s homemade-porn festival], became big revenue streams.

Why couldn't *The Onion* do something like this? *The Onion* could become a production studio. Staff could write other kinds of books. They could give talks and presentations. The Mohonk retreat had already generated many ideas. Brian Janosch described interconnected digital story experiences filled with Easter eggs where, for instance, a character in a story would have their own Twitter feed or YouTube channel, so readers/viewers could travel to different digital places and expand a story in multiple ways. More smart comedy. Not more stupid advertising, which, as Josh Modell told me, doesn't do anything anyway. He said in our interview that he'd seen probably a hundred web ads that day and didn't remember a single one. "I'm sure I can be proven wrong by science," he said. "But, like, I don't think *The Onion* doing a sponsored article about Home Depot sent anyone to Home Depot."

THE FUTURE OF THE ONION

★ ★ ★ ★   a proposal   ★ ★ ★ ★

We love The Onion and are proud of its 23 year record

* Thurber Prize & a Peabody
* At least 6 NYT best-sellers
* 30+ Webby awards
* 1 to-be-awarded Pulitzer Prize

* High cultural impact special issues (China, 1783, 1000th issue)
* Cited and revered by politicians & revolutionaries
* Strong, loyal alumni network

But The Onion has serious problems

* Core Onion revenues and traffic are down or flat
  * Overly dependent on a volatile quarterly ad model
  * Have not meaningfully expanded sources of revenue
* The creative team is suffering from record low morale
  * Non-competitive compensation and investment
  * Growing content demands, especially video, without resources

Chicago move does not fix these problems. It exacerbates them

* Will lead to an unsustainable loss of talent
* Has already negatively affected quality and productivity
* Exposes severe lack of trust between creative and management
* Invites poaching from competitors
* Will result in irreparable damage to the company and brand
* This scenario is the opposite of a win-win. Everybody loses

The Onion can survive and grow with investment in:

* Marketing: commit to supporting content investment
* Merchandising: multiply digital and physical goods revenues
* NYC Sales: expand sales team in the largest ad market
* Data Analysis/Traffic Acquisition: provide insights for business & creative; intelligently target users
* Community: engage user base and monetize creatively
* Talent: attract and retain with new staffing, compensation and career development

We see three broad options for the future

* Status Quo:
  + Overstretched teams and stagnant business
  + Geographically separate and inefficient operations

* Chicago Move:
  + Unsustainable loss of talent, quality and brand value
  + No underlying change in business strategy

* Another Way:
  + Inspired NYC-based team
  + Expanded business strategy and tech integration
  + New investment

Steady Decline

Extreme Risk

Vibrant, Growing Business

The Onion has faced this challenge before

* In 2001, business performance lagged creative potential.
* David Schafer and Steve Hannah stepped in to rescue and grow The Onion, leading to another 10 years of life
* In 2011, business performance again lags creative potential. Digital revenues hover near $10M (franchise and television revenues are not sustainable)
* We believe a similarly dramatic move is needed to rescue and grow The Onion at the next level

We propose a management buyout in whole or in part

* We have found strategic investors to back our buyout
* The entire creative team supports the proposal
* While we would consider The AV Club, we are focused on The Onion alone

Next Steps

* Our backers are successful investors operating multiple digital businesses and possess a deep understanding of media
* They are committed to maintaining the editorial independence and integrity of The Onion
* We ask that you consider this opportunity and notify us of the direction of your intent by end of week

In November, they were ready. They made a brief but detailed nine-slide deck and arranged to meet with Schafer and Hannah at Schafer's New York apartment, which was in "a gleaming, glossy black tower that looked like something out of *Planet of the Apes* or *The Dark Tower* from Stephen King, a shiny obelisk next to St. Patrick's Cathedral in Midtown," Thurston said. Schafer and Hannah did not know why they called the meeting.

They made their pitch and showed the deck and talked about the history of *The Onion* and how important this moment was in that history. And all the great things they wanted to pursue that would both extend *The Onion*'s legacy and keep it thriving as a business. "And we turn this page and it's like, 'So we want to buy it.'"

They had no idea that was coming, Thurston said. "They were just like, 'What? We thought you were going to quit.'" But it was not a mass resignation. "We think it's time for new blood and a new generation," Thurston said. "We think we are that blood. And we have partners who are willing to back us. So let go, because *we're not trying to leave.*"

And to their credit, Thurston said, "they didn't fire us all on the spot." Hannah and Schafer told the insurrectionaries that they needed to think about it, "and we left and went straight to the bar to drink whiskey. Official drink of *The Onion*." The bar was Jimmy's Corner, the old-school Times Square dive bar owned by Jimmy Glenn, a former boxer, trainer, and cutman who'd covered the walls with images of fighters. Not long afterward, Hannah and Schafer met with Betaworks. Then the team waited to hear what might become of it.

In the meantime, however, another bomb dropped. Steve Hannah had contacted Scott Dikkers and asked if he would return, move to Chicago, and run the show. And Dikkers had said yes.

Hannah told me:

We offered Scott the job because he was an immensely talented guy and he had a long and storied history with *The Onion*. He had talent and credibility. In fact, I never met anyone in my years at *The Onion* who knew more about

---

(opposite page): The slide deck Thurston and associates presented to Schafer and Hannah.

its particular satirical voice than Scott. We wanted someone to embrace the idea of putting editorial and business in the same space in Chicago, and Scott was open to that idea. He saw the obvious synergistic—as well as economic—benefits of having one company working in one place, not the fractured arrangement of having editorial in New York while the people who ran the business were half a continent away. Scott wasn't in the least bit afraid of the "business" side of comedy. Plus, David and I really liked Scott.

To the editorial staff, however, this was a sneak attack so shocking it was almost unbelievable. Will Tracy—who would go on to write for the HBO series *Succession*—said, "It was very unfortunate. Because now they had a pretty good piece of leverage." He continued:

Before they talked to Scott, the press release they would have had to put out would be "*Onion* management fires entire writing and editorial staff of *The Onion*, and it will start fresh with a completely new staff in Chicago." That doesn't sound good, does it? Most people would read that and think, "Oh, *The Onion's* dead. Fuck. *The Onion* was so great. Now it's gone. It's over, it's dead."

And now they can put out a press release, if need be, which is: "*The Onion* returns to its midwestern roots with original genius editor Scott Dikkers at the helm again." And that looks quite appealing optically, doesn't it?

Joe Garden was baffled because he remembered Dikkers hating management before—it was why he quit in 2008. Regarding Dikkers, Hannah told me, "Some people you may hear from will differ. I thought he was probably the creative genius behind *The Onion* editorial." Joe Randazzo said, "I think what people saw is a shill. Just sort of like, 'Fuck off, dude, because you couldn't make it on your own. Now you come crawling back, and you were never that great to begin with.' I'm not saying this is my feeling of him, because I have a great deal of fondness and admiration for Scott, while also recognizing his creative limitations. But yes, there was definitely that sense."

Thurston said finding out Dikkers was "behind the scenes talking about taking his old job back was really fucking infuriating." He hadn't checked in with any of them. Thurston did try to make Dikkers understand, but got nowhere. "You're meddling, and you're hurting us, and you used to be our leader. Like, what is happening here?" Thurston said, "It just felt clear, in aggressive and dramatic language, that he had been turned and he was no longer one of us. He was one of them."

Randazzo said Adult Swim had approached him around this time to see if he wanted to start something there—and take as many *Onion* people with him as he wanted. How he felt about it deep down, though, was obscured. "Again, I found myself in a situation where I was the oldest brother trying to keep everybody happy and maintain as many relationships in good standing as possible," he said, while putting out "as many fires as I could, and also keep the paper going, and try to get eleven different people a job after this all fucked off. I don't feel like I even had a ton of time to think about how I personally felt about things."

On December 5, 2011, Dikkers came up to the office from Brooklyn to meet with the staff. Trying one last time, Hanson and others again explained what was going on and why it was so important for them all to stick together. And they begged him not to take Hannah's offer.

Tracy said, "The tenor of the meeting was all of us trying to say, 'Scott, you've really handed them a gift here. And this really fucks us a bit. Please don't do this.'" Hanson said:

Everyone explained to him what was wrong. And he just kept saying, "Well, you just don't understand. I know what this company needs. I know how to make this work in Chicago." And they're just like, "But you just entered the situation, like, two days ago. We've been working on this for months. And you're insulting us." I remember Randazzo saying, "Don't you see how what you're doing is insulting to us, because you're claiming to know more about it than us? That's an insult."

And I said—you know, I'd given this whole speech—and I was looking right into his eyes. And I said, "Scott, look in your heart; you know that you're going to betray all of these people that are the creative staff of *The Onion* if you do this." And he kept insisting, "Well, I'm the only one who's in a position to save *The Onion*. I have to do it. I just have to." And he refused to listen.

Several people remembered Hanson yelling at Dikkers, "You think you're going to go down in history as the man who saved *The Onion*. You're not. You're going to go down in history as the man who destroyed it."

"When we all walked out of that meeting," Hanson said, "everybody hated Dikkers. I'm not even talking about myself. I'm talking about all kinds of people who didn't have a history with him. They just knew of him as this guy who had been in charge in the past. They all felt stabbed in the back by him." Dikkers, Hanson said, "took decades of goodwill and burned it up in a sixty-minute meeting."

A few more developments occurred. Dikkers actually withdrew himself from consideration for a few weeks—probably to allow time for everyone to calm down, not because he was wavering in his decision. Schafer talked about letting people work remotely. Other possibilities were explored. It seemed like maybe some sort of compromise could be reached.

But it wouldn't be Betaworks. That deal was dead. Thurston said, as he understood it, that Schafer and Hannah asked for "an absurd, absurd price. Well beyond the enterprise value of the business that could be justified at the time." Josh Modell said of the attempted coup, "It was ridiculous, like an ant trying to kill an elephant. It was never going to happen."

Hannah saw the Betaworks deal as "a frivolous, silly, time-consuming move that I would say, all these years out, that we decided to indulge. I would say they had no idea what they were doing." But also, Hannah added, if Betaworks had offered them some ungodly sum of money, they would have said, "It's yours." But they didn't. "It was a PE [private equity] firm trying to do what PE firms do, and that is get the price down as low as they possibly could and get the most for their money. It had no appeal to us whatsoever." To be honest, I'm not sure why the rebels thought a tech zillionaire's ownership would ultimately be all that different from David Schafer's. Because *The Onion* would still have been an investment to be sold later at a profit. Not a public service to be maintained in perpetuity.

On February 5, 2012, an email announcement came from Kate Palmer to the entire *Onion* staff: Scott Dikkers had accepted the position of general manager, effective the next day.

It's obviously an understatement to say the last few months have been trying for everyone. It's my hope that this move helps close that difficult chapter even as the hard work of this transition begins. I've been incredibly proud of each of you for making tough decisions about the Chicago move that are best for you and your families. And for keeping the quality of your work incredibly high through it all.

Janosch told me he learned a "harsh, harsh, harsh lesson" about "the cruelty of the universe." Sometimes, "this is just how businesses are run. And it doesn't matter how much creative brilliance is in the room or in the organization. They don't have the power."

Dikkers offered his own version of the story. He said, "Some of the problems with management continued after I left [in 2008], and the writers became very disgruntled." Management "wasn't really aligned with the sort of cool, hip, funny, edgy brand identity of *The Onion*. And the writers were really feeling that, and they were feeling like they were like missing out on opportunities and weren't being teed up for the kind of success they could be having if they had better management."

Then Dikkers heard what was going on with the Chicago move; he said he visited the office "frequently" to talk with the staff. Dikkers also said he was the one who suggested to Thurston that he take over. Recalling the big show-down meeting, Dikkers said the writers "were angry at me for even talking to management.... There was a lot of anger in that room.... I know a lot of those writers really hated me for that. And that's that."

Dikkers said he heard the staff was going to start something new. He told them they were wasting their time. "It's going to fail. It's not going to work. You're going to have zero leverage with Steve Hannah. He's going to go hire hacks to write *The Onion*, and the culture is going to completely die." But the writers, he said, didn't believe him. Then, he said, he called up Steve Hannah and asked if he could do anything to help. Hannah said, "Can you come and be the manager or the boss of the staff when we move to Chicago?" And that's when Dikkers realized what he had to do. He would go to Chicago and save *The Onion*.

I said to him, "But Scott, your version of the story is really different from everybody else's." He replied, "I read that *Saturday Night Live* book, I'm sure you've read it, where people tell stories of what happened. They're, like, completely different. Albert Brooks remembers something totally different from Lorne Michaels. It's very amusing."

Tu Stultus Es

⌀ the ONION®

MARCH 1, 2012 • VOL. 48 ISSUE 09 | AMERICA'S FINEST NEWS SOURCE • ONION.COM | Copyright © 2012 Onion, Inc. All Rights Reserved | MSN

INSIDE

LOCAL
Yard Sale Reeks Of Divorce
Page 12B

LOCAL
Road-Kill Squirrel Remembered As Frantic, Indecisive *Page 3B*

HIGHLIGHTS

Red Lobster Offers New 'Top Hat Full Of Shrimp' To Attract Wealthier Customers
NATIONAL, Page 21A

Cute Couple On Same Antidepressant *NATIONAL, Page 4A*

SPORTS

Wheelchair-Basketball Players Stunned By Thunderous Slam Dunk *Page 3C*

A.V. CLUB

ONION SPECIAL REPORT

COST OF LIVING NOW OUTWEIGHS BENEFITS

WASHINGTON, DC—A report released Monday by the Federal Consumer Quality-Of-Life Control Board indicates that the cost of living now outstrips life's benefits for many Americans.

"This is sobering news," said study director Jack Farness. "For the first time, we have statistical evidence of what we've suspected for the past 40 years: Life really isn't worth living."

To arrive at their conclusions, study directors first identified the average

yearly costs and benefits of life. Tangible benefits such as median income ($43,000) were weighed against such tangible costs as home-ownership ($18,000). Next, scientists assigned a financial value to intangibles such as finding inner peace ($15,000), establishing emotional closeness with family members ($3,000), and brief moments of joy ($5 each). Taken together, the study results indicate that "it is unwise to go on living."

AMERICAN FOCUS

see COST OF LIVING, page 5

K-Y Introduces New Line Of Jam

NEW BRUNSWICK, NJ—Johnson & Johnson, manufacturer of the nation's most popular personal lubricant, K-Y Jelly, held a press conference Monday to unveil its new line of K-Y Jam, which the company has touted as having "that thick, homemade feeling you've been craving." "Our new K-Y Jam contains no additives and is made from only the finest natural ingredients, resulting in a luscious blend that's packed with rich, jammy goodness." Johnson & Johnson CEO William Weldon said as he spooned out a dollop of the clear, glycerin-

based jam. "A heaping spoonful of this stuff every morning will help you start your day off right." Weldon went on to say that Johnson & Johnson had also begun production on a new line of K-Y Preserves targeted at the 65-and-over set. *ø*

National Endowment For The Arts Funds Construction Of $1.3 Billion Poem

Massey says a small group of two or three deserves as good a reading as a buzzing crowd of nine.

WASHINGTON—The $1.3 million interpretive-National Endowment dance budget of 1985. for the Arts announced "America's metaphors Monday that it has begun construction on a $1.3 billion, 14-line lyric poem—its largest investment in the nation's aesthetic-industrial complex since the $850

poems, they are in danger of completely falling apart," said the project's head stanza foreman Dana Gioia. "We need to make sure America's poems remain the biggest, best-designed, best-funded poems in the world."

Gioia confirmed that the public-works composition will be assembled letter-by-letter atop a solid base of the relationship between man and nature. The poem's metaphors, laid out extensively on lined-paper blueprints, involves a traditional three-quatrain-and-a-couplet framework, which will be tethered to an iambic meter for increased stability and symmetry. If

have become strained beyond recognition, our nation's verses are severely overwrought, and if one merely examines the internal logic of some of these archaic

see POEM, page 6

Meth Addicts Demand Government Address Nation's Growing Spider Menace

Harlowe pleads with senators to ask the King of America to do something about "all the goddamned spiders."

WASHINGTON, DC—Following the tragic falling death of 32-year-old methamphetamine addict Phillip Diggs, who was reportedly attacked by spiders while scaling a large construction crane near Palo Alto, CA, thousands of outraged and confused meth addicts marched frenetically on Washington as part of a week of activities urging the federal government to address the nation's growing spider epidemic.

"Something needs to be done and it needs to be done soon—these spiders are everywhere," said Rich Harlowe, event organizer and founder of Tweakers' NowNowNowNowNowNow-

NowNowNow!, in testimony before a Senate committee Tuesday. "The government must address this problem before the situation gets out of hand and these poisonous, acid-shooting spiders develop the powers of mind control or—God forbid—flight."

"America cannot afford to ignore this any crisis any longer," Harlowe added.

The rally drew addicts from every part of the country, many traveling on foot through the night, trading sex with truck drivers for rides, or stealing their brothers-in-law's bicycles. At dozens of rambling public speeches, organizers de-

see ADDICTS, page 5

One of the first issues after Dikkers took the general manager position but before the editorial move to Chicago. Randazzo was still editor.

The only thing the staff could still do for *The Onion* was make sure it didn't turn into a bunch of second-tier beginners being taught how to write funny by Scott Dikkers. So even though most of them ended their time at *The Onion*, a handful decided they would go—especially younger people who had fewer ties to New York.

Kate Palmer said they gave a lot of thought to how they could make the best of the situation, and one of the ways was promoting the careers of younger people on staff. Ben Berkley was one of them. He recalled the older staff urging him to leverage the situation into a raise and a promotion "and to just help keep *The Onion* strong. Which they also at the same time wanted to see burn." He became editorial manager. Berkley said, "It hurt so much for the staff to be broken up, but it would hurt so much more to see the whole thing turned to dust." Will Tracy became editor and Seth Reiss the head writer. J. J. Shebesta from ONN became creative director of video. A few others stayed on as remote freelancers, including Hanson. Krewson agreed to keep writing too. Chad Nackers also moved, taking the role of *Onion* sports editor. But about 85 percent of the staff quit for good. Jun Ueno said, "Those were really dark times. Because it felt like we were kind of ending the run." So much of their best and most experienced talent was now gone. "And it's kind of like, how are we gonna survive the next few months?"

After the New York office closed, but before Chicago began, the remaining staff worked in horrible temporary shared office space. (Randazzo told me that during the transition from the old office, *The Onion*'s writers' room conference table was put up for sale on Craigslist and taken away by its new owner in the middle of a headline meeting.) The newspaper staff were sent to a place called Sunshine Studios. "It was so depressing," Seth Reiss said. "Oh my God." Berkley said they had two pods of open cubicles on a floor that was shared with an online auction site. While they were there, an employee of the site was going through a very loud divorce and custody situation on the other side of the cubicle wall. "We're doing book proofs while this is happening; we're trying to keep putting out issues," Berkley said. "Onion, Inc., by the way, very kindly only paid for two key cards for the space. I had one. And nobody could access the bathroom without it. So I got to play bathroom escort for months." The video staff went to similar space in DUMBO, across the Brooklyn Bridge.

Hannah displayed no regret about the move. The writers, he said, "thought New York was the center of the media universe. And despite the costs of it, they wanted to stay there. And I believe that they were honest in their assessment that you could do better work in New York." However, "I think the move to

Chicago proved that that wasn't true at all. Not only did we not skip a beat, I think that *The Onion*, with fresh talent that came in, and more money to spend on things, and getting everybody together to communicate in one office, I thought it brought the company much closer together. And I will go to my grave believing that it was the right thing to do." The New York staff thought *The Onion* needed them to stay in business. But, as Hannah said, "It did not turn out to be true. And you know, I'm wrong 50 percent of the time, but [the move was] part of the 50 percent when I was actually right."

Once the closing date of the New York office had been announced, Whiskey Friday intensified. Brian Janosch said he wouldn't quite use the word "debauchery," but he said it was "a very fun place to be in your twenties" on a Friday night. There was romance; there was laughter. "We were going to have a fucking blast on the way out. It was a bunch of Gen X guys. You knew they were gonna, like, punk rock, put a hole in the wall before they go." Graphic designer Nick Gallo actually had a small hole in his office wall. He made it a little bigger, stuffed all the dildos and sex toys into it, and sealed it up again. Someday, he said, "somebody will remove that temp wall and a lot of things will fall out."

On the last night, Dan Mirk said, "Everyone was just taking things from the office, everyone was drinking . . . taking mementos, like *Onion* framed front pages. There was an *Onion* newspaper box I think somebody took. Just kind of looting the place. I remember everyone was drunk, and we had these huge rolls of bubble wrap that we were just unrolling and sending down the hallways. It was just crazy. Throwing paper through the air." Hanson also remembered the bubble wrap, which was "huge, the size of a bale of hay or something." People were unrolling it and walking on it so that it made popping sounds. "Everybody was drunk, and I was all drunk. I remember there was music playing that was really loud. And then the popping of the bubble wrap." It was like, "This is our last Whiskey Friday because, you know, we lost the fight."

Reflecting on what being at *The Onion* had taught him, Janosch said, "Once you start seeing the world through the eyes of this place, it's a beautiful thing. And it's also a curse. It's the curse of a comedian's eyes or a satirist's eyes, because you start to see the greed and the wickedness and the cruelty and the injustice" as the source of what the satire is about. They were all now being affected "by what *The Onion* believes the world to be, which is greed and idiocy."

Steve Hannah said, "You asked me why I was attracted to *The Onion* in the first place. I started reading it when it first came out. It had exactly the kind of smart-ass humor, parody, hyperbole, and mockery that I love in satire. I mean, it was perfect for that.

"I think I heard a guy once say that *The Onion* was the perfect refuge against rage in society. I couldn't have agreed more. I absolutely loved the product. Product sounds a little harsh. I loved *The Onion*. It was wonderful. Nobody loved *The Onion* more than I did. And believe me, I hope that everybody you talk to says nobody loved *The Onion* more than they did. I'm sure Scott would say that. And Rob Siegel would say that. Carol would say that. And Will Graham would say that. We were all, I think, in lockstep about that. We just loved what we were doing. We loved the havoc that we created. We loved puncturing the inflated egos, the politicians.

"And never did a publication have a more appropriate slogan on the masthead. And I'm not talking about 'America's Finest News Source.' I'm talking about the Latin, which was 'Tu stultus es,' which means, 'You are stupid.'"

Chapter 17

In Chicago, editorial and business were now under the same roof for the first time in more than fifteen years. Though the final party in New York had felt like a wake, new editor Will Tracy and new head writer Seth Reiss knew that wasn't the case. "I just got done packing the truck to move out there," as Tracy put it. Cole Bolton and Jermaine Affonso, who had been working remotely for a couple of years as writers-at-large, joined the Chicago staff as well. Everyone made an informal deal that if it didn't work out within a year or so, they would all quit.

Many people were still reading *The Onion*. According to a *Chicago Tribune* article about the move in April 2012, they had about seven million monthly digital visitors, with an additional three million for the A.V. Club. Chicago print circulation alone was fifty thousand, and overall profitability had returned in 2010. Digital ad revenue had doubled in 2011 and was projected to increase even more in 2012.

Ben Berkley, who had come on as an intern only about two years earlier, was now the only remaining operational editorial employee, covering the two jobs formerly held by Janosch and Palmer by himself. He said Onion, Inc., did go out of their way to welcome them. And despite the complaints of the New York staff, it wasn't like being sent back to Podunk, Wisconsin, at all. On Lake Michigan with miles of beaches and shoreline, Chicago was the third-largest city in the United States and had long been filled with artists and musicians and writers and performers, had several outstanding universities and museums, and was home to the *Chicago Tribune*, the *Chicago Reader*, and WBEZ, one of the largest public radio stations in the country. The city's historic fortunes were based more in material goods like meatpacking, grain markets, and chopping down midwestern forests than imaginary things like skyscraper high finance and movie stars, sure, but that's America too. Hannah was also correct that you could get a lot more apartment for your money, and from an organizational and office-rent perspective, it made perfect sense for everyone to be housed in the same spot. Still, the elephant in the room remained. They were now a full-time editorial staff of six; in New York they'd had almost twenty. As Berkley put it: "You've got a group moving into a city they didn't want to live in, without probably a good 80–90 percent of the people we loved working with back in New York."

A historic paradigm shift was also at hand. "As much as we were welcomed," Berkley said, "we were immediately under pressure to deliver for the business." The old Dikkers-Haise agreement that a firewall would forever remain between the creative side and the money side—an agreement that both physical distance and a previously more generous advertising paradigm had helped to maintain even after *The Onion* went corporate—was now over.

Whiskey Friday remained in name, occasionally, but as a shadow of its former self. Joe's Cold Beverages was gone along with Joe Garden, who was now at Adult Swim. When Jay Rath visited one day from Madison to help Scott Dikkers with a project, he thought the editorial staff was the business team. A 2017 NPR "deep dive" feature on the office said it looked like "a Silicon Valley startup office or something. Sleek cubicles and young people with headphones on and hoodies," and very quiet.

There *were* some produced-in-jest oil portraits of Hannah, Schafer, McAvoy, and T. Herman Zweibel hanging in the boardroom. It was so funny that *The Onion* now had real corporate bosses along with their fake one. The Hannah portrait was eventually purloined to the writers' room and decorated with stuffed arms and a cigarette in the portrait's mouth, and McAvoy's apparently made him look so bad he took it down and hid it somewhere. But otherwise, in Chicago there just wasn't the kind of downtime required for a lot of office decorating. Because now, the goal was quantity, pretty much the only choice in the digital media environment if you were trying to support yourself without a paywall—and turn a profit sufficient for investors—with ad sales. Every single *Onion* article, slide show, video, podcast, web page, and so on was now a place to park an ad.

There was sort of a classic supply-demand problem, though. Online, you could theoretically have infinite advertisement sales, very different from a physical newspaper, which really did have to stop at some point because of that relentless printer deadline. For *The Onion*, this included both premium advertisers attached to particular creations that the sales team sold, and the programmatic ads that displayed automatically on the web page according to each user's cookie history. If the sponsorships went a step further and became branded content, then the story itself could be an ad.

In other words, *The Onion*'s deeply developed joke-crafting methods, based on multiple layers of revision and discussion and research and arguments and editing created over many years in a prior era, were now to be used for mass production of not literary satire but "content." And content is *not* literary—that is, not metaphorical, multilayered, complex, ambiguous, difficult, or illuminating, something from which you can gain new insights every time you pick it up to read. Instead, as scholar Lisa Dush wrote in an issue of *College Composition and Communication*, content is "conditional, computable, networked, and commodified." It's also usually meant to be seen once, after which it vanishes forever. Dush quotes writer Tim Kreider:

> The first time I ever heard the word "content" used in its current context, I understood that all my artist friends and I—henceforth, "content providers"— were essentially extinct. This contemptuous coinage is predicated on the assumption that it's the delivery system that matters, relegating what used to be called "art"—writing, music, film, photography, illustration—to the status of filler, stuff to stick between banner ads.

Of course, news and publishing has long been a for-profit enterprise, and what readers supposedly paid the most attention to has been basic to media since it was invented—violence, sex, food, fear, gossip, scandal, and cuteness, pretty much. Stuff that activates our lizard brains. That's how Pulitzer funded his famous investigative reporting. Now, though, reader attention was measured— and manipulated—in seconds or minutes rather than weeks, months, or years, and anything that didn't motivate an impulsive click and hold your gaze for at least a moment or two was valueless. Writers and readers now served the technology rather than the technology serving us, and what worked was reducing humans to our most basic, knee-jerk responses and keeping us all in a state of anxious, jumpy, close-focused "now." Cole Bolton said:

272

The Chicago era of *The Onion* was defined by many efforts, mostly hare-brained, to game the number of clicks that the *Onion* website received. Clicks were king, and we were contorting ourselves to appease an inscrutable Facebook algorithm, an algorithm that changed regularly and may have even been restricting the spread of our content in an era when "fake news" and concerns about its propagation were growing. . . . It is no way to run a good satire business to make your North Star blindly chasing clicks from mercurial social media gods.

Bolton said it was also "frustrating and conceit obliterating" when Facebook started putting the label "Satire" on all *Onion* articles around August 2014. On top of this frustration, he said McAvoy tagged stories that did well in this momentary-attention model (unsurprisingly, hot topics of the moment online and stuff that was NSFW) and pushed them to do more, such as content that required more clicking, like slide shows. It also meant phasing out long-form articles and op-ed pieces in favor of shorter "News in Brief" articles and "skyboxes"—one-liners with images. No more Jean Teasdale or Jim Anchower, Point-Counterpoints, or advice columns—or not many of them, anyway. (McAvoy objected to this characterization. He said it was not a mandate at all and people didn't write those things anymore because they didn't want to.) "Moreover," Bolton said, "there were lots of calls to drastically expedite or remove steps from *The Onion*'s editing process to get more out faster—basically to turn us into a content factory."

The print edition would still be produced for a little while longer, with Tracy and Reiss lovingly attending to the supposedly old-fashioned (really the more humane, nuanced, and interesting) paper paradigm that gave much thought to story mix, visual layout, and structure in a format that still had a beginning, middle, and end. That is, an *Onion* made for humans to read and enjoy, not computer algorithms to game. But such tactile, intellectually/emotionally manageable media experiences were rapidly being obliterated. Now, what a human being might see as brilliant work was immediately subsumed by the infinite feed of content all around you, like a cupful of clean, living water dumped into the cesspool rivers flowing endlessly online that were now hard to avoid even if you were reading on paper. Until our economic system undergoes fundamental change, until health and well-being for all in the real world becomes more important than conceptual abstracts like shareholder profit and GDP numbers, until we stop fetishizing "efficiency" and behaving like technology and quantification are deities to be obeyed rather than tools to be used, we will never not overdo the machinery that makes mass production and mass consumption possible. *The Onion* had long fought this ever-expanding media pollution and stupidity through courage, locality, and iconoclasm. Its leaders—and the 2010s digital media paradigm—were now demanding it become just another part of it.

Just as Tracy predicted, soon after his arrival in Chicago, Dikkers was immediately spun in the media as the former editor-in-chief returning to his roots. But even though a *Chicago Tribune* article reporting on the move said Dikkers would be stepping into his old editorial role, this was not actually the case—or at least not for long. It appears Dikkers had either been misinformed or just truly didn't understand that he was signing away his soul when he became general manager. Tracy guessed Dikkers thought he was going to be a sort of "editor above the editor," while Onion, Inc., thought of him as an insurance policy in case these "youngsters" (Tracy was twenty-nine) didn't work out.

Dikkers figured it out soon enough. He told me his experience in Chicago was "horrible." The writers didn't like him, and management didn't like him either. "They thought of me as kind of this necessary evil," he said. "I think what they were doing was pitching me to advertisers as 'Hey, one of the original guys is back. He'll make sure that *The Onion* is just as funny as it always was. No worries.' But to the writers, they were saying, 'Don't worry, Dikkers isn't going to be involved at all. You guys will run the show. He's just a figurehead.' And that's exactly what it was. I was just there to keep a chair warm." He told me the one thing he regretted about his *Onion* career was selling his ownership shares.

The personnel situation was also just different than it was back in the day. Dikkers, as he said in the *Tribune* article, liked to work with inexperienced, "green" young people. The argument was usually that writing for *The Onion* was so difficult and specialized, writers needed to be trained from the ground up. Tracy, however, put it in terms of motivation. The '90s staff, as brilliant as they were, did need to be pushed a bit—and Dikkers had done a lot of the pushing. But by the time they got to Chicago, it was no longer a staff of slackers.

Back in the writers' room, Tracy said it didn't take long before it was clear that the new editorial staff was working just fine. Which meant the big insurance policy that Onion, Inc., had taken out on Dikkers wasn't needed. Tracy said

Dikkers, styling himself as some sort of *Onion* "guru," would occasionally come to headline meetings and say things like, "You need to have the right mix of oats and marshmallows," as in the correct mix of serious satire and silly stories. He would also "give these pep talks or dissertations on his thoughts about *The Onion* and thoughts about comedy and how we should be doing it."

Tracy said he understood Dikkers was in a difficult position. "Especially as a guy who was one of the founding figures in *The Onion*, he probably felt justifiably like, 'They should listen to me. I know how to do *The Onion*.'" To Tracy and the staff, though, the feeling was, "I also know how to do *The Onion*. I've gotten pretty good at this." Tracy needed to have editorial authority on his own.

One day, Berkley said, Dikkers gave the editorial staff a "very unpopular" presentation about how their satire was "too dark and real and serious." Dikkers told them his ideal *Onion* was gentle, for both "nine-year-olds and ninety-year-olds." I think we can all agree the only response to this is: What? "It did not go well," Berkley said. "They mocked it for years after." Tracy also recalled a meeting where Dikkers drew some graph of "silly versus smart" on a whiteboard, "and you're too far on this end of the graph." Tracy told me he said, "Well, thank you, Scott. Thank you, we'll take that into advisement." After Dikkers left, he turned to the writers and said, "Yeah, forget all that. Don't worry about any of that. You guys are doing great." And then he went to visit Hannah and McAvoy. "I guess this was the advantage of having them right down the hall," Tracy said. "Because I went right down the hall, and I kind of said, 'You know, maybe there's been a few things with Scott that I don't think have been very helpful. . . . Maybe there needs to be a little bit of a rethink on exactly what Scott's duties are here.'"

Berkley also told me Dikkers tried to get him removed from his position. One day Hannah came up and said, "We hear you're going to be a writing fellow going forward!" Berkley said, "Excuse me?" It seems Dikkers had decided to demote him to writing fellow—a temporary entry-level position—and replace him with an old friend who was an occasional *Onion* headline contributor. Luckily, Berkley said, "Will, Seth, and Chad mobilized so fast to smash that out, which I'll always be grateful to them for."

Dikkers was also, of course, dealing with the high level of animosity he'd created in New York. Berkley didn't think Dikkers was a bad person. But it was hard not to see him as a villain. It couldn't have been a fun time for Dikkers. No longer a co-owner or even an editor, as general manager he seems to have had no clear or consistent duties, roaming from one place to another as his not-so-distant fiftieth birthday hung in the air.

Dikkers said, "Seth and Will literally didn't even want me in the writers' room. I get that it was their turn. They wanted to do their thing." But when he saw them making mistakes, he needed to mention it. "Like one time they started having just way too many words in the headlines. It was getting out of control. I said, 'Cut half the words,' you know? And that was like the limit of my involvement." (Dikkers had a point about headline length. Both Robert Siegel and Stephen Thompson told me they'd finally had to stop reading *The Onion* because the new staff was writing headlines too long, and it was driving them insane. The one that apparently did Thompson in was from April 20, 2005: "Papal Election Brings End to Worldwide Unsupervised-Catholic Sin Binge." He told me it should obviously have been, "Unsupervised Catholics Embark on Sin Binge"—30 percent funnier. Their dedication to the form was being lost. "It just made me crazy," Thompson said.)

Todd Hanson was still involved, but mostly on the sidelines. As Berkley put it, "I would talk to Todd on the phone like every other week for what was scheduled for thirty minutes and probably always ended up being hours." They would fly him out to Chicago sometimes so that Hanson could spend time with the writers as a "spiritual advisor," Berkley said, though he wasn't someone they could lean on for production. Mitch Semel said, "Todd, to his credit, could see where things changed in the voice or the presentation or whatever, but also was a real tie to the roots." (Hanson was asked how he wanted his role to be listed on the masthead. He chose "Éminence Grise.") John Krewson lasted only about a week before leaving to take a job at a car magazine. In other words, other than Nackers, Tracy, Reiss, and Bolton, the editorial staff, including interns, was now mostly very young people a couple of years (or weeks) out of college. *The Onion* was no longer a place to spend a career but instead an entry-level gig into late-night television, the world of TV and movie writing in Hollywood, advertising, or some other field related to putting words and pictures on a screen where anyone over forty was considered useless and old. In this way, *The Onion* became like any other media or tech company, cranking through one group of twenty-somethings after another and bringing in a fresh one whenever the prior group aged or burned out—which not only kept personnel and benefits costs low but also avoided any entrenchment of "legacy" staff. (In the course of my interviews for this project, I spoke with more than one over-forty former *Onion* editorial staffer who was now struggling to find appropriate employment.)

Indeed, few people over thirty-five or with caregiving responsibilities would have tolerated the new content demands. On Twitter, for instance, the staff was now expected to come up with something new every fifteen minutes from 8:00 a.m. to 8:00 p.m. Berkley said in that first year and a half, "We tripled our output. We more than tripled our traffic. And we did that after having more than halved our staff." For a while, the staff did get bonuses for extra clicks, but that didn't negate the intensity of the environment. At age twenty-three, Berkley broke out in shingles from the stress. There was even talk of mandating a weekend staff to keep fresh clicks coming in seven days a week. Berkley began spending as much or more time with the business staff as he was with the editorial team, usually to "try finding creative workarounds for terrible sponsored content deals they were making." (McAvoy disputed this characterization as well. One, he said, their output expectations were not unreasonable. Tracy and Reiss did just fine—in fact, they produced even more than subsequent editorial staffs. Two, Berkley was kind of an Eeyore who brought a lot of his stress upon himself.)

The video staff was also tasked with creating and managing ginormous quantities of content. Most of the videos appear to have been created in a few hours by a skeleton crew with a modest budget and bore little resemblance to ONN's former brilliance; they were all branded content or existed mostly so ads could be attached to them. Some were even pretty funny, but the mass-production aspect is apparent.

And no matter how many videos they did, editorial staff told me, business wanted more. On July 23, 2012, the staff did a story and video called "Blood-Drenched Berserk CEO Demands More Web Videos." In the story, the CEO yells out random media buzzwords such as "social presence," "responsive site," "integration opportunities," and "eight-episode web series." "Toward the end of the verbal and physical onslaught, he relieved his bowels in the middle of the office floor, rubbed his body in the excrement, and told employees that nobody was leaving until there were forty more videos online." (McAvoy told me the piece was shot in Steve Hannah's office.) Staff who went on to late-night comedy-show writing told me what they missed most about *The Onion* was being able to write whatever they wanted. But as Josh Modell put it, the deal with the devil at *The Onion* in this era, "a place that's not making money hand over fist," was sponsored content.

It is true that the staff were still writing regular *Onion* articles and that the writers' room was still the writers' room. Plenty of great satire was still coming out that had nothing to do with brands. As McAvoy put it, not everyone was being "managed to business outcomes"; they did the business stuff outside the traditional editorial. "I can't imagine Seth [Reiss] saying he was oppressed at *The Onion*," he said. But it is also true that sponsored content was not a very *Onion*-y thing to do.

Mike McAvoy became president in February 2013. Cost-cutting seems to have appeared soon after. Early in 2013, designer Jun Ueno, who had been with *The Onion* for twenty years and probably had one of those "legacy" salaries, was fired. "We could have run that operation for one hundred years," he said. "But management screws it up every time." The print edition was still around too, but not for long. It was also a remnant of the 1990s. As Welyczko had anticipated, the print franchises failed one by one. Finally, in December 2013, *The Onion*'s beloved weekly print edition—cherished by readers for twenty-five years, altering and influencing culture for a longer, more frequent, and more consistent period of time than any humor publication since *MAD* magazine or *National Lampoon*, and inspiring imitators around the globe—came to an end.

Tracy said, "We tried to shut it down in the funniest possible way. The whole issue is a special issue about '*Onion* ad sales up 5,000 percent,' all this stuff about how well it's going. 'Digital revolution still twenty to thirty years away, say experts.'" He said, "It was sad that it ended for me, because I always just thought and still think it's the funniest way to read *The Onion*. . . . And that was a shame." Reiss said even as the digital side was getting bigger and bigger, "and the paper was dying, you know, city by city, slowly but surely, we still thought of everything as 'the issue.' As opposed to a running stream of headlines."

Unfortunately, former editorial staff suspicions were confirmed with the shutdown: McAvoy said in an *American Journalism Review* article at the time that "we planned for this long ago," beginning in 2007 when the company began "a push toward a digital-first strategy." (This initiative explained the millions pumped into ONN while the print side languished.) Revenue from the print franchises had actually been channeled into building up the digital operation—not into print sustainability—while also allowing *The Onion* to get someone else

⌀ the ONION

WEATHER *Page 8D*

Perfect for curling up with a real tangible copy of a newspaper

"Tu Stultus Es"

DECEMBER 12, 2013 · VOL. 49 ISSUE 50 | AMERICA'S FINEST NEWS SOURCE · ONION.COM | Copyright © 2013 Onion, Inc. All Rights Reserved | 10¢

INSIDE

INK The Rise Of The Most Enduring And Trusted Player In Modern Journalism

PART ONE OF AN EIGHT-PART SERIES

HIGHLIGHTS

Nation Just Prefers Feel Of Newsprint In Hands
NATIONAL, *Page 14B*

City Planners Call For Widened Sidewalks To Alleviate Congestion Around 'Onion' Newspaper Boxes
NATIONAL, *Page 7B*

COMPLIMENTARY **ONE YEAR SUBSCRIPTION**
Redeem at onion.com/redeem · Enter code 'PRINT'

'ONION' PRINT REVENUES UP 5,000%

Company sources say The Onion's print business continues to be an unstoppable source of profit.

WASHINGTON—A report released this Monday from the U.S. Department of Commerce confirmed that, consistent with the past 60 years, The Onion's revenue from print media and other print-related ventures has increased a resounding 5,000 percent in 2013.

"According to our analysis, in just the last month alone, we've seen The Onion's already dominant print empire nearly triple its revenue stream, all while continuing to meet the rampant international demand for newsprint," said the report's author, Jeffrey Larson, explaining that despite a slower-than-average first quarter of just $41.8 billion in growth, The Onion's print division ended the year having added over 850,000 jobs to the U.S. economy in key sectors such as printing press operation, page layout design, and newspaper distribution. "At this point, we estimate that the lucky investors who got in at the ground floor of this unstoppable print media cash cow have made somewhere between $15 to $20 billion—if not double that. In fact, in the current climate, I anticipate The Onion newspapers will make up well over 45 percent of the nation's GDP next year."

The report concluded by noting that revenues for The Onion will likely only continue increasing through 2014, with experts estimating that readers across the country would likely continue flocking to Onion boxes every Thursday morning and pulling out a fresh copy of the paper for generations to come. ⌀

Demand for digital content "simply isn't there yet," experts say.

Experts: Digital Media Revolution Still Another 70 Or 80 Years Away

NEW YORK—Confirming that the current media landscape has so far shown virtually no sign of shifting away from the lucrative print trade, a group of experts told reporters today that the so-called digital media revolution, long rumored to one day transform the industry as we know it, remains at least 70 to 80 years away.

see DIGITAL MEDIA, page 17

Google CEO Fondly Recalls 'Onion' Print Ad That Put Company On Map

MOUNTAIN VIEW, CA—Discussing the company's evolution from a two-man graduate research project to a global multimedia company employing thousands of workers, Google CEO Larry Page fondly recalled to

see GOOGLE, page 13

INSIDE

Study Finds 97% Of Happily Married Couples Met While Going For Same Copy Of 'The Onion' Newspaper
Page 12C

ONE CALL THAT'S ALL
GRUBER LAW OFFICES, LLC.
gruber-law.com
INJURED? (414) 276-6666

Thanks for all the laughs
⌀ the ONION

The end of a 25-year print run in December 2013.

---

to take the economic hit around the end of print. Legacy media and its copier salesmen had still been good for something. Now, "the majority of the ad campaigns the company uses revolve around custom content for advertising, such as branded content and native advertising."

Reiss escaped in 2013 to write for *Late Night with Seth Meyers*, and Tracy in 2014 to write for *Last Week Tonight with John Oliver*. Hannah and McAvoy both considered them two of the best editorial leaders *The Onion* had ever had. Before Tracy left, on July 29, 2013, his team posted a short piece called "Merger

279

of Advertising Giants Brings Together Largest Collection of People with No Discernible Skills":

> Not a single person involved in the merger has ever made anything with his hands, knows anything about information technology, or is capable of doing quality writing or research. "These two ad behemoths will have the industry's largest and most formidable talent pool of people called 'creatives' who have never created a single thing in their lives and whose only apparent ability is to trick other people." At press time, over $500 billion was spent on advertising last year.

The next editor was Cole Bolton, with Nackers as head writer. Bolton grew up in a small town on an island in Vermont's Lake Champlain called South Hero, "all apple orchards and dairy farms." His mom was a psychiatrist, and his dad was a classic-rock deejay, sort of the perfect parents if you want to go into comedy writing. They divorced when he was in first grade. Bolton went to college at Brown University and studied economics. He had read *The Onion* since high school, however, and after college, persistence and luck got him a freelance-contributor gig while he was working at the Federal Reserve in Chicago. Finally, Bolton was asked to be a writing fellow for a summer. Joining the New York writers' room was a thrill and a challenge. "It was so hard as a person who had been on the outside, just like writing headlines, to get a word in. . . . I would describe it to people as like stepping into traffic." Bolton took a job as a writer "at large" for a while and finally joined the group in person in Chicago. But *The Onion* he got to edit was not *The Onion* he had grown up with. Bolton soon realized his primary job wasn't to take *The Onion* to new and better places. It was to do whatever he could to keep it from sinking any deeper.

Much of the branded content was done through a new in-house ad agency, Onion Labs. Founded in 2012, headed by advertising industry veteran Rick Hamann after 2014, and apparently one of McAvoy's proudest accomplishments, the agency made *Onion*-style ads for clients from David's Bridal to White Castle that could appear outside *The Onion*. In a university adjunct-instructor bio, Hamann said of the role, "As a young copywriter, I studied *Onion* headlines like they were gospel. . . . They are fiercely protective of everything that bears their name, and they agonize over every headline, video, and photo. That kind of dedication to craftsmanship is becoming increasingly rare in our industry, and to work with that kind of talent is a dream come true." (Hamann would go on to oversee *The Onion*'s entire editorial operation and all creative development from 2017 to 2019.) You can find articles about how millennials needed edgy, nonbullshit marketing and how Onion Labs was just the thing to reach them, something I'm sure nobody has ever said about any prior generation of young people.

Onion Labs apparently began after *The Onion* was hired to do a campaign for Microsoft's reboot of Internet Explorer. I'm not sure what it means when the tech giant that helped start this entire nightmare wants to portray itself as a joke thirty years later while still continuing to go about its business hoovering up the life energy and attention of billions of people from cradle to grave, like some extremely nerdy Stephen King horror clown, but . . . we are living in a strange time. In an odd hybrid of *Onion* sarcasm and actual advertising doublespeak, the old Onion Labs website reads:

> *The Onion* has long believed that advertising is the true bedrock of any first-world economy, which is why America's Finest News Source decided to finally enter this sacred arena—creating smart content on behalf of brands. Comedy is at the heart of who we are and what we do. Our work stands out because we don't create ads. We create content that your target audience actually wants to watch.

One former staffer's LinkedIn profile described his job as "work[ing] with some of the world's largest companies to solve brand challenges using *The Onion*'s iconic voice" that included "video series, articles, commercials, social content and 360 campaigns." In a *Shots Magazine* article, Hamann said his work at *The Onion* "really changed the entire process of how content is created. . . . It's been a revolution rather than an evolution."

Like the idea of *Onion* sponsored content, the idea of an *Onion*-inspired advertising agency seemed ludicrously tone-deaf when I first learned about it. But here it was. (The Onion Labs video archives on YouTube do include a couple of projects so surreal and disorienting, it's questionable viewers even realized they were ads. Maybe that's the "we don't create ads" part, or perhaps the work of gifted filmmakers trapped in a sponsored-content job to pay the bills.) Onion Labs apparently brought in at least $10 million a year and provided 80 percent of *The Onion*'s revenue for a while.

McDonagh said, "This is where they may hate me. The branded-content piece was a necessary move for our business. I think getting *Onion* writers to do it probably was not the right move and would probably have to be rethought. But I think Onion Labs ended up being a very important part of the business if you just look at the numbers." Modell said the problem was really the digital advertising industry, which demanded more and more while paying less and less. He said, maybe as a joke, that rates were now around two cents per thousand impressions. Still, in Baratunde Thurston's day, it was eighty dollars. McAvoy told me they once sold ONN ads for $80,000 a pop. A few years later, the same ad space would be lucky to get $800. As long as your funding model was ad sales, the only way out of that math was to make a lot more content while also drastically dropping how much time and money you spent on each piece. Or pimping out *Onion* writers. "I don't understand how things that are only sites and that's the only way they're making money are even still around," Modell said. Maybe it's good *The Onion* never truly sold out. "Because you're fucked if you do and you're fucked if you don't."

At first, *The Onion* apparently used its regular writers for Onion Labs, though Dikkers told me he hired a separate writing staff. The way it worked, he said, was that the writers would not be told who the advertiser was. "We would just say, 'Come up with jokes about laundry,' and then they would have to focus on laundry. They wouldn't know that the client is Clorox Bleach." And the situation "morphed from total separation to advertising basically having total control."

Dikkers said that early on they did say if a story was an advertorial, but then that fell away. It's from a few years later, but one example is clearly "Bounty Scientists Scream as Experimental Paper Towel Absorbs Entire Lab," from 2021. Dikkers said:

> The model is *Vice*. *Vice* is a company that has these really gritty guerrilla journalism—type investigative pieces. They're all ads. Some big company will say, "I want a piece about the way Sherpas are discriminated against in the Himalayas." And it'll be like Red Bull, because they want to be associated with this extreme adventuring or whatever. And *Vice* will make this totally gritty, seemingly purely journalistic, "comfort the afflicted, afflict the comfortable" report about the plight of some marginalized group, and it's just an ad.

The staff also had to deal with advertiser ideas for stories. Berkley said the sales team would bring the writers some "absolute flaming pile of shit and lay it at our doorstep," like "The CMO of Pepsi really likes *The Onion* and wants there to be a story about how Coca-Cola was voted the worst soda ever." Another one was Red Robin, which was sold a deal for a bunch of sponsored articles with headlines that would include their new slogan, "Let's Burger." Berkley said after weeks of negotiating, the editorial staff finally got Red Robin to accept a ton of extra ads in exchange for not having to include this unbelievably stupid catchphrase in their work. This was part of what the staff called "*Onion* fantasy camp," where the sales team was essentially selling the chance to make an *Onion* story. (Quite a few of these prospective campers seem to have come in with amazing, hilarious ideas for ad campaigns about how stupid advertising is.)

Layering it all even further, these requests seemed to have then prompted ironic advertising-is-great *Onion* stories, some of which may themselves have been sponsored. (Once the concept of sponsored content arose, I started questioning whether any *Onion* story mentioning a brand name after 2012 wasn't bought and paid for somehow.) See May 17, 2013, "Sponsored Content Pretty Fucking Awesome."

Sources confirmed that while a majority of Americans can't get enough sponsored posts, an even greater number "really fucking love and appreciate" when content written for advertisers is seamlessly woven into a publication's regular material, thereby leaving readers confused as to whether or not they are reading an advertisement or original writing from the publication's creative staff.

The article concludes with "Buy Doritos."

At the end of 2013, Berkley put together an end-of-year recap for the staff showing their "obscene" success. All records had been beaten. Millions of people were seeing their output. "And that was undercut a day later by a Mike McAvoy email that said, essentially, 'Thanks for all your work, people! Next year, we're going to come back harder; we're going to do this all 3x!'"

McDonagh said, "I think what nobody probably really understood was how good we actually were at monetizing every page view on *The Onion*. Much better than a lot of other websites." McAvoy echoed this. He also said a primary problem with satirizing the news was that *The Onion* did not have the kind of budgets real news had—especially, I expect, as news got more and more indistinguishable from entertainment—so achieving verisimilitude, as with ONN, was expensive and time consuming and required a lot of staff. You simply couldn't fund it by selling ads—you needed a far larger source of cash. That's where Onion Labs came in. (Onion Labs also apparently was the place where writers who weren't good enough to write for the regular *Onion* were steered, including the many ad salespeople who actually wanted to be editorial staff.) McAvoy also said he shielded the satire writers from stupid advertiser requests all the time—they just didn't know about it. *The Onion* always put editorial first. In 2014, *The Onion* was a finalist for *Digiday*'s 2014 Publishing Awards in the categories of "Best Branded Content Integration by a Publisher," "Best Editorial Achievement by a Publisher," "Best Use of Native Advertising," and "Best Use of Social Media by a Publisher."

I asked McDonagh what the point of it all was. What were they making the money *for*? "That's where the clash between the business side and the creative side was," he said. "There wasn't any clarity. And then if the writers and the creatives don't have any skin in the game, why are they incentivized to do anything that's going to help us to sell?" McAvoy told me, "Anyone who owns a company, they want it to grow in value. I was employed by the people who owned the company. They wanted it to grow, make more revenue, make more money in profit." Berkley said, "We were growing steadily, organically at this time. The only discernible reason for Mike pushing the pace was growth for growth's sake. Companies apparently aren't allowed to produce modest, gradually increasing profits anymore."

The pressure was on for other reasons, too. Berkley said he was told, "Do this if you don't want layoffs on your hands." Or—as probably seemed possible spiritually if not economically—let *The Onion* die. That, more than anything, seems to have been the motivating factor behind tolerating the bullshit. "There were some red lines that we set out," Berkley said. "And we're like, 'If this is crossed, you're not going to have an editorial staff anymore.'" Meanwhile, the business side was reading articles in *Digiday* and saying "*Vox* did this; *Vice* did this; we should do it," while the young, clinging-to-idealism editorial staff tried to make them understand they were degrading the value of the entire thing.

The Onion was now a multiplatform media brand, a business whose primary goal was not to speak truth to power or write timeless literary satire—though they did still do that sometimes—but to prep itself for sale and make more money for people who were already wealthy after the staff salaries were paid. Or just, you know, make more videos. "So many places have gone under," Berkley said, "so many jobs have been lost, because we set the expectation that content was free."

Though diminished, *The Onion* was not dead yet. Remember the YouTube money Thurston mentioned coming in right as the move to Chicago was announced? The remaining ONN staff used it to create two comedy-horror masterpieces: *Sex House*, a reality-show satire, and *Porkin' Across America*, a travel-documentary satire starring Jim Haggerty from ONN's *Today Now!* traveling across the United States eating pig meat in various forms and slowly de-evolving. Both were released in 2012. (The internet is not forever, despite popular belief, so watch them now.)

This was essentially *The Onion*'s version of Peak TV. Both shows were very dark and very well written, acted, and produced. I read them as a colossal middle finger to Onion, Inc.'s lack of imagination and shortsightedness, as well as an expression of the way the world represented by media was even more rapidly separating from lived reality even as it insisted, *Everything is great! What are you getting so upset about? Maybe you should work on yourself more. Here, have another video.*

Television had always lived in a mostly stupid alternate world, adding little of value to how people talked and thought about things. But the sheer quantity of 24/7 media now being taken in by millions of people through their anxiously clutched, designed-to-be-addictive devices and apps was setting up an uncanny valley situation in which huge chunks of the population really did seem to be living in an alternate reality where every thought and emotion was shaped by their portable glowing rectangles. We were deep in triple-latte, Adderall-Ritalin land, a world where stimulants were pretty much required just to keep up with it all—a long way from Gen X and boomer weed and beer consumed as an escape from corporate reality, not as a way to fuse with it.

Sex House and *Porkin' Across America* weren't literally about any of this. But to me they did what *The Onion* does best: re-create the *feeling* of the media experience while magnifying it enough to reveal everything that is normally left out—emotionally and philosophically. And in both shows, the revelation is how profoundly narcissistic and abusive our for-profit culture and media have become. And how hard we try to get that culture to love us and accept us and give

285

us attention—a quest that cannot and will not ever be fulfilled in any sustaining way, however "interactive" we are told that system is. It's all just a con and a lie.

The Onion was at least making an effort to create new styles to attach ads to. These would include *Onion*-style TED Talks (2014), a true-crime podcast (2018), and a nature show (2012). (A project called Onion Studios was an attempt to do movies and TV—taking an office in New York for a while since that's where the action was—but it didn't get very far.) Also in 2013, Dikkers, now cast out of the writers' room, was assigned to create *The Onion*'s first onstage comedy show in cooperation with Second City, to be called *Onion Live*. In a *Chicago Tribune* article, Steve Hannah described it as a "funny, biting new incarnation of *The Onion*." The intention was to tour it nationally in the fall and winter of 2013, with Second City providing the backbone for the show.

Because Dikkers lacked experience with live theater, he again enlisted his old standby, Jay Rath, for help, who had written and produced for local theater in Madison. Rath said, "Scott called me down, and I was very glad of it and pleased and proud and got paid a lot of money." However, he also said he didn't think the show would "ever fly." Tracy said, "It felt a little bit like, 'Let's give Scott something to do so he's not going to bother the writers,' if I'm being completely honest." Unfortunately, early performances didn't go over very well. Josh Modell went to see it "out of morbid curiosity" and told me, "It was fucking abominable. . . . So far from the spirit of *The Onion*." The national tour was canceled.

Not surprisingly, Dikkers's time at *The Onion* soon came to an end, and this time it would be for good. "I think I was there for all of two years," Dikkers told me. I asked him if he was fired or if he quit, and he said it was "a combination of the two things." Tracy said, "That's kind of what happens, I think, when you allow yourself to be used as a piece of leverage by management to strong-arm editorial."

Even though he was no longer part of the company, Dikkers apparently retained an *Onion* email address for a while, which it seems had to be somewhat forcibly extracted from him. At another point, Dikkers was also apparently issued a cease-and-desist letter forbidding him to use the *Onion* logo in his presentations and websites (where he also often calls himself *The Onion*'s "founder" or variations thereof and says he personally won *The Onion*'s Peabody Award and Thurber Prize, wrote *Our Dumb Century*, and other interesting things).

McAvoy said, "Was he hard to police? For sure, because his version of reality is different than everyone else's." When *The Onion* had their thirtieth anniversary comedy festival in 2018, important former editorial staff were brought back for a panel discussion. Dikkers was not invited. During the panel, however, to the shock of his former colleagues, Dikkers suddenly climbed onstage out of the audience. Hanson said he hugged everyone, shouted something like, "It's great to see all my old friends again!" and jumped off the stage. Afterward, he tried to join the group backstage but was barred by a security guard. Hanson found out and let him in. Dikkers then, Hanson said, "made himself the center of attention."

I asked Dikkers how he felt about his *Onion* career. He said he was really proud of all the work he did and of everybody he worked with. "So much good work," he said. "So much good comedy."

Since we are in Chicago now, and facing the classic American corporate-capitalism-versus-art-and-humanity situation, I'd like to digress a bit and tell you about a man named Steve Albini.

Albini, who died too soon in May 2024 at the age of sixty-one, was a famously outspoken underground Chicago musician, producer, music writer, and leader of the 1980s band Big Black. He is associated with an intense, powerful, punk/hardcore sound, and after Big Black became a sought-after recording engineer for many bands, including 1990s icons like the Pixies, the Breeders, PJ Harvey, and Nirvana as well as more underground groups like The Jesus Lizard.

Albini was known for his anticorporate attitude and outspokenness, as well as his insistence that he not be given any credit for the soul and creativity of the bands he recorded. Unlike other producers, he asked to be paid like a "plumber" rather than take a percentage of sales—even for the million-selling Nirvana when they asked him to record their next album after *Nevermind*, *In Utero*. A 2023 article in the *Guardian* described him:

> Albini—and I can't say this without it sounding a little silly because of the way the music industry has conspired for decades to sand off the edges of any once-transgressive cultural movement . . . is a genuine punk rocker. Not because he plays music with distorted guitars or exudes contempt for pretentious establishment figures—though he has done plenty of that—but because

throughout his career he, perhaps more than anyone else, has attempted to embody the righteous ideological tenets that once made punk rock feel like a true alternative to the tired mainstream.

Regarding the "manipulative and unhealthy" corporate people around Nirvana after their huge success, Albini said at the time, "They want, somehow or another, to claim authorship of the creative output of these other people who are actually doing the heavy lifting for their career. I can't have any respect for somebody like that, who's not involved in the creative process but then decides that they wanna snipe at it from the outside and manipulate people into doing things to suit them. Fuck every one of those people."

Albini was admired by *Onion* writers going back to Matt Cook, who reviewed a Big Black album in *The Onion*'s first year. One day in around 1994, back in Madison, Dan Vebber found out Albini was an *Onion* fan. He brought in a picture of him that he'd drawn as a UW–Madison freshman with the words "ALBINI IS WATCHING" underneath it and hung it over his desk—a role model, inspiration, and monitor for *The Onion*'s writers. And a warning for its owners. Past, present, and future.

On May 15, 2015, *The Onion* posted an article called "Media Organizations Make Pilgrimage to Facebook Headquarters to Lay Content at Foot of Mark Zuckerberg" satirizing the iron grip Facebook now had on traffic to news and media websites:

> "Sir, I humbly offer you this 650-word feature on community gardens in New Jersey in hopes that you will, in your great enlightenment and wisdom, find it to your liking," said visibly trembling *New York Times* executive editor Dean Baquet, setting the journalistic token down before the Facebook CEO after having waited many hours alongside fellow pilgrims from *Slate*, the *Chicago Tribune*, *The Atlantic*, *Time*, *Al Jazeera*, and scores of other news outlets in a line that stretched through the social media site's Silicon Valley offices.

In 2017, however, Facebook began destroying the click-through advertising model used by media publishers around the world by cutting off the spigot through which a zillion links had once flowed. Facebook-originated traffic to media websites had accounted for a huge percentage of visitors to those sites. Now, though, Facebook was changing to a focus on personal posts. As a result, by 2018 traffic to basically all media sites on the planet had dropped into the basement, as did their revenue. No traffic, no clicks, no money. Many media outlets, their ad revenues erased, laid off staff or went out of business. Want your views and clicks back? Well, Facebook said, now you had to pay. It was a classic bait and switch. Or the old trick of giving someone their first taste of a highly addictive drug for free to get them hooked, after which you could charge whatever you wanted.

On the other hand, sensing it was dangerous to put all your eggs in the Facebook basket, this scenario had inspired media sites to try new ways of getting clicks outside of Facebook referrals even before this plug was pulled. In 2014, *The Onion* decided to try a spin-off website venture, to be sponsored by one lucky advertiser. This was the genesis of ClickHole, *The Onion*'s brilliant clickbait site that launched on June 12 as a parody of Upworthy (which was actually cofounded by former *Onion* managing editor Peter Koechley after he left MoveOn.org) and BuzzFeed. The pitch was created by Berkley and J. J. Shebesta, and Jack Link's Beef Jerky sponsored it for $600,000. Berkley said, "And what resulted was the world's very best beef-jerky ad." Jermaine Affonso was hired as the first editor.

Affonso was born in Dubai in the United Arab Emirates. His father worked in the petroleum industry, and the family lived in Saudi Arabia, Indonesia, and Houston. Affonso attended the University of Texas, where he wrote for the *Texas Travesty*, their *Onion* knockoff, and did a little stand-up. He was chosen to become a writing fellow at *The Onion* right after college, in New York. Affonso said that since his parents were Indian American, they had it "drilled into their mind early on that if you can be a doctor or an engineer, get your MBA, that's a key to having a stable career." But of course, one generation removed, Affonso said, "I'd like to pursue poverty." It was an incredible experience to be in the room with the people he'd read and heard about for so long, Affonso said. It was also a "brutal" training ground where writers got accustomed to the experience of rejection.

When I first saw ClickHole, I was so happy. I thought they absolutely nailed it. I wasn't a clickbait reader (the look and feel of it makes me want to instantly flee), so for me it was more like a satire of what it felt like to be on the internet in general: the place where in the space of ten minutes you can have flash before your eyes cute puppies, rotting corpses, the *New York Times*, a note from your boss, fifteen spam emails, a video from 1987, idiotic data-mining quizzes, your middle schooler's Chromebook report on their YouTube views at school (cooking shows, veiled pro-Trump videos), your friend's invitation to their new play about how language creates reality, and a notification that your Wayfair order is out for delivery. Never was Marshall McLuhan's observation that electronic media cause everything to infinitely return more true than now, where you can live virtually in multiple generations and realities at once simply by retrieving their associated images and information. It also means being stuck in a world that *feels* like it's constantly changing, but where in fact nothing actually changes that much, except the speed and intensity with which these associated virtual experiences arrive. The entire internet has become a sort of massively immersive video game. (It also often just feels like tacky, infinite-channels 1980s cable TV—just with more surveillance and better graphics.) The word "samsara" also comes to mind—no, not the "cloud-based platform that helps organizations manage complex physical operations and the people that power them," but the Buddhist concept of never-ending suffering caused by wanting and clinging that fuels an endless cycle of death and rebirth that can't be escaped unless you step out of it all entirely.

In other words, ClickHole brilliantly reproduced the absurd, hilarious, baffling horror show that is the internet. It also reads like it was written by artificial intelligence (or at least an AI circa 2023; by the time this book comes out you will no longer be able to tell). Given that *The Onion* often seems to be ten years ahead when it comes to predicting the future, you can't say you weren't warned. Berkley said ClickHole is "always so excited about the most nothing or dark or upsetting thing. It's just this smiley dope that's unleashing the havoc of the world."

ClickHole got a lot of attention when it first appeared because the uncanniness was so high. In an interview on Splitsider, Affonso said, "It's really just the way the internet is at large and how it's affecting culture as a whole. . . . There's a desperation to it, so instead of being frustrating it's almost more sad at this point." ClickHole also represented a return to *The Onion*'s absurdist roots. It is darker than the Keck/Dahm/Vebber days. But it's easy to imagine Vebber's "RUN FOR YOUR LIVES!" repurposed here without many modifications. ClickHole posted piles of content: surreal quizzes, videos, articles, celebrity quotes, and "clickventures"—choose-your-own-adventure type stories like "Get the Whole Online Experience by Trying Our Internet Simulator." (Koechley told me his favorite ClickHole piece was the video "This Stick of Butter Is Left Out at Room Temperature; You Won't Believe What Happens Next." The video is a single three-hour shot of a stick of butter slowly melting on a counter.) I also recommend "What This Adorable Little Girl Says Will Melt Your Heart," one of the first videos posted on the site: two minutes of an eight-year-old girl explaining she is nothing more than a ploy to get you to watch a web video. "Let's look at the big picture for a second," she says. "If even one hundred people saw this video on Facebook, the website is automatically guaranteed thousands of more page views, which in turn means thousands of more dollars in ad revenue. Why would anyone spend time writing up an eight-hundred-word article when they could just put up a video of a cute little girl?" Just remember, though, "no matter how many videos you watch, how many lists you read, you're still going to feel all alone." The goal was to post one new video on ClickHole every day, replicating the methods of clickbait sites while skewering them at the same time.

Back at theonion.com, 2014 also saw one of the most important stories *The Onion* ever published: "'No Way to Prevent This,' Says Only Nation Where This Regularly Happens," written by Jason Roeder, about the latest mass shooting (this one was the misogynistic attacks in Isla Vista, California, carried out because the shooter wanted to punish women who had rejected him). The staff would always call a special brainstorming meeting when a huge news event happened. And the number of mass shootings was really starting to get them down—for emotional reasons, but also because they were simply running out of jokes. Finally, someone said, "Why don't we just run the same story each time and see if that resonates?" And boy, did it. *The Onion* first republished it after the 2018 Parkland school shooting. Now, each time a mass shooting occurs, *The Onion* repeats the same headline and the same copy, just changing the number of victims, the location, and the media photo. As of September 2024, the story has been published at least thirty-seven times.

In 2015, Hannah and Schafer decided it was time to retire, and *The Onion* was put up for sale. In the process, McAvoy became CEO. Mitch Semel pointed out that when Schafer originally invested in it, it was still only a print and rudimentary website operation—and a unique one. That's why Schafer had valued *The Onion* in the first place. Now, though, *The Onion* was a digital media business similar to many others and much less distinctive.

As editor, Bolton was at first invited into the discussions. It was discouraging. Some potential buyers were private-equity groups that did not care what they were buying. "It could be providing health care to people," he said. "And if they can find a way to save money, they'll do that and eliminate jobs and remove the soul of anything." News Corp. was also interested—the company owned by Rupert Murdoch. Then an investor wanted to combine Cracked, Funny or Die, and *The Onion* into a "behemoth of comedy." Bolton asked why *The Onion* would want to be part of a behemoth. After that he was no longer invited to the meetings. Still, "for a while, it genuinely seemed like this merger was going to happen," Bolton said. "They even had a dumb name picked out for the merged entity: Punchline." It was a "deep relief" to him when the deal fell through; the investor, he added, was "staggeringly ignorant about *The Onion* and, I'd say, comedy in general." (McAvoy said in his opinion Bolton was one of the most conservative editors *The Onion* had ever had. He and Berkley "shrank what *The Onion* was" compared to Tracy, had "the least outside creative ambitions," and "didn't want to deviate at all from what *The Onion* was at a point in time." Bolton also thought his job was about "protecting" the writers, a "kind of archaic view of things.")

The Onion sold a 40 percent stake to Univision in 2016 under its Fusion Media Group (FMG) division and was merged into the Gizmodo Media Group along with Gizmodo, Deadspin, Jezebel, The Root, and several other "diverse" sister sites. (Univision wanted to appeal to a younger crowd.) McDonagh believed the sale was for between $85–$100 million, the bulk of which went into the pockets of the already extremely wealthy Schafer. Since the few remaining editorial shareholders were from many years ago—Bolton said "there certainly wasn't any opportunity in my era for editorial members to have an ownership stake"—most of the writing staff got nothing.

McAvoy, now tasked with overseeing ad sales at FMG as well as *The Onion*, got a raise. A big one. By 2019, his salary was $500,000 per year—a huge bump that came with the Univision sale. They wanted to bring him in line with other media company compensation. (Other senior *Onion* executives also got big raises.) McAvoy also apparently began experiencing the frustration of not being clued in on Univision management goals and decisions.

Then, out of the blue, an opportunity came to Bolton and Berkley from an unexpected place. Elon Musk, who had apparently been among those with potential interest in buying *The Onion* in 2016, made an offer to the editorial staff. He would fund a comedy enterprise, and if they came over to him, *Onion* writers could do whatever they wanted. By that point, working for Elon Musk (who back then was seen as an "ecoconscious visionary," as Bolton put it) looked appealing compared to working for *The Onion*. Bolton said, "We felt like it was a good way to give people who were really frustrated and wanted to just focus on writing satire a chance to just go and do that in a more pure space. And we did that. And it was really fun for a little bit. And then it really wasn't fun." Berkley also left *The Onion* to pursue the project. It was not an easy decision. But this felt like having the Medicis say, "Here, you can go make your Renaissance frescoes." And it was like, "Wow, can we? Can we just go do that?" McAvoy said Bolton and Berkley took several of the best staff with them.

The multigenre project was called *Thud*. And for a while, they thought they had a writers' room with no businesspeople in it. But when they had a few things ready to go, *Thud*'s benefactor changed his mind. He also started getting investigated by the SEC [Securities and Exchange Commission] and other things. *Thud* soon ended (though the website is still up).

After Trump was elected in 2016, Berkley said, "Not surprisingly, fake news came up a lot." He and other editorial staffers were doing a lot of public talks then, and they would lay out the case that satire and fake news have opposite intentions. The talks included a slide that read, "Fake news exploits truth to gain power, satire employs truth to check the power." Nuance, Berkley said, "isn't really a thing that we do a lot in the world now. But if you really look at the two, they are so not the same."

Despite having to make jokes about Trump filling the staff with "comedic dread," as Nackers put it at the time—it's hard to satirize someone who is basically already a stand-up comedian—*The Onion* did its best, portraying him as a sad, lonely man whose life is missing something important. (They did have some Hillary Clinton headlines ready, like "Desperate Woman Settles for Asshole Nation Without Much Money.") In 2017, they published another intricately detailed book called *The Trump Leaks: The Onion Exposes the Top Secret Memos, Emails, and Doodles That Could Take Down a President*. The book contains much silliness and absurdity, albeit with running themes of madness, torture, self-absorption, and death. It ends with several letters to "Donald" from a malevolent being lurking in "the dark and hidden places of the earth" called The Director who will soon walk forth and, with the help of Donald's people, carry out his long-planned machinations. The volume ends with a Trump executive order to close down *The Onion*, seize all its works, and try all *Onion* employees for treason.

Also in 2017, Mike McAvoy fired Todd Hanson. Hanson said *The Onion* had been paying him about $15,000 a year, enough to maintain the health insurance he needed for his psychiatric care. He also said he'd been promised he'd never be fired. McAvoy said he hadn't been to work in about three years. (Hanson had actually contributed a lengthy section about Sean Spicer to the Trump book.) Others had wanted to fire him, McAvoy said, but he had been the only one willing to do it. "How long can something be financed like that?" McAvoy said. (It was something, McAvoy said, that every legacy company goes through.) It was also unfair to the other staff—and maybe also illegal—to pay someone who wasn't working. He told me a story about a cleaner in the New York office who'd been borrowing money from staff, not paying it back, and not cleaning anymore. But they stayed on payroll because the staff felt bad for them. The cleaner got fired too. "One of the things that's charming about *The Onion* was that there's so much empathy, right?" McAvoy said. "But you have to still operate in a world where bills are paid." The job of the editorial staff wasn't to protect Todd, he said. It was to do what was best for *The Onion*. Hanson told me that looking back, the biggest mistake *The Onion* ever made was moving to New York.

Berkley recalled something Hanson said long ago. There should be a National Satire Foundation, a nonprofit that would allow *The Onion* "to exist as a public utility, essentially, as a satirical check and balance in society, without having to be a brand. Without being this big old piece of fruit that some rich people are going to try to squeeze the life out of for every dollar."

In 2019, *The Onion* (along with the other Gizmodo sites) was sold again, this time to Great Hill Partners—a firm that owned dozens of other entities along with *The Onion*. Univision got "a heck of a lot less" than they paid for it, as McDonagh put it. Great Hill Partners was a private-equity group, "a $4.65 billion fund that invests in exceptional high-growth companies across various sectors" with little interest in what these companies did other than whether they could make Great Hill money when they sold them again. Great Hill packed the Gizmodo sites together and called it G/O Media, which produced "Fearless Journalism, Provoking Comedy, and High-Impact Storytelling." G/O Media then became another of about a hundred companies listed on Great Hill Partners' website, from RetireeFirst to PuppySpot (I wonder what the graphic designers who created all those logos are doing now, and the status of their creative dreams), with *The Onion* reduced to an entry in the G/O Media site list.

Bill Wernecke told me *The Onion* was now doing all the things they said they would never do. McDonagh said of Great Hill Partners, "I know the people running it, and they don't care about *The Onion*." Mike Loew said Chad Nackers told him: "*The Onion* has had a lot of bad owners over the years, but the current one is the worst."

In 2019, a year before his fortieth birthday, McAvoy was unexpectedly fired from his *Onion* CEO position by new G/O Media CEO Jim Spanfeller. McAvoy filed a lawsuit due to the violation of his employment contract, which stated he would receive his $500,000 salary as severance if he was let go. McAvoy told me he learned a ton at *The Onion* and loved his time there. He also said that G/O Media shut down Onion Labs after he left, and *The Onion* went from being a $20 million company to $2 million in a few years.

McAvoy bought Upright Citizens Brigade with a partner and became its CEO in 2022. When I told Hanson about the UCB purchase, for the first time ever in my life I saw him struck dumb.

Chad Nackers became editor when Bolton left for *Thud* and has held the role ever since. He has now been at *The Onion* longer than anybody: twenty-seven years. He is also the only original Madisonian left on staff. Much of his career has been spent educating new staffers in institutional knowledge and how *The Onion* works, which has helped maintain consistency even in the face of the demands from the moneymaking side. He is also the keeper of *The Onion*'s flame. Albini is watching him, and he knows it.

The Onion unionized in 2018, with 90 percent of the staff signing on with Writers Guild of America East. At that time, Caitlin PenzeyMoog, the A.V. Club's deputy managing director, said in *Deadline* that "digital media is a precarious industry," especially without union protection. In January 2024, a strike was narrowly avoided over a push by management to use AI to write *Onion* stories, an "existential threat" to their careers. A press release stated: "The Guild must receive 20-day notice of any AI policy changes and the company must consider the union's input in good faith. . . . Further, stories, articles or graphics created by [generative AI], in part or in whole, shall first be reviewed by an editorial employee and will have distinct signifiers in the byline indicating that the content is GAI [generative AI]-generated."

ClickHole was sold in 2020 to Cards Against Humanity. The A.V. Club was sold in March 2024 to Paste Media.

There is a stark reality in *The Onion*'s recent history. *The Onion* was once the singular go-to place for satiric insight and humor, but—after more than a decade of investor-profit-driven ownership that changed its satire into "content," as well as the ocean of other online comedy now appearing alongside it—as of 2024 it's safe to say this is no longer the case. *The Onion* is still very good—a testament to the solidity of its editorial methods—but I doubt there are many teenagers now who are devoted fans like the ones who became *The Onion*'s first interns, and I suspect much of the readership is the same people who have been reading it for decades. (McDonagh told me that when his daughter wears her *Onion* T-shirt to school, the only people who know what it is are her teachers.)

However, right as I was finishing this book in the spring of 2024, the announcement came that *The Onion* had been sold again. The new owners created a parent company, Global Tetrahedron (named after Todd Hanson's recurring joke in *Our Dumb Century*), owned by Jeff Lawson—former chief of the technology communications company Twilio and a longtime fan—to provide *The Onion* with a solid financial foundation, free it from content-farm hell, and start a new era of creativity. *The Onion*'s new CEO is former NBC journalist Ben Collins, whose news specialty was digital disinformation (and who was also born the year *The Onion* was founded, 1988). Former TikTok and

Tumblr executives completed the team. They say the staff will remain the same, the office will stay in Chicago, and the goal is to fund *The Onion* to do whatever they want. And the creative team will share in the wealth. Could Thurston's 2011 dream actually be coming true?

Collins told me their goal was to allow *The Onion* to grow and tell jokes in new formats, including TV and film. He said they didn't buy *The Onion* to change it but to set the staff free. Collins told me, "Truth doesn't exist anymore. It has been totally murdered and massacred by the worst people in the world." *The Onion*, however, is "impervious to the bullshit in a way that nobody else has been." In August 2024, *The Onion* brought back its print edition using a paid subscription model. It appears that sign-ups surpassed expectations. One of the first public distribution sites was the Democratic National Convention in Chicago. Collins also said in a media article that café and record-store owners wanted racks of *Onions* to place in the store so patrons could take copies home with them. Many delighted reader comments on articles about the renewed print edition revolved around "I am so incredibly sick of having to read everything online."

It could work. The *Stranger* is publishing a print edition again—and Tim Keck told me it makes a lot more money than the digital version. He thinks alt weeklies might make a comeback. Print also has the benefit to the reader of not being able to surveil you or require expensive technology to read, and both selling and acquiring it often means leaving your house and interacting with other actual human beings. Vinyl records are back too—kids are even making and buying cassette tapes again—and I hear that brick-and-mortar bookstores are coming back as well. Chad Nackers told me, "We are very excited, and *The Onion*'s future looks bright."

I'll still reserve a bit of my Gen X cynicism—battling the for-profit corporate media is not easy, especially when you may have unintentionally absorbed their priorities, and it would be foolish to think digital media is leaving its central location in our lives anytime soon. But I agree with Krewson, who said, "It seems to be pretty endemic in the tech sphere that because they think of technology as what leads the human race forward, they seem to think they have found the silver bullet to everything, and they haven't." Being at the mercy of a single zillionaire feels risky too. I also confess that when I first heard there was going to be a sale, I hoped it would be the staff themselves that were taking over. And indeed I learned later there was in fact a group of former *Onion* staff in the running.

Nobody would give me numbers, but the price was probably in the single-digit millions, making *The Onion* in 2024 worth less than Comedy Central was apparently going to pay back in 1999. The rich guy won again. He'd better do a good job. Still, with a disinformation journalist as CEO, maybe this will be a good thing for *The Onion*—as long as Global Tetrahedron remembers where *The Onion* came from. And whose interests it serves.

The Onion's best satire has always been based in both emotional honesty and clearly stated, well-researched facts—in other words, the truth. Its writing staff has now given us decades of brilliant, compassionate, blunt, and hilarious critical thinking about news, the media, and human nature—and a lot of fun and silliness too. Even after almost forty years, they have not given up the fight—for you, for me, or for themselves. That is something worth protecting.

AFTERWORD

The idea for this book came to me in 2018 on an especially absurd news day during the first Trump administration. (I don't even remember which one it was.) What, I wondered, did the old *Onion* people think about all this? Not just the real-life insanity, but also the new forms of fake news that were now being discussed constantly.

After thirty years of *Onion* news satire—good fake news—we now had bad fake news, manufactured deliberately as propaganda. And as social media "news" feeds narrowed to the level of the individual, as it became evident just how siloed online algorithms had made our points of view, we also now had fake news as in "news you do not agree with." "Help us, *Onion* writers," I thought, not entirely in jest, and started researching and interviewing people.

In the back of my mind, all the time, were climate change and right-wing nationalism. I didn't see a direct path between *The Onion* and addressing these things. But I kept thinking about it. How were we going to solve these huge communal problems when everyone was so fragmented and distrustful and scared? Maybe there was something on a human scale, something simple and basic, that *The Onion* could offer. Something relational rather than doctrinaire.

Todd Hanson, being an old friend, was one of my first guinea pigs. It wasn't a happy conversation. After Trump got elected in 2016, he said, he despaired. "I felt like a priest who wonders if he still believes in God," he said. "I went through a crisis of faith in satire. Because for fifteen months, all the best satirists in the country were firing away with both barrels at the man, and doing some of the most brilliant work of their careers, and it had no effect on protecting the country from him."

Hanson said the idea of fake news at *The Onion* once felt like culture jamming. But now:

When I think of fake news, I think of it as the thing that got fucking Trump elected. And that it is destroying truth. So it kind of took the wind out of my empirical sails. People can't tell the difference between a fact and a falsehood anyway, so it's not really culture jamming to fool them with satire.

I mean, I have "Satire" tattooed on my arm, Christine. It's like a religion to me. And I can't exactly turn my back on it and go "It's all bullshit" now. You need a straight line to juxtapose with your punch line. But there are no straight lines anymore, because no one can agree on the basic fundamental definition of reality.

The term "culture jamming" comes from the 1980s–1990s; the name was reportedly coined by the band Negativland in 1984, though the idea goes back further than that. It's a creative way to subvert corporate media methods, tropes, and imagery, often by repurposing them, to fight the for-profit takeover of the public and personal spheres that was really ramping up then. And that today, alas, seems to be nearly complete.

Carol Kolb told me she thought *The Onion* was funnier in the old days, "because we weren't saturated with twenty-two thousand different types of unreal stuff coming at us." Joe Garden said "You Are Dumb" meant "You will believe anything. We are the source of knowledge, and you are the sponges that will receive our knowledge." It was all part of the old character of *The Onion*. But that didn't feel good anymore. Ben Karlin said, "It's really funny to think about how kind of naive and, in some ways, optimistic we were that we could do this thing that so squarely spun off something as solid and immutable as the objective truth of journalism. And now, that's gone. I don't know how people try to do what I used to do."

"Let me tell you the dumbest thing I have ever thought in my entire life," Stephen Thompson said. "I believed that *The Onion's* great gift to society was teaching people not to believe everything they read. Can you imagine a more wrongheaded way to think about the way the internet would shape society than to think it's really great if people don't believe everything they read?"

Some, however, might argue that saying satire failed because it didn't change anything is misunderstanding the purpose of satire, which is to make us laugh, and then think about what we just laughed at. Not to change election results. Satire is *comedy*—an art form—with a point. It's expressing something about a specific time and place. *The Onion* probably affected politics about as much as Bob Dylan did. (I'm not saying Dylan didn't affect politics, by the way.) Still, satire *does* still matter, as scholar James Caron told me, "in that it is one important way to push back. I think we need it more than ever, given the crisis of confidence we are in. It's not that we all need to first agree on how to define 'reality.'" One of the most important functions of satire is as a morale booster; it says you are not the only one who thinks what's happening is ridiculous.

Still, it did cross my mind, uncomfortably, to wonder if *The Onion* had somehow actually accidentally contributed to our fake-news problem. When I first spoke to her back in 2019, scholar Amber Day said that because satirical news sources set a precedent to see fake news as a joke, they may have helped the bad stuff slide under the radar at first, especially leading up to the 2016 election:

> But I personally would not draw a direct line from one to the other. I think I would draw it backwards, in that it's now making it much harder for satirists to do what they do. The satiric stuff is meant to *reveal*. To show us something about our reality that we might not have noticed. And to point to hypocrisy and inconsistencies, to pull back the curtain. At heart, it is a media literacy project.

> Whereas the current fake news that we're talking about is so clearly the opposite. Its intent is entirely to obfuscate and throw smoke bombs up into the conversation so that nobody knows what's going on and just sow confusion and chaos.

Indeed, the first time I saw Fox News, around 2008 in the Amtrak lounge at New York's Penn Station, I thought it was a parody—and I blame this entirely on having read *The Onion* for twenty years. Still, when I saw Glenn Beck's show, or first heard Alex Jones, it seemed obvious these guys were just right-wing performance artists. The only weird thing was hearing paranoid far-right ranting instead of excoriations of sexism and racism and capitalism. (See "Performance Artist Shocks U.S. Out of Apathetic Stupor," September 20, 2000.)

Carol Kolb told me, "It's like professional wrestling or something. You're like, 'How can people think that's real?' And then you realize that they don't, exactly. They kind of just like it. They're rooting for those characters." She said she definitely didn't think *The Onion* was part of the problem, "but on the other hand, it's not something that is as impressive in this day and age. It's not impressive to confuse people anymore, because everything is confusing."

It's complicated. The ability for anyone to go online and state their version of the truth gave us QAnon and Pizzagate. But this ability also drew attention to police violence against unarmed Black people and sexual harassment in the media and entertainment industries. The consensus reality that many of us thought we were living in was largely a product of our position in the world. Many people's experiences were left out of that consensus. Still, in the digital era, citizen journalists are raising awareness of important real issues at the same time conspiracy theorists, white supremacists, and all kinds of charlatans and frauds are using the same technologies to do their thing.

As I kept reading and talking to people, I also learned the uncomfortable fact that the idea of comedy and satire "speaking truth to power" had gone conservative (though I do find it weird that liberals are supposed to be "the power"; somebody is not doing their research). See the *Babylon Bee*, the right-wing Christian version of *The Onion*, which I confess I laughed at a couple of times a few years ago. *The Onion* did used to make jokes about liberals, after all. The majority of it, though, is not my cup of tea, and they seemed to have swerved pretty hard into the "liberals are trying to crush free speech" thing.

I was also one of those people who thought "conservatives don't do comedy," or at least not very well. Then I read *That's Not Funny: How the Right Makes Comedy Work for Them* by Matt Sienkiewicz and Nick Marx, who write it's a big mistake to think comedy has a liberal bias. One of the most popular late-night comedy talk shows now is *Gutfeld!* on Fox News. According to *Forbes*, in the first quarter of 2024 *Gutfeld!*—which operates in the *Daily Show* mode—was the highest-rated late-night comedy talk show on TV, with 2.5 million viewers. And *Gutfeld!* is part of an ecosystem of right-wing comedians that now exists strategically, "supported by our increasingly bubbled and siloed media industry structure." The Right also now styles itself as the only place where people have freedom to play and speak their minds anymore.

Norm Stockwell, publisher of the *Progressive*, told me: "There's no question that the Right has a much better understanding of the role of media" than the Left. The Right has used media in a deliberate way to achieve their goals, funded by wealthy conservative foundations and guided by conservative think tanks, for decades now. The Left, however, Stockwell said, "thinks of media not as *part* of the social movement, but as something that *covers* the social movements," and in comparison gets much less support. The Right also seems willing to tolerate a wide range of viewpoints (all the way to neo-Nazism, in some cases) and works from an evangelical philosophy that's trying to bring people *into* the fold—while the Left too often focuses on finding reasons to cast people out. As Jesse David Fox put it in *The Comedy Book*: "Every time we see the left or any group trying to move forward politically in a radical way, when they're humorless, they fail."

The old *Onion* staff weren't the only ones rethinking their past positions. Back in the 2000s, a whole crew of scholars made their careers studying *The Daily Show* and *The Colbert Report*, investigating whether TV news satire was saving democracy by teaching critical thinking about the relationship between media and politics. Recently, though, the group has been taking another look at their earlier work, and I attended a panel discussion featuring many of them at a 2023 conference. Geoffrey Baym led the discussion and gave an overview of the changes in media and politics that news satire was commenting on in the 2000s. Those changes have since only accelerated, which has profoundly complicated the study and practice of satire, "along, I think, with everything else. . . . Were we wrong? Or has the world changed so much that maybe what we used to think doesn't apply?" In today's state of deep fragmentation, it was no longer clear what the political function of satire might be. These days, he said, it's more about "the performance of outrage," with very little of what Jon Stewart once called "the better conversation" that engaged across difference in pursuit of the common good.

In a separate interview, scholar Sophia McClennen said comedy does still have the power to disarm what feels scary or threatening. McClennen gave the example of a white supremacist march. Protesters using typical tactics of waving signs and becoming angry can just spike the tension and give a weird legitimacy to the white supremacists. A bunch of people dressed as clowns dancing around the same marchers has a very different effect—and exposes who the real clowns are. Satire helps people think critically and have fun at the same time.

Tim Fontaine, a screenwriter, journalist, and the founder and editor of *Walking Eagle News*, the Canadian online satirical news source centering

Indigenous perspectives, told me, "In many ways, media is a pack animal. So if one person says something, they often mimic that same language." (The ease with which digital media activates our fight-or-flight response and the "performance of outrage" make this even worse.) Using that same language *against* the system, however, was what Fontaine loved about *The Onion*.

He also said journalists sometimes don't state the obvious because they're worried about being called biased. "And so we don't often just say what the truth is." As Karlin put it in a 2004 *New York Times* article, "There's some weird handcuffs on the mainstream news so that they feel that no matter what, they have to present both sides of the argument, even if one side of an argument is wrong." Comedy, though, is under no obligation to do so.

Matt Cook told me that satire should make *everybody* a little uncomfortable. "If you're really good at satire, you're going to be able to point out things that even the most progressive intelligentsia didn't realize was fucked up." Day said satire can also "push issues that were super niche into a sort of more mainstream venue and bring it to people's attention. It can also change the frames and the vocabulary that we're using to talk about something, which I think is actually really substantive."

But, she said, "that becomes really problematic if there isn't a central conversation happening. That's the scary part."

Dan Kaufman, author of *The Fall of Wisconsin*, said, "We're at this stage where there's a fork in the road, like a Robert Frost kind of moment but for humanity, so I think it's still unclear which path we're taking." It's funny, though, he said. "In some ways my book is very dark, but in some ways it's very hopeful, because it really is about these people in Wisconsin who refuse to accept defeat—despite defeat after defeat—and in them, I feel like they want to reclaim the state's democratic ideals of the past. I think the heart of it is really a testament to their perseverance. Their doggedness."

"The thing that I kind of love most about *The Onion*," Karlin said, "is that without this word ever being stated in the entire time that I was there, there's a ton of integrity. It was filled with people who feel like we should have rules in society that make sense, that are fair, that are compassionate." And when people don't play by those rules, "shit starts breaking down, and we need to work towards a world where we're all playing by those rules that still respects people's freedom and everything like that. That's ultimately what *The Onion* is about."

When they were making fun of greedy corporations that try to circumvent the rules, or politicians who lie, "it's ultimately like this little kid saying, 'Why are you doing that? That's not fair.' There's something beautiful about that."

I hear these days, in fact, that sincerity is the new punk rock. And as I was finishing this book, still thinking about the reasons I started it, a fundamental improv concept came into my mind: "Yes, and." That is, a *method*, rather than an ideology, where the goal is to cooperate, not to dominate—and which doesn't work very well unless you carry it out sincerely. A *structure*.

"Yes, and" is when you agree to go with the flow of what your improv partners say or do during a scene and build on it. Or, if you don't think it's great, artfully transform its direction, ideally without scapegoating or humiliating. (Is this concept now being used in corporate training scenarios by visiting improv instructors making their rent for the month? No doubt. Doesn't mean it doesn't have more socially productive uses.) We could also take a lesson from the *Onion* writers' room and understand that most of anybody's ideas might not be perfect, including our own. Bring them on anyway, and we'll go through them, choose, and polish our choices together. *The Onion* also values research, fact-checking, and editing.

Combine all this, and you have something interesting. A method that helps us make something together that is more than any of us might be as individuals, in a way that also—ideally—lets everyone feel like their voice is heard and valued and is carried out in a space where the health and well-being of the people and the environment are more important than a rich guy making even more money.

I still don't know what the answers are to my questions. I do think, however, that this sounds a lot like democracy. The biggest culture jam of them all. That may be *The Onion*'s most important message.

BIBLIOGRAPHY

Abramson, Jill. *Merchants of Truth: The Business of News and the Fight for Facts.* New York: Simon & Schuster, 2019.

Alesia, Tom. "Thousands Get *Onion* Online." *Wisconsin State Journal,* November 27, 1998.

Amarasingam, Amarnath. *The Stewart/Colbert Effect: Essays on the Real Impact of Fake News.* Jefferson, NC: McFarland, 2011.

Ananny, Mike. *Networked Press Freedom: Creating Infrastructures for a Public Right to Hear.* Cambridge, MA: MIT Press, 2018.

Andersen, Kurt. *Fantasyland: How America Went Haywire, a 500-Year History.* New York: Random House, 2017.

Anderson, C. W., Leonard Downie Jr., and Michael Schudson. *The News Media: What Everyone Needs to Know.* Oxford: Oxford University Press, 2016.

Anderson, Laurie. "From the Air." *Big Science* (1982).

Anderson, Stacy. "*The Onion* Finds a New Slice." *Capital Times,* November 5, 1994.

Arnold, Amanda. "Why Literature and Pop Culture Still Can't Get the Midwest Right." *Literary Hub,* March 27, 2017.

Associated Press. *The Associated Press Stylebook and Libel Manual.* Reading, MA: Addison-Wesley, 1987.

———. "Staff of the Satire Website *The Onion* Has Unionized." Associated Press, March 29, 2018.

———. "UW Madison Underground Paper Pokes Fun at Just About Everyone." *Racine (WI) Journal Times,* Sunday October 24, 1993.

———. "Wisconsin Recount Confirms Biden's Win over Trump." PBS.org, November 29, 2020.

Bagdikian, Ben. *The New Media Monopoly: A Completely Revised and Updated Edition with Seven New Chapters.* 20th ed. Boston: Beacon Press, 2004.

Bakalar, Nicholas. *American Satire: An Anthology of Writings from Colonial Times to the Present.* New York: Meridian, 1997.

Barrodale, Amie. "Letter from New York, 2005." *Paris Review,* January 26, 2015.

Baughman, James L., Jennifer Ratner-Rosenhagen, and James P. Danky. *Protest on the Page: Essays on Print and the Culture of Dissent Since 1865.* Madison: University of Wisconsin Press, 2015.

Baym, Geoffrey. *From Cronkite to Colbert: The Evolution of Broadcast News.* Boulder, CO: Paradigm, 2010.

Baym, Geoffrey, and Jeffrey P. Jones. *News Parody and Political Satire Across the Globe*. London and New York: Routledge, 2013.

Benton, Joshua. "Facebook's Message to Media: 'We Are Not Interested in Talking About Your Traffic . . . That Is the Old World and There Is No Going Back.'" NiemanLab, August 13, 2018.

Bethea, Charles. "*The Onion* Struggles to Lampoon Trump." *New Yorker*, March 13, 2017.

———. "What Happens When the News Is Gone?" *New Yorker*, January 27, 2020.

Bing, Jonathan. "Miramax, *Onion* Ink First-Look Deal." *Variety*, February 15, 2001.

Boczkowski, Pablo J., and C. W. Anderson, eds. *Remaking the News: Essays on the Future of Journalism Scholarship in the Digital Age*. Cambridge, MA: MIT Press, 2017.

Boczkowski, Pablo J., and Zizi Papacharissi, eds. *Trump and the Media*. Cambridge, MA: MIT Press, 2018.

Bradley, Jane, and Katie J. M. Baker, "Unlimited Power: A *BuzzFeed News* Investigation." BuzzFeed.com, May 17, 2019.

Bridle, James. *New Dark Age: Technology and the End of the Future*. London: Verso, 2018.

Bucknell, Claire, and Colin Burrow. "On Satire." *London Review of Books Close Readings*, 2024. www.lrb.co.uk/podcasts-and-videos/podcasts/close-readings/on-satire-what-is-satire.

Callison, Candis, and Mary Lynn Young. *Reckoning: Journalism's Limits and Possibilities*. New York: Oxford University Press, 2020.

Campbell, W. Joseph. *1995: The Year the Future Began*. Oakland: University of California Press, 2015.

Carey, James W. *Communication as Culture*. Rev. ed. New York: Routledge, 2008.

———, ed. *Media, Myths, and Narratives: Television and the Press*. Thousand Oaks, CA: Sage, 1988.

Caron, James E. *Satire as the Comic Public Sphere: Postmodern "Truthiness" and Civic Engagement*. University Park: Pennsylvania State University Press, 2021.

Channick, Robert. "After 10 Years in Chicago, *The Onion* Is Navigating Fraught Times with Its Unique Sense of Humor." *Chicago Tribune*, June 3, 2022.

———. "No Tears for *Onion*'s Departure from Print." *Chicago Tribune*, April 13, 2014.

———. "Nothing Fake About *The Onion*'s Move." *Chicago Tribune*, March 31, 2012.

Cole, Bill. "A Little Light Data." *Baffler*, December 1994.

Colton, Michael. "Paper Provides Jokes, Pain: *The Onion* Grows on Nation. Read It and Weep." *Washington Post*, October 25, 1998.

Courtwright, David. *The Age of Addiction: How Bad Habits Became Big Business*. Cambridge, MA: Belknap Press, 2019.

Cramer, Katherine J. *The Politics of Resentment: Rural Consciousness in Wisconsin and the Rise of Scott Walker*. Chicago: University of Chicago Press, 2016.

Cramer Brownell, Kathyrn. *24/7 Politics: Cable Television & the Fragmenting of America from Watergate to Fox News*. Princeton, NJ: Princeton University Press, 2023.

Crisman, Julie. "All the News That Fits." *Wisconsin Badger* 108 (1994).

Cronon, William. *Nature's Metropolis: Chicago and the Great West*. New York: W. W. Norton, 1992.

Cryns, Jim, and Kathy Buenger. "Area Man Sells & Tells." *Greater Milwaukee Today*, January 19, 2004.

D'Allessandro, Anthony. "UCB Theater to Reopen; Comedy Brand Acquired by Mosaic Founder Jimmy Miller & Former *Onion* CEO-Owner Mike McAvoy." *Deadline*, March 25, 2022.

daSilva, James. *The Onion: 20 Years Later*. https://onion20.substack.com/.

Davis, D. L. "9 Key Fact-Checks About the Presidential Election in Wisconsin." *Politifact*, January 4, 2021.

Day, Amber. *Satire and Dissent: Interventions in Contemporary Political Debate*. Bloomington: Indiana University Press, 2011.

DePaul College of Communication. "Richard Hamann." https://communication.depaul .edu/faculty-and-staff/faculty/Pages/Adjunct%20Inactive/hamann.aspx.

de Waal, Frans. "The 'alpha male' myth, debunked." Big Think video, June 21, 2023.

Dickey, Colin. *The Unidentified: Mythical Monsters, Alien Encounters, and Our Obsession with the Unexplained*. New York: Viking, 2020.

Digiday. "'A Builder and a Fixer': New Gizmodo Boss Jim Spanfeller Is an Old School Digital Media Vet." *Digiday*, April 10, 2019.

———. "'Comedians Are the New Public Intellectuals': Why Univision Took a Bite of *The Onion*." *Digiday*, January 16, 2016.

———. "Once a Newspaper, *The Onion* Is Growing Its Digital Ambitions." *Digiday*, April 10, 2015.

———. "*The Onion*, Urbandaddy Lead *Digiday* Publishing Award Finalists." *Digiday*, March 26, 2014.

Dikkers, Scott. "The Funny Story Behind Funny Stories." Presentation, Wisconsin Union Directorate Distinguished Lecture Series, Memorial Union, Madison, WI, October 11, 2021.

———. *How to Write Funny: Your Serious, Step-by-Step Blueprint for Creating Incredibly, Irresistibly, Successfully Hilarious Writing*. Self-published, 2015.

———. "Making a TV Show." *No Dikkering Around*, July 31, 2023.

———. *Outrageous Marketing: The Story of "The Onion" and How to Build a Powerful Brand with No Marketing Budget*. Self-published, 2018.

———. "Who Are These Guys? They're Everywhere." *No Dikkering Around*, December 20, 2023.

Dionne, Alexandria. "*The Onion* Moves to the Internet: The History of the Madison, WI, Weekly Newspaper." *Entertainment Weekly*, January 8, 1999.

Dush, Lisa. "When Writing Becomes Content." *College Composition and Communication* 67, no. 2 (2015): 173–196.

Edwards, Danny. "Chicago: Rick Hamann; The Labs' Comedic Layers." *Shots*, October 8, 2014.

Egendorf, Laura K., ed. *Satire*. San Diego: Greenhaven Press, 2002.

Elliott, Robert C. *The Power of Satire: Magic, Ritual, Art*. Princeton, NJ: Princeton University Press, 1960.

EW Staff. "The It List: Digital." *Entertainment Weekly*, June 26, 1998.

Foer, Franklin. *World Without Mind: The Existential Threat of Big Tech*. New York: Penguin Press, 2017.

Fox, Jesse David. *Comedy Book: How Comedy Conquered Culture—and the Magic That Makes It Work*. New York: Farrar, Strauss & Giroux, 2023.

Glass, Ira. "Tough Room." *This American Life*, February 8, 2008.

Goldberg, Chad Alan, ed. *Education for Democracy: Renewing the Wisconsin Idea*. Madison: University of Wisconsin Press, 2020.

Gordon, Jeremy. "Albini: 'If the Dumbest Person Is on Your Side, You're on the Wrong Side.'" *Guardian*, August 15, 2023.

Gournelos, Ted, and Viveca Greene, eds. *A Decade of Dark Humor: How Comedy, Irony, and Satire Shaped Post-9/11 America*. Jackson: University Press of Mississippi, 2011.

Gray, Jonathan, Jeffrey P. Jones, and Ethan Thompson, eds. *Satire TV: Politics and Comedy in the Post-network Era*. New York: New York University Press, 2009.

Greenfield, Jeff. "State of *The Onion*." Webcast of panel discussion with *Onion* editorial staff, Toyota Comedy Festival, June 6, 2000. https://web.archive.org/web/20000815075850 /http://www.comcentral.com/festivals/.

Griffin, Dustin. *Satire: A Critical Reintroduction*. Lexington: University Press of Kentucky, 1994.

Guardian. "@ Future of Journalism: *The Onion* News Network and the High Art of Satire." *PDA, the Digital Content Blog*, September 5, 2008.

Hamm, Theodore. *The New Blue Media: How Michael Moore, MoveOn.org, Jon Stewart and Company Are Transforming Progressive Politics*. New York: New Press, 2008.

Hanson, Todd. "Sloth." *The Moth*, May 3, 2006.

———. "The Triumph of Apathy." *The Moth*, December 3, 2006.

Harrison, Colin. *American Culture in the 1990s*. Edinburgh University Press, 2010.

Harvey, David. *A Brief History of Neoliberalism*. Oxford: Oxford University Press, 2005.

Heller, Chris. "*The Onion* Is Not a Joke: How a Fake Newspaper Is Turning into a Real Media Empire." *Atlantic*, May 1, 2015.

Hemmer, Nicole. *Messengers of the Right: Conservative Media and the Transformation of American Politics*. Philadelphia: University of Pennsylvania Press, 2016.

Hendershot, Heather. *When the News Broke: Chicago 1968 and the Polarizing of America*. Chicago: University of Chicago Press, 2022.

Herman, Edward S., and Noam Chomsky. *Manufacturing Consent: The Political Economy of the Mass Media*. 1988. Reprint, New York: Pantheon Books, 2002.

Hersey, Curt. *A History of Television News Parody in America: Nothing but the Truthiness*. Lanham, MD: Lexington Books, 2022.

Hodgart, Matthew. *Satire*. New York: World University Library, McGraw-Hill, 1969.

Hoekstra, Dave. *Beacons in the Darkness: Hope and Transformation Among America's Community Newspapers*. Chicago: Midway Books, 2022.

Hoganson, Kristin L. *The Heartland: An American History*. New York: Penguin Press, 2019.

Holiday, Ryan. *Trust Me, I'm Lying: Confessions of a Media Manipulator*. New York: Portfolio/Penguin, 2012.

Holland, Edward C. "*The Onion* and the Geopolitics of Satire." *Popular Communication* 16, no. 5 (2017): 1–14.

Holm, Nicholas. "The Political (Un)Consciousness of Contemporary American Satire." *Journal of American Studies* 52, no. 3 (2018): 642–651.

Hudson, John. "*The Onion*'s Bumpy Ride to Chicago." *Atlantic*, March 22, 2012.

Hyde, Lewis. *Trickster Makes This World: Mischief, Myth, and Art*. New York: Farrar, Straus & Giroux, 1998.

"In Focus: Right-Wing Media." *Cinema Journal* 51, no. 4 (2012).

Jeffries, Norman. "The McSweeney's Store." *Free Williamsburg* 29 (August 2002).

Joyella, Mark. "King of Late Night Greg Gutfeld Signs New Multi-year Deal with Fox News." *Forbes*, April 24, 2024.

Kalk, Samara. "Book Deal Has *Onion* Laughing Way to Bank." *Capital Times*, September 10, 1998.

Karp, Josh. *A Futile and Stupid Gesture: How Doug Kenney and "National Lampoon" Changed Comedy Forever*. Chicago: Chicago Review Press, 2006.

Kaufman, Dan. *The Fall of Wisconsin: The Conservative Conquest of a Progressive Bastion and the Future of American Politics*. New York: W. W. Norton, 2018.

Keck, Tim. "Dead Guy Found: Early Days of The Onion." Presentation at Seattle Interactive Conference, November 7, 2013.

Keighley, Jeff. "*The Onion*: Funny Site Is No Joke. A Diversified Media Company Built on Sardonic, Topical Humor." CNN.com. August 29, 2003.

Kendrick, Lyle. "How Will an Online-Only *Onion* Make Money?" *American Journalism Review* (December 9, 2013).

Kenzior, Sarah. *The View from Flyover Country: Dispatches from the Forgotten America*. New York: Flatiron Books, 2018.

Klein, Naomi. *Doppelganger: A Trip into the Mirror World*. New York: Farrar, Straus & Giroux, 2023.

———. *No Logo*. 10th anniversary ed. New York: Picador, 2010.

Klosterman, Chuck. *The Nineties: A Book*. New York: Penguin, 2022.

Kovarik, Bill. *Revolutions in Communication: Media History from Gutenberg to the Digital Age*. 2nd ed. London: Bloomsbury Academic, 2018.

Krassner, Paul, ed. *Best of the "Realist": The 60s' Most Outrageously Irreverent Magazine*. Philadelphia: Running Press, 1984.

Krewson, John, and Joe Garden. "*The Onion*'s Creative Power to Persuade." Presentation at the Cambridge Forum, WGBH, August 15, 2012.

Kruse, Kevin M., and Julian E. Zelizer. *Fault Lines: A History of the United States Since 1974*. New York: W. W. Norton, 2019.

Kuhn, Thomas S. *The Structure of Scientific Revolutions*. 3rd ed. Chicago: University of Chicago Press, 1996.

Lancetta, Joel. "*Onion* Editors: We Are Anti-stupid, You Are Dumb." *Chicago Maroon*, October 24, 2004.

Lauk, Jon K. *The Lost Region: Toward a Revival of Midwestern History*. Iowa City: University of Iowa Press, 2013.

Lauk, Jon K., Gleaves Whitney, and Joseph Hogan, eds. *Finding a New Midwestern History*. Lincoln: University of Nebraska Press, 2018.

Lazeroff, Leon. "Smarty-Pants Newspaper Seeks World Domination. Satirical Weekly Plants Self in Twin Cities; Growth Plan Includes 6 Additional Editions." *Chicago Tribune*, August 6, 2004.

Lyall, Sarah. "How to Satirize This Election? Even *The Onion* Is Having Trouble." *New York Times*, November 4, 2016.

Madison, Lucy. "Republican Congressman Falls Victim to Old *Onion* Article." CBSNews.com, February 5, 2012. www.cbsnews.com/news/republican-congressman -falls-victim-to-old-onion-article/.

Marantz, Andrew. *Anti-social: Online Extremists, Techno-utopians, and the Hijacking of the American Conversation*. New York: Viking, 2019.

Marek, Lynne. "Area Men Agree Print Is Dead." *Crain's Chicago Business*, November 11, 2013.

Maron, Marc. Interview with Todd Hanson. *WTF with Marc Maron*, July 7, 2011. www.wtfpod.com/podcast/tag/Todd+Hanson.

Marx, Nick, and Matt Sienkiewicz. *That's Not Funny: How the Right Makes Comedy Work for Them*. Oakland, CA: University of California Press, 2022.

McChesney, Robert W. *Rich Media, Poor Democracy: Communication Politics in Dubious Times*. New York: New Press, 1999.

McChesney, Robert W., and Victor Pickard, eds. *Will the Last Reporter Please Turn Out the Lights: The Collapse of Journalism and What Can Be Done to Fix It*. New York: New Press, 2011.

McClennen, Sophia A. *America According to Colbert: Satire as Public Pedagogy*. New York: Palgrave Macmillan, 2011.

McClennen, Sophia A., and Remy M. Maisel. *Is Satire Saving Our Nation? Mockery and American Politics*. New York: Palgrave Macmillan, 2014.

McDermott, Claire. "*The Onion*'s Custom Content Agency Makes Brands Seriously Funny." *Content Marketing Institute* (April 19, 2015).

McGovern, Kyle. "Read Steve Albini's Four-Page Proposal to Produce Nirvana's *In Utero*." *Spin*, September 26, 2013.

McMillian, John. *Smoking Typewriters: The Sixties Underground Press and the Rise of Alternative Media in America*. New York: Oxford University Press, 2011.

Meyerowitz, Rick. *Drunk Stoned Brilliant Dead: The Writers and Artists Who Made the National Lampoon Insanely Great*. New York: Abrams, 2010.

Michael McAvoy vs. GO Media Inc., Onion Inc., James Spanfeller. Filed 05/30/2024. Case no. 2024L005858.

Michael McAvoy vs. Onion, Inc., James Spanfeller, G/O Media Inc. Filed 11/01/2019. Case no. 2019L012149.

Miller, James Andrew, and Tom Shales. *Live from New York: The Complete, Uncensored History of "Saturday Night Live."* Rev. ed. New York: Little, Brown, 2014.

Miner, David. "How David Letterman Drove Fringe Comedy Mainstream." *Hollywood Reporter*, May 20, 2015.

Moore, Powell A. "The Newspaper Press of the Calumet Region, 1836–1933." *Indiana Magazine of History* 52, no. 2 (1956): 120–122.

Mumford, Lewis. *Technics and Civilization*. 1934. Reprint, New York: Harcourt, Brace & World, 1963.

Munger Kahn, Virginia. "Investing With: David K. Schafer; Strong Schafer Value." *New York Times*, October 12, 1997.

Neff, Glenda Tenant. *Writer's Market 1990*. Cincinnati: Writer's Digest Books, 1989.

Nesteroff, Kliph. *The Comedians: Drunks, Thieves, Scoundrels, and the History of American Comedy*. New York: Grove Press, 2016.

"New *Onion* Fake News: Actually Fake, Not So Funny." *New York Magazine* Intelligencer, March 27, 2007.

Nichols, John. *Uprising: How Wisconsin Renewed the Politics of Protest, from Madison to Wall Street*. New York: Nation Books, 2014.

Nichols, John, and Robert W. McChesney. *Tragedy & Farce: How the American Media Sell Wars, Spin Elections, and Destroy Democracy*. New York: New Press, 2005.

Olszanski, Mike. "*Times'* Keck Forced Out by Inland." *Local 1010 Steelworker*, February 1979.

The Onion. *Dispatches from the Tenth Circle: The Best of "The Onion."* New York: Three Rivers Press, 2001.

———. *"The Onion" Ad Nauseam/Complete News Archives*. Vols. 13–17. New York: Three Rivers Press, 2002–2006.

———. *"The Onion" Book of Known Knowledge*. New York: Little, Brown, 2012.

———. *"The Onion" Magazine: The Iconic Covers That Transformed an Undeserving World*. New York: Little, Brown, 2014.

———. *"The Onion" Presents: Christmas Exposed*. Philadelphia: Quirk Books, 2011.

———. *"The Onion" Presents: Love, Sex, and Other Natural Disasters*. Philadelphia: Quirk Books, 2011.

———. *"The Onion"'s Finest News Reporting*. Vol. 1. New York: Three Rivers Press, 2000.

———. *"Onion" Sports: The Ecstasy of Defeat*. With a foreword by Anabolic Steroids. New York: Hyperion, 2011.

———. *Our Dumb Century*. New York: Three Rivers Press, 1999.

———. *Our Dumb World*. New York: Little, Brown, 2007.

———. *Our Front Pages*. New York: Scribner, 2009.

———. *The Trump Leaks: "The Onion" Exposes the Top Secret Memos, Emails, and Doodles That Could Take Down a President*. New York: Harper Design, 2017.

The Onion A.V. Club. *The Tenacity of the Cockroach: Conversations with Entertainment's Most Enduring Outsiders*. New York: Three Rivers Press, 2002.

"*The Onion* Political Humor." C-SPAN, October 22, 2003.

Overholser, Geneva. "How to Best Serve Communities: Reflections on Civic Journalism." *Democracy Fund*, November 2016.

Paley Center for Media. "Behind the Scenes at the Onion News Network on IFC." Paley Center for Media video, November 11, 2011.

———. "Media as Entertainment: Upright Citizens Brigade." Paley Center for Media video, November 8, 2007.

———. "*The Onion*: Celebrating 1,000 Issues of Prize-Worthy Journalism." Paley Center for Media video, June 21, 2011.

———. "*The Onion*: An Evening of Polite Mockery with America's Finest News Source." Paley Center for Media video, October 17, 2023.

Patel, Nilay. "How *The Onion* Is Saving Itself from the Digital Media Death Spiral." *Verge*, August 22, 2024.

Patel, Sahil. "Parody Site ClickHole Isn't Aping BuzzFeed's Distributed Strategy." *Digiday*, January 26, 2016.

Peter Haise vs. Onion Inc. et al. Filed 01/08/2014. Case no. 2014CV000258.

Pew Research Center for People and the Press. *Perceptions of Partisan Bias Seen as Growing—Especially by Democrats: Cable and Internet Loom Large in Fragmented Political Universe.* Washington, DC: Pew Research Center for People and the Press, 2004.

"Political Humor and 2016 Campaign." *Washington Journal*, September 26, 2016.

Producers for Bob. *Bob's Media Ecology* [CD]. Time Again Productions, 1992.

Provenza, Paul, and Dan Dion. *¡Satiristas! Comedians, Contrarians, Raconteurs, and Vulgarians.* New York: HarperCollins, 2010.

Reilly, Ian. "From Critique to Mobilization: The Yes Men and the Utopian Politics of Satirical Fake News." *International Journal of Communication* 7 (2013): 1243–1264.

———. "Informed Comedy: Do Mock News Shows Make for a More Informed Public? Yes: New(s) Parodies, New(s) Alternatives." In *Communication in Question: Competing Perspectives on Controversial Issues in Communication Studies*, edited by Joshua Greenberg and Charlene Elliott, 281–288. Toronto: Nelson College Indigenous, 2012.

———. "Satirical Fake News and/as American Political Discourse." *Journal of American Culture* 35, no. 3 (2012): 258–275.

Rich, Frank. *The Greatest Story Ever Sold: The Decline and Fall of Truth in Bush's America.* New York: Penguin, 2006.

Romenesko, Jim. "Philly Editor Thought *Onion*'s 9/11 Issue Was Pulitzer-Worthy." Poynter, March 22, 2004.

Sacks, Mike. *And Here's the Kicker: Conversations with 21 Top Humor Writers on Their Craft.* Cincinnati: Writer's Digest Books, 2009.

———. *Poking a Dead Frog: Conversations with Today's Top Comedy Writers.* New York: Penguin, 2014.

Sanders, Sam. "Inside *The Onion*." *It's Been a Minute*, August 22, 2017. www.npr.org/2017/08/22/545049924/inside-the-onion.

Sangal, Aditit. "*The Onion*'s Mike McAvoy: 'There's No Money in News Feed Video.'" *Digiday*, August 23, 2017.

"Satire Today." Special issue, *Studies in American Humor* 5, no. 1 (2019).

Schillinger, Liesl. "Award-Winning Local Journalists Reflect Own Self-Hatred Back on Nightmarish World." *Wired*, March 1, 1999.

Schudson, Michael. *The Sociology of News.* 2nd ed. New York: W. W. Norton, 2011.

Scown, Nick Fituri, and Julie Seabaugh. *Too Soon: Comedy After 9/11* [film]. 2021. https://toosoondoc.com.

"Second City, *Onion*, Delay Live Show." *Chicago Tribune*, August 6, 2013.

Sinkovich, Justin, and Terry Brindisi. "The Art, Influence, and Business of Satire: Peeling Back the Layers of *The Onion*." *International Journal of Arts Management* 18, no. 2 (2016): 75–85.

Sontag, Susan. "Notes on Camp." In *Against Interpretation, and Other Essays*, 275–292. New York: Picador, 1968.

Soren, Emma. "Inside *The Onion*'s New Clickbait Parody, ClickHole.com." *Vulture*, June 12, 2014.

Spicer, Robert N. "Before and After *The Daily Show*: Freedom and Consequences in Political Satire." In *"The Daily Show" and Rhetoric: Arguments, Issues, and Strategies*, edited by Tricia Goodnow, 19–41. Lanham, MD: Lexington Books, 2011.

St. John, Warren. "The Week That Wasn't." *New York Times*, October 3, 2004.

Stephen, Jessica. "Wauwatosa Business Spotlight: Bridgetown Framing Gallery." *Wauwatosa Now*, December 16, 2014.

Stibbe, Arran. *Econarrative: Ethics, Ecology and the Search for New Narratives to Live By*. London: Bloomsbury, 2024.

Stivers, Richard. *The Media Creates Us in Its Image, and Other Essays on Technology and Culture*. Eugene, OR: Cascade Books, 2020.

Stokoe, Rachel. "*The Onion*." *Penthouse*, March 2002. https://penthouse.com/legacy /the-onion/.

Sullivan, Margaret. *Ghosting the News: Local Journalism and the Crisis of American Democracy*. New York: Columbia Global Reports, 2020.

Tatum, Christine. "Successful Satire." *Denver Post*, October 4, 2005; updated May 8, 2016.

Test, George. *Satire: Spirit and Art*. Tampa: University of South Florida Press, 1991.

Thompson, Stephen. "Here's to the Losers." https://vdocuments.mx/heres-to-the-losers -s-to-the-losers-have-looked-at-our-rag-tag-bunch-of.html.

Tortorello, Michael. "Peeling the Onion." *Minneapolis City Pages*, March 19, 1997.

Tucher, Andie. *Not Exactly Lying: Fake News and Fake Journalism in American History*. New York: Columbia University Press, 2022.

USA Today. "About *USA Today*." https://static.usatoday.com/about/timeline/.

Usher, Nikki. *Making News at the "New York Times."* Ann Arbor: University of Michigan Press, 2014.

US Securities and Exchange Commission. "Strong Capital Management and Richard Strong Agree to Pay $140 Million to Settle Fraud Charges Concerning Undisclosed Mutual Funds Trading: Richard Strong and Two Executives Permanently Barred from Mutual Fund Industry." US Securities and Exchange Commission, May 20, 2004.

Vaidhyanathan, Siva. *Anti-social Media: How Facebook Disconnects Us and Undermines Democracy*. Oxford: Oxford University Press, 2018.

VanHooker, Brian. "An Oral History of *The Onion*'s 9/11 Issue." *MEL Magazine*. https://melmagazine.com/en-us/story/onion-911-issue-oral-history.

Vitaris, Paula. "He's More than Your Average, Cold-Blooded Killer. He's Spaceman." *Cineaste* 33, no. 4 (2001): 12–15.

Waisanen, Don J. "An Alternative Sense of Humor: The Problems with Crossing Comedy and Politics in Public Discourse." In *Venomous Speech: Problems with American Political Discourse on the Right and Left*, edited by Clarke Rountree, 2:299–315. Westport, CT: Praeger, 2013.

———. "Crafting Hyperreal Spaces for Comic Insights: The Onion News Network's Ironic Iconicity." *Communication Quarterly* 59, no. 5 (2011): 508–528.

———. "*The Onion.*" In *Encyclopedia of Social Media and Politics*, edited by Kerric Harvey, 913–914. Los Angeles: Sage, 2014.

———. "The Problem with Being Joe Biden: Political Comedy and Circulating Personae." *Critical Studies in Media Communication* (September 12, 2015): 1–16. https://doi.org/10.1080/15295036.2015.1057516.

Wendling, Patrice. "*The Onion* Likes to Raise a Stink." *Capital Times*, April 29, 1989.

Winters, Joseph. "Culture Jamming: Subversion as Protest." *Harvard Political Review* (March 23, 2020).

Woolley, Samuel. *The Reality Game: How the Next Wave of Technology Will Break the Truth*. New York: PublicAffairs, 2020.

Young, Dannagal Goldthwaite. *Irony and Outrage: The Polarized Landscape of Rage, Fear, and Laughter in the United States*. Oxford: Oxford University Press, 2020.

ACKNOWLEDGMENTS

This book is as much a creation of the dozens of former *Onion* staffers I interviewed as it is my own. *The Onion* has always been a deeply collective enterprise, and I wanted this book to represent that spirit. A heartfelt thank-you to everyone I spoke with—some of you multiple times over the six years it took me to finish and as the format changed from an oral history to a prose history. Your trust in me, and your willingness to explore along with me as I figured out how this story wanted to be told, made this book what it is. Special thanks to my old friends Matt Cook, Rich Dahm, Andy Dhuey, Todd Hanson, Tim Keck, and Johanna Wilder, who indulged my early rounds of questions and many follow-ups with wonderful insight and conversation. Thank you to Pete Haise and Scott Dikkers. Thank you also to Deidre Buckingham, Heather Donohue, Randy Jones, Peri Pakroo, Joe Pickett, Mark Pitsch, Jay Rath, Susan Rathke, Amy Reyer, Dan Savage, James Sturm, Lucky the Chimp, and everybody else from back in the day. If your name is not mentioned here, it does not mean you weren't important.

It was also great to finally spend time with members of the 1990s Gen X staff whose names I'd heard over the years but whom I'd never actually met or spoken with until I started researching this project. These include Mark Banker, Joe Garden, Tim Harrod, Ben Karlin, Chris Karwowski, John Krewson, Sean LaFleur, Chad Nackers, Maria Schneider, Robert Siegel, Jack Szwergold, Scott Templeton, Stephen Thompson, Jun Ueno, Dan Vebber, and Andrew Welyczko. (I had met Carol Kolb and Mike Loew before, but we hadn't yet talked at much length!) I hope this book can show the world the magnitude of your accomplishments. Extra thanks to Scott Templeton, Stephen Thompson, Tim Harrod, and Jack Szwergold for sharing your incredible personal *Onion* archives. Scott Templeton also improved the images in this book and Stephen Thompson—who is indeed a damn good copy editor—took a pass through the page proofs. I am so grateful for their incredible attention to detail and willingness to help with one more *Onion* book project. Thank you also to Al Yankovic and Alan Zweibel.

Meeting later generations of *Onion* staff was also very fun and key to helping me understand just how important and influential the work of the first generation was. Thank you for working so hard to maintain the spirit created by a bunch of brilliant, cranky, weirdo, midwestern Gen X cynical idealists—and for adding so much of your own spirit to the mix. The words "protect" and "love" came up a lot from this group. You were what *The Onion* needed during some difficult times. Thank you also to the former *Onion* business staff who provided essential insight and perspective on the commerce side of *The Onion*'s story. Thank you to James daSilva for his website "The Onion: 20 Years Later."

Heartfelt thanks also to the Madisonians (former and current) I spoke with about the local context of *The Onion*'s origins, as well as the scholars, writers, journalists, editors, artists, comedians, and everyone else who helped me understand the larger context of *The Onion*'s story. Like the 1880s–1920s, our current era is a pivotal transitional period, with long-lasting consequences we are only beginning to understand.

In the end I was not able to include everybody I interviewed, nor was I able to speak with everybody from *The Onion* I would have liked—but even if your words are not in this book, your spirit is there and helped shape and drive everything. I feel honored to have made the acquaintance of so many brilliant, interesting, compassionate, and hilarious people through this process. It was also just really fun. Please forgive any errors in fact or representation.

Thank you also to Janet Keck and Mike Olszanski for fighting the good fight. As Mother Jones once said: "Pray for the dead and fight like hell for the living."

So much about *The Onion*'s story was beyond the scope of this project. This includes but is not limited to thousands of *Onion* headlines, articles, and videos; a TV pilot; books; many writers, editors, designers, directors, producers, photographers, videographers, ad reps, office staff, and business staff; the people whose faces appear in "American Voices" (I do know that one of them was *The Onion*'s Madison UPS driver); a cease-and-desist letter from the George W. Bush administration; a 2022 Supreme Court amicus brief; countless incidents when people thought *Onion* stories were real; and countless *Onion*-inspired newspapers and websites on college campuses and other places across the United

States and around the world. "Not *The Onion*" has been an Internet trope for years, and there are many articles out there about *The Onion*'s accurate future predictions. I also could have made a list of *Onion* writers who went on to jobs writing for late-night talk shows, sitcoms, and other interesting places.

Thank you to Madison for being the perfect place at the perfect time. Thank you also to the Chicago branch of the Awesome Foundation, which awarded me a grant supporting the writing of this book, and to the Paley Center for Media for allowing me access to archived *Onion* panel discussion videos. Thank you to the University of Wisconsin–Madison.

Finally, thank you to my old UW–Madison undergraduate creative writing thesis advisor, Peter Smith, who connected me with my literary agent, Daniel Greenberg, decades after my college days ended. Daniel happened to be *The Onion*'s old agent and a UW–Madison grad himself, keeping it all in the family. Thank you, Daniel, for your invaluable expertise and advice—and for being willing to lend your talents to one more huge *Onion* book project. Thank you also to my editor at Running Press, Randall Lotowycz, for his enthusiasm, support, and belief in *The Onion*'s story, as well as copy editor Annette Wenda and production editor Amber Morris.

A fundamental reason I was able to write this book at all was the federal, state, and county pandemic-era emergency funding that provided benefits to the self-employed and to parents of school-aged kids. I am deeply grateful for this government-funded safety net that helped not only me and my family, but also so many others during a very difficult period—even as I acknowledge the loss of millions of lives due to COVID-19 taking place at the same time and how this loss still echoes everywhere. Since challenging times still lie ahead, and since we remain one of the wealthiest countries on earth, this safety net—and its spirit of mutual cooperation for the benefit of all—should be made permanent.

This book is also dedicated to Milo and Alexi. I love you.

ABOUT THE AUTHOR

Christine Wenc was a member of *The Onion*'s original staff from 1988 to 1990 as a UW–Madison undergrad. She has played central roles in highly regarded public history projects for Harvard University Libraries, Brigham and Women's Hospital, and the National Library of Medicine and has received grants from the Awesome Foundation and the National Endowment for the Humanities. She is also trained in midwestern prairie ecosystem restoration and likes to spend time helping to revitalize one of the rarest, most diverse, most beautiful, and most ecologically beneficial landscapes on the planet. She grew up in rural Spring Green, Wisconsin.